THE FRONT RUNNER

THE FRONT RUNNER

THE LIFE OF
STEVE PREFONTAINE

BRENDAN O'MEARA

MARINER BOOKS
New York   Boston

HarperCollins books may be purchased for educational, business, or sales promotional use. For information, please email the Special Markets Department at SPsales@harpercollins.com.

The Mariner flag design is a registered trademark of HarperCollins Publishers LLC.

FIRST EDITION

Designed by Renata DiBiase

Library of Congress Cataloging-in-Publication Data

Names: O'Meara, Brendan, author.
Title: The front runner : the life of Steve Prefontaine / Brendan O'Meara.
Description: First edition. | New York : Mariner Books, [2025] | Includes bibliographical references and index.
Identifiers: LCCN 2024060597 (print) | LCCN 2024060598 (ebook) | ISBN 9780063348967 (hardcover) | ISBN 9780063348981 (ebook)
Subjects: LCSH: Prefontaine, Steve. | Runners (Sports)—Oregon—Biography. | Long-distance runners—United States—Biography. | Track and field athletes—United States—Biography. | Track and field—Oregon—Eugene—History—20th century. | Track and field—United States—History—20th century. | Olympic athletes—United States—Biography. | University of Oregon—Track and field.
Classification: LCC GV1061.15.P74 O64 2025 (print) | LCC GV1061.15.P74 (ebook) | DDC 796.42092 [B]—dc23/eng/20250212
LC record available at https://lccn.loc.gov/2024060597
LC ebook record available at https://lccn.loc.gov/2024060598

ISBN 978-0-06-334896-7

25 26 27 28 29 LBC 5 4 3 2 1

For Melanie,
we eat our candy with the pork and beans

Pre was stubborn. He insisted on holding himself to a higher standard than victory. A race is a work of art. That's what he said. That's what he believed. And he was out to make it one every step of the way.

—Bill Bowerman, Prefontaine eulogy,
Hayward Field, June 3, 1975

CONTENTS

THE FRONT RUNNER

PROLOGUE

COOS BAY, OREGON, June 2, 1975: Clouds flecked the sky and the sun cast a gentle pre-summer warmth while wind whipped off the bay over the tall, infield grass. Flowers and ferns adorned the casket of Steve Roland Prefontaine. Floral wreaths provided a somber backdrop behind the podium. Close to 3,000 friends and colleagues—runners, jumpers, throwers, veterans, coaches, teachers, and acquaintances from all walks of life—gathered to recall the life and mourn his death. Some knew him as a teammate and peer and called him "Pre." Those closest to him called him Steve. Most, though, knew him as the greatest middle-distance runner in America—a man who by 1975 owned all seven American records between 2,000 meters and 10,000 meters; a front runner on and off the track, who ran for gold and settled for fourth in the 1972 Olympics, an emblem of the athlete as activist; and as a gentle yet rebellious spirit.

Steve died at the age of twenty-four in a single-car accident, at the height of his popularity. Earlier that spring, he had been named by *Track & Field News* as the world's most popular athlete. His mother once said, "He no longer belongs to us. He now belongs to the world." Now the world was grieving over what many would recall as a deeply tragic moment of a life taken far too soon with far too much to give.

People from all parts of Steve's life had gathered for his funeral. Steve's parents, Ray and Elfriede Prefontaine, sat in the front row of those closest to Steve at Marshfield High School's Pirate Stadium, barely ten feet from the casket. Sitting with them were Steve's older half-sister, Neta Fleming, thirty-three, with her young son, who wore a "Go Pre" shirt; Steve's younger sister, Linda, twenty-one; and Steve's girlfriend.

Frank Shorter, wearing his 1972 Olympic uniform, a close friend of Steve's and gold medalist in the 1972 Olympic marathon, was one of the six pallbearers. Members of the Finnish national team, who were in Oregon as part of an unprecedented series of track meets conceived of and organized by Steve Prefontaine, bowed their heads. From Madras, Oregon, the entire Gauthier family, who had provided Steve sanctuary from his growing celebrity in their high-desert town, mourned. And then, of course, there were two of the most important influences of his life in his head coaches, Walt McClure of Marshfield High School and Bill Bowerman from the University of Oregon.

With Steve's body in repose, those present were left to reflect on their own remembrances of the great young runner. Steve Prefontaine was warm and confident, as charismatic as he was fast, a middle-distance runner who incited animalistic desire, someone who partied as hard as he ran. Phil Knight, cofounder of Nike and an Oregon alumnus, said, "In the track and field world Pre is eternal."

Bowerman, a cofounder of Nike and the track coach who oversaw the 1972 Olympic team, said, "Pre's legacy to us is that the good things of track and other sports may be freely enjoyed by athletes and spectators, won by truth, honesty, and hard work. With his characteristic courage and persistence, through difficult communication, Pre opened that door. He was able to get that final step in athlete emancipation through our national organization. I pledge to Pre to fulfill his great dream—to keep that door open."

Abroad, some foreign runners thought little of him, didn't "get it," but at home he became a symbol for those looking to take the power back. When offered a professional track-and-field contract, he remained an amateur, fully committed to the Olympic ideal, his Ahab-ian obsession. To this day, he embodies a purity of spirit in a sporting culture awash in myopia and cynicism. Though he greatly wanted money, stability, and structure for himself and others, he rebuffed the opportunity to fully sell out, thus he remains untainted. To his detractors, he was just a blowhard whose mouth ran faster than his legs and an unpatriotic ingrate more concerned with his own image than that of his country's.

McClure, who, along with brilliant distance coach Phil Pursian, coached Steve as a budding star, said, "He was always in a hurry, his destiny could not allow for a wasted effort. Greatness is for only a few. The accomplishments of such an individual are often recognized years after the deed, the act. Steve Prefontaine achieved this level during his brief lifetime. I would not say that Pre was the last to leave the gym after a workout as many might believe, but rather he was generally the first, so intense was his concentration in a workout, so great his effort, and so valuable his time." With that time, he wasn't merely running, he was organizing; he, along with a small cohort of athletes, were at the dawn of a new athlete, one pushing against the power structures of track and field. He sought institutional support for track-and-field athletes, to free them from the stodgy, antiquated, and suffocating rules of the amateur establishment, long governed by the anemic Amateur Athletic Union. Before Tiger Woods and Serena Williams, before Bo Jackson and Michael Jordan, there was Steve Prefontaine, the one who started it all. Steve was a front runner on and off the track.

But the plight of the front runner is the vulnerability of getting run down by those less prone to risk, those who inherently feel they have more time, and Steve, perhaps instinctually, knew not to waste his waiting. In dying young, his legacy lived on; he became timeless. And this is his story of how he embodied a new athlete for a new era, someone who didn't shut up and run. Far from it.

PART I

CHAPTER 1

FORGED

STEVE ROLAND PREFONTAINE took off running, smiling, laughing hysterically.

As children, Steve and Ray Arndt, his first cousin, had taken their bicycles cruising around Coos Bay, Oregon, their hometown in southwestern Oregon. Arndt, named after Steve's father, was just a couple years older than Steve; the pair were practically brothers. Growing up, Steve always seemed in motion. He could be draining and some kids in the neighborhood didn't care for his boundless energy, the incessant high motor. Arndt, however, was the perfect balance, often by Steve's side, someone who could hang with Steve, even put him in his place. Steve, Arndt recalled, "used to jabber incessantly," before quickly adding, "so did I."

The pair often suffered road rash at the hands of each other as they horsed around Coos Bay. One time, they separated, and Steve hid in the hedges, grabbing a sturdy tree branch and waiting for Arndt to pedal by. At the right moment, Steve stuck that branch into the front spokes of Arndt's bicycle and flipped Arndt over the handlebars and off the bike. Steve doubled over, laughing so hard he could barely breathe. Arndt brushed the grit off his wounds and glared at Steve, and thus Steve took off running.

Arndt, a bit burlier, wasn't as quick, but he knew more shortcuts than Steve, and he knew where Steve would surface, so he cut through yards and waited for Steve, out of sight, like a panther. Steve ran past and Arndt pounced and knocked Steve to the ground. While on top of him, Arndt noticed that while Steve was on his side lying on his elbow, his legs never stopped running. Steve's entire body was pivoting about his elbow trying to avoid getting punched and kicked by his cousin. In the way boys of a certain age were, they were always at war. But within minutes, they were friends again. Arndt said, "I could see what kind of a running spirit he had just because of the way he ran away from me."

That was Steve's nature, always on the move, from dawn until the dinner bell rang, and he'd come running home to be with his older half-sister, Neta, and his younger sister, Linda. Steve's parents—Elfriede, Steve's mother, a German émigré and war bride, and Ray, a hard-working carpenter—had little patience for nonsense.

At the age of twenty-one, Ray, small in stature with tightly cropped hair and a neat mustache, had moved to Portland, Oregon, by way of Devil's Lake, North Dakota, where he was a plumber's helper. In 1940, he married Jennie Redmond, age seventeen; with America on the brink of entering World War II, they settled in southwestern Oregon, in Coos Bay, a little city pinned against the Pacific Ocean, booming in big timber. Come March 1942, the pair had a child, whom they named Neta. Yet soon their little family was in upheaval.

Jennie had grown restless and unhappy. She spent many nights drinking in bars and taverns and sought the company of other men, often coming home at two or three in the morning intoxicated. She abandoned her toddler, soiled and developing a nervous disorder, for hours at night. She frequently beat Neta, and when Ray was drafted into the Army on August 4, 1944, he petitioned for his daughter to be made a ward of the court and placed her in the custody of trusted neighbors. On December 2, 1946, Ray filed for complete divorce and full custody of Neta.

After the war, Ray met Elfriede, a platinum blonde, blue-eyed German woman, marrying her on July 2, 1948, in Berlin. She emigrated to the United States, and on January 25, 1951, Elfriede delivered Steve Roland Prefontaine into the world, both new to a booming country.

Nine years older, Neta looked after Steve and babysat him. She'd dress him up like a girl and put makeup on him. Neta put him in a playpen out in the sunshine when he was six months old, and he developed the most gorgeous bronze skin. Steve won the prettiest baby contest because he had a tan nobody could compete with. She needed him, pretended he was her baby. A photograph from Christmas 1952—a month before Steve turned two—showed Neta with a big smile beside her chubby-cheeked brother.

On November 5, 1953, a baby girl, Linda Prefontaine, was born, and it was Linda much more than Steve who was the apple of Elfriede's eye. When Linda was a baby, she got all the attention. While Neta adored Steve, Elfriede did not, leaving Neta as her little brother's caretaker.

She also was his protector.

As a toddler, if Steve damaged anything, spilled his milk, bumped his tricycle, Elfriede beat him. When Neta returned from school and witnessed it, she would scoop him up and shield him, and "I would let her hit me," she recalled. "Sometimes I really wanted to hit her. Because God said, 'You must honor your father and mother,' I didn't. I was big enough to."

After a long day at a construction site, Ray, now a carpenter, would come home drawn and tired, hands dry, cracked. Elfriede greeted him with a list of transgressions by Steve or Neta, and he was urged to take out the strap. Neta thought he didn't really want to, but Elfriede insisted they be taught a lesson, so he lashed them. Neta would ask her father why he beat them all the time and he said, "I have to teach you to be good." She pleaded, she *was* good, but there was no use arguing. When Neta was twelve and Steve three, she tried asking the neighbors for help, but they didn't want to intervene. When Elfriede found out, she made Neta confess to the neighbors that she was lying. If not, she'd have Ray beat them when he got home. Corporal punishment was far from uncommon—even commonplace—during this time, but it must have been especially toxic for Neta to seek help, and all the more dispiriting to admit the painful falsehood that it was all a lie.

Outside the home, school didn't come easily for Steve. Perhaps it was because he had to shake the German off his tongue (he would always remain mildly fluent in German and could translate when competing in Germany), but when he inevitably brought home bad grades, he was embarrassed, afraid to show his parents. To them, Steve was an embarrassment. Many times, Neta would come home to find her father beating Steve. Powerless to help, she'd run crying to her room. She worried about him constantly.

Neta was not the only one who saw the abuse. Ray Arndt, Steve's cousin and fellow rabble-rouser, witnessed Ray take out his belt and "beat the crap out of Steve in front of my eyes." Steve used to cry at first, but, according to Arndt, after so many beatings, he'd sit and not whimper. A seething intensity emerged on Steve's face. He wanted to show his father that he was tough. In private, Steve told his cousin that when he got big enough, he'd swing back.

Back then, Coos Bay was a working town and working men insisted on hardness, where a lumberman "will cold deck you if you hold your glass the wrong way." A generation of men returning from World War II sought an idyllic setting to find work and build a life. For many, the woods called. Acre upon acre of dense old-growth forests practically begged to be felled. The roar of chainsaws echoed through the woods and the trees moaned as they fell. These were grizzled men, and though it wasn't war, they took their lives in their own hands in the surrounding forests where blade met blood. A job in timber could provide for a decent life, but just as easily take it. On coming home from the woods or a work site, a man's hands might be swollen, bloody, and chapped. It was proof that you were tough, and toughness would be handed down one way or another. Boys wouldn't become men; they would be forged into men and shaped accordingly, a brute-force initiation where youth must measure up.

By the time Steve turned ten, Neta was nineteen and had since left the house to live in a girls community center in Medford, Oregon. She made him a card for his birthday and wrote him a note telling him how sorry she was that she couldn't stay there with him. She felt terrible. Neta barely had any money, but she placed $1 in the card. As a keepsake, Neta included in the card an innocent photograph of herself in a swimsuit so he wouldn't forget her. Steve tucked it away, for safekeeping, in his wallet.

Years later, when Steve pledged a fraternity as a freshman at the University of Oregon, he bonded with John Van Zonneveld, an upperclassman. His parents had emigrated to the United States in 1947 from Holland. Van Zonneveld said his father "ruled with an iron fist." Van Zonneveld wasn't a competitive runner, but to escape his father, he took up running. "Pissed off," he laced up his Converse tennis shoes and ran out the door, time and again. One day, Van Zonneveld shared a "rather bad episode" with Steve. Steve nodded, said he could relate, "Yeah, that's kind of how I got started." It could be why, for a time, running was so important: not only did Steve have a talent for it, but if he was running, he was free. It would also prove to be a means for Steve to mete out pain on his own terms; levied on his rivals, yes, but, just as often, drawing on the unforgiving masochism inherent to distance running. He ran with an intensity you rarely saw in a distance runner. Steve was going to make you hurt. While it is a stretch to connect a straight line from being beaten as a child to Steve wanting to then "abuse" his competition, the pain he endured at the hand of his father was, without question, a condition of his upbringing, in the same way that the pervasive culture of masculinity endemic to Coos Bay also was an ingredient to the roundness of Steve's character and burgeoning sense of self.

Van Zonneveld noted how much Steve ran from the gut, from a will that transcended his meager stature. "He was running with a purpose," Van Zonneveld said, "and that purpose might have been to relieve the anger. I think a lot of it stemmed from his childhood." For a time, Steve found a friend in Van Zonneveld because they felt that all-too-familiar paternal rage, a generational pain that often found its way from father to son.

With Neta carving out, as best she could, a life for herself, Steve was effectively on his own. Instead of swinging back with his fists, Steve saw the validating power of his emerging athleticism. Steve would later say, "You don't have many ways to jump. You can be an athlete. Athletes are very big in Coos Bay. You can study, try to be an intellectual, but there aren't many of those. Or you can go drag the gut in your lowered Chevy with a switchblade in your pocket."

Despite the "running spirit" that Arndt saw in his cousin, whatever Steve's natural aptitude for running as a boy was, initially it wasn't his focus. Sports ruled in Coos Bay, providing entertainment for the locals and giving the young athletes a chance at status and prestige. The politics of growing up in Coos Bay were apparent to anyone walking the halls of Blossom Gulch Middle School or Marshfield High School, high up on the hill, a white, institutional-looking building above the bay. If you were a standout athlete, no matter the sport, you had the respect of everyone. You could walk the halls with your letterman jacket unbuttoned, chest puffed out.

And of all sports, football was king.

It didn't matter that Steve was small. Steve wanted to play football—

the most aggressive and manly of the major sports—in middle school. After all, he was tough, knew how to take a beating. The helmet atop his head made him look like a bobblehead doll. The shoulder pads rattled atop his bony body and the jersey hung off him like a nightgown. Steve's legs were that of a great blue heron, barely more than skin-wrapped bone. He rarely made it into an actual game. One look at him and you figured he was a liability. At ninety pounds, he mainly watched from the bench. "Football was suicide," he would say. He stood on the sideline looking out onto the field, waiting for a shot at glory that was unlikely to arrive. Like many generations before and after, a misplaced football player might find his way into a singlet, short shorts, and running flats. Once Steve had the courage to give up football and pursue an altogether different sport, he proved capable. In the desperation to find his place in the Coos Bay athletic hierarchy to belong, distance running grabbed hold.

While he wasn't yet great, a byproduct to his newfound study surfaced: when Steve proved fast, as he started to win, the beatings at home stopped. "Lo and behold, what happened? He was a good runner," Arndt recalled. What Arndt couldn't stomach was how quickly Steve's parents changed tenor from shame and indifference to boastfulness once Steve showed a skill for running. Arndt said, "Steve probably did feel good or glad that the days of getting strapped on the ass were replaced by his dad in the stands, clapping and cheering for him."

In the years that followed, Steve grew closer to his parents and never said a bad word publicly. They would travel to many of his meets, often going as far as southern California, even Europe. Steve loved his little sister Linda; and he loved and always stayed connected with Neta, though Linda and Neta would grow estranged. Future friends would say how much Steve loved his father, but it was just as likely that Steve ran so furiously, so far and so fast, so early in the day and so late, for refuge. Running earned him love, his speed a shield.

CHAPTER 2

DANGEROUS

THERE WAS ALWAYS a watchful eye scanning the football field for kids who looked, let's say, out of place. Steve didn't know it when he was playing football, but Walt McClure, the high school track-and-field coach, had his eye on him.

A sturdy six foot one, McClure was trim and athletic. In high school, he had played basketball and football, but he excelled on the track as a middle-distance runner. McClure's father had run the 1,500 and 800 meters for Team USA in the 1912 Stockholm Olympics, and McClure himself went on to run at the University of Oregon for legendary coach Bill Hayward, the namesake for Hayward Field in Eugene. McClure bridged two generations of running royalty, beginning his collegiate career under Hayward and ending it running for Bill Bowerman, who would one day be the most revered coach in all of college track and field and a cofounder of Nike. McClure graduated in 1951 to start a life as a high school coach and biology teacher at Marshfield High School in the bustling seaside town of Coos Bay.

Steve Prefontaine later said McClure was like a second father to him. Steve wasn't alone, as many would attest. Where a boy's home life might be chaotic and frightful, McClure, though stern, brought comfort and stability to his teams, his Boy Scout troops, and the boys that composed them. As a coach, McClure didn't make each athlete conform to his program. Rather, he looked at each athlete as the individual they were, be it a possible state champion or someone looking to earn their letterman jacket. He set a date pace for each runner (the time you could run *that* day) and a goal pace (a stretch, something you should strive for).

The thought of running for its own sake did not come naturally to many, as cross-country runners and distance runners were just as often "failed" football players or basketball players. Steve Prefontaine was no different. Steve wondered, *What kind of a crazy nut would spend two or three hours a day just running? I'll never do that.*

Steve wasn't the only one skeptical of his running ability. Roger Bingham, a classmate of Steve's and a close friend going all the way back to the seventh grade, thought Steve was too small, too short, too slow—a sentiment shared by many. At the time, Bingham, by his own account, was the best distance runner in their grade. In an event called the 1,320—three-quarters of a mile—Bingham dusted his peers, with Steve never coming within ten seconds of him, or about sixty yards. Still, Steve showed some talent, though raw, for running. High in energy, he endured despite not being the quickest.

At the end of the 1965 school year, Howard Kubli, who was a sophomore at Marshfield High School when Steve and Bingham were finishing the eighth grade, was part of a crew that organized a track meet for the incoming freshmen. It was partly for fun, but it also was a showcase so the upperclassmen could see who was coming up the pipeline. More importantly, McClure could evaluate a diamond or two in the rough. The eighth graders would challenge the freshmen. Kubli had heard Steve could run a mile in just more than five minutes, not half bad for a fourteen year old. Nobody remembered the result of this meet, but the feeling remained: Steve had talent; he was tough; he had a punishing way of moving.

And yet, despite the small buzz around Steve, come cross-country season, he didn't show up at first. McClure found Steve in a physical education class and successfully lobbied him to come try out for cross-country. At Marshfield, the cross-country team was desperate for bodies, which meant a freshman could compete on the varsity level. However, Steve also turned out to be, at least for the early part of the season, a non-factor.

Part of the problem might have been mindset—something that in a couple of short seasons would come to define Steve but was lacking at the start. Tom Huggins, a year ahead of Steve and one of the best runners on the team (and a captain as a sophomore), saw something in Steve, even though Steve couldn't see it in himself. Huggins noticed some of the upperclassmen, who lacked his own commitment to excellence, would take cigarettes with them on training runs. Out of sight from the coaches, they'd smoke when they should have been hammering out the course. Huggins couldn't believe it, but he kept it to himself. They would never listen to him.

The team had a running route they called the Blue Course (every route McClure mapped out had a name), on which they ran up a hill and stormed down the other side. At the bottom of the hill, a road jutted to the left that was perfectly flat and circumvented the hill—a shortcut. The slackers took this route. One day, Huggins sped around the corner and saw Steve hanging out with those guys burning down cigs. Huggins knew he had to intervene. Maybe it was insecurity, but Steve chose to fit in with the smokers. When Huggins finished the workout, he caught up with Steve and took him around to the side of the bus.

"That's not going to help you," Huggins said. "You start cheating on this stuff and hanging out with those guys, you're never going to become as good as you have the potential to be."

Steve nodded, receptive to a slightly older peer showing him a better way. Inherent to growing up in Coos Bay were the disparate paths that could lead to an unsavory, hard-scrabble existence. He saw a very real future where he was headed for the streets, which could very well land him in the woods or the mills, honest but bludgeoning work. To Steve's credit, he listened, because after that moment, Huggins never saw him cheat again. Huggins never told the coaches. Never told anybody. He recalled, "If there was an incident that turned the switch, that was it. The Blue Course."

With a renewed sense of purpose, Steve kept running that fall of 1965, his freshman year at Marshfield, casting aside cigarettes and filling his lungs with the crisp air blowing off the bay. Once Huggins straightened him out, Steve's focus revealed itself to everyone. On training runs, some of the up-perclassmen would hide in the high grasses of the dunes and pounce on unsuspecting teammates as they ran by. They knew better than to tackle

Steve, though. He was out for himself and wanted to improve. The seniors could still beat the little upstart, but they were seventeen and eighteen years old; Steve was fourteen and slowly started to see how increased effort translated into better results.

During an early season cross-country race, with points on the line, the athletes jogged and stretched in their purple and gold racing singlets and shorts that barely covered their legs. Bingham was primed and so was Steve, who had a bit more bounce in his step. Some fifteen runners from Marshfield started tearing up the trails. Though Bingham wasn't quite as fast as the upperclassmen, he was running a fine race by his standards as the finish line neared. Just behind him, he could feel a runner gaining. Then, seemingly out of nowhere, Steve edged Bingham by two strides. Bingham couldn't believe it. With gained confidence, as the season progressed, Steve routinely beat Bingham by a few strides—others too. All he needed was that initial taste of competition and the satisfaction of climbing through a field . . . and he was hooked. Bingham said, "I never saw the front of Steve Prefontaine again." Few would.

Jim Villanueva, Gary Matthews, and Huggins were the returning veterans to this 1965 squad, a team that won the District 5 championship and finished fourth place in the state in 1964. Villanueva, a senior, was the best runner on this team, and it was his time, as it were, to shine. He wasn't very big, but despite a slight upper body, he had powerful thighs with white socks pulled halfway up his chiseled calves.

While Villanueva started the season with several wins, Steve hovered around the back of the top ten. Despite Villanueva's wonderful season, McClure was bullish on Steve, "a wisp of a boy who's come on like gangbusters and has challenged . . . the team's No. 2 runner." McClure needed Steve to step into bigger shoes as Huggins, "last year's outstanding freshman," and Clyde Blakely, "who's been a hard worker this fall," were injured.

With the season winding down, Marshfield traveled to the District 5 championships. North Eugene High School won easily over South Eugene High School and Marshfield. Villanueva finished sixth overall to lead his team; Steve finished nineteenth. Despite it being Steve's first district meet—a step below state championships—McClure quickly noted there was something . . . *different* about Steve. More than any other boy, McClure saw composure from Steve. He showed promise. McClure wasn't the only one to notice.

Attending this meet was the looming figure from the University of Oregon, famed track-and-field coach Bill Bowerman, with NCAA track titles in 1962, 1964, and 1965 to his name. McClure had told Bowerman "about this little guy who was a good one." It was the first time Bowerman laid eyes on Steve. Bowerman noticed he ran about as good as any freshman could under those conditions and with that level of experience—or lack thereof. Bowerman would later say that Steve "wasn't necessarily born to run, but he was born to compete." Bowerman saw that in action; he saw fight. But there were many young, talented ruins across all sports who peaked too soon. There was no sense in getting his hopes up about the potential of a relatively untried freshman who was finding, but hadn't yet found, his stride.

DESPITE SHOWING AN aptitude for distance running, for Steve there was an element of wanting to belong, to impress his elders. As he grew more confident and transitioned from fall cross-country to spring track and field during his freshman year, he began to reveal a feistiness that surprised many. What stood out the most was how Steve began to talk.

In 1964, the year before Steve really leaned into running, Muhammad Ali—then Cassius Clay—chirped. He proclaimed how he was raising ticket prices for his fights, how he was putting people in the stands and filling up stadiums, and what does he tell the reporter ahead of his fight with Sonny Liston? He was going to "float like a butterfly and sting like a bee!" At the time, athletes, especially track-and-field athletes, barely uttered a word of conflict or confrontation. There was a gentleman's quality to the sport, a country-club air to the primarily white distance runners that cast the lanky and skeletal bodies as more than boring: milquetoast. But in 1964, Steve was thirteen years old and still very much unsure of himself and what his athletic path would be. There was something in the brashness of Ali that awakened an inner part of Steve's psyche, that as long as you could back it up, you could say whatever you wanted. Whether Steve saw it on television, heard it on the radio, or read it in the papers, he must have loved Ali's confidence, probably laughed, and *definitely* stowed it away for future use. What he heard or saw in Ali was someone not only speaking up but also speaking out. Talking trash was a means to agitate, but also to hold himself accountable. Time and again Steve would talk; time and again he backed it up, which, among distance runners, made him an altogether new species of competitor.

Before a track meet in the spring of 1966, McClure told Kubli, now a junior, and Steve they would be running the mile. Steve, barely 100 pounds, cornered Kubli and said, "Man, I'm going to kick your butt. I'm gonna float like a butterfly and sting like a bee!"

Kubli said, "Get out of here, you're a freshman punk. You're not gonna do anything."

Kubli was determined to show Steve what it meant to be stung like a bee, only to have McClure change his mind and have Kubli run the two-mile, sending another upperclassman, Steve Prescott, to run the mile instead. Kubli then saw Steve corner Prescott and spout off the same line, how he's going to "float like a butterfly and sting like a bee." Kubli couldn't believe it, and later recalled, "But that was just kind of *him*."

Nobody remembers if Steve won or not. Nevertheless, he made an impression.

Steve's teammates weren't the only ones noticing. Phil Pursian, tall, narrow shouldered, came to Marshfield High School from the state of Washington to teach English. He had grown up on thirty-eight acres on a small farm in Renton, Washington, "out in the tilly weeds," as he recalled.

After graduating from Linfield College, where he excelled as a runner, and taking a teaching job at Marshfield, Pursian laced up his shoes and ran on the Pirate Stadium track. Standing on the fringes of his fiefdom was McClure. McClure watched Pursian's technique. "I can tell you did a lot of running," he said.

"Yeah, yes, I did," Pursian said.

"If you get time, go down to the track and check out what we're doing."

Pursian did, and before long McClure entrusted Pursian to coach the distance runners, including a still-scrawny Steve Prefontaine.

The spring of 1966, Steve and the other freshmen ran in several junior varsity meets, gaining a sense of what it meant to compete and win. In one early season meet the "frosh spikers" won thirteen of fifteen events, with Steve winning the two-mile in 10:54.4. About a month and several meets later, Steve stepped to the line for the varsity two-mile against his good friend Tom Huggins, teammate Steve Peterson, Bandon's Dan Fraser, and North Bend's Arleigh Allen. For the first seven laps, they remained in line, likely with the leaders trading the pacesetting. When the meet official fired the gun for the eighth and final lap of the race, Huggins surged to the front and drew away with a winning time of 10:02.2. Allen took second, Peterson snagging third. Steve finished fourth but set the school's freshman record for the two-mile in 10:08.6, a drop in time of some forty-five seconds in one month.

Running gives an athlete immediate feedback: the stopwatch doesn't lie. The work pays off. This improvement gave him all the validation he needed that he was on the right path.

SUMMER GAVE WAY to fall and a new school year. The Marshfield High cross-country team found itself on a rugged, pitted course, part of it on sandy beach for the Gold Beach Invitational in October 1966.

Bob Hylton, running for Siuslaw High School in Florence, was a couple years older than Steve. Hylton, undefeated at this point in the young season, lined up beside Steve. One of Steve's teammates got Hylton's attention, pointed to Steve, and said, "You know who this is?"

Hylton looked back at him, looked to Steve, and said, "Um, no." Hylton's impression was that Steve was awfully scrawny. According to Hylton, some of his teammates were "screw offs," and one of them who was none too impressed with Steve, pointed to Hylton and said, "Do you know who *he* is?" They lined up and leaned over at the waist and—BANG—off with the pistol.

Steve shot to the front. He likely had heard about runners like Washington State University's Gerry Lindgren or Australia's Ron Clarke, maybe even John Landy (the second man to break the four-minute-mile barrier), runners who relished being on the lead, thought it immoral not to be. To run behind the leaders and try to outkick them—to sit and kick—would make them sick. But in this race Steve contended with Hylton, and Hylton, older and stronger, went right with him, and the pair pulled clear of the field. Hylton noted how fast this Steve Prefontaine was, that unsettling feeling that it took a little too much effort to keep pace. Hylton did what many runners would do with Steve in the lead: he tucked in behind and drafted. Hylton stared at Steve's feet, hypnotized by Steve's rhythm. Steve didn't appreciate this. He would have choice words for people like this. He cussed at Hylton for drafting. Steve said, "You're not gonna outkick me!" all while continuing to swear his head off at Hylton. Had Steve shut his mouth, he might have had more reserves, but his impetuousness was winning out, as it sometimes would. Hylton couldn't jaw back, too tired.

Steve led the entire way and cruised 15 yards ahead of Hylton with 400 yards to go. Steve hit the bottom of his reserves and was tying up. With 170 yards remaining, Hylton had just about pulled even. The pair, practically by themselves, charged down the straightaway toward the finish. Hylton churned harder, and in the final 20 yards eclipsed Steve in the final sprint, a near photo finish to win in 15:40. Steve's time was 15:41. The next closest finisher was Steve's teammate, a full 14 seconds back, roughly 80 or so yards. Hylton certainly knew Steve's name now, and he wouldn't be the last upperclassman in the area to leave a race wondering—even in victory—what the hell had hit them.

By the time of the District 5 cross-country meet that same year, Steve had emerged, if not the best in the area, at least one of the best. Not bad for a sophomore. This did wonders for his confidence, something rarely in short supply and, frankly, never would be. Qualifying at districts would vault this team into the state championship meet the following week in Salem.

McClure figured North Eugene High School's Bill Keenan and Thurston High School's Jan McNeale, talented upperclassmen, were favored. His handicapping was spot-on. The course took place on a sports car racing track between Eugene and Creswell and McClure watched Keenan and McNeale set a fast pace, putting a great deal of distance between them and the rest. Except there was one "little guy in purple and gold." Steve clung to their heels like a Jack Russell. Keenan recalled, "Who's this young fool who thinks he can run with us? We're waiting for his lungs to explode and to call an ambulance."

The course was a few loops—the leaders would dip out of sight and re-emerge. McClure and Pursian watched with each lap how Steve kept pace with the upperclassmen as the rest of the field fell farther back. At the three-quarters mark in the race, Steve passed Keenan and McNeale and took a short lead. McClure noted that this came as quite a surprise to Keenan and McNeale. Had Steve run his own race, the outcome might have been different. Steve periodically peeled off to chastise his own teammates for not keeping up with the leaders. Then he turned around and caught back up to Keenan and McNeale. In the final 300 yards, the strength of Keenan and McNeale outkicked Steve. Keenan won with McNeale finishing second. Steve, for all his jawing, was third.

Steve shocked Keenan. Not one to offer counsel to a competitor, he approached Steve and said, "You know, buddy, I don't have any idea who you are, but if you ever learn to shut your fucking mouth, you're gonna be dangerous."

McClure would later say, "It was, however, apparent that if competitive spirit is an ingredient for athletic success, 'Pre' had a good start toward becoming a giant among runners." He also thought, *We've got a good one! It was the way he ran, how he carried himself, how he accelerated, what he had left that made us believe he could be a great one if he wanted to be.* Indeed he did want that, and he wanted others to know it as well.

Come spring track in 1967, it wasn't just his running that made him memorable—his mouth did some of that work. At the Indian Club Relays, Roseburg High School's Greg Barnett, a 1:56 half-miler, edged away and left Steve in the final lap of the mile winning by seven-tenths of a second. It was a race that stuck in Steve's craw, so much so he turned to Barnett and said, "Who are you?" There was a measure of audacity in Steve's voice, that he didn't expect to lose and certainly not to someone he hadn't heard of. Barnett's reply was even better, "Well, who are *you*?" Barnett made note, this was one God darn cocky son of a bitch.

———

THE LONGER A sprint became, the harder Steve was to pass, yet despite his growing confidence, the end to Steve's sophomore track campaign proved a bitter disappointment.

At districts, Steve failed to hit the two-mile standard of 9:45 necessary for states, finishing fourth overall in 9:52.3. Six Marshfield athletes qualified for states—but shockingly none in the distance events, including Steve. The beauty and pain of track and field is the brutal objectivity of the clock or the measuring tape. During the season he had met the standard of 9:45, but not in the meet where it mattered most.

His season was over.

This abrupt end shook him. Steve had already been measuring his worth in sport—in minutes and seconds—and that growing confidence he had forged sprinting up eroding dunes and braving the cunning headwinds with flecks of sand peppering his face suddenly appeared more fragile. Sure, that season he had produced personal bests, even state-qualifying times. The problem was he didn't run those times when it mattered, and it ate at him. Steve was, by now, the best runner on his team and one of the better runners on the coast. Not good enough.

When athletics awards were handed out for spring participation, Steve, and many others, were merely handed their letter that year. That letter meant little to Steve. He had failed, this in a year when he told his mother one day he was going to run in the Olympics. "You're crazy," she said. Maybe he was, but he would later tell her that she had to think positive and things would fall into place.

Steve wasn't as discouraged as he was sickened by his failure. He knew he was better. He believed he was better, and he sought out to prove it. His resolve deepened. Steve began to get ideas; he was thinking far into the future and mentally putting himself on the medal stand on the biggest stage imaginable. Lofty as those ambitions were, he couldn't even earn his way into a championship field of Oregon high school runners. This was merely a setback, a defining moment that propelled him, not a moment that pegged him as a loser.

McClure would write in an essay long after Steve graduated from high school that, "Spring track (of his sophomore year) seemed to bring nothing but frustration to Steve. The final disappointment was his failure to make the state high school meet in the two-mile. A possible contributing factor to Steve's poor sophomore year was his strong concern for and interest in the other members of the team: this took some of the concentration away from his own task. His failure to make the state meet in the two-mile bothered him greatly at the time. This, however, may have been a determining factor of things to come."

He had reached a tipping point of leveling off or leveling up. He wanted to make sure that the piss-poor race he ran at districts never happened again. He would keep this failure at the forefront of his mind to fuel the ever-punishing workouts he would endure. His trash talk had failed him. As an inflection point in his burgeoning career as a distance runner, this failure to qualify was the most impactful, where he knew, in his bones, he needed to double down in his training. More work was to be done, more pain to endure. There were lessons in losing, and he never let a loss define him. He looked forward. A loss was merely data, though it angered him deeply, gnawed at him. He had won races his sophomore year. Some races. Some wasn't enough. He wanted them all.

With the help of McClure, Steve's resolve deepened. All summer, all he thought about was coming back. He "flogged" himself. All he did was run. On the beaches. Up the hills.

He vowed to never lose again.

CHAPTER 3

CHAMPION

IN THE SUMMER of 1967, ahead of Steve's junior year at Marshfield, he asked McClure and Pursian to meet with him. McClure, with Pursian by his side, asked Steve, "What do you think about this cross-country season?" He looked them dead in the eye and said, "I'm going to be state champion." Then Steve told them he didn't plan on losing another race. He asked them to draw up a plan in line with his ambition. If nothing else, Steve had already proven his capacity to compete. Now, they saw something else: hunger to train. They got to work.

McClure and Pursian later grabbed a cup of coffee. McClure said, "What do you think about Steve's statement?"

"That's a tough goal," Pursian said.

"I don't know if he can do that this year."

There were plenty of strong returning distance runners in the state. That said, by the end of the first week of practice, McClure and Pursian noticed a shift in Steve's mentality, a ruthlessness to his training. He was going to punish himself and, by extension, his competition. Perhaps it was a product of his upbringing, but he sought to impart his will on anyone who should challenge him. Distance running isn't unto itself an aggressive pastime, but Steve ran with a near pathological violence. One way or another, Steve wanted you to hurt.

Not wanting to squander what they had in Steve, and wanting what was best for his development, McClure and Pursian phoned a friend: Bill Bowerman.

In addition to leading his Oregon Ducks track team to back-to-back

NCAA championships in '64 and '65, in 1966, Bowerman also published a slim book, *Jogging*, to wide acclaim, making the case that, when it came to coaching and training talent, he was one of the sharpest minds in modern distance running. A WWII veteran, tall, lean, with graying, close-cropped hair, Bowerman was putting something in the water down there in Oregon. His résumé in the distance races, to that point, was unprecedented. In 1960, twenty-year-old Dyrol Burleson became the first Duck—and second American—to break four minutes in the mile. Over the decade, he'd be followed by six more: Keith Forman, Archie San Romani, Wade Bell, Dave Wilborn, Arne Kvalheim, and Roscoe Divine. As a result, Bowerman became a sub-four whisperer and runners who were under 4:10 in high school often found Oregon irresistible. Bowerman sent runners to the Olympics. He forged champions.

He was equal parts teacher, coach, and mad scientist. Where most coaches of that era believed in bludgeoning a runner with relentless mileage, Bowerman favored an alternating hard-easy approach. For instance, when Steve would enroll at Oregon, a typical week of workouts looked like this:

Monday: AM 3–6 (miles), PM 3–6
Tuesday: AM 4–7, PM 6x330 in 48–52 seconds,
    7–10 mile run, 6x330 cut down
Wednesday: AM 4–7, PM 7–9, squad meeting 5 p.m. lounge
Thursday: AM 3–6, PM 6–8 laps with Pat and Randy, 2–4 sets after
Friday: Light AM + PM
Saturday: 7–10 mile run at 6:00
Sunday: 12–15 easy or 3:00 PM with other runners

Bowerman wanted runners to finish workouts "exhilarated, not exhausted." Many coaches of the day preached "more" as their mantra, with excess mileage becoming a top down, system-wide approach. Bowerman believed in the individual, what some at the time might have considered coddling, and he would favor stress, recovery; hard, easy; and thus he began grooming great distance and middle-distance runners.

Bowerman, far ahead of his time, took to optimizing the athlete instead of cramming his schedule with garbage miles for the sake of mileage and running the risk of breaking down an athlete's body and, just as important, his spirit. A phrase heard all the time today but put into practice in the mid-twentieth century by Bowerman is train smarter, not harder.

Bowerman also believed in light shoes and fabrics, often designing the squad's uniforms and footwear, figuring that if an athlete can shed a few ounces in his uniform and footwear, that would equate to several pounds of burden saved over the course of a long race. He wanted shoes as light as if "I drove nails through your bare feet." Indeed, Duck feet were the envy of every rival.

McClure had run for Bowerman, so they were more than passing acquaintances. When McClure and Pursian drove up to Eugene to visit the great guru, they told Bowerman they had a special talent with out-size ambition in Steve. Had McClure not run for Bowerman, it's unlikely the Oregon coach would have shared his secrets. With Steve, and the rest, Bowerman recommended they alternate between hard and easy days—smarter, not harder. Bowerman would later say that given the choice, he'd rather undertrain an athlete than overtrain him. They would incorporate date pace and goal pace. They would have test runs and they would plot the times on graph paper. The hope was, come the end of the season, the athlete will have hit goal pace. Once the runner hit goal pace, reset. That was now date pace. And so on.

The plan was ostensibly for Steve, but everyone would benefit from the new playbook.

Steve, a junior, and his running partner Tom Huggins, a senior, were Nos. 1 and 2 on this team and they reveled in the training. McClure marveled at Steve's strength. Steve had been soaring around the 2.4-mile course at Mingus Park in workouts stopping the watch at 11:55. Quite a ways back, along came Huggins, the only runner on the team capable of staying with Steve.

Huggins was a brilliant long strider. That fall he woke early, at those unforgivable hours. If it wasn't already apparent after the previous season, Huggins, as fast as he was, was nearing his ceiling. As long as he kept waking up early with Steve, Huggins would ensure, at least for a time, that his ceiling might grow a touch more, even if Steve's ceiling revealed itself to be somewhere in the clouds.

But those mornings . . . they were brutal. Soon, they didn't need an alarm clock; habit roused them. They laced up and hit the road running. Huggins woke at 5 a.m., puffy eyed, face still creased from his pillow, and headed out the door, feet pop-pop-popping toward 921 Elrod Street, where Steve would be waiting, puffy eyed, face still creased from his pillow. Huggins always liked it when it was Steve's turn to wake up first and trot over to the Huggins' house, so Huggins could steal a few more minutes of sleep.

The wind whipped and the rains pummeled. It rarely got too cold in Coos Bay, often in the 40s and 50s with a peaceful—though sometimes vengeful—rain showering them. Their favorite runs were on the sand dunes, especially in "bad" weather, because the sand was clean and they didn't get muddy. And, well, Huggins could, at times, beat Steve on their runs on the dunes because Huggins' feet were bigger—think snowshoes—and Steve's feet were little hooves by comparison.

The pair would talk on runs; Steve could always talk, so great were those incongruently massive lungs. In high school, it was usually about girls. It was always these two on the runs. Someone might experiment and step in for one workout, but they quickly deduced that waking up at 5 a.m. was one thing—but waking up at 5 a.m. to get drummed into the ground on these runs was far from worth it. Some runners grew frustrated that they couldn't beat Steve or Huggins and Huggins said, "Well, you don't work out as hard as we do." By 1967, Ron Clarke, the great Australian runner and owner of several world records from two miles to 10,000 meters, wrote in *The Unforgiving Minute*, "Consistent training, not over two or three months, but over two or more years, is the only secret to success."

Those morning runs had the desired effect. Save for a dead heat (still a win) with Huggins, Steve was undefeated through all nine races that cross-country season, still adhering to his promise not to lose again.

Earlier in the season in a triangular meet with Roseburg and Medford, Steve ran into a familiar face: Roseburg's Greg Barnett. Barnett had beaten Steve in the mile the previous spring during track season. Barnett was pleased to beat him, especially when Steve had the audacity to question who Barnett was. Here was Barnett again, though his lungs were charred from fighting forest fires all summer.

McClure approached Steve before the race and asked, "Do you remember Barnett?"

Steve nodded. Steve told McClure he'd like to settle things.

The pistol fired and Steve shot to the lead to clear the field. Barnett pulled even with Steve 200 yards into the race—it was roughly two miles long, the distance of most high school cross-country races at that time. In a questionable and brilliantly antagonistic move, Barnett slapped Steve on the ass and said, "Show me something, Prefontaine."

As if Steve needed any more motivation to grind Barnett into dust, Steve ripped ahead by 40 yards in the bite of an apple. There would be no catching Steve that day, or any day, and he won by thirty-nine seconds, roughly 200 yards.

Years later, Barnett marveled at Steve's transformation, the incredible leap Steve took from mortal sophomore to something untouchable. At the end of the race, with Steve fully recovered by the time Barnett huffed across the finish, Barnett asked, "What the heck did you do this summer?"

"I ran ten miles a day," Steve said. "I ran ten miles a day, but to tell you the truth, I had to walk a lot of it."

Barnett admired Steve's vulnerability, that he admitted he needed to walk at times. It took work, even for someone as seemingly gifted as Steve. Barnett would always remember that.

Ahead of districts on Friday, October 27, 1967, McClure told Steve and Huggins they had to finish one-two, and don't let anyone get ahead of you. Take it to the field. When ruminating on Huggins and Steve, McClure said Huggins had more speed, but after two miles, "he can't stay with Pre." On average, Steve beat Huggins by eleven seconds in all their races and as much as seventeen seconds. Steve was the toughest competitor McClure had ever seen.

On a typical late October day in Oregon, meaning lots of rain and soggy conditions, the kind where spikes get waterlogged and feet smoosh around inside, Steve was one of the favorites along with fellow junior, North Eugene's Doug Crooks. As a sophomore in the spring of 1967, Crooks became the fastest sophomore miler in Oregon prep (meaning high school) history, one of the few rivals Steve could claim in high school.

With his hair greased to his head by the rain, Steve took charge of the race early and by the halfway point was all alone. The "diminutive bundle of energy," as the papers called him, covered the 2.5 mile course in 12:40, thirty-four seconds ahead of Huggins, the pair finishing one-two—just as McClure had hoped—despite both getting lost and running an extra 50 yards to get back on course. Post-race, Steve—with a gentle, knowing smirk on his face, his eyes heavily shadowed by his prominent brow, head slightly tilted, a swoosh of wet hair—looked like he had just gotten out of a pool. Crooks finished third.

On that day, Bowerman was in Corvallis at Oregon State University laying out the cross-country course, but he sent his deputy, assistant coach Bill Dellinger, to scout. Three days after the race, Bowerman, in what was the first recorded outreach to Steve, addressed a letter to Mr. Steve Prefontaine, Marshfield High School: "Bill Dellinger and I have watched the newspaper with interest this fall in your cross-country races. We congratulate you on your steady improvement. . . . Bill reports . . . that you look like a real champion. Congratulations, hit the books and if we can be of help to you here at the University of Oregon, we would be more than pleased to do so."

Bowerman was always quick to say that he didn't recruit, that he wasn't going to swoon some kid. It would appear there were exceptions to every rule. Much to Steve's chagrin, Bowerman rarely wrote letters to him. But it didn't mean he wasn't interested.

Bowerman left it to Dellinger to spearhead Steve's recruitment. Steve and Dellinger had a lot in common. Dellinger was one degree of separation between Steve and Bowerman. Dellinger competed for Bowerman at Oregon, ran in three Olympics, and won a bronze medal in the 5,000 meters at the 1964 Tokyo Olympics, which would eventually become Steve's signature race. Also, Dellinger grew up in Springfield, a town that shares an identity with Coos Bay—a bit rough around the edges, a little rusty.

A few days before the state championship meet, Dellinger addressed a letter to one Mr. Steve Prefontaine wishing him luck. At that moment, all Dellinger could hope for was that Steve remained academically eligible, grounded, healthy, and still loved to run. Likewise, it must have filled Steve with a greater sense of confidence to be courted in such a way, to be recognized for his achievements. Steve was officially a prospect, but any number of things can befall a young athlete with potential. A precocious runner often levels off as the competition rises up to meet him. But at this juncture in the season, as many runners peaked, Steve kept improving and his determination kept pace with his fury to lead from beginning to end.

Schools traveled to Willamette University in Salem for the state championship meet on November 4, 1967, set for a 10:45 a.m. gun. That day, the foot traffic was thick at Bush Pasture, and as 10:30 a.m. approached, more than twenty teams warmed up their best runners. The morning had that mid-fall chill of 45 degrees, but there was no rain and barely a breeze blowing in from the northwest. Steve, still unbeaten on the year, stepped up to the line.

Steve whipped to the lead as the course curled around the grandstands. Then came a hill, the first of several, and Steve, with shorter legs, powered up the incline. Doug Wellman of Parkrose High School coasted roughly 10 yards behind Steve and would be the primary threat to Steve's assault on an undefeated season. Wellman thought Steve was too strong for a runner and awfully muscular, which made the hills navigable; Wellman's longer legs made it more difficult for him to climb. The hills were long but gentle with sharper, swifter downhills. Try as he might, Wellman watched as stride after stride, Steve got smaller and smaller in the distance. Though Steve was in his sights, Wellman never felt in contention. Steve covered the 2.5-mile course in a walloping 12:13.8, ahead of Wellman by about 100 yards. Huggins finished fifth to give Marshfield the No. 1 and No. 5 positions, good enough to help Marshfield finish third overall.

As Steve crossed the finish line, he looked like he was in shock. His eyes wide, mouth agape, fists raised above his head; he had done it. No goal could've been loftier that season, and perhaps that realization led to that look of surprise that he was the best of them all.

Over the years, there would be hundreds of photographs of Steve Prefontaine. There'd be photographs of him so rung out he could barely stand;

photographs rather matter-of-factly hitting the tape with that rounded chest, eyes peering up over his left shoulder at the clock; photographs of him merely swiping the tape with his hands as he trotted past. But this one from 1967, taken by Janet O'Dell with the caption title "Straining Winners," is the only one where he looks positively shocked at what he had done. There was no anguish, nothing put-on, no heavy-handed performative fatigue. It lacked that been-there-before pastiche because, in this context, he had never been there before. He had won races in dual meets but to win a BIG one, to defeat the best of the best, was uncovering new territory on the map and planting his flag. In that moment, there was no certainty, no swagger. It might just be the most human portrait of Steve Prefontaine ever taken.

STEVE'S PERFORMANCES IN the fall earned him an invite to the Oregon Indoor meet-up in Portland—where he was considered the favorite to win the high school mile—except he got sick with a severe cold and a fever and scratched. He was disappointed, even crestfallen.

A few days later, Dellinger heard the news. Based on Dellinger's reply, and that it was addressed directly to Steve at his house on 921 Elrod Street, Steve worried about what it would mean to his ascendant career as a runner. Offering Steve words of encouragement, Dellinger wrote: "I am very sorry that, because of your illness, you did not get to run in the Oregon Invitational Indoor meet. I am sure you could have won your event. However, you still have one year to look forward to that race and the record that stands up there. Do not panic because of your illness. You will come back very fast. The main problem is not to start too hard, too soon. I know your coach will do what is right as far as your training. With the work that you have been putting into it, and are putting into it, and with the desire you have, I know you can look forward to a rewarding outdoor season."

Dellinger proved a comforting voice as Steve turned his gaze to the bigger picture. One of Steve's burgeoning superpowers was his ability to focus, to set goals for himself, to visualize. His disappointment at missing a premier indoor meet at the start of the new year was palpable. He wanted to keep proving himself on bigger stages and missing an event felt like a loss, like he was losing ground. But he soon put it behind him and refocused.

Ahead of the 1968 track season, Steve took out a sheet of paper and a marker. Atop the sheet, he wrote:

'State'
'Champ'
Remember last year?
3:5(?) <== 4:08 or better
1:4(?) <== 1:54 or better
8:(??) <== 9:00 or better
Run with the best??????????????

And taped it to his bedroom desk.

Steve believed in goal setting, so he kept his litany of goals in plain sight. Years later, at running clinics, he would always speak of the power of goal setting and clear intentions—things that athletes of all kinds take for granted now, but few gave voice to back then. Sports psychology didn't become a formalized discipline until the late 1970s. Steve intuited long before such concepts would become the norm that if he wrote it down and visualized where he wanted to go, he had a better chance at scaling the highest peaks. Here, in 1968, he ensured that he didn't forget the sting of not qualifying for states in 1967. He picked at the scar of that pain to refresh it. By the time spring track started, Steve had heeded Dellinger's advice—do not panic. When the Indian Club Relays at Roseburg headlined a Saturday in southern Oregon on March 23, 1968, Steve became the fourth fastest miler for an Oregon high schooler ever. The "seemingly tireless junior" was a "show stealer . . . when he ran away from the field for a 4:13.8 mile." His goal was 4:08, so Steve still had a way to go, but the 4:13.8 bettered his time as a sophomore by some fifteen seconds. He now stood at five foot nine and 142 pounds—right around where he'd race for the remainder of his career, give or take a few pounds, his face slimming and narrowing, looking less like an innocent Boy Scout, and more like a strapping, confident young man.

Steve wasn't happy with his performance at the relays, something of a trend to come in the following years. When he ran fast, he always felt he could run faster if the conditions were better or if he had more help on the lead. His speed isolated him. His commentary about how he ran isolated him, as there were peers who grew frustrated when hearing his voice or reading his words. Be that as it may, McClure readied to drop Steve's time down a notch, maybe as low as 63-second laps, which would put him at 4:12. Steve put all his trust in his coach. He always would.

Steve wanted any clipping he could get, so he spoke to Dellinger asking for any story from any newspaper that might have a record of his achievement. As it happened, Dellinger clipped the article from the *Register-Guard* and wrote another letter to Steve. "Enclosed is the clipping which you wanted me to send you from our area. Again, my congratulations on your very fine race. I am sure you can look forward to greater things to come. Looking forward to seeing you up here on the weekend of the thirteenth when we go against USC."

Attending the Oregon-USC meet as a recruit would give Steve the chance to see and experience what world class, Division I athletes could do, what a sub-four mile might look like in person, how that might just help him further visualize his time creeping ever closer to his goal of 4:08.

And Oregon's Hayward Field was the place to see it.

The Oregon-USC meet took place on Saturday, April 13, 1968, and Steve, along with his father and uncle, was an enthusiastic spectator. The Ducks lost 92-53 to the Trojans (who, because of a cold, were without their best 220 runner in Orenthal James Simpson, better known as O.J.), but Steve saw some electric performances. Six thousand five hundred fans shouldered into Hayward Field to challenge USC, the defending NCAA champions. Unlike in cross-country, where it was quiet for most of a race, save for the final fan-lined chute, here Steve saw how runners could ignite the crowd with every lap, even perform for the crowd and feed off each other. Like football players visiting Notre Dame, an aspiring track star visiting Hayward Field felt like they were walking into a cathedral. It undeniably infected him, the speed, the cheers from the mighty crowd.

Steve intently watched the Duck milers—Dave Wilborn and Arne

Kvalheim, among others—tactically approach the race, alternating leads every 330 yards, then, in the final lap, fight it out. For the crowd on hand, they knew they were in for a sub-four mile, by now an expectation at Oregon. Midway through the backstretch, the leggy Kvalheim led the shorter Wilborn by 3 yards. Wilborn moved up to meet Kvalheim on the turn but downshifted a bit to save his ever-fleeting stores of energy. The two straightened out down the homestretch and with the crowd roaring, Wilborn's rations gave him enough to inch in front of Kvalheim 30 yards from the tape in a riveting finish. They jogged together after the race, Kvalheim grimacing, Wilborn with eyes downcast, gasping for air, a race properly run. Wilborn seared the track with a 3:58.4 mile—still a smashing time for the day. Kvalheim earned a 3:58.5. Steve's eyes glued to that race, knowing—deep in his bones—that one day he could break the four-minute barrier himself. And listen to the crowd! Wilborn, looking up to the stands, said, "This is the greatest crowd in the world, right here in Eugene. Can we hear it? We sure can, and it sure does help."

Steve heard it, too. Bill Bowerman was responsible for popularizing distance running in Eugene, and with so many sub-four minute milers at Hayward Field, Eugene quickly became known as "TrackTown USA" throughout the state and the region.

But Bowerman wasn't on his own in popularizing the sport throughout the country. Indeed, American distance running in the mid-1960s saw a boom of success. At the 1964 Olympics in Tokyo, Japan, Billy Mills won the gold medal in the 10,000 meters over Ron Clarke, the world record holder at the time. In those same Olympics, Bob Schul and Bill Dellinger won the gold and bronze in the 5,000 meters. Similarly, the success of Gerry Lindgren at Washington State University added to the fervor of distance running in the Pacific Northwest. Also, in 1964, Lindgren shocked the U.S.S.R. by winning the 10,000 meters in the U.S. v. U.S.S.R. dual meet in Los Angeles, becoming an Olympian that same year.

But in the 1960s, no one stirred the hearts of American runners like miler Jim Ryun. The mile was the glamour event of middle-distance running in the mid- to late 1960s. In 1967, Ryun, an American from the University of Kansas, broke his own world record (3:51.3 originally set in 1966) in the mile in Bakersfield, California—3:51.1, a record that would stand until 1975. Later in 1967, Ryun also set a world record in the 1,500 meters (3:33.1). All of this success by Americans on the track meant that heading into the 1968 Mexico City Olympics, Steve and his peers had role models on their own soil.

While Steve wasn't yet breaking four minutes himself in 1968, he was inching close enough to the four-minute barrier that comparisons were made to another University of Oregon miler—Dyrol "Burley" Burleson, who had been Oregon's first sub-four minute miler. Yet, their styles were diametrically opposed. Burley, coached by Bowerman in the early 1960s, sat off the leaders and then outkicked them in the final 220 yards. It was effective, but . . . boring, and a bit sleazy.

Steve, on the other hand, lived and died by being at the front, setting a hard pace and daring anyone to stay with him. It wasn't merely a fool's errand and a means of commanding attention; there was a strategy to it as long as you had the mid-race strength to carry that early speed. He dictated the terms of the race. For runners who waited to kick—which was practically everybody—Steve would set so fast a pace that their kick would be systematically drummed out of them as they struggled to keep pace. It was a fearless approach that put him on the line, without compromise. If you wanted to beat him, you were going to suffer.

People were quick to say Steve didn't possess tremendous speed, and what they meant was he didn't have electric footspeed or a long stride. McClure knew this and Steve knew this, which was why they knew the longer the race, the more Steve could grind his competition under. McClure looked around at the other talent in the area. It was unmistakable that Oregon high school runners were emerging like never before. And beyond state lines, just a few more hours north, it had only been two years earlier, in May 1966, that a runner from Spokane, Washington, Rick Riley, had set the national high school two-mile record running 8:48.3. Steve often spoke of "getting ideas," and ideas meant records. This two-mile record piqued his interest.

—

IN CORVALLIS UP Interstate 5—"the five"—from Eugene, it practically rolled out the red carpet for Steve. A headline read "Top Prep Distance Star to Compete Here Friday." From sophomore year to junior year,
Steve had improved nearly sixteen seconds in the mile (4:29.1 to 4:13.8) and
twenty-nine seconds in the two (9:42.1 to 9:13.9).

On the day of the meet, April 26, 1968, there was not a drop of rain, a
gentle breeze, and a soft-to-the-skin temperature of 62 degrees at 5 p.m. On
the bus ride north, the Marshfield squad went from talking to a hush as they
neared Corvallis and McClure gave the signal to be quiet and focus on
the event, and so the bus grumbled north. Steve thought about the two-
mile, eight laps, on Corvallis' all-weather track. He thought back to the
conversations he had had with McClure. They spoke of hitting 9:04 on
sixty-eight–second laps, but hoping to break nine minutes.

Toward the end of the meet, with the sun setting and the temperature
dropping five degrees, Steve approached the line, leaned forward, and bolted
at the sound of the gun. Off he went to the front, though a bit slow through
the first six laps. McClure was, according to Pursian, very much a "watch
guy." McClure peered down at his stopwatch with worry that Steve wasn't
hitting his marks. Through six laps, he was averaging roughly 68.5 seconds
per lap, just off goal pace to break nine minutes, but right on point to get
under 9:04. On the seventh lap, far in front, Steve clipped off a 66.7 lap
setting up a final kick.

Some athletes need to feel the breath of another runner on their neck to
push and find that extra something. Steve appreciated someone pressuring
him, but he didn't need that external sense of urgency; he drew that from the
well within. He was equally driven while out in front, all by himself, taking
the energy from the people who stood witness. And so he ran faster than he
had the previous seven laps, faster despite having spent one and three-quarter
miles setting the stage for what he hoped would be something worth remem-
bering. With the shadows lengthening over the track at Spartan Field, Steve
approached the finish line with a vacant look in his eyes, eyebrows climbing
up his forehead, his arms lifted and his torso twisted, hair blown back. His
cheeks were sunken and if he wasn't still standing you might think him dead.

As his navel broke the tape, the time was 9:01.3, the best-ever prep two-mile in Oregon, ninth best all-time nationally for a prepper and the best prep nationally so far in 1968. McClure stopped the watch and thought Steve looked strong at the end. They expressed mild disappointment, however short-lived, as he'd been within a whisker of breaking nine minutes. They must have been thinking how Steve could have found a mere 1.4 seconds—0.175 seconds per lap—over eight laps so he could've broken nine. So close as to question what more could have been done. The next closest runner was a full thirty-six seconds behind, roughly a half-lap. Steve was, not for the last time, all by himself.

Setting records—or coming close—put a spotlight on Steve and he would never again simply be listed in agate type. Steve had become a headline; he had become a headliner. In a town like Coos Bay, that mattered, even if you were a skinny kid running in circles. Steve, for the first time, began to feel the heat of that light. A week after his smashing two-mile effort, for the forthcoming Coos County Track and Field Championships, Steve wanted to break the state mile record by running 4:08, his goal pace put forth by McClure. The local paper touted Steve as the next great hope and the pressure was, without question, on Steve's mind. The sun dropped and the air cooled. Steve warmed up to cheers.

Steve wore his singlet with the No. 29 on the chest above the winged "M" for Marshfield for the meet. More than a thousand people filed into Pirate Stadium, turning out to see history, far from the last time Steve stood before a demanding crowd. With tensions rising, McClure readied his stopwatch. Steve was as excitable as he was exciting. This was problematic from a pacing perspective. McClure knew Steve had to keep a steady pace: 62s. He could lead, but he shouldn't go out too fast. Better to give himself a chance late in the race. McClure could tell Steve was keyed up.

The gun went off and Steve, true to form, shot for the front. McClure couldn't believe what he was seeing. Steve was practically sprinting. This was a nightmare. McClure yelled for Steve to slow down. Steve ran the first 100 hundred yards in 13 seconds. What McClure wanted from Steve was a good, solid 15.5 through that first 100–110 yards. He thought to himself, *There she goes*. Instead of running the 62-second lap pace he needed for a shot at 4:08, his first lap ended in 58 seconds—a 3:52 pace!—suicidal and, for a coach, dispiriting. McClure saw Steve go beyond his limit to a point of no return. To ration speed, Steve could have run the next lap in 66 seconds, but, instead, he ran through the half-mile in 2:01. Steve was in trouble.

Lap 3 went in 67 seconds and the wobbly-legged junior could only muster a 66.1 final lap, for a final time of 4:14.1, not even close to the goal, or close to the time he had set a few weeks before. He had failed.

After the race, a photograph of Steve showed him sitting on the edge of the track by a chain-link fence. He took his shoes off and let his bare feet air out. His head hung low as he messed with his gear. His slumped body language showed the weight of his disappointment. It didn't matter that he had broken the meet record by some fourteen seconds. In his mind, he let all those people down who came to see him. It was one of his first brushes with the burden of expectation. Steve soon saw running as a partnership between him and the fans. He wanted so desperately to perform for them.

McClure consoled Steve. "People came to see you run. You're that type of runner." Steve learned something from it, that sometimes wins can feel like losses, and losses can feel like wins.

Steve was crushed by not living up to the hype, but he wasn't about to dwell on it. He redeemed himself and easily qualified for the state championships in the two-mile, "his real talent," as McClure noted, at the District 5 meet on May 18, 1968, redeeming his failure to qualify from the previous year. He was asked if he was ready for states. "Ya, I'm ready."

Temperatures never crested 60 degrees on Saturday, May 25, 1968, at Corvallis High School. Perfect. Although Steve had recently earned a mini-profile in the national publication *Track & Field News* lauding his triumphs in the mile that season, for the remainder of this campaign, the mile would be tabled for the two-mile. On a perfect day for Steve, he had a sub-nine effort in mind, "money in the bank" for the Pirates.

Steve took his mark and—pow!—the gun fired. For fear of burning out too early, something he could easily be accused of, he tethered to the pack through the first lap. After the second lap went in 71 seconds—practically walking—he did what he did best: lead.

Frustrated by the early pace, he took off and lengthened his lead on the third lap and carried it lap after lap, so much so that everybody in the race knew they were running for second place. He easily could have coasted and won the championship, but he sprinted as hard as he could in the final hundred yards, so hard that at the finish "his face was twisted from the strain." Overall, though, Steve ran with poise. His fingers were loose, brow furrowed, thigh muscles bulging. Steve set a new meet record of 9:02.7, 6.7 seconds faster than the previous record set a year earlier in 1967. Steve finished a full 16 seconds—roughly 100 yards—ahead of Mark Hiefield. Dellinger wrote to Steve again, as each performance gave him an excuse to touch base.

Nice as it was to receive letters from Dellinger, it was Bowerman who Steve wanted to win over. But in the power structure of coach and athlete, the coach always reigned. Bowerman, known to urinate on athletes in the team showers, or burn them with hot keys in the team sauna as a form of initiation, mailed a letter not to Steve, but to McClure. There was an undercurrent of pride from Bowerman given that McClure had sought his counsel with how best to coach Steve: "My congratulations to you and your fine team, also, my admiration for the fine way you have brought Prefontaine along. Your biggest problem is now ahead. This young man is going to get so much adulation and contacts from all over the USA that it will be a very hard thing to keep his feet on the ground. Please remember that if we don't blow as much smoke up his shirttail that it's not because we don't want him here. We want him, and we hope to help him achieve his very best in education and on the track. . . . Again, congratulations and all the best."

Bowerman didn't tell Steve he wanted him; he told Steve's coach. Bowerman was explicitly playing hard to get with the greatest distance prospect in the country.

THE ALARM CLOCK didn't have to ring before the sun peeked over the towering Douglas firs of the coastal range. Nevertheless, it did. The end of the school year didn't mean Steve stopped running or competing. He logged those miles to the beat of his own metronome.

Training had turned lonely over the summer of 1968. It took singular devotion and focus, often alone, and with nobody to motivate him but himself. His friend Tom Huggins was nursing a knee injury, and besides, Huggins had just graduated—his time at Marshfield was over. Steve was on his own. He confided all this to Dellinger, who, showing increased interest in Steve, replied: "You are right, it is lonely having to run by yourself. When I finished college in 1956, for the next eight years, my training was done almost solely by myself. It is nice to have buddies to visit with while running. On the other hand, I know it is possible to train by yourself." In 1956, having just graduated from Oregon and pointing to the 1960 Rome Olympics, Dellinger, who had enlisted in the Air Force, was stationed at a radar station on the Washington Olympic Peninsula, eighty miles from the nearest track. Bowerman mailed Dellinger interval workouts and, knowing his stride was six feet long, Dellinger counted how many strides it took to run 220s, 440s, and 1320s on hard, sturdy beaches. He trained that way for eight months, by himself, without a watch or knowing the exact distance of his running, back and forth along the beach. Out of necessity, Steve grew to like running alone.

Though Steve had McClure and Pursian to lean on, he felt rudderless without the keen oversight provided by the structures of class and practice. Left to his own devices, he likely would push himself too hard, a maximalist approach that would inevitably lead to burnout or injury. Dellinger continued, "You should be a little careful about overdoing your training this summer. If you are taking a morning run, make sure it is only 1.5 to 3 miles of easy running with, occasionally, a few fast 110s. I would not run during the noon hour, but take a light swim. Be sure this is a nice, relaxing swim and not hard. On your evening running, make sure you alternate going hard and easy."

With little to do but train and think about the season behind him, Steve nitpicked his times, thinking he could have squeezed a few more seconds out of the watch, namely breaking nine in the two-mile, and dipping closer to four minutes in the mile. Part of the problem, as Steve identified for himself, was that he was all alone out there in the front, with no real competition to speak of. Dellinger wrote, "I thought you had a very successful season this year and, certainly, you should not be dissatisfied with your times. I, too, feel that the only thing that kept you from running faster was not having competition. I am sure you will have the opportunity to run well under 9 minutes next year and under 4:05 for the mile."

During the early summer, Steve heeded the guidance of McClure, as well as Dellinger's insistence on ease, lifeguarding at the Mingus Park community pool, pumping gas at a service station, and working as a policy evaluator for a local insurance company. By mid-July though, he'd ramped up his training. There were never enough hours in the day to do all he wanted.

Steve's active mind planned for the forthcoming cross-country season, and part of that preparation was attending a pre-Olympic meet at Hayward on August 23, 1968, that Dellinger had invited him to in a letter. By this point, Steve had earned the attention of other colleges. He didn't know how to handle it. He sought Dellinger's advice. Steve, left-handed, wrote in a childish script with charmingly poor grammar and punctuation:

Dear Mr. Dellinger,

Yesterday I got a letter from Colorado State, with the whole works, admission papers, and everything. What do I do with it. I don't plan on going, but I don't think It would hurt to fill it out.

My running is coming along great. I'm only running about four miles a day, I can hardly wait for C.C. to start. I think this year is going to be a good one for us in Cross country.

Well, I have to go to work now.

Your's truly,
Steve Prefontaine

A week later, Dellinger told him not to waste the money or the time applying to colleges as a courtesy. He said that Oregon charged a $10 fee for admission, and he only encouraged athletes who were serious about attending the U of O to apply. He told Steve he would be getting many offers and that he owed it to himself not to "obligate" himself to anyone. Dellinger shared the pressure he once felt to attend Oregon State University because it had provided him a summer job. "Believe me, I am very happy that I did attend the University of Oregon and ran for Bill Bowerman." He signed off his letter looking forward to seeing Steve.

For that pre-Olympic meet, a late weekend of August 1968, Dellinger also invited a runner named Pat Tyson to Eugene. He and Steve watched the many runners at Eugene's Hayward Field who were tuning up for the Olympics, runners like the Russian slayer Gerry Lindgren, Martin Liquori (as he was then called before going by Marty), Kenny Moore (who would one day write for *Sports Illustrated*), and Bob Schul (1964 5,000-meter gold medalist). No better way to inspire the next generation of runners than by seeing the country's best cut divots in the Hayward cinders.

Tyson, a recently graduated senior from Tacoma, Washington, was an incoming freshman at the U of O, and he had heard of this kid from Coos Bay, Oregon. Tyson was an up-and-coming runner from an upstart high school program. There wasn't much of a pond in Tacoma, but, as luck would have it, Tyson was the big fish in it. Tyson's high school coach was aware of what Bowerman was doing down there in Eugene, Oregon, and he figured if a kid had the skills to be a college runner and walked onto a team coached by Bowerman he could, in the words of Tyson's coach, "become somebody special."

In Tyson's senior year, 1967–68, when he had decided that, yes, maybe Bowerman could make him something special, he read about a junior from Coos Bay named Steve Prefontaine who ran a state record 9:01.3 in the two-mile. Tyson's high school coach was also his science teacher, and in his classroom stood a pile of *Track & Field News* magazines—the bible of the sport, as it was called. Today, it's hard to imagine a scarcity of information about running or training, but back then, each issue became this holy text of features and analysis, an encyclopedia of times and records, a portal to an entire subculture. Getting your name in *Track & Field News* elevated your status, you were a somebody. And Steve was listed as the next great Northwest runner, sharing the pages with Australia's Ron Clarke, who held the world record in the two-mile at the time, 8:19.6; Lindgren, the impish, bespeckled, distance maven; and national high school two-mile record holder Rick Riley, in what was a sure-to-last-several-years 8:48.3.

Dellinger boarded Tyson in a dorm room across the street from Hayward Field. There were two beds to the room so, naturally, Tyson figured he'd have a roommate.

That's when Tyson first met Steve Prefontaine.

Up until that point, Steve had merely been a godly name in *Track & Field News*, a name and a time: 9:01.3 for the two-mile. Then here he was, in the flesh, just another about-to-be senior in high school, clean cut, wide-eyed, Eagle-Scout handsome with the swagger of Joe Namath. Steve captured Tyson's imagination, that a kid could be a distance runner and emit that degree of cool, not the misfit, lanky, scrawny, geeky mold most distance runners—Tyson included—embodied. "He was a 9:01-kid," Tyson said, the ultimate signifier: your PR.

Steve was every bit the opposite of Tyson. Tidal wave to mirrored lake. As would become evident throughout Steve's life, many of his closest friends were people of great stillness and introversion, while also not being a threat to him on the track. With time to socialize, Steve and Tyson walked downtown and entered an athletic shoe store. They held the shoes, turned them over, admired the contours, the weight (or lack thereof) in their hands, even the smells of glue, rubber, and upper materials.

The running shoes of the day were dominated by Adidas and Puma, though Reebok, Wilson, Karhu, Riddell, Spalding, Rawlings, Citius-4, Brooks, and New Balance all also populated the pages of *Track & Field News*. There also was a lesser-known brand emerging in popularity with connections closer to home: Tigers, made by the Japanese company Onitsuka and distributed in North America by Blue Ribbon Sports, a company cofounded by University of Oregon alumnus and shoe maven, Phil Knight, along with Bowerman.

In 1963, after a trip to Japan and a chance meeting with the leadership of the Onitsuka, Knight, a CPA and former 800-meter runner for the University of Oregon, hatched an idea to distribute what he thought were a superior brand of shoe at a far more affordable price, taking advantage of the lower Japanese labor costs: Tigers. Come January 1964, Knight sent Tiger samples to Bowerman. He told Knight, "I like the looks of your Tiger shoe." Bowerman was a cobbler of sorts, always tinkering with shoe materials to make the lightest spike possible. The partnership with Onitsuka offered Bowerman a chance to share shoe designs as long as Knight and Bowerman could be in cahoots in this new venture. By the end of January 1964, sitting by a roaring fire and sipping hot chocolates, Knight and Bowerman became near-equal partners in Blue Ribbon Sports, Knight 51 percent, Bowerman 49 percent.

By August 1965, Blue Ribbon Sports—America's exclusive Tiger distributors—ran its first full-page ad in *Track & Field News*. Its fourth ad ran in January 1967, "Tired of road shock? Twice as much cushion at half the price." Come the Mexico City Olympics in August 1968, a half-page Blue Ribbon Sports ad for the Tiger "Marathon" shoe was constructed with patented "SWOOSH FIBER" (the first known use of "swoosh" tied to Knight) uppers, "a synthetic nylon resin, specially woven to form a unique track shoe upper" that was "lighter than leather, stronger than leather, permanent ventilation. And comfort? Putting it on is half the fun." Blue Ribbon Sports would, in a few years, become Nike with its ubiquitous "swoosh" logo emblazoned all over the world's best athletes for decades to come.

Yet in the 1960s, the world's best track athletes were entirely absent from the ads—in fact, each shoe ad was similar in one way: the shoes were not shown on an athlete's feet. It would violate the amateur code to be sponsored by a company or for an athlete to leverage their likeness for celebrity or monetary gain. An athlete would lose their eligibility and be unable to run in the Olympics, still the ultimate goal for every athlete. As such, an athlete didn't win medals or break records; it was the shoe. One ad: "In the long distances, *TIGER* (emphasis added) ran a 2:09.36 marathon, the fastest of all time"; and, "adidas with the 3 stripes was the only sportshoe in the world to win 33xGold 34xSilver 32xBronze."

While Tyson and Steve gawked at all the gear, the store's proprietor noticed these young men and talked to them about the buzz about a kid by the name of Steve Prefontaine, "Pre," he said. "The kid's been on a roll. Crazy, he still has one more year left of high school." The pair nodded along then Steve, flipping his hair out of his eyes, said, "That's me. I'm Pre."

Tyson admired how Steve wasn't the least bit timid. Steve had these wide eyes, and he bounded around as if walking on water. Tyson marveled at the confidence Steve exuded, the charisma. Even as a seventeen-year-old kid,

Steve had a degree of celebrity Tyson had only read about, and here he was, hanging with him. Tyson was bashful and shy; Steve was most certainly not.

Steve and Tyson attended a nearby fair with its funnel cakes, pop, fried foods, and Ferris wheels, and Steve found, to his taste, countless cute girls. He talked them up, flashed that teeny-bopper smile. Steve and Tyson were ostensibly in Eugene to watch a track meet, see the possibilities should Steve attend the University of Oregon. But, as Tyson said, "It wasn't so much about the rides. It was more about him trying to hook up."

Of course there was the track meet on Friday night, August 23, 1968, where Moore and Lindgren slugged it out in the 10,000 meters, stealing the headlines away from the likes of Jim Ryun. It had rained all day, and the cinder track was soaked through making for "soggy footing." The sun was setting and just about the only things lighting the track were a series of portable lights. In front of 8,000 "frenzied spectators," Moore and Lindgren electrified the crowd that screamed and stomped the wooden bleachers. Moore broke the tape after a gut-busting sprint that saw him rip the lead away from Lindgren on the backstretch. Moore strained to the finish on the inside. He couldn't hide his exhaustion as he set a new Hayward Field record in the 10,000 meters in 28:54.9. One track coach on the scene said it was without a doubt the distance run of the year, "one of the most sensational distance race duels in the long history of Hayward Field."

Moore, wearing his old Oregon singlet and nearly a foot taller than Lindgren, rested his left arm atop the Spokane Sparrow's head, who wore his classic Washington State University singlet and wrapped an arm around Moore's waist. The pair were soon mobbed by autograph seekers.

Lindgren yelled over to Moore, "That was a good one."

"This one is sweet," Moore replied.

"I'm not in shape yet," panted Lindgren.

"I'll accept that," Moore said through a smile.

In the stands, Tyson and Steve watched the race and saw how two Pacific Northwest distance runners raised the rafters and shook the earth.

CHAPTER 4

PREVIOUSLY UNKNOWN SPEED

CROSS-COUNTRY SEASON STARTED in earnest on August 15, 1968, heading into Steve's final year of high school. On training runs, the distance runners would barrel out of Pirate Stadium down 9th Street, turn left on Elrod running past Steve's house, hang a right on 10th and begin the long climb past the Mingus Park pool where Steve worked over the summer, then turn left on Koos Bay Boulevard. They often could run down the middle of the roads, or along narrow foot-worn paths on the road's shoulder. Steve charged ahead all on his own, with the pack far behind.

Without Huggins, Steve was peerless on the team, reliant on himself and what McClure and Pursian could do to push him. The first meet laid bare this problem when Steve finished a full 48.5 seconds ahead of his teammate Kirk Gamble, who placed second. Steve posed a challenge to McClure and Pursian. It was a team sport but at the current moment, it was Steve . . . and everyone else. His performances often suffered when he focused on trying to pull his teammates along.

Still, McClure noticed a "steady growth in maturity and endurance throughout late summer and into the fall." McClure and Steve knew he had to find goals elsewhere. Though track season was months away, McClure and Steve were already plotting, the better to keep him engaged. They spoke of an assault on the national high school two-mile record. The work started now.

As the fall season progressed, with his hair a mess, Steve rolled the District 5-A-1 field in Eugene to win a second-straight district championship.

He was dubbed Marshfield's "super-type" runner. After three-quarters of a mile in the 2.5-mile race, Steve opened up an 80-yard lead on the entire field. He glided over the course; he felt good, but in the last half-mile, he started tightening up—shoulders knotting, stride shortening. It mattered little. Doug Crooks of North Eugene High School finished anywhere from 125 to 140 yards behind Steve in second.

Crooks, roughly the same size as Steve and pale as a ghost, was, like Steve, one of the state's best milers and two-milers in track. They were friendly rivals, though Steve won head-to-head every time. After Steve trounced the District 5 race with Crooks, who later admitted that this race was one of the worst races he ever had in high school, the pair were seen later trading insights about the race. A spectator approached Crooks and said, "You must hate his guts!"

It was a sign of what *The World*'s Kenn Hess eloquently wrote "narrow-minded sports followers fail to comprehend that a bond of sincere comrade-ship, friendship and mutual admiration truly exists between rival athletes, particularly those engaged in individual sports where it's competitor against competitor and the athlete against time and distance—or both." Though Steve would, at times, come off in print as antagonistic, arrogant, and conde-scending to his rivals, he had tremendous respect for his peers.

Steve and Crooks grinned. Crooks mockingly replied, "Yeah."

The person walked away, and they resumed their conversation. Crooks turned to Steve, "They just don't understand, do they? I just didn't have it today. I wish I had been closer to you."

"So do I," Steve said.

For Crooks, he didn't hear what Steve said as being untoward, rude, or insulting. Crooks later recalled, honest in his appraisal that Steve wished he'd been pushed harder, "He was real about it. Because I'll say this about Steve: He loves to get in people's heads, and that's part of his brashness."

Steve's success led to greater confidence with the press and, at times, right to his rivals' faces. Though Steve was maturing, he continued to find strength in trash talk. It held him accountable. Martin Hagger, a sports psychologist for the University of California, Merced, has seen the sci-ence behind Steve's approach. "Trash talk builds your self-efficacy, your self-confidence, self-affirmation. Voicing it is a way of reinforcing it." The instigation was every bit to psych himself up as it was to get into others' heads. They could hate him all they wanted, but he backed it up. Even in this regard, Steve was, indeed, ahead of his time.

Unlike the previous year where Steve entered the cross-country state championships with something to prove and a seemingly unreachable goal to manifest, this year he entered as the defending champion, a favorite. It was time for his final cross-country race as a high schooler, set for a chilly 10:30 a.m. start on November 2, 1968, at Bush Pasture in Salem. A year before, Steve blitzed the 2.5-mile course in 12:13.8, but he'd have his rival Crooks on his heels this year. The 27.2 second margin over Crooks at districts was, as McClure said after the race, "as close as anybody has been to [Steve] this year. Steve is still hungry."

After a false start and reset, the stampede charged, and Steve, "off hard" and in characteristic fashion, struck the front. He was soon by himself, some 20 yards ahead of the field early in the race. This would prove much closer than districts, only it wasn't Crooks on his heels, but Mark Hiefield of Milwaukie, following close and pressuring Steve—pressure he hadn't felt all season. Steve plowed ahead, his spikes kicking up grass and his singlet and shorts pressed tightly to his skin. Brow furrowed and charging forth, Steve maintained the lead with Hiefield closing, the sound of his breath within earshot, the presence of a hard gainer. The gap narrowed, but Steve still held strong heading down the final straightaway. He hit the finish first in a time of 11:30.2, a smashing time, four seconds ahead of Hiefield.

The time was brilliant. A little *too* brilliant. Turns out, the Bush Pasture course was mis-measured and was 150 yards too short, not a true 2.5 miles. Steve's goal was to break twelve minutes over the course. If he was at a full sprint, and factoring in fatigue, conservatively he would have run the final 150 yards in 25 seconds, maybe faster. Doing the math: sub-twelve.

He was state champion in cross-country once again, but it didn't take long for him to turn his attention to the track.

Keeping in tune with his penchant for good-natured trash talk and the subtle art of mind games, Steve took out a sheet of paper and wrote "Beat Crooks" in prominent letters. Not that Steve had ever lost to Crooks, but he wanted to rib his rival every chance he got. Crooks, the reigning state mile champion, then received a phone call. On the other end of the line was Steve inviting Crooks to visit Coos Bay to train on the dunes and maybe run in a random indoor meet that winter in Reedsport. Crooks agreed. The forthcoming track season would allow runners to double in the mile and the two-mile. Steve had his sights on repeating in the two, but now the mile added to Steve's temptations and Crooks was Steve's foil.

When Crooks arrived at Steve's house, Steve showed Crooks his bedroom and there, prominently displayed, was the sign: "Beat Crooks." Crooks laughed. In a time before "visualization," perhaps this was Steve's way of putting his chief rival in the mile on the forefront of his mind. If Steve could plant doubt in a rival's head, whether it worked or not, it didn't matter as long as *Steve* believed it gave him an advantage. It boosted his mental approach.

Much to Steve's chagrin, the race at Reedsport was canceled. It didn't matter that it was an obscure, off-the-wall race—he wanted to compete. So Steve suggested they go for a long run anyway, make a game of it.

The two set out. Eight to ten miles. They ran side by side and Steve pointed to a spot. "He wanted to race to *that* point," Crooks recalled. They powered on. "Then he wanted to race to *that* point because he loved pushing himself. Steve liked to run up front. A part of his personality was that way."

After that long run, Crooks went back to Eugene. They'd meet again soon enough.

IN FEBRUARY 1969, STEVE and his coaches were planning something big. It wasn't enough to be state champion anymore. Steve had done that three times: twice in cross-country and once in track and field in the two-mile.

McClure and Pursian utilized Bowerman's training plans: the date pace/goal pace philosophy. Red ink in the training log was goal pace and black ink was date pace: the pace the athlete could run on that day. And on Monday, February 10, 1969, in Pursian's distance logbook, atop the list of distance runners was PREFONTAINE. To the left of his name was his current date pace for the two-mile: 9:12. Written in red ink just below that was 8:40.

To the untrained eye you'd say that's awfully swift . . . but what did it mean? If Steve ran within 8.2 seconds of that time, he would break the national high school record set in 1966 by Rick Riley.

McClure spoke to Steve about his spring goals and McClure walked away knowing that the more challenging the goal Steve set for himself, the more rewarding the training. Put another way, without ambitious goals, training was a drag. Steve had a vision, and his training fed into his goal setting. Goals born "not from over-confidence, rather from a desire to explore the unknown," McClure wrote.

On a Monday, the "warmups" were hellish unto themselves. The first set was 8x220 with a 110 shag—so eight 220-yard sprints, followed by a 110-yard jogging recovery. One and a half miles, roughly. They did that one more time, another round of 8x220s. After that, 8x110s with a 55-yard shag. Good and loose? Okay, let's do the real working sets at date pace.

- One 1,320 (3 laps) at 3:23 with a 440 shag
- One 1,100 (2.5 laps) at 2:52 with a 440 shag
- One 880 (half-lap) at 2:18 with a 440 shag
- Two 440s (quarter-laps) at 69 seconds with a 220 shag
- Six 165s between 34.5 and 25.7 seconds with a 110 shag

Workouts of this nature were commonplace for Steve. The hope, of course, was that these brutal track sessions would translate into eye-popping results, records. And so it was during an early season track meet when Pursian looked down at his stopwatch at Steve's first mile race of the season. Pursian yelled, "How's that for openers!"

A haggard-at-the-finish-line Steve, looking like he had more in common with a mummified pharaoh than an eighteen-year-old high school boy, finally broke the Oregon high school mile mark with a time of 4:11.1 in the first dual meet of the outdoor season. He then parlayed that by winning the two-mile. Overcast, windy, Oregon Coast weather in early spring, "biting cold nipping at his heels," the wind took a lot out of him. Steve felt "dried out," and the image of his face would suggest how spot-on a comment that was.

These hard miles primed him for speed. For six months, Steve and his two-headed brain trust had worked toward this final season, and questions surfaced about whether Steve's best event was the mile or two-mile. The mile was still the marquee event of the day, no less diminished with American Jim Ryun still holding the world record. Steve looked up to Ryun. Everyone from that time did—after all, he was only a few years older. McClure conceded Steve's desire to run as close to four minutes in the mile as possible, but McClure knew Steve's strength could carry his speed farther, making him a far more dangerous two-miler. "In the two-mile, he would like to get that national prep record." Just shy of three weeks from the Corvallis Invitational, on April 8, 1969, McClure put it out there and let the greater area know the full scope of Steve's ambition on the school's rubber asphalt, all-weather track, which was practically state of the art.

Surveyors set up at Corvallis High to ensure the track was of regulation distance. For the record to be legitimate, the track had to be within a whisker of a quarter-mile. It would be devastating to break the record only to find the track was deemed too short. The track coach for Corvallis was inconvenienced by the ordeal. He called McClure and said, "Next time you want to set a national record on my track, you might get a 'no.'"

Workouts for Steve had been going well. Mainly in the mile range and mile tempos, but McClure and Pursian knew that Steve craved more. They told him to only run three to four miles in the mornings, easy runs, that's it. He said, "Yeah, sure, that's what I'll do." Wink, wink. Steve's morning runs, for him, were too boring.

Steve woke for his clandestine workouts with an easy half-mile, usually up a hill that could use a chairlift. In the middle of these four-mile jaunts, with the punishing hill as part of his warmup, he surged beyond workout pace to Steve pace. He made notes in his mind about certain markers on the course. He might mark out a telephone pole or another landmark and think, *This is how far I got before I felt tired enough to want to slow down.* The next morning, he pushed himself harder to go beyond yesterday's limits. He wended his way home, coasting in with little more than a slab of cheap foam between his feet and the ground. Steve's coaches had no idea what Steve was up to these mornings. Had they known, they would have been deeply upset. Steve risked injuring himself, but he also was bucking the plan set out by their prescribed workouts with the intention of peaking at a specific time and place.

If Steve was feeling the pressure, he didn't show it. Pursian witnessed how carefree Steve's attitude was by how fast he sped out of the parking lot after practice to see his girlfriend in nearby Coquille. Contrary to what people might think of the elite athlete, so valuable was Steve's time that he often was the first to show and the first to *go* after practice.

McClure and Pursian started to dial him back, tapering. Yet as they prepared for race day, around the state, runners knocked on the nine-minute door threatening Steve's hegemony. A runner near Portland logged a 9:03.3 and Doug Crooks ran 9:03 flat, becoming the second-fastest two-miler in Oregon prep history behind only Steve. Newspapers zeroed in: "Don't look over your shoulder, Steve Prefontaine!"

Steve wasn't the only runner improving. As the Corvallis Invitational neared, Crooks was "pretty prepped," even excited. Most track meets came and went, barely a footnote in the largesse of a school year. But Crooks admitted this meet was, in fact, a big deal. Rare was it that he thought about a meet in the week leading up. Somewhat out of character, he couldn't stop thinking about this one.

It was on everyone's minds in the week leading up to Friday, April 25, 1969, but Crooks' high school coach, Bob Newland, race promoter and confidante of the one and only Bill Bowerman, knew Steve's goal. Newland told Crooks he didn't think Steve could pull it off, so stay on pace, don't get sucked into Steve's vortex. Let Steve run himself ragged, and we'll stick to a plan that'll earn us an 8:55 and be the first sub-nine two-miler in Oregon history, and one of the rare high schoolers nationally to ever do so. The goal, Newland told his star runner, was to run the first mile in 4:30, then pick up a bit each lap until the finish. "You should easily be able to get to 8:55," Newland told Crooks.

Rick Riley, now a sophomore at Washington State University and the reigning high school record holder in the two-mile, was tasked by Jack Mooberry, the WSU coach, with calling Steve to pitch him on coming to Pullman, Washington, to be a Cougar. Few people thought Steve would leave the state of Oregon, but Riley, being a good soldier, dialed up Steve anyway.

Riley exchanged niceties with Steve. Before long, Steve told Riley, "I'm gonna break your record."

Riley, not particularly adversarial or the least bit egotistical, said, "Well . . . that's cool."

"I'm going to run 8:40 this week," Steve said. Few college runners could run that fast. The world record at the time was 8:19.6, held by Australia's Ron Clarke. Riley was taken aback by the brashness of this "irreverent youngster." Riley, reflecting on his record, would later express that you ran those races and those times for someone else to break them. When he hung up the phone he thought, *That was an interesting conversation. Shit, my record was 8:48.3 and he wants to break it by nearly eight full seconds? Well, good luck.*

And then it was time.

By now, everyone knew Steve's plan. In 1968, Steve ran 9:01.3 on Corvallis' all-weather surface. Though it wasn't his home track, the mental edge of having already broken a record there gave him extra confidence. By design, Steve and his coaches hadn't entered him in many two-mile races that spring. The few he did run were rehearsals to run 66-second laps with a 4:24 opening mile with the ultimate target being somewhere between 8:40 to 8:45, well clear of Riley's record.

McClure knew what this meant to Steve. It was the only thing he thought about. He had been building to a moment where he could leave a mark. McClure's worry boiled down to Steve's excitement level, his pacing. Steve didn't have the benefit of a rabbit—a pacesetter. He had to modulate his pace on his own knowing everyone behind him would be reading him, waiting on him to make a mistake, to burn out. He needed to run relaxed and remain tall. If a front runner went out too fast, there was no recovering.

The tactical advantage always favored the followers. Clarke, the Aussie who would soon be retiring, held five world records at the time, and as it related to Steve, "Clarke defied the one edict that, in contests among equals, approaches law: The Pacesetter Never Wins," wrote Kenny Moore. "Ron Clarke was a front runner out of principle. He accepted each of his races as a complete test, an obligation to run himself blind." It nauseated Clarke to watch superior runners coast behind the field until 200 meters remained and then sprint ahead of the field and win. "That is immoral," he said. A sentiment Steve would share, saying, years later, "I hate to have people back there sucking on me."

Rivals knew the book on Clarke, and knew it on Steve, too. That didn't stop the front runner from attacking a race. In modern-day sport psychology, an athlete's tendencies—like Steve's front running—are a mental tactic as much as a race strategy. By dictating the pace and slowly turning the screws lap after lap, doubt can creep in among the others who aren't comfortable drafting in that wake. It gets in someone's head.

Early spring in Oregon can bring anything from drizzly rain to torrential rain, to persistent pulsating rain and tree-bending winds, with a chill to the air that could tighten up a runner's shoulders, arms, and legs. That mattered little to McClure. "Regardless of the weather, we're going for it."

As confident as Steve appeared, the moment was, in fact, subsuming him. He told McClure, "My stomach has been upside-down for three days."

"Mine has been that way for five weeks," McClure replied.

The night before the race, Steve had a dream he ran 8:40. It was so vivid, so real that when he woke up, he thought he had done it, tired as if he had run it. When he realized he was still in his bed, he thought, *Hell, I've got to run the whole thing again.*

People in the area were calling the Corvallis Invitational the meet of the season. A bold statement in normal times. This wasn't the state championship meet but, given the stakes of an open attempt at a major record, people were going to turn out to watch a track meet made all the more special since it was under the lights.

Working in Steve's favor was something he rarely had: strong competition. His brilliant inner drive had carried him to this point; the question now was what the others would do in reaction to him. Record attempts need several ingredients, not just an athlete primed and peaking. Some runners wilt when challenged, so used to dominating that pressure crumbles them. Not Steve, though. "He will be pushed this time," Mel Boldenow, the Corvallis High track coach, said.

Admission to the covered grandstand was $1 for adults and 50 cents for students. The main meet was set to start at 7 p.m. If all went according to plan, the two-mile was set for the fitting and coincidental time of 8:40 p.m.

Visions of 8:40 dancing in his head, Steve took his seat on the team bus. The ride up to Corvallis for the meet was quiet. Most of the team knew what was up, but it was a dead-silent ride, just the way McClure liked it, the better to focus on the events at hand. Steve sat by himself visualizing his race. Ron Apling, a junior on the team and one of Steve's close friends, was so excited. He couldn't believe he was friends with someone who had the ability—the capacity—to shoot for such a record. And Steve was just a kid from the southwest corner of Oregon, of all places.

Wearing his North Eugene colors, Crooks put his trust in Coach Newland, who still didn't think Steve could break the record. Crooks didn't question his coach. So Crooks did what he usually did. He ran a few warmup laps, then he performed some sprints, and some stretches. His stomach fluttered—racing against Steve did that to a runner—as he signed into the race with the clerks. Steve was in Crooks' head. *Beat Crooks.*

As the race neared, McClure and Pursian talked about their main concern for Steve: pace. Everyone else knew he was going for a big time. He must not flame out early. McClure and Pursian wanted him no faster than 4:20 for that first mile. Maybe even a little slower by a second or two but no faster. If they looked down at their watches and saw 4:16, they knew he'd be toast. He might still win, but they weren't there merely to win.

They monitored Steve's warmup and a reporter approached McClure inquiring about Steve. Pursian, by McClure's side, who by now was more nervous than Steve or McClure, snapped, "Get out of here! We got a race to run! The kid's running the race! We don't need to deal with your questions right now!"

McClure calmly swiveled to face Pursian and pulled him back. Pursian was now standing. McClure gently urged him to relax. The reporter backed away and left the two coaches. "That's how uptight we were," Pursian recalled. "McClure was the same way, but he was more reserved. He was all business."

The temperature on this Friday night, April 25, 1969, was a cool 52 degrees with a light breeze. Not a drop of rain to be found and the sun had long set.

The lights hummed and illuminated the track. So rare for these high schoolers to run under the lights. It wasn't so much a track meet as it was a spectacle. A thousand people eagerly awaited the featured event. The runners trotted on the track, slowly made their way to the starting line, and waited for the gun.

Pursian, up in the stands near the finish line, his heart in his throat, thought to himself, *Hold your pace!* The starter raised his pistol and pulled the trigger.

Steve was the pace. He shot out early and cleared the field, bending into the first turn, the empty expanse of the track laid out before him. Up in the stands, Pursian and McClure, stopwatches in hand, thought, *Hold your pace! Hold your pace!*

Steve breezed around, hugging the inner white line. The field followed several yards behind. If Crooks were to believe Newland, it was only a matter of time before Steve burned himself out and started the slow erosion back to the field. McClure had looked down at his watch and saw that Steve was two seconds slower on his first lap than he was hoping, but, he figured, better to be a bit off pace early than late.

The first few laps, Steve's lead grew, but McClure and Pursian didn't panic. Steve looked comfortable, within himself, and he was holding pace out there on the lead, running to his own internal clock, making the race his own.

Three-quarters of a mile into the race, McClure and Pursian looked at each other, their eyes widening in disbelief. There was still a lot of race left, but . . . *This is happening. He's gonna get there.* Steve was approaching 4:20 for the mile—right on pace—and looking fresh. In fact, he was a tad slower, 4:25, which meant he'd likely have the juice to perhaps run 4:20 or faster over the next mile. But anything could still happen. He could trip. Another runner could move up on him and clip his heels.

At the mile, Crooks was 50 yards behind Steve, roughly seven seconds back. Still, he trusted his coach, not his own instincts. Crooks sped up, per his coach's plan, and now he had to start a new race. But despite running the fifth lap faster than his previous ones, he was farther behind after accelerating.

Steve had found another gear.

Crooks coasted in second place, but futility had set in. If he couldn't close the gap, it was likely better to power down and be a spectator, save some juice for the rest of the season. With three laps to go, that much was clear. Crooks thought, *Wow, he's really out there*. At this point, he started to downshift. It was all Steve's race.

Every 200 meters, McClure and Pursian peeked up and down from Steve to their stopwatches to see if he was holding pace. A half mile to go, they willed Steve to hang on; they were witnessing something that had never been done and he was doing it by himself.

Steve's teammate and friend, Apling, who was on the infield watching the race, ran to the finish line and yelled, "Go, Pre!" Seven laps down in 7:40. One lap remaining. Steve thought, *I think I got it now, but I'm going to have to go for it*. He revealed the hint of a confident grin. On that final lap, it was Steve against the specter of Riley. A tepid final lap would still give him the record, but he ran harder. He would never be satisfied to glide into the finish line even with the time secure and the race long won; he needed to fully wring himself out. After running one and three-quarter miles, Steve throttled up, his head swiveling and the stride remaining long and true. Apling then sprinted to the top of the stretch, roughly 220 yards from the finish, and yelled again, "Go, Pre! You got this!" Steve bent around the curve and straightened out for the final sprint with the crowd screaming. Apling did his best to dash back across the infield to the finish line on a diagonal. "GO, PRE! COME ON! YOU CAN DO IT!" Looking over his right shoulder he saw Steve all alone with the numbers on the clock in the low 8:30s.

The crowd cheered him as his limbs began to flail and his head bobbed from side to side. He was drained, fully drained, but upright, and swift. He poured it all out, scraped his insides. The crowd gave it back. He carried them; they carried him. He hit the tape.

8:41.5 for the "Marshfield Machine." It might not have been the time in his dream, but it smashed Riley's record.

Pursian, bespectacled, wearing a shirt and tie, blazer, and dark, sensible slacks, with two stopwatches around his neck, told McClure, "I gotta get down there before the reporters. I gotta get down there and make sure he gets a lap in before he gets hung up with reporters, that he gets a chance to cool down."

He ran to the track. Steve threw his right arm around Pursian and Steve's right hand lay dead over his coach's shoulder. Steve closed his eyes, his head was thrown back over his right shoulder. Pursian smiled at Steve, a big smile that signified all the vision and work that went into this moment where Steve broke his own state record by nearly twenty seconds and a national record by nearly seven. Apling held Steve's left arm at the finish. Steve could barely stand. It wouldn't last because when he heard the final time announced (erroneously as 8:40, the same as in his dream), he jolted awake from his witless deliverance and yelled, "This must be the Olympics!" And he went off trotting around the track in a victory lap. The crowd gave him a standing ovation. Crooks thought the Olympics comment was a bit silly but then he saw the time and said to himself, *Wow. Well done.*

For Crooks, it was disappointing for what might have been. He finished 200 yards behind in second place with a time of 9:07.2—25.7 seconds back. He put his faith in his coach's handicapping and ran his pace on the assumption that, perhaps, Steve would carelessly tire too soon. Crooks wasn't even tired at the end of the race. He could have run so much faster, not thirty seconds faster, but maybe twenty seconds. He wondered what would have happened had he stayed within striking distance, running right off Steve's shoulder.

In the meantime, Steve bounded around the track, waving to the fans. He delivered on his promise. Nobody embraced a victory lap quite like Steve. "Man, isn't this something," Steve said. "I can't believe it. It's something I've looked forward to for a long time." He said it with a "smile of satisfaction as wide as the Willamette Valley and in his effervescent style."

It had been six months in the making, all the way back to the fall of 1968. That time was the goal. This meet was the venue. It was likely the adrenaline talking, but Steve said how much he enjoyed the race and that he had been more tired after other races.

All the more impressive was that Steve wasn't pressured on the front end. He ran to the beat of the clock. His pacing was pristine, amazingly popping off 68, 66, 66, and 65 seconds through the first mile for a 4:25. The second mile charged in 66, 65, 64 and 61.5 seconds for a 4:16.5 mile—not much slower than his Oregon state mile record of 4:11, this after running a blistering opening mile. Never threatened, he ran with remarkable discipline and, as one paper noted, "previously unknown speed." It was enough for the *Oregon Journal* to call it "'Pre'-mendous!" atop a photograph that showed Steve's head cocked to the right, mouth agape, legs knock-kneed and faltering.

Steve's father Ray said, "He's worked tremendously hard for this. He's always moving. Even around the house he can't sit still." Ray mentioned that during the winter when the snow flurried down and blanketed their city, Steve was "like a caged cat . . . He wanted to run in two feet of snow." He lauded his son for the years of waking up at 5:30 a.m. for his morning five- to six-mile run, this in addition to his afternoon workouts.

As Steve ran around the oval, waving to the fans who stood for him and rained down applause, this record was far from the end of something, but, rather, the start. Years later, Steve would remember this night as his most pure moment, the highlight of his life.

CHAPTER 5

GRADUATION

THE HIGH FROM the race lasted through the weekend and into the next week. Steve Prefontaine stood atop the track-and-field world. The sports community was desperate to know what was possible for this young man. Steve energized the Oregon running scene, with one official from the Corvallis Invitational saying, "You have to realize that this boy ran a tough 4:25 mile and then kept right on going for a 4:16.1 (actually 4:16.5)—and obviously he had a lot left at the finish! And he doesn't just have endurance, he also has speed. How fast can this kid run?"

The "backwoods sports buffs" of the Coos Bay Quarterback Club convened in town to honor Steve. Mildly embarrassed, he sat to the side, quietly listening to McClure praise him. "Coos Bay is a proud town," McClure said. "As long as I've been here, it always has been proud of its kids who have gone on to do well. Coos Bay can be extremely proud of this boy."

McClure's words spoke to the gravity of Steve's achievement, which, to all of those of the inner circle, knew that it wasn't a solo effort. This record *meant* something. It brought national attention to the seaside city best known for its lumber exports. McClure said, "He has been willing to pay the price. He has been more dedicated than any other athlete I have ever had." The record set things in motion that couldn't be undone. He would one day say, "That kind of brought everything on. Without that record I probably wouldn't be where I am now."

All this said, the pressure wasn't about to cease or relent. Breaking the prep national two-mile record came at a cost. Steve was now bombarded with letters from track coaches all over the country, many from schools he'd never heard of. Steve admitted that about thirty-five colleges expressed interest in him. He got so much mail that it took him an hour and a half every night to read through it all. Beyond the mail, the Prefontaine phone rang off the hook. Stanford University, Princeton University, and Villanova all expressed interest in Steve, but the odds-on favorite was either the University of Oregon or Oregon State. Steve was forever at his core an Oregon boy.

Eventually, to take pressure off Steve, McClure began fielding the calls. Southern California's coach asked if Steve could come and visit. McClure said, "Where were you last year?"

"We hadn't heard of him last year," he said.

"Steve was the third fastest two-miler in the country as a junior. USC ought to pay better attention," and he hung up. For a time, Steve almost regretted breaking the record.

After the Coos Bay Quarterback Club meeting, McClure admitted that he had felt "deflated," and that he "had a monkey on his back." True, the pressure was substantial, and they made it to the other side. They could savor the moment, but the season wasn't over yet. It's hard not to read between the lines of what McClure was saying when expressing the thrill of the opportunity to coach the boy: it was soon coming to an end.

"LET'S GO FOR the mile," Steve told McClure.

Of course they'd give it a shot, though in McClure's bones he thought it might be a stretch to break four minutes. Feeling invincible off his record-breaking performance, Steve figured he could cut back at the Coos County Meet on May 9, 1969—his final high school race over the Marshfield rubber-asphalt track. He could serve the hometown fans one lasting, surging memory. He was their national record holder.

Jim Ryun, who would be graduating from the University of Kansas in the spring of 1969, was still the star of the day and invincible at the mile as the world record holder. He still owned the best record of only three high schoolers to have broken the four-minute barrier (3:55.3), (along with Tim Danielson [3:59.4] and Martin Liquori [3:59.8]). To date, Steve's best time at the four lapper was 4:11.1, an Oregon state high school record, but nearly thirteen seconds—close to 100 yards—off Ryun's mark. McClure, though, pointed out that Steve's mile races in 1969 had "all been under controls of one type or another." Controls, of course, to break the two-mile record. But in the next week they would shoot for something spectacular. After all, there'd been a governor on his earlier mile times. He'd already chased the two-mile rabbit. Steve wanted to turn it loose in the mile, energized, perhaps, by having, at last, chosen his college. Was there ever any doubt? It was Bill Bowerman and the University of Oregon Ducks . . . but Oregon still needed to court Steve.

Over the previous winter, before the national record, Bill Dellinger remained in touch with Steve. Dellinger told McClure at a cross-country meet in the fall that when he looked at Steve he saw a level of intensity that you rarely saw in an athlete. Dellinger had arranged for the upperclassmen Roscoe Divine and Arne Kvalheim to visit Coos Bay and run with Steve, make him believe that becoming a Duck sure as hell beat any other option. Steve expressed interest in running one of the more difficult courses that he trained on. It involved the immutable dunes and soft sand. Divine and Kvalheim weren't too keen on doing something too trying, but, as Dellinger said, "If Steve wants to do it, we're going to do it."

Pursian, McClure, and Dellinger dropped Steve, Divine, and Kvalheim just off Highway 101 near North Bend, the neighboring city to the north of Coos Bay. They ducked down the trail and out of sight. It had been raining steadily for days. At times it could feel like the rain was coming up from the ground. The three traversed the first dune-like area and, thanks to the incessant rain, the sand was packed down, not quite as slippery under foot. Once they trod toward the bottom of the dune, there was a massive puddle. Steve didn't slow down, and they plowed right into the puddle, splashing all the way through. Up came another dune, and by now their feet were soaked through. Once they cleared that dune and powered down the other side, there was yet another puddle, but far larger and deeper. The rain poured and the wind whipped the rain into a frenzy. The water came up to Steve's waist. But they waded through, and Steve kept pounding the pace. Steve showed them no shortage of confidence and willingness to endure discomfort at a level very few could. His parents and his city had drilled toughness into him. Steve called back to them, "Getting tired? Am I going too fast for you?"

By the time the run was over, soaked and sandy, Divine and Kvalheim must have thought, *This punk better come to Oregon . . .* or maybe not.

Rumors circulated that Steve would choose Oregon State University over Oregon. But there was never any real decision. Steve allegedly wanted to hear from Bowerman himself—not Dellinger—if he so desperately wanted Steve to become a Duck, a "Man of Oregon." Bowerman relented. He scribbled a barely legible letter to Steve saying that if he came to Oregon, he could be the greatest distance runner ever. When Steve got that letter and tore it open, Steve's father remembered him being in "seventh heaven." In late April 1969, Steve Prefontaine and his 3.0 to 3.45 GPA said, "Where's the dotted line?" On a Tuesday night, April 29, 1969, Steve proudly said, "I'm going to become a Duck."

Oregon loves nothing more than its homegrown athletes who remain in the Pacific Northwest. Steve added his name to the roster of other Oregon running royalty: Dyrol Burleson of Cottage Grove, Jim Grelle of Lincoln, and, of course, Bill Dellinger of Springfield. Handicapping Steve vs. some runners in the Pacific 8 Conference, Steve's 8:41.5 two-mile was surpassed by just four college runners.

On May 8, 1969, satisfied by Steve's decision, Bowerman penned a letter to *The World*. Bowerman wrote of his great appreciation for the Coos Bay community, for McClure's outstanding coaching, and Steve's family for making Steve's accomplishments possible. "Believe me," he wrote, "we are honored, flattered, and of course pleased that he has chosen the University of Oregon. . . . I do feel that our accomplishments in the running events, where we have had more sub-four minute milers, as well as more runners on the United States Olympic team, than any other area, probably had something to do with his choice."

Steve's ambitions were to make an Olympic team some day—the Munich Games were three years away. Bowerman wanted to let the community know that he was "aware of the great responsibility" to assure Steve had the best possible chance to achieve his goals on the track while not forgetting the need for a good education. Bowerman expressed that if Steve "keeps his eye on the target," his dedication, along with the toughness endemic to his background as a native of Coos Bay, Steve could, quite literally, "become the greatest runner in the world."

Bowerman also added a note chilling in its prophecy. More likely he referred to the known obstacles any young man setting off on his own for the first time would face: independence, competition, friendships, women, drugs, alcohol, a brazen spirit let loose on the world. He wrote, "There are many pitfalls along the way."

For now, Steve couldn't see the pitfalls. Instead his future was secure ahead of the sixtieth annual Coos County meet slated for Friday night, May 9, 1969. Expectations were high. People would file in by the 4:15 p.m. start with the mile going off at 7:30 p.m. For $1.25, a Bay Area sports fan might see something special.

For Steve, breaking four minutes was the dream; every miler wanted to. It was also a measure of status: in the fraternity, or not. 3:59.9, welcome in; 4:00.0, try again. As with anything, it all depended on how Steve felt, the conditions, the weather, whether he could handle his pace, whether he had any help on the lead (he wouldn't). Steve had never been down that close, but it wouldn't stop him from shooting for it.

He delivered for the two-mile record two weeks before, but he had failed other times in front of his people when the pressure was too much; he didn't want to disappoint, he *never* wanted to disappoint. It wasn't enough that he already had the Coos County mile record at 4:14.1, which seemed like child's play at this point. He had the state record already, but to be sub-four? That's why the stands were packed on a cool, breezy evening at Pirate Stadium. Nearly 2,000 people filed in. One of the earlier events was the two-mile and, no, Steve Prefontaine wasn't running in that. His focus was solely on the mile . . . sort of.

When the two-mile went off, his friend Kirk Gamble, a fellow senior who was in Steve's shadow, whipped around the track. Much of his improvement he owed to Steve, chasing after him day after day. "He runs me until I'm ready to drop sometimes." "Gamby," as he was sometimes called, strode around the track. There, in the infield, zigging and zagging across the field from the backstretch to the homestretch was Steve cheering on Gamble. With every lap, Steve followed Gamble. It got to the point where Steve's coaches yelled at him to conserve his energy. But he didn't listen. For this moment, Gamble charged ahead; Gamble was out of Steve's shadow. Gamble crossed the line with a career best 9:26.5 and broke the old Coos County meet record by thirteen seconds. Friends would later quiz people and ask, "Who set the Coos County meet two-mile record set in 1969?" And when they inevitably said Steve Prefontaine, they would be wrong. The record then rested in the hands of Kirk Gamble, Class of 1969.

If nothing else, Steve was already warmed up from cheering Gamble on. Steve readied for his race, began visualizing the pace. To break the four-minute barrier without a rabbit would mean he'd have to pace himself. There wasn't a runner on the coast who could push him, so it would have to come from within.

In his gold singlet with No. 13 on the chest, Steve burst from the line. The crowd cheered as Steve leaned into the inside lane hugging the white stripe around the first turn and down the backstretch. A year ago at this time, Steve wanted to break 4:10, but settled for 4:14.1.

Tonight, he went out fast. Not again. That was always the peril of the front runner: they may take the kick out of closers, but they risk their capacity to fend off the late charge. The front runner is the most exciting runner to watch because it is all tension. They are out there doing the work, cutting a hole in the wind. McClure and Pursian called out Steve's split: First lap, 58-59 seconds. Pursian thought it was too fast.

Steve knew it, too.

He thought he was pacing at 60 to 61 seconds, but when he heard the split, it rattled his cage. Up to that point, he knew he had a good warmup. He had felt good all day and in less than a minute, he was in trouble. The air was chilly, but not so much that it would have a great effect on his body.

Three laps remained and his arms and shoulders tightened up. For the rest of the race, he'd be fighting his body. At the end of two laps, the call was 2:03. McClure, Pursian, and Steve had hoped to be around 3:01 or 3:02 for three laps, and then let it all out for Lap 4, but that quickly became fantasy. McClure thought before the race that a time under four was possible, but they hadn't worked as hard on this effort as they did for the national two-mile push.

But onward Steve charged through his third lap and into the final. The people were on their feet urging and pleading for Steve while the clock climbed ever closer to four minutes. Steve closed his eyes as he lunged toward the tape. His hair had whipped back, and his mouth gasped for air.

4:06.9.

It broke his own state record by more than four seconds. It was the fastest time for a prep runner in the United States that year and sixteenth fastest prep mile ever.

He slowed to a jog and soon trotted away. McClure thought that perhaps Steve didn't break four minutes because of the success he had with the national two-mile record. It could have been "the pressure he felt by the presence of all these people who came out just to see him—twice as many as at Corvallis when he ran the two-mile—the physiology and the psychology of it. But how can you be disappointed with a boy like that?"

McClure would always maintain that Steve's strength meant the longer the race, the better. But also there was something intangible at play with Steve: "the price he is willing to pay." The physical, yes, but also performing for thousands of people who paid admission to see *him*.

Athletes of a certain caliber all have a power that unlocks their greatness. The best have many, but it could be that Steve's was, as McClure noted, "the price he is willing to pay." If someone was hurting, Steve would hurt more. If you were going to beat him, you'd remember it in more ways than one. He would take you to your limit and even if he beat you, if you looked down at your watch, odds were you ran a PR keeping pace. Sacrifice, dedication; he was willing to bleed for the people and, really, for himself. Few high school athletes felt what he felt. Even at eighteen, he had the self-awareness to know he was the draw. People came to see him, and he wasn't about to win with ease, though he could have. There was no next time; only now. Though McClure was not the least bit disappointed in Steve, Steve was crushed.

Steve's friend Ron Apling watched Steve turn himself inside out to break four minutes. Shortly after finishing the race, Steve ducked around the corner and out of sight. Steve was sitting on the ground, head hung low, taking off his spikes. He was crying.

Apling asked, "Steve, what's the matter?"

"They all came to watch me break four minutes," he said. "And I failed them."

Apling told Steve he ran an amazing race, told him that the time was still awesome.

"Yeah," Steve said, "but they came to watch me break four minutes and I didn't do it."

The pain, the letdown, it was part of the price, but despite Steve's disappointment in himself for not breaking the four-minute barrier, he would brush it off and win state championships in the mile and the two-mile just a few weeks later. In the two-mile, he was pressed all the way by Mark Hiefield and proved he could win a dog fight just as often as he could by day light. He ended his high school career as he'd always intended: in front.

STEVE WAS NEVER one to dwell much on the past. He knew he was on to bigger and better things. If anything, the two-mile record unlocked something deep inside him. Steve said, "It proved that if I set myself to do something, I could do it. It was like the sun coming up in my mind. I really began to get ideas."

High school was over. And in the summer that followed, Steve was courted for the tenth annual Golden West Invitational Track and Field Meet on June 14, 1969, at Hughes Stadium in Sacramento, California. Steve's goal, as it had been at the Coos County meet, was simple, though not easy: break four minutes in the mile.

Pursian joined Steve as his coach and chaperone. But he was also a voice of reason for Steve. The officials for the Golden West pressured Steve to double in the mile and the two-mile. Steve told Pursian, "They keep telling me I should double. I can be the MVP of the meet if I'll just double." The organizers were all too keen to play to Steve's ego, far from the first bureaucrats to squeeze what they could from rank-and-file runners. This happened, according to Pursian, two to three times. In conversations with McClure and Pursian, they had agreed that Steve would run the mile. Period. This was an especially important boundary because the following week was the Amateur Athletic Union (AAU) track-and-field championships in Miami, Florida, against older athletes. Until the AAU had called saying it'd love to have Steve run in its meet down in Florida, the Golden West was going to be a culmination of sorts. But now it was a detour en route to running against men and closing a boyhood chapter.

Knowing this, Pursian bluntly asked Steve, "What do you want to be? MVP of a high school meet or maybe make the U.S. travel squad?"

Steve nodded.

It made sense.

It was confirmation that selling out for MVP of a high school meet in the grand picture was foolish. Steve had nothing left to prove among high school peers. And while he garnered many headlines over his last two years at Marshfield High School, this experience with the Golden West was Steve's first true exposure to celebrity. The officials, according to Pursian, treated Steve like royalty and even provided him with at least one pretty high-school-aged girl to keep him company. He never let the preferential treatment blind him to the task at hand, though. Steve went to the lead, won in 4:06 flat, and cut anchor from high school for good.

With the Golden West behind him, Steve fixed his gaze to racing the next level of athlete, even if it meant getting schooled. Steve may have graduated, but McClure wasn't through with him yet. Thanks in large part to telling the organizers of the Golden West Invitational that Steve would not double, it left Steve fresher for the AAUs, where McClure would be his chaperone. Performing well in an AAU meet could lead to international travel, and, most importantly, competing with the best runners in the world.

Coos Bay area businessmen raised money to subsidize the trip for Mc-Clure and Steve, the pair's first foray into the machinations of the AAU and its draconian rules regarding amateur athletics. Steve had energized the entire town, and they opened their wallets and raised $1,000 for him, $8,400 in 2024 dollars.

Track & Field News gave Steve "little chance to win but a definite chance to place in the first six," which, for a recent high school graduate stepping up to his first open track meet, was not a terrible forecast. For the first time in two years, Steve would not enter a race as the favorite, or even one of the favorites. McClure knew Gerry Lindgren, the pixie-size runner from Washington State University, had the prep record of 13:17 for the three-mile. McClure thought Steve capable of 13:30. It would be Steve's first competitive race at three miles. But Steve was feeling the weight of such an aggressive senior campaign. He was mentally fine, but physically tired.

Wide-eyed and out of his element, Steve hung around Lindgren and Florida's Jack Bacheler "like a groupie." Where before Steve took up space and commanded attention, he was now content to sit back and absorb, listen. If anything, Steve would be nothing but a passing curiosity. The real attention focused on Jim Ryun running in the mile against Marty Liquori, a rematch of the 1969 NCAA championships that Liquori had miraculously won just a week prior to the AAUs. It was a "heralded rematch." Heralded because, up to that point, Ryun was untouchable, an automatic win when he stepped to the line, running with the ever-present bull's-eye on his back.

Losing to Liquori in Ryun's final race as a college senior in the spring of 1969 shocked the running world. In 1966, Ryun had made the cover of *Sports Illustrated* twice, once when he first broke the world mile record (3:51.3, though he would later break his own mark in 1967 at 3:51.1) and a second time when he was named *SI*'s Sportsman of the Year. He would be *Track & Field News*' athlete of the year in 1966 and 1967. Winning "only" the silver medal in the 1968 Olympics was a letdown for many. He was the next great American distance runner in a proud lineage through the early '60s that saw Billy Mills, Bob Schul, and Bill Dellinger win Olympic medals.

In the end, the Ryun-Liquori rematch didn't amount to much. Ryun dropped back in the race, slipped to last on the second lap, and then quit. The crowd jeered. Liquori, confused, heard someone in the crowd cry out, "Forget Ryun! He dropped out!" Liquori took over and won the race; Ryun tried to escape.

Ryun was upset. He said he didn't care to talk. He was in tears. Still wearing his University of Kansas red and blue track uniform, he put his arm around his wife and walked the half mile to his car. His head down and a hand over his face, photographers snapped pictures, and he drove away without speaking to a soul, with no explanation as to why a world-class athlete like him would just . . . stop. Someone following him blurted, "Are you hurt, Jim?"

"Nope," he said.

Ninety minutes later, Ryun, twenty-three years old, still the world record holder, still an Olympic silver medalist, returned. He felt guilty. The experience and the jeers bothered him, so much so he was contemplating his future in the sport. He had no immediate plans and needed to do some serious thinking. He hadn't just quit this race; he was giving serious consideration to quitting running all together. The world record . . . it was a gift, but also a burden—heavy is the head that wears the crown. He was "stale from too much competition, too much pressure." He saw the field pull away from him and he had no drive to keep pace. It was then that he knew he was, in his words, "stale," but it could be two other words, "burned out." He motioned to his wife and said they'd have to discuss how to proceed. He had a lot of thinking to do. Someone else said, "He doesn't seem to want to run anymore."

Looking back now, Ryun could be forgiven for feeling that way. No longer in college, he was entering a terrible, unsupported period in the career of the amateur track-and-field athlete: without the structure of class and coaching, he, like generations of track athletes before him, were turned out to pasture, left to fend for themselves. They had to thread their training around a career: a career that could not capitalize on whatever celebrity they had earned from running (or risk losing their amateur status and thus any shot at running in the Olympics again). With no centralized federation, it fell to the individual to, simply put, *find a way*, or be done with it. And thus there were many brilliant athletes who retired not from lack of ability but a deficit in institutional support. Ryun would be left to find a day job that allowed him to train on his own time and dime in the hours before and after work. Such an athlete no longer had at their behest coaching, teammates, nutrition, medical care . . . the things four years of college had granted them. Ryun, like others of his caliber, was alone and, like many before him, it was weighing on him.

Ryun was still the biggest draw in track, but there were cracks in the facade and his invincibility had wilted at the AAU meet. Here he was a cautionary tale laid bare at the feet of any upstream talent. With Ryun, you no longer knew what you were going to get. Seemingly overnight, Ryun's narrative in the sporting landscape of the late 1960s shifted from the epitome of dominance to leading man of the fall from grace, head hung low, exiting, worst of all, a quitter.

Steve, along with everyone at the AAU meet, witnessed this firsthand, but he had work of his own to do and was preoccupied with his nerves. Entering the three-mile, Steve was afraid. He had rarely left the borders of Oregon, let alone traveling across the country. This was the first time he was stepping up this much in competition since he was a sophomore during that 1966 cross-country season when he shadowed the two seniors, when everyone that day asked themselves, *Who the hell was that?* For the first time in a long time, nothing was expected of him.

It was 82 degrees in Miami with a 70 percent humidity you never felt in Oregon. The summers are hot in Oregon, but the air is never heavy; those on the east coast and certainly those in Florida know of the sweltering air.

As Steve shook out his legs at the starting line, he looked over and saw tiny Lindgren about to enter his final red-shirt semester at Washington State (since he sat out the fall of 1968 due to the Olympics, Lindgren had an extra semester of college eligibility), former Oregon State University runner Tracy Smith, and Juan Martínez of Mexico. These weren't seniors in high school. These were grown-ass men.

Steve fashioned himself a front runner, but Lindgren was even more swift on the front end, though not from the outset in this race. Jerry Jobski of Arizona State ran a measured pace on the lead. The half went in 2:12 and the first mile in 4:32. Those were splits that would otherwise invite Steve to take the lead, but he was understandably timid. Smith and Steve cruised in fifth and sixth through the first four laps, closely bunched. Steve was getting banged around, the other runners elbowing and jostling as they raced. He learned another lesson: running at this level was physical beyond the simple act of running. It further cemented in his head the greater utility of being a front runner: you're free from traffic.

Lindgren, his tiny strides quickening, zipped ahead of Jobski with a 65-second lap. This triggered Smith to follow Lindgren. Steve, being a strong-willed leader himself, tried to keep pace through that opening mile. But feeling the weight of the Florida sun in the second mile, he slipped all the way back to twelfth place, in way over his head. Steve's feet were killing him, and while he had run plenty of training runs longer than three miles, he had never raced at three miles, and he was laboring. Steve rarely trailed in races but to be at the back of the field was poison. For the final mile, he started to climb through the field, dueling with Jobski and a young runner from Mexico. He thought, *I can't come all this way without giving everything.* So, he took off. Given what he'd endured, he was surprised he had anything left.

Into the final lap, Lindgren surged ahead of Smith as the two ran side by side in a match race of their own making. Turning for home, Smith and Lindgren dueled all the way down the stretch with the pair hitting the tape at the same time, though the race was awarded to Smith.

McClure, always with the stopwatch, saw Steve's second mile slow by four seconds to 4:36.5, but in the final four laps, he saw Steve rise. McClure witnessed that Steve had quite a bit of "snap" at the end. Through the field he rose, past more than half, into sixth, then fifth, then with "long hair flying and an eager grin on his face" stormed past Mexico's Benito Perez into fourth. Those who had finished ahead of Steve turned around and saw the "future come charging up at them."

Steve Prefontaine, the high schooler, outlasted many older, seasoned, more polished runners to finish in 13:43 with a punishing 60.7-second final lap. McClure stopped the watch and admired it, and said, "Steve didn't look like any prepper at the end. He left an awful lot of people with the feeling that he's one to watch in the future."

McClure was indeed pleased with Steve's fourth-place finish and expressed as much to Howard B. Thompson, a Naples, Florida, man attending the track meet. Thompson, impressed by what he saw in Steve, wrote a letter to the editor of the Coos Bay *World* and mailed it across the country: "We were fortunate in meeting this young man, Steve Prefontaine, just prior to his event and were impressed greatly by this fine young athlete. During the race, he displayed the courage and stamina we hear about but seldom see in action. Although he was a youngster, experience wise, he made the winner earn his win. The young man's coach (Walt McClure), who happened to be seated next to us . . . was justifiably proud and happy when Steve placed fourth in the three-mile event. We could not help noticing the bond between runner and coach and the pride of accomplishment they shared. We need more teams like these two."

After the race, once everyone had cooled down, the athletes headed back to the bus. Steve Savage, a steeplechaser entering his junior year at the University of Oregon, who had finished seventh and one spot from winning a medal in his event, boarded the bus and sat a few seats from the back. Savage watched Steve—his future teammate—board and walk toward the back. Steve ripped his fourth-place medal off his neck and hurled it as hard as he could at the back of the bus. Savage watched in mild disbelief. He would have loved to have won a medal and here was this petulant teenager showing a performative sense of displeasure at finishing fourth. Anything short of first place was clearly unacceptable.

On the heels of that, roughly two weeks later, Steve traveled to Los Angeles for a triangular meet between the United States, the Soviet Union, and the British Commonwealth. His parents also made the trip to watch him potentially run in the 5,000 meters (3.1 miles) as a member of Team USA, proud as they were now that Steve excelled on the track. But Tracy Smith, the runner who defeated Lindgren in the three-mile at the AAU nationals in Miami, was the top pick. There was a chance Smith wasn't going to return from a trip to Europe in time for the meet and Steve was the alternate in case he didn't. Alas, Smith returned and relegated Steve to the bench for this meet. Steve, chagrined, said, "This is the last time I'm ever going to be an alternate."

On Friday, figuring he wasn't going to compete, Steve charged through an intense workout in the L.A. smog; no sense in sitting around. Afterward, he heard Smith contracted an intestinal bug from drinking the water in France. Twelve hours later—"That isn't sufficient for me psychologically"— Steve would get to run in the triangular meet in the 5,000 meters after kicking his own ass the day before in a workout. Had he shown greater maturity and experience, he would not have trained so hard with the possibility of being called in as an alternate. Steve knew by now his racing was finely tuned to his training, even his mental preparation. His mind slipped, and so too did his body. He set himself up for a disappointing effort. Even at eighteen, he should have known better. Also at eighteen, he should have known better than to chuck his AAU medal in front of others, especially those who would have gladly taken that medal. The great ones have a burning competitive furnace that few understand and even fewer live up to. Given that he wasn't expected to do anything, that charging up for fourth was in and of itself a victory, throwing his medal in performative angst did more to show how ungrateful he was, indeed how childish, that, in this instance, how much more mature his body was than his mind. He didn't look intense; he looked like a brat.

Steve, heavy from his ill-timed workout and running for Team USA for the first time, led through a disastrously slow 73.5 first lap, and "soon dropped away." At two miles, Steve eroded back a full five seconds and winced with pains in his side. He "wobbled noticeably" on the last curve and staggered to the line, finishing a distant fifth, some forty-two seconds behind the winner, Rashid Sharafetdinov of the U.S.S.R.

After the race, Steve told Kenny Moore, a teammate and fellow Oregonian acting as a correspondent for the *Register-Guard*, that he felt okay at the start but halfway through the race he experienced a terrible stitch, the effects of which were compounded by the heat, what he attributed to hard running in his ill-timed workout.

Following the triangle meet in L.A., Steve was scheduled to be off to Sweden as part of Team USA, but was left off the team . . . again . . . momentarily. There was no reason for being dropped from the fifteen-man team. He was still reeling over how his race was handled in Los Angeles. He was being pulled one way then another. "I almost have to find out everything for myself," he said. "The AAU is about the worst organized group that has been brought together."

This was the first time in print—and far from the last—where Steve voiced his discontent toward the AAU. He got a rude awakening as to the machinations of this inept, dictatorial organization. Steve was surrounded by other more seasoned—and jaded—runners' opinions, but it had been a while since an athlete expressed such displeasure over the AAU, and even more jarring that it should come from the mouth of an eighteen-year-old kid. That he, of all people, would feel the agency to do so. Eventually, the AAU explained that Steve couldn't run because he ran in the triangular U.S.- Soviet Union-British Commonwealth meet. Instead, he'd be named an alternate in the 5,000 meters for a meet in Stuttgart, Germany.

So the team left for Sweden on Monday without Steve, and on Wednesday, July 23, he was told that he would be heading to Europe on the very next day. *The World* wrote, "The bureaucracy and organization—or lack of it—of the Amateur Athletic Union is something else . . . After only three world class meets . . . Steve Prefontaine is learning fast."

Indeed, he was learning, as many wide-eyed, innocent track athletes figure out—the AAU held the keys and the doors. It was the governing body, the gatekeeper for Olympic qualification, an authoritarian private organization that sanctioned every major track meet in the country, named the U.S. national team, and, most notably, the Olympic team.

Dating back to the AAU's inception in the late nineteenth century, its power grab was incremental and went largely unnoticed. The latter part of the nineteenth century saw any number of athletes touring the country like circus freaks enjoying, as Joseph M. Turrini wrote in *The End of Amateurism in American Track and Field*, "a large measure of individual control and athletic freedom," which, on its surface, couldn't be any more American. Up until the 1860s, athletes benefited from the independence to choose where and when to compete, be it as side attractions to horse races, picnics, or parades. But soon this idea of amateurism, more a gentlemanly pursuit among the privileged castes and classes, took hold, as Turrini wrote, the "primary tenet of the new sporting philosophy . . . true athletes competed not for monetary gain but for the love of sport. . . . Compensation gained from athletic success created contaminated competitions and caused illegitimate outcomes." The definition of amateurism, brought forth by New York Athletic Club (NYAC) founder William Curtis in 1869, was "any person who has never competed in an open competition, or for admission money, or with professionals, for a prize, public money, or admission money, and who has never, at any period of his life, taught or assisted in the pursuit of athletic exercise as a means of livelihood." An athlete couldn't even coach.

By 1888, the NYAC and eight other track clubs formed the Amateur Athletic Union to regulate and organize amateur sport, replacing, as Turrini wrote, "the open professional running competitions with organized, standardized, elite-controlled, and formally amateur track and field." It seized control of track and field and its officials demanded sanctions to hold meets.

Over decades, the AAU spread its tendrils into every facet of the sport. By the first modern Olympic Games in Athens, Greece, in 1896, AAU meets dominated competitive track. In 1904, the International Olympic Committee granted the AAU power to rule on an athlete's Olympic eligibility. Once the modern Olympic Games gained traction—and needed a steady flow of athletes—so too did the AAU's influence. Both grew in power and stature and braided concurrently as to be indistinguishably tethered. The AAU was building a near impenetrable wall should an athlete want to compete in the Olympics—and of course they did. Abide by the AAU rules or else. By 1906, the American Olympic Committee, comprised primarily of AAU leaders, selected the athletes for the U.S. team. Athletes needed AAU eligibility to compete in AAU meets, one of which being the Olympic Trials. By 1908, the AAU had secured the only ticket to the Olympic Games. The power brokers of the AAU didn't hide their intentions. As AAU president James Sullivan once said, "Registration, gentlemen, is the backbone of this organization. It means centralization, it means control. It gives us what we certainly should have, *absolute control* [emphasis added] over the individual athlete who competes under our protection." By 1912, and the Olympics having become a major international event, the AAU, not the U.S. government, effectively named the Olympic track-and-field team.

Seeking greater international influence, the AAU provided $1,000 to help form the International Amateur Athletic Federation (IAAF). In something of a *quid pro quo*, the newly formed IAAF "granted the AAU the American track franchise in 1913." By 1921, the IAAF "affiliated" with the International Olympic Committee (IOC). Given the AAU's influence in each of these satellite bureaucracies, the AAU further secured its power and clout over domestic track and field. The AAU was insatiable in its reach for power and, before long, its over-reach and arrogance could largely go unchallenged. The AAU cared little about athlete welfare, and athletes didn't have any sway, not for decades. By mid-century, the AAU's vice grip on American track and field was ironclad. The AAU brass grew bloated while the athletes had to eat crow. Petty travel expenses and per diems were meted out by AAU officials, like parents handing out an allowance to children. And make no mistake, the AAU treated athletes like children. When athletes voiced discontent, an AAU leader said, "I don't know what the kids want, and I don't think they do either." Steve Prefontaine would one day say, "A cheap hotel, a red-eye flight, and three bucks a day." AAU officials leveraged the athletes' dream for their own meal ticket.

Once Sullivan died, Avery Brundage took charge and became, as Turrini wrote, "the most virulent, oppressive, devoted, well-known, and despised supporter of amateurism in American sport." Brundage evangelized, "The amateur code, coming to us from antiquity, contributed to and strengthened by the noble aspirations of great men of each generation, embraces the highest moral laws. No philosophy, no religion, preaches higher sentiments."

Time passed, the AAU grew more institutionalized, and athletes grew fearful and resentful. In the 1950s, Wes Santee, the brilliant miler from Kansas, brought to light ideas like "broken-time" payments, athletes seeking reimbursement for lost time from work due to an AAU track meet. Brundage, of course, denounced this: "Everyone knows that reimbursement for lost wages is not compatible with amateurism." Naturally, this priced out many of the best athletes. Santee's struggles with the AAU began during the 1952 Olympic Trials, where he qualified for the 5,000 meters. He was less experienced in this race and hoped to qualify in his better event, the 1,500. If he qualified for both, given the choice, he would have opted for the 1,500. AAU officials gave him no choice and "grabbed him by the arm" and pulled him off the track at the Trials, and he made the Olympic team only in the 5,000. He said the AAU, "Did whatever the hell they wanted to." True believers in amateurism—the AAU chief among them—posited that the athlete had free will to go wherever they pleased, race wherever they wanted. Government subsidization of athletes would make them beholden to the government, who would then have total control of where and when they raced. Fact is, the AAU wielded the same exact power but outsourced the time and cost of developing athletes to the athletes themselves. The AAU's "free will" logic was downright laughable, hypocritical. The AAU still told athletes where and when to run. As future AAU president Nick Barack said, "The voluntary, democratic model of participation in sports in the United States can meet the challenge of the compulsory mass program of a totalitarian country." Athletes were growing fatigued by this notion of amateurism.

In Santee's pursuit of the four-minute mile, he was described as "very outgoing" and the media "loved him. He did all the interviews, made the circuit, all the papers, TV." In a convoluted series of events that proved how doggedly obsessed the AAU was with putting Santee—a proto-Prefontaine—in his place, the AAU found a way to make an example of him that nobody was, is, or will be bigger than the AAU. It maintained that Santee earned too much in travel expenses doled out in a three-meet stretch in Fresno, Los Angeles, and Modesto, and banned him for life.

The Santee saga soon gave way to a war between the NCAA and the AAU. Dating back to 1961, Oregon's Bill Bowerman and Kansas's Bill Easton, among others, led a "secret revolution that seems certain to wreck the all-powerful AAU." Wrote *Sports Illustrated*'s Tex Maule in 1961, "The sprawling Amateur Athletic Union of the United States, long in iron control of almost every amateur athlete in this country, began to die . . . While the AAU will not die overnight, it cannot survive long." Bowerman, Easton, and fifty distinguished U.S. track-and-field stars, aimed to form their own union—the U.S. Track and Field Federation—that would give them control over track and field. As college coaches, *they* trained the bulk of the athletes at *their* facilities, so it stood to reason why they wanted out from under the AAU's thumb, or at least have an equal seat at the table.

At the time, Bowerman corresponded with New Zealand track coach Arthur Lydiard about sending four American athletes—his treasured miler Dyrol Burleson among them—to compete in New Zealand. Per the rules, Lydiard mailed the invitation to the AAU and never received clearance. Bowerman grew impatient and didn't wait for permission; he sent his guys, consequences be damned. Bowerman said, "[The AAU] seem to be more concerned with perpetuating themselves in power than with the development of track and field." Added Easton, "This has become a political operation—the selection of coaches for foreign trips, in the selection of sites for track meets and certainly in the selection of AAU officials."

"We've had the same ones ever since I can remember," said Al Oerter, then the 1956 and 1960 Olympic discus champion (he would also win in 1964 and 1968), who also complained about horrible living conditions. Resentments were simmering, even boiling over.

Once an indomitable facade, the AAU now showed signs of wear. Bowerman was growing older and the fight, though virtuous, would have to be handled by a younger generation, a counterculture serendipitously timed to push back against the legacy institutions of the first half of the twentieth century. At the close of the 1960s, when Steve was on the rise, the AAU was proving to be anemic royalty, but it still wielded surprising amounts of power.

Through it all in the summer of 1969, the men's track athletes were in a feud with the AAU and threatened to boycott the upcoming meet in London. Bob Beamon, the world record long jumper, needed to return to the United States for a personal emergency. He wasn't supposed to jump in Augsburg because he recently had stitches removed during a dental surgery. The AAU "told him he could not return home unless he jumped tonight in the Augsburg meet." Most of the team supported the boycott, putting pressure on the AAU.

Steve learned much on this trip from his elders, either directly or by osmosis. He was immersed with far more weathered competitors, many near the ends of their careers, bitter, resentful, tired. The boycott was eventually dropped, but their protests still thrummed. Steve was learning first-hand the painful reality of running for the ol' red, white, and blue. Several athletes placed tape over the AAU insignia on their warm-up suits, a "silent protest against unsatisfactory treatment on the trip," according to Neal Steinhauer, a shot-putter and U of O alum. Several posed for the cameras pointing to the tape covering those three letters, laughing at the absurdity.

And so, Steve would run under the auspices of this necessary evil. In the summer of 1969, Steve didn't know if he'd be running in any of the European meets, but they wanted him there just in case. He hurtled across the sky to Germany, to Stuttgart, where he would speak German (thanks to his German mother) and act as an interpreter for his teammates. He was an alternate but trained accordingly while occasionally sightseeing.

Far from the days of running around Mingus Park or the rutted logging roads of his hometown, instead he was staying at the Hotel Am Schlossgarten and rooming with Lindgren and Moore. Steve appreciated that they were distance runners like him and native to the Pacific Northwest. When Steve touched down in Europe, he practically sprinted from the tarmac. "I just got to Stuttgart a couple hours ago and went for a run . . ."

On the Stuttgart Tartan track, Lindgren was brilliant in an "electrifying" win in the 5,000 over East German defector Jurgen May. While 30,000 German track fans filled the stadium with noise as it poured down rain, Lindgren led most of the way. Steve ended up third, some fourteen seconds back. "You know me," Steve later wrote home. "I don't like fourth places." It was a humbling experience to be in contention then suddenly . . . not. Reluctant to assert himself in the way that Lindgren did, Steve had a long way to go in these amateur meets. Yet though this meet at Stuttgart was Steve's first overseas, Lindgren, who was in his fifth year of international competition, was impressed with Steve.

Still, the U.S. team was trounced by the European team overall. Steinhauer said, on the way to Augsburg, Germany, for the next triangle meet, "We'll win to save some American pride." Lindgren suffered a bruised leg muscle and planned on sitting out the next meet, which left Steve as the "American hope" in the 3,000 meters.

Admittedly, after a grueling—though fun—campaign that had really started in the late fall of 1968, Steve was ready to get home, ready to rest. The tread on Steve's tires was starting to slip after he finished second in the 5,000 behind Werner Girke in Augsburg. After running several 5,000-meter races in a short amount of time, he desperately wanted to run the 1,500 in London. He wanted the variation. So many 5,000s in a month's time was "something you should not do," he said. He was denied this chance to run the 1,500 and had to run the 5,000. In his final race abroad in London, Steve finished fourth, beaten by, among others, Great Britain's Ian Stewart and Dick Taylor, who won in "crushing style." On the sixth lap of this race, all Steve could do was laugh: Taylor and Stewart ran a 61-second lap, which "just killed me." He was cooked. He finished a full seventy seconds behind the winner and twenty-three seconds behind Lindgren, who finished in third place. At this point, Steve was running on fumes. Rare were the times he didn't fully show up. For this final race, tired and travel-weary, he didn't feel like running at all. He was sluggish, in part because he had gained thirteen pounds—from 147 at the start of the trip to 160 at its end.

For a kid who, as a prepper, had lost just a single race since 1967, he lost all of his races that summer of 1969, finishing as high as second and as low as fifth. Yet losing can be good for a runner—it teaches more than winning— and this was especially true for Steve. After all, failing to make states in his high school sophomore track season had launched him onto a trajectory of excellence that he otherwise might never have discovered. Likewise, losing this summer with such punishing regularity was an awakening, a demonstration of how far he still had to go and an invitation to level up. And critically, his belief in himself remained unshaken—if anything, his winless summer campaign heightened his ambitions. The way he saw it, in three years, he might be ready for the Olympics.

While in Germany, he had quickly visited Munich, the site of the forthcoming 1972 Olympics. He perused the site of the new Olympic stadium and snapped a photograph of it—a growing hobby of his—and thought how badly he wanted to be back there competing for the United States. He closed his eyes and visualized what it would mean and how it would feel to be there. He mounted the photograph on his wall and put a pin in the picture where he envisioned the victory stand to be. That was the bull's-eye; he was the dart.

PART II

Steve Prefontaine as a junior for the Marshfield High School Pirates, the year he declared he'd never lose again. Here, Steve won the mile in 4:23.4 at Silke Field in Springfield. © *Register-Guard*—USA TODAY NETWORK via Imagn Images

On April 25, 1970, Steve set new school, meet, and field records in the three-mile as a freshman in a time of 13:12.8. If there ever was a breakout race, it was this three-mile against Washington State University, one year to the day when he broke the high school national two-mile record. © *Register-Guard*—USA TODAY NETWORK via Imagn Images

Every spring, the University of Oregon track team would head south to escape the cold rain of the Willamette Valley. Here, in March 1970, a few Ducks crossed the border into Juárez, Mexico, to drink lots of beer. *From left to right*: Stan Rotenberg, Pete Shmock, Rick Ritchie, Mac Wilkins, Steve Prefontaine, Roscoe Divine, Tommie Smith, and Jim Gorman. Courtesy of Pete Shmock

An illustration from the *Register-Guard* from the 1970s. Never shy about his love of beer and people, Steve long wanted to open a sports bar in Eugene named the Sub-Four.
© *Register-Guard*—USA TODAY NETWORK via Imagn Images

Steve Prefontaine, ready to make his first—and only—Olympic team, took command of the 5,000-meter final in the Olympic Trials at Hayward Field over the veteran George Young, who would make his fourth Olympics. © *Register-Guard*—USA TODAY NETWORK via Imagn Images

Bill Bowerman, cofounder of Nike, the University of Oregon head track-and-field coach, and the head coach of the 1972 U.S. Olympic team, applauds his star runner after winning the Olympic Trials and qualifying for the Olympic team.
© *Register-Guard*—USA TODAY NETWORK via Imagn Images

The leaders turn for home in the 5,000-meter final. Exhausted from leading most of the final mile and attacking a number of times on the backstretch, Steve can't keep pace with Lasse Virén and Mohammed Gammoudi, the eventual gold and silver medalists. In the race's final strides, Great Britain's Ian Stewart would eclipse Steve in the shadow of the wire. AP Photo

Left: Pat Tyson, *rear*, was one of Steve's best friends and his roommate at the famous trailer in Glenwood. They loved few things more than a good cookout at the trailer. Courtesy of Pat Tyson | **Right:** Steve Prefontaine and Ralph Mann, the 1972 silver medalist in the 400-meter hurdles, stand atop a ski jump in Finland during the summer of 1973. Steve would run and recreate in Finland. Due to Mann's friendship with the Finn coach Jaakko Tuominen, Steve was inspired to organize his own series of track meets in the Pacific Northwest. Courtesy of Dave Wottle

Left: Bob Williams, *left*, and Steve Prefontaine clear a hurdle in a steeplechase race in 1972. Courtesy of Bob Williams | **Right:** Steve and Dave Wottle, the 1972 gold medalist in the 800 meters, pose here in Leuven, Belgium, in 1973. Back on U.S. soil just a few weeks before this photo, Steve paced Wottle to the third fastest mile of all time at Hayward Field, 3:53.3. Courtesy of Dave Wottle

In 1973, Steve, trying to look tough for the camera but not being able to keep a straight face, posed with Dave Wottle in Munich, the site of Steve's most crushing defeat in the 5,000 meters. Courtesy of Dave Wottle

An exhausted Steve Prefontaine at the end of a race at Hayward Field. The photo was taken by Eugene native Debra Roth, a runner and one of the few athletes Steve coached in 1974. Few people knew, but Steve drew up workouts and oversaw the training of a handful of women runners. Courtesy of Debra Roth

Left: Steve Prefontaine and Bill Bowerman attend a community running event in Eugene. Bowerman, who won four NCAA track-and-field championships with Oregon, abruptly retired from coaching in 1973. But he always stayed plugged into the running community he helped build in Eugene. © *Register-Guard*—USA TODAY NETWORK via Imagn Images | **Right:** Steve running in his final race at Hayward Field on May 29, 1975. © *Register-Guard*—USA TODAY NETWORK via Imagn Images

In an uncharacteristically black singlet, Steve Prefontaine wins his final race at Hayward Field on May 29, 1975. © *Register-Guard*— USA TODAY NETWORK via Imagn Images

Left: Mere hours after winning his final race at Hayward Field, Steve Prefontaine crashed his 1973 MGB on the morning of May 30, 1975. © *Register-Guard*—USA TODAY NETWORK via Imagn Images | **Right:** At the site of Steve's accident on Skyline Boulevard, Pre's Rock, fans, admirers, and runners make pilgrimages to this spot and leave medals, shoes, bibs, and nutrition packets, paying tribute to their favorite runner. Photo by Brendan O'Meara

To this day, Coos Bay, Oregon, celebrates its most famous son. Here, a mural in downtown Coos Bay shows Steve as a high school senior.
Photo by Brendan O'Meara

CHAPTER 6

LIMITLESS

THE UNIVERSITY OF Oregon's Hayward Field has an aura. It is a place where a runner feels the weight of history, not for the grandiosity of its aesthetic, but more for the legendary performances, the sub-four milers, the pop of a starting gun.

The footprint of Hayward Field was originally a cow pasture to provide students with fresh milk. In 1919, the pasture gave way to a new football field (where the Ducks would play until 1966), and in 1921, a six-lane cinder track was installed. The iconic roofed, wooden bleachers were transferred from nearby Kincaid Field—where the track-and-field team competed—and re-situated on the western perimeter along the homestretch with Spencer Butte's 2,000-foot, fir-coated peak looming to the south. The East Stands were added a few years later, and by the late 1920s, thousands of people could cheer from the backstretch to the homestretch creating a cacophonous arena, none louder than the roaring thunder of the fans banging the boards in the West Stands. Jim Bush, UCLA's head coach, said, "You don't know what noise is until you've been in Eugene. They go wild when one of their guys bends over to tie his shoelaces." At the southern end of the field stood an electronic scoreboard that myriad runners breaking the tape would peer up at to revel in—or sneer at—their time, the wide eyes of Steve Prefontaine chief among them, the clock, just as often, being his only competition.

Come spring 1970, volunteers and track junkies—faculty, administrators, junior varsity track team members, and the Oregon Track Club—would fix up Hayward Field's rickety bleachers, working all day to replace rotten and crumbling portions of the "unsafe" grandstand. These stands were every bit for percussion as they were for sitting. Anyone in the community who wanted to help was urged to bring a hammer. Leaning on the community—TrackTown USA—saved the university thousands. The DIY project cost about $1,000 to $2,000. A complete renovation, which would be needed for the enchanted old ruin in the future, would cost upwards of $30,000, perhaps more.

Also in the spring of 1970, Hayward Field would unveil a new urethane, all-weather surface. The people of Eugene deserved a state-of-the-art track to rain praise on their athletes, a facility worthy of TrackTown USA, of one day hosting the Olympic Trials. These were the days before the "running boom" and people jogging on the roads were often seen as freaks. Not here. These were people who didn't throw rocks when they saw an athlete running through town; they waved. Steve would say of the people, "When you're on the final lap, and you have fans like they do here at Oregon, they actually lift you up—carry you to the finish. A runner feels like a new man."

But before the new surface and the renovations, Steve arrived on campus in the fall of 1969 with a reputation befitting of the tongue-in-cheek sobriquet that javelin thrower and classmate (and eventual discus champion) Mac Wilkins gave Steve: World, as in "world famous." Steve whipped around the cinder oval running "fartleks," speed play, whereby a runner in a group sprinted from the back to the front. And Steve was primed to live up to his reputation as a full-scholarship freshman runner. If there was a culture shock about acclimating to collegiate running, it didn't show.

In a few months' time, Bush watched in awe following an indoor race where Steve wiped the floor with the competition. He pointed to Steve, who, donning a track jacket, took a victory lap, and said, "There goes the world's next great runner." Bill Bowerman added, "He's got talent and a lot more to go with it."

Through fall and winter, Bowerman and Dellinger handed him workouts and he gladly performed them. He didn't need oversight, didn't care for it. Steve thrived on the long leash, something his future roommate and close friend, Pat Tyson, recognized. Other runners would have preferred more hands-on guidance and mentorship from the likes of Bowerman and

Dellinger, but that wasn't their style, nor was it Steve's. Long accustomed to isolation, Steve could be himself, push himself. Tyson said, "Albert Einstein probably needed a long leash. Otherwise, if you controlled him, he probably wouldn't have been as good of a scientist, maybe he wouldn't have been who he was."

One day during his freshman year, Steve returned from a grueling six-mile workout and limped down the hallways of MacArthur Court. Hal Cowan, who worked as the chief of sports information, noticed Steve hobbling by. "What's bothering you?" Cowan asked.

"Oh, I just worked out six miles," Steve said.

Like any good sports PR person, Cowan coaxed out a time from Steve before Steve scampered off: he was always scampering off. For plodders, the thought of a six-mile run took closer to an hour. Steve ran this workout in 28:20. Gosh, Cowan thought, the six-mile isn't even his race. The Oregon record for the six-mile was held by alumnus Kenny Moore, who ran the race in 28:50. The winning time in the 1969 NCAAs in the six-mile was 29:30. Steve was posting championship times in workouts . . . as a freshman.

For that track season, Steve focused primarily on the two- or three-mile, much to his chagrin. All evidence pointed to Steve's endurance—his strength—not speed. But he was in love with the mile. In time trials, he ran as low as 4:01.8, knocking nearly five seconds off his best high school time. He still hadn't broken four minutes, his white whale. With a three-way meet at Fresno State approaching, Steve was defiant with Bowerman. "I'm running the mile," he said. Bowerman disagreed and entered him in the two. Steve rebuked, "I'm not a two-miler. I'm a miler." To which, Bowerman told the stubborn freshman, "You might want to give some thought to the university you'd be running for if you don't try this particular two-mile because it won't be ours."

Steve ran out of the room. Fifteen minutes later he said, "Okay. Fine. Got it."

Bowerman looked at Steve and thought, *Ah, with the talent comes the temperament*. Steve was of the mind to push back against authority, Bowerman included. There'd be photographs of Steve and Bowerman punctuated with a quote from Bowerman's wife, Barbara, saying, "There's not a picture where they're not asking, 'Who's boss here?'" Steve, more often than not, listened to Bowerman.

Steve did not run bitter and took over the lead after he covered the first mile in 4:21. The pace in the race gave way and he threw in fast laps to grind them under. He never looked back and even tallied a 62.1 final lap, a "study in smooth efficiency," helping to lead his team over Stanford and Fresno. His two-mile time of 8:40 flat was the second-best in school history, as he outlasted Stanford's Don Kardong by a full seven seconds. It being early in the season, Steve felt sluggish from the gun, and the head wind on the backstretch hit him hard. Still, as per usual, he was displeased with his overall performance. "Even when he feels bad he runs pretty good," Bowerman dead-panned. Just under a year prior, running a record 8:41.5 was all out; now it was no big deal, such was his growth as he showed no signs of plateauing.

The Ducks continued their trip south to El Paso, Texas, for a meet against the University of Texas at El Paso (UTEP). El Paso shares a border with Mexico's Ciudad Juárez, and the UTEP campus wasn't much farther away. For an entire crew of college kids, Mexico beckoned. No drinking-age issues. "Good weather, no school, no distractions, and we just went away to train," said Pete Shmock, one of Oregon's throwers. Bowerman also had to know that as good of a business trip as it was, it was equally inviting for his team to let loose south of the border.

Steve and a group of athletes crossed the border and found the nearest bar. They sat around a table with cans of beer scattered about. Steve, dressed in a too-large blazer over a white shirt, dark pants, and wearing a dingy pair of Tigers, rested his right elbow on the table and held up a can of beer, his face beaming, cheeks rosy. "We had way too many beers," Shmock said. "Pre was a fun-loving guy. No more or less than any of the rest of us. This showed Pre could have a couple of beers after training." Stan Rotenberg, then a writer for the school paper, *The Daily Emerald*, added, "I remember how comfortable everybody was with everyone. You forgot that Pre was a world-class athlete," he said. "His public persona tended to be a bit more serious, more focused, more goal-oriented than it was when he was just being one of the guys."

Back in El Paso, Steve bought a postcard with the drab UTEP campus on the front. He wrote to former Duck runner Dave Wilborn, "Well we are all here layin in the sun and living it up. We had a pretty good meet at Fresno but we are going to have to be great this weekend. Last night a few of us went across the border and raised a little hell, we took a picture of us in a bar you will have to see that its [sic] to [sic] much. Well I best go."

At this point, even as a freshman, Steve was dubbed Oregon's best performer with conference best times in the mile, two-mile, and three-mile. The attention was merited, if a bit overblown. He wasn't the least bit shy when it came to victory laps, even on the road, something few runners did but he relished.

The impression Steve made on those around him on the track was unmistakable. American sport culture then as now loves brilliance at a young age. Steve embodied a new wave of athlete, one who could be candid and brazen with the press as well as bombastic in his sport. He embraced the spotlight, thrived on the give and take between him and a rabid audience. If Steve was a gladiator, his aim was to deliver blood. It could be his own.

Bush, fresh off one of the most intense dual meets against the Ducks, said that Steve would surpass most or all of what Jim Ryun had accomplished. Ryun was still in a self-imposed exile after walking off the track after the AAU championships in Miami in 1969. Again, Bush said, "Steve is going to be the greatest distance runner this country has ever had. He is cocky but not in a negative sense. He has the kind of cockiness a coach loves to see—real confidence."

And he had an awareness for what other runners were doing around the country . . . and how he might best shape his efforts to return serve. On April 25, 1970, Steve read in the Saturday sports section that Jack Bacheler, a post-collegiate runner for the Florida Track Club, had recently run the three-mile in 13:13.4 at the Drake Relays in Des Moines, Iowa. Steve wanted to better that mark when Oregon ran against the Washington State University Cougars, but Steve had been battling a cold all week, so his hopes weren't too high.

Steve left the Hayward Field corral after registering and jogged onto the track. He stood near WSU's Rick Riley, the same person whose national high school two-mile record Steve had broken a year ago to the day. The gun popped for the three-mile and the field curved around the southern turn of Hayward Field. Lap splits and mile splits are the toeholds for the distance runner. Grabbing hold—or not—tells the runner all they need to know about what is possible in a race. The field cruised around, Steve thinking he wanted to be at nine minutes for the first two miles, maybe then he could punch out a 4:10 final mile, which would vault him past Bacheler. During the race, Steve thought, *I'm not scared. I don't know what I can do, but crossing two miles in nine? Well, then maybe somewhere between 13:10 and 13:15 is within reach.* Steve's rhythm was on point, but when he saw he ran a 4:17 first mile, he slowed down so as not to burn himself out. He surrendered to how he felt: he wasn't excited; he didn't let the pressure cook him. Riley, who earlier in the meet ran a personal best 4:02.8 to win the mile, hung with Steve for five laps, but ultimately peeled off the track and dropped out.

Steve didn't slow down too much. That would be, in his words, ridiculous. He eased a touch, logged a 4:28 second mile, and he felt almost like he was out for an easy training run. Two miles in 8:45 in a relative trot. Steve took one look at that split and realized he'd never been here before. This was unexplored territory. He knew he had gone two miles faster in Germany the previous summer but he had been dead—dead!—in that final mile. But not this day. He saw the clock and felt good. By now, Steve knew Bacheler's mark was his prey. Steve figured it was time to quit fooling around and get out and do something.

Eleven laps down, 440 yards left; he sprinted. Steve felt he could have begun his kick earlier. He charged into that senseless drive pulling something up from the deep. The crowd roared and Steve felt a newness in his body as he fixed his gaze on the running clock, never relenting though a win was secured many laps before. Often the biggest race is the race within. "I'm always exploring myself," he'd say. With his spikes clawing at the earth, he gained a shocking amount of distance on the rest of the field. Coming down the finish, Steve threw his hands in the air setting a new conference, meet, and field record in the three-mile in 13:12.8, the fastest three-mile in the world that year. He broke Oregon alum Arne Kvalheim's record, though Kvalheim did it on a cinder track. To what extent that track had an effect or not shouldn't be discounted. With a hand on his hip, Steve walked around the track waving to the fans.

It wasn't even an all-out effort, and he did it with a cold. It was the rare moment for any runner of any skill where high speed came easy, a frictionless glide. Dellinger was amazed at how easy Steve was running. The best have ways of making the difficult look effortless, and yet . . . watching Steve run typically was watching effort pour forth. He could, at times, appear wounded. Not this time.

Oregon's Steve Savage, who finished second in the race in a personal best 13:50.0—thirty-eight seconds behind Steve—remembered running down the backstretch and looking across the track and seeing Steve 200 meters ahead with the crowd in frenzy.

If ever there was a breakout race, according to Savage, this was it; this was the three-mile where Steve put immeasurable distance between him and his closest rival for the sake of performance, treasure on display. Steve could have coasted in, but he defied rationality: the race was won, yet he sought a different kind of victory. He didn't win extra points because of how he ran or how far ahead he was of second place. This wasn't the crowning moment of a track season, rather it was just another dual meet. He wasn't about to give anything less than his best to the 6,200 fans screaming and stomping those beleaguered bleachers to see something people might just be talking about for weeks, months, or years from now. That day, he superseded the team and became the draw itself.

Larry Standifer, an athletic trainer at Oregon, smiled at Steve. He brought out a warmup suit. Steve told Standifer, "Easiest three-mile I ever ran." Standifer shook his head, thinking, *What is he going to say when he runs one where he has to work hard?* Just as likely, Steve was posturing and publicly discounting his effort, the better to suggest to his rivals: *imagine what I can do to you if I tried.*

After Steve completed his requisite victory lap, he told his teammates, "That was easy. I'm ready, man. I'm ready to do anything." He felt he could have gone faster. He grinned at the thought.

The buzz around Steve's rising celebrity extended to the more obscure corners of southwestern Oregon. Mary Dufort Harris, sports editor for the

Western World out of Bandon, Oregon, sent a letter to the editor to the Coos Bay *World*, that Steve was, in essence, a greater export than its billions of board feet of timber. She wrote, "Oregon's most prized commodity is a slight-built sandy-haired youth named Steve Prefontaine who is rapidly emerging as a world-class distance runner."

Just a year before, in 1969, Steve had broken the national two-mile prep record. He seemed just a talented boy back then. Graduating to the rigors of college running and runners did nothing to deter his drive or dampen his spirits, meaning he wasn't drowning in the deeper waters of the next level. He already was becoming the next level unto himself. Back in high school, what drove him was a sense of finding his place. He had to be an athlete to show everybody—his family, his community, his peers—that he could excel at something. Steve felt a swelling of his powers in college. Though still technically a teenager at nineteen, he said he wasn't a "teenybopper anymore." Steve secured himself with the fact that a runner got stronger as he got older, and, "Man, if I keep getting this much stronger every year, I don't know what I'm going to be doing."

For now, he felt somehow more confident. From his limited time abroad, he experienced how the Europeans treat running as a contact sport, more jostling, something foreign to most U.S. athletes not wanting to incur a foul. "I know what the big boys do to you," Steve said. "There's an offense and a defense to a race. People don't realize you just don't go out and grind, grind, grind. A lot of psychological factors are involved. You're trying to hurt the other guy and he's trying to hurt you."

Steve was predictable in many ways, and that was part of his daring, but he was learning to play with his own tendencies, including front running. "Like Bill Bowerman says, you change it around . . . and I'm going to keep people guessing. It's like a football game in a way." More revealing was how he came to view his running and how it harkened back to the more physical and confrontational sports he tried, but ultimately was too small to play, as a boy. His tone as a runner was hyper-masculine and he wanted to inflict as much pain on the competition as he did himself. One thing he could never outrun was where he came from, how men were made and must measure up, the ethic of the city he called home. People wanted to see Y.A. Tittle—the former New York Giants quarterback—on his knees, bloodied and beaten, as he was in 1964, the final year of his career. A boxer's eye swollen shut. A runner so deep in oxygen debt they flail and stumble at the finish line. The people wanted you to suffer for them.

Steve sensed their devotion in a way that made him want to send it back, a thank-you note in the form of a memorable race, perhaps an American record, a gift from Steve to them. Hearing them roar for him as he was a furlong clear of second place, well, "For some reason," he said, "that just built up my confidence 100 percent on top of the 100 percent I already had. I feel now that anytime I come on the track I can break anything I want. It's really funny . . . a feeling like no goal is too high, no record is too far out of sight." Giving voice to it might make it happen.

Entering May 1970, Steve's goals were modest: run a sub-four-minute mile, win the NCAAs, and win an AAU championship in the three-mile. No bigs. Dellinger said a distance runner didn't hit his peak until his mid- to late twenties. Steve, nineteen, had a long way to go, and he didn't want to hear that. Dellinger maintained that age gave a runner experience, confidence, and a bigger engine. With Steve by his side, he said Olympic champions in the distance races of the past were all twenty-five or older. The issue with the American system of amateurism wrought by the AAU was few athletes could compete at their physiological peak because of careers and families. By adhering to dictatorial edicts of the amateur establishment, the AAU was, in effect, interfering with sending the best possible distance runners abroad. That was why so few runners made it to their physical peak. Dellinger had bucked that trend and won a bronze medal at age thirty in the 1964 Tokyo Olympics. Steve chimed in, "We'll have to make an exception in the 1972 Olympics." If he could stay healthy, motivated, and not plateau. Steve would be twenty-one. He was not joking.

These were the thoughts zipping in and around his head at night. He hadn't been sleeping well, so he thought even more about running and his place in it. Running this three-mile race faster than anyone in America had in two years, than any Oregon Duck had ever, and anyone in the world to that point of the year, Steve asked himself, *What are my limits?* His belief in himself was so strong that the only answer to that question was simple: none.

———

STEVE PREFONTAINE'S PERFORMANCES on the track, not to mention his penchant for pithy quotes and being preternaturally photogenic, invited greater visibility. Over the year, many local publications gave Steve preferential attention, even the esoteric "bible of the sport" *Track & Field News*. This was nothing out of the ordinary.

And then along came *Sports Illustrated* to profile Steve.

It's difficult to contextualize just how meaningful a feature or profile in *SI* was. It was the premier weekly publication that showcased the best writing and photography in sports, heavy with coverage on the popular and the fringe, often exceeding one hundred pages per issue swollen with ads for cigarettes and alcohol. To cross over from the track-and-field media into the mainstream was nothing short of a moment for Steve, for Bowerman, for Oregon. And *Sports Illustrated* wanted to not only write about Steve and Bowerman, it also wanted to put Steve on the cover. Suddenly the nineteen-year-old freshman was experiencing something very few athletes could relate to, transcending his sport and arriving in mainstream culture in a way that further separated him from his peers. There would no longer be such a thing as obscurity with Steve.

Sports Illustrated called Bowerman and, when he took the call, he heard a woman on the other end, likely a writer's assistant. It was posited that *SI* couldn't find a man "venturesome" enough to haggle with Bowerman, so *SI* elected to send a "sweet voice" to find "sweet reception." This unnamed woman, doing outreach for the man who would ultimately write the piece, reportedly said, "Mr. Bowerman, in order to get him the proper exposure, you should run him in this meet . . . that meet . . . If you do, then we will be justified in doing a cover story on him."

"Ma'am, I will run that young man where and when I think it is best for him and his career," Bowerman replied. He just as likely, "responded with a suggestion of what *SI* could do with its idea."

After a pause, he said, "But if you want to do a story on him, we will have our Twilight Meet on June 5, and we would welcome you out that week."

An exhibition and the final meet the Ducks would run before the NCAA championships in Des Moines, Iowa, the following week, the Twilight Meet was an institution, something unique to Eugene, more an act of service for the U of O track program to the denizens of TrackTown. The Twilight Meet at Hayward Field was born on May 24, 1961. There's rarely a better time to compete in the Willamette Valley than in late May, this just as the rain clouds march off until October, before late-day heat becomes stifling, and the wildfire smoke blows in. What made this meet so . . . personalized . . . was Bowerman's knowledge of the grounds. It went far beyond what was underfoot, but also which way the wind blew and, more importantly, when the wind stopped. Sunny afternoons usher in winds from the north, a frustrating resistance down Hayward Field's backstretch, but when the sun sets, the wind dies, and the air calms with it. A stillness, except for the people. Bowerman would later say, "Eugene, Oregon, had all the attributes that let Paavo Nurmi, Gunder Hagg, and John Landy set records in Scandinavia. We had the calm air. We had the demanding crowd."

Steve had been taking aim at a sub-four-minute mile—and missing— since his junior year of high school in 1968. In his first college track season he had been clocking second by second closer to that coveted barrier. Based on his desire, it was fair to say he wished he was a true miler. Steve lacked the turn of the foot runners like Oregon senior Roscoe Divine and Jim Ryun had, *true* milers. Kenny Moore would write that speed, unlike stamina, could only be improved so much by training, much like a pitcher's fastball. Roughly a month before, on May 2, 1970, Steve led a sweep of the mile against Oregon State in 4:00.4 facing "chilly, gusting winds," so close to becoming the ninth Duck to run sub-four.

Bowerman put Steve in his place ahead of the Fresno meet earlier in the 1970 season, which wasn't to say that Steve could never run the mile; Steve wasn't going to be a *miler*. Given his competitive instincts, he wasn't going to let such a designation keep him from crossing into the sub-four club. Steve would bend the mile to his will and run below four minutes against a quality field.

Ten races were slated for the Twilight Meet on Friday, June 5, 1970, at 6:50 p.m. "We think we're going to have a heck of a mile," Bowerman said.

Roscoe Divine, a senior miler on the team, was on something of a farewell tour as he rounded back into shape. After a long career, one where he often didn't square with Bowerman—a commonality among his many athletes—Divine was finally healthy and energized by the end. The past year had left him largely unmotivated, this in a sport where self-motivation is tantamount to a runner's success. It can be a lonely sport; that's simultaneously its curse and appeal. In the 1969 track season, Divine had won the mile in the Northern Division and Pac-8 meets. But come NCAAs, he loped home last in his heat. He had lost the fire.

He had suffered a "fatigue fracture" in his leg prior to the 1968 outdoor season, which was the beginning of a long march toward the 1968 Olympics in Mexico City. He failed to make the team in the 1,500 meters. How dispiriting, to give so fully only to be left behind. There would be no foreign trips in the summer of 1969 because he was required to attend ROTC camp. Divine went back to the U of O where he was then tasked with recruiting Steve, this hot-shot high schooler from Coos Bay. But once he got away from the rigors of the track and traded it for the rigors of military training, the flame rekindled. His strength, hunger, and confidence returned. "The thing is," he said, "even when I ran well as a sophomore, I was always afraid. I put all kinds of pressure on myself. Before a race I'd get so scared I'd have shot myself if you'd given me a gun."

Now Divine was running free. In a recent race against Oregon State, Divine had been looking forward to competing. Win or lose, his opponent would know he had been in a race. It was a lot easier to run if you didn't care if you lost. But he desperately wanted to win this Twilight Mile. He especially wanted to beat Steve, and with good reason.

Roughly two months prior, in April 1970, the Ducks had traveled to Seattle for a dual meet against the University of Washington Huskies. The score of the meet was closer than Bowerman had anticipated. He was scrambling for points, and he saw an opportunity to seize the meet with a strong effort in the mile. He decided to run Steve and junior steeplechaser Steve Savage in the mile. Divine had been training for the two-mile all week, but Bowerman couldn't waste his best pure miler, so he ripped Divine from the two and entered him in the mile.

The wind howled. "A superstition exists hereabouts that, no matter how nice the early spring weather may have been previously, the first Pacific-8 dual track meet brings with it a return to winter," wrote the *Register-Guard*. The wind blowing off Lake Washington into the UW football stadium created the physically anomalous and diabolically mysterious phenomena of "the only stadium in the country where the wind blows two ways at once." Twenty-five mile-per-hour winds toyed with these teams.

For the mile, Steve, along with Divine and Savage, had an arrangement, like many teammates did, usually trading pace-setting duties with the final lap being every man for himself. The arrangement was that after the first 220, Divine would assume the lead for 330 yards, Savage would take time in front next, then Steve. Share the burden.

The first 220 crept by, and then Divine "hammered" the next 330. When it came time for Savage to do his part, he said, "Roscoe, I can't take it, I'm hurting." So Divine took Savage's place and kept acting as a windbreak. He was never a front runner, but here he was taking on the headwinds. Onward . . .

Steve never showed up to relieve Divine. In high school, Steve had been characterized as a good teammate as he'd cheer them on, but nobody could ever run with him; they were never a threat to his dominance. College was the first time Steve had teammates who could run with him, especially in the mile. Whether Steve knew it or not, he let his selfish drive get the best of him at the cost of his relationship to Divine. You don't renege on a deal, and you don't hang a teammate out to dry. Steve did exactly that as Divine gasped for air. This, to Divine, was a key difference in the next wave of runners: they seemed more out for themselves.

Steve drafted for most of the race, Divine acted as a windbreak, taking on that inescapable headwind while Steve and UW's Bill Smart fell in line. During the final lap, Steve felt something going wrong and picked up the pace with 330 to go, accelerating to outpace Smart. Divine hanged tough, but the wind had taken its toll. Divine recalled, "Prefontaine never showed up until 100 yards from the finish. He passed me and I was stumbling by then. I'd been taking this wind. . . . And I was pissed." With the wind blowing him all over the place, Steve ran 57 seconds for the final lap to win in 4:03.2. Smart closed for second, Divine third in 4:06.7. Divine remembered, "Pre fucked me over. I was ready to quit the team. Bowerman didn't hold him accountable." The star got star treatment.

After the race, Divine was visibly upset. Gassed from being a windshield, incensed with Steve, he took a seat off to the side by himself. A handful of guys on the team consoled Divine and said, "We saw what happened. You'll get your chance."

Steve doubled back and won the two-mile easily that day and the Ducks secured the 89–65 win over Washington, but Divine still seethed. Divine was in the right and justified in his anger. He could take losing to Steve if Steve had pulled his weight. Compounding Divine's anger was the notoriety Steve kept receiving as if he was the messiah. Steve did the same thing he hated other people doing: drafting off him, letting him do all the work, then sprinting by. If revenge is a dish best served cold, Divine stuck that in the freezer. He'd get his revenge, but it was a matter of how and when, and if his body would hold up so he could, when the time came, drop the hammer on that freshman.

The timing of the Twilight Meet could not have been better. Nearly two months to the day since Steve screwed over Divine, Divine would get his chance in front of the "demanding crowd." The day before the meet, *The Daily Emerald* ran a headline that said, "Divine-Pre dual Twilight feature." This was Divine's time. It was the senior vs. the freshman. One nearing the end of his career and one ascendant. Elder statesman, punk.

Meanwhile, Steve, Divine, Savage, and Dellinger spent time at Bowerman's property up the McKenzie River. *Sports Illustrated* writer Pat Putnam joined them, as well as a photographer. Earning this kind of attention from *Sports Illustrated* was exceptional. Back in high school, Steve had received a silver dish from *Sports Illustrated* for being one of the "Faces in the Crowd." Every week, *Sports Illustrated* highlighted four athletes from the amateur ranks who performed remarkably well nationally. To be recognized by the premier magazine of the day was nothing short of monumental. Steve was unimpressed, saying, erroneously, that *SI* gave those out to everybody. As great as being a "Face in the Crowd" in high school was, a cover story in *SI* could not be understated. Mickey Mantle, Muhammad Ali, Jim Ryun made the covers. Bona fide stars. And now Steve Prefontaine was one of them.

Dellinger rested a hand on a paddock fence, wearing a light jacket and jeans. Behind him was Savage. Tallest of them all was Divine, and sitting on the fence over Divine's left shoulder was Steve, leaning around to peer at something just off camera. Where Divine had the stoic demeanor of a subway commuter, Steve's countenance was of cocksure confidence bordering on smug. He hadn't lost a race all track season. The photographer had them run a bit on Bowerman's property and he snapped a photo of Steve jogging up the hillside with straw-colored grass at his feet. The view overlooked the serpentine McKenzie River, which was the deepest blue imaginable. Spiking through the sky were the evergreens hugging the river giving Eugene the name of the Emerald City.

Divine, feeling healthy for the first time in what felt like ages, had been spitting out 220s in practice in 22 seconds flat. Bowerman loved it. Make no mistake, though: *Sports Illustrated* hoped to see Steve not only win but run his first sub-four. The story practically wrote itself. Here was the freshman prodigy and the great guru. Bowerman said, "*Sports Illustrated* could come out to take a picture of Prefontaine and he could come in fourth . . . and still run a sub-four-minute mile."

As much as Steve longed to win every race, he could stomach losing if he broke four minutes. He acknowledged there were five or six guys, in his estimation, who could win the race. Steve had won all ten of his outdoor races to date, three of them at the mile. Breaking that barrier, win or lose, was and is a badge of honor. The elegance of one minute (or less) per lap. The math was simple. Runners could easily tell if they were on pace. Fans could tell. Short enough not to bore, long enough to watch the drama unfold. Short enough not to think too much, but just long enough where you could think too much.

The Twilight Meet, though an exhibition, was a meet where, as the *Register-Guard* noted, "things happen." Given Steve's growing love affair with the people at Hayward Field, the electricity sparked in Eugene. All eyes would be on Steve. Just as well for Divine, who planned to strike. As Kenny Moore would write in *Bowerman and the Men of Oregon*, "It didn't sit all that well with Divine that a self-absorbed kid who wasn't a true miler was the focus of attention in his event."

The sun dipped and the temperature held at a comfortable near-70 degrees, right on par for the regional average and oh-so-perfect for a track meet.

Mile weather. The people poured into Hayward Field, 8,400 strong for what was essentially an intrasquad meet between current and former Oregon Ducks.

Divine lived about a mile away from Hayward Field and the "handsome, dark-haired Oregon senior" waited until just an hour before the race to jog over. When he arrived, tanned face, eyes with piercing intensity, he stretched on the infield grass, alone. One look and people could tell Divine was ready to run a smashing mile.

People felt the tension. For the fans, it didn't matter who won. They were rabid for a sub-four mile, and the more who could run under it the better. It had long been publicized that *Sports Illustrated* would be on hand to witness what they hoped was Steve's baptism by mile.

In the corral before the race, Divine started to lock in and block out his surroundings. He was ready. Wendy Ray, Hayward Field's track announcer, called Divine's name and he jogged out toward the starting line. The crowd roared. It was the biggest sound he'd ever heard being introduced here. The West Stands with the overarching roof acted like a megaphone, projecting sounds right down onto the start/finish line. He was locked in and fired up by the reaction. "The whole Oregon team was there," Divine recalled, thinking to himself, *Okay, motherfucker. You gonna cry or walk the walk?* Several teammates stretched out their hands for Divine, slapping him five. Rooting him on. *Put the kid in his place, Roscoe.*

The conditions were brilliant. Warm, windless, still. The wind would be provided by the screaming horde packing Hayward Field. Before the gun, standing in the front of the group was Divine, Steve, and Savage. Divine stood in Lane 1, eyes cast down at the track, hands on his hips. Steve stood beside him in Lane 2, his hair sun-streaked blond and his skin copper-bronze like a statue. He, too, cast his eyes down toward his feet, picturing the perfect race. Steve was never short of confidence, but he thought, *There's no way I can win this race. But I'm going to try. But if I don't win and I get under four minutes, that would be just as beautiful.*

Bowerman entered Wes Smylie, Oregon's half-miler, as the sacrificial rabbit. He was tasked with running at least a 60-second opening quarter to keep the prospective winners on pace for the insatiable sub-four fans. His plan:

blitz through his lap and pull off the track. "I wanted to WATCH that race," he joked.

The runners took their mark. One more deep breath . . . and—pop! The pistol blasted and Smylie shot to the front and leaned into the first turn. He didn't sell out full throttle but cruised at a satisfying speed. Quarter-mile done, 59 seconds, Smylie peeled off the track. Now he could watch.

Jim Gorman assumed the lead with Steve, a willing shadow. By and large, Steve's strategy was always to strike the front, but now that the baseline talent of runners had risen, he could no longer just drum them to death on the lead for four laps in a mile. Plus, he wasn't a bona fide miler; he needed to take shifts, though he was never far from the tip of the spear. The suspense was building as the field moved as one, strung out over several yards, the fans in the East Stands providing wind down the backstretch. The goal at this point was to clock a half-mile between 1:58 and 2:00. Fast, but not too fast. Coming down the stretch for the second time, Steve struck the front, a half-mile down in 2:01. Divine thought it would be 1:57. Steve had told Divine that he and Dave Wilborn, who had recently graduated and was running for the Oregon Track Club, were going to push the pace. Instead they were off pace. And yet this played better into Divine's strengths. The cheers escalated, imploring the field, the front runner to pick up the pace. Steve, still on the lead through the three-quarter mark, peeked at the clock.

3:00.

For the people who turned out to see a sub-four-minute mile, they must have let out a groan. Whoever was going to win this race and break four minutes would have to run the final lap in a swift time of just under sixty seconds. Steve hadn't pushed it fast enough and now the entire expectation of the race shifted. The officials held up the card for the final lap and drew the tape across the finish. Now the real race started.

Steve held the lead with his head rocking, chest pressed out, and shifting to a higher gear. Wilborn, knees high, sat just a stride off Steve's right shoulder. Norm Trerise drafted behind Wilborn. Stoic as ever with ramrod posture was Divine on the inside, two strides behind the leader. Savage rounded out the top five. These would be the top five finishers, but what order and how fast? Over . . . or under?

Halfway through the second-to-last turn of the race, Steve poured it on. Wilborn followed suit and closed the gap. Steve, feeling the pressure, dug down and fended off Wilborn down the back straightaway. Knowing, on some level, that surge squeezed some juice out of Steve's kick, Divine pounced. With 220 yards to go, Divine rocketed in front and curved around the final bend to the riotous West Stands. Steve had felt Divine breathing up on him and knew he was dead. He knew that Divine had greater foot speed. Nevertheless, Steve went to the gut for the last vestige of his strength as Divine flew by. He vaulted past Steve like the freshman was standing still, like he was a boy among men. *Am I going too fast for you?* The crowd was in a frenzy, a "standing, foot-stomping, screaming throng."

With every stride, Divine, cheeks inflated, breathing hard, put more distance between him and Steve. Divine made a statement, prodigal upsetting prodigy. His face placid, his posture unwavering, high up on his toes, Divine neared the tape and people on the infield raised their arms because they saw the time as Divine hit the tape: 3:56.3 after a searing 54.3-second final lap.

For his effort, Steve sprinted in behind Divine—his first loss (though unofficial) of the outdoor season—but a win of sorts. At long last, he finally broke four minutes: 3:57.4. "Nobody likes to lose, but I'm too happy just becoming a sub-four-minute miler. I'm glad I made Divine run; he had to work for it. And I'm glad he won. I would have been bitter if it would have been from another team," Steve said.

But wait . . . Divine and Steve weren't the only two to break four minutes. Wilborn, who back in 1967 recorded the fastest mile at Hayward Field to date, followed in third place: 3:58.2. Before the race, he was most worried about Divine and Steve. "One is faster and the other is stronger . . . and they both got me."

Trerise took fourth in 3:59.1.

And in fifth was Oregon's star steeplechaser, Savage, finishing in 3:59.2.

The 8,400 fans couldn't contain themselves. They witnessed the second fastest mile in Hayward Field history, Steve's first sub-four-minute mile, and a total of five runners break four minutes in the same race. Divine entered the race as confident as ever and knew he was practically unbeatable that night. The race unfolded perfectly for him and his running style. Years later,

Divine said, "I could always focus. I didn't hear a sound that whole race until the end of the race, like somebody slapped me across the face with noise."

After the finish, Bowerman, in a short-sleeved shirt, a tie knotted around his neck with a tie bar, met Steve, whose eyes were wide, mouth open and smiling, his hair tousled, and chest rounded. Bowerman smiled brightly at the young man. He pressed a palm against Steve's heaving stomach and looked into Steve's eyes like a proud father. Steve had, at times, been defiant, lobbying to be a miler vs. a two- or three-miler, but here, in this moment, Bowerman could not have been happier for what Steve had accomplished for himself.

The Twilight Meet was, for a time, a magical event where many Oregon athletes showed up as if it were AAU nationals or the NCAA championships, all this for an intrasquad meet. Bowerman imparted on his team to perform their best to show appreciation for the people in the community, the fans "teethed on stopwatches," and the Oregon Track Club, all those who bleed track and field the way Notre Dame fans bleed football.

After the race, Steve looked up into the eyes of Divine, who stood several inches taller. Divine stuck out a big hand to shake Steve's. In another photograph, Steve wrapped his left arm around a smiling Divine and leaned his head on Divine's right shoulder, the freshman leaning on the senior. If there were resentments still bubbling, it didn't show. Divine entered the race fueled by a sense of renewal and, well, revenge. Nothing could take away the joy of that moment and the sweetness of delivering one of the greatest miles of all time—and against the rising star who had, to date, stolen much, if not all, of the attention.

It would never be as good again on the track for Divine. Due to the hard urethane track, Divine had partially torn a few strands of his Achilles tendon during the race, which would force him to undergo two operations over the next three years. He asked his body for all it could give him that night. He would never again regain the magic of that mile.

THE HIGH OF the Twilight Meet ushered in the official end of the 1970 track season, Steve's collegiate freshman year. A week following the Twilight Meet, on Saturday, June 13, 1970, Bowerman and eighteen Ducks touched down in Des Moines, Iowa, to compete in the NCAA championships. This was an area of the country few of them had likely seen, flat as a checkerboard and corn everywhere. The weather called for heat so, as was Bowerman's custom, he wanted to acclimate his athletes. This meet was a culmination of bruising miles dating back to rain-soaked mornings where cotton sweats dragged down their spirits as they ran up the punishing hills of Willamette St. and around Spencer Butte.

To date, it was, in Iowa, the hottest and most humid day of the year. It got hot in Oregon, but it almost never got humid, and competing in that heavy, burdensome air would dampen their chances of winning NCAAs. Thinking of the humidity as some sort of historical allegory, Bowerman said, "Lord Nelson was asked by a reporter to what he attributed his success. The admiral answered, 'Being fifteen minutes early to every engagement.' Well, we're here a week early. It may, or may not, help. But then we're not fighting the Spaniards." As it turned out, acclimating his athletes to the weather would be the least of Bowerman's worries.

That Sunday, the Ducks gathered around the motel pool to swim and cool off. The diving board had been removed, save for several exposed bolts sticking straight out of the concrete and into the air. Steve trotted along the pool deck and, as he ran by, stepped on a bolt and tore the skin of his foot apart. The bolt had gouged the skin of the webbing between the big toe and the second toe of his right foot. Steve was taken to the hospital where he needed six stitches to sew it up. After the doctor knotted the final suture, he told Steve and Bowerman that Steve couldn't walk on it for two weeks. The air sucked out of the room. This was unacceptable. Bowerman placed a call back to Eugene to Dr. Donald Slocum. Slocum knew of another doctor in Des Moines who might offer a second opinion that just might keep Steve suited up and ready to run. This doctor advised Steve to soak his foot every hour. Do this for the next five days. No training. Just soaking. That was Bowerman's directive. Bowerman tried to downplay it, saying, "He tore a little gash and needed six little stitches." Still, it had the papers saying Oregon's title chances were shot.

Given how hard Steve trained, it likely was a blessing. Rest—forced rest in this case—could be the best form of preparation. He was used to running ten to twelve miles worth of intervals on Mondays and Tuesdays. Followed by "medium hard" sessions on Wednesdays for eight miles. Thursdays were a light track workout to "loosen up." Fridays were for rest before Saturday duals. On Sunday, he'd run anywhere from ten to fifteen miles. Going back to his senior year of high school, he hadn't taken much by way of a break. His aggressive high school campaign gave way to several AAU meets, then running in Europe, which fed right into his first year at college. It was too much to ask of a nineteen-year-old body.

For now, Steve soaked his foot in the sink and spent much of his time in bed. His roommate was none other than Divine, ax buried. Divine, who was one of the favorites to score points in the mile, had a flare-up of his troublesome Achilles tendon. Unbeknownst to Divine at the time, a third of his Achilles was torn. Divine dunked his foot in an ice bucket, and the two nursed their lower extremities to something resembling health in their makeshift motel infirmary. Bowerman routinely poked his head in their room calling them "Champs."

Someone of Steve's unwavering energy couldn't sit for long. He tested his gashed foot Monday but found it too sore. He was told to walk one mile. Steve planned on giving it a test run on Tuesday. He laced up and trotted around. It felt a lot better. He felt confident that he could jog, but he wisely thought to give it another night's rest. Still, you never could tell. "You might see a hobbling Duck out there," he said.

If the three-mile event was just the one race—the final on Saturday—hopes would have been higher. But preliminaries were scheduled for Thursday evening, June 18, 1970, and there was no way his foot would be fully healed. Initially, there were forty-five entries in the three-mile. That number plummeted with the knowledge that Minnesota's prime freshman Garry Bjorklund would be running the three over the six-mile; throw in a still-hobbling Prefontaine, and the entries dropped to twenty-five.

Bowerman held a meeting with rival coaches and posited whether a three-mile prelim was even necessary. Send them all to the final, he said. Among the deliberations, Bowerman grew impatient and threw up his hands and said, "Go ahead and have a prelim. I don't give a damn. My guy is used to running two races." The entries needed to drop to twenty or fewer for the

NCAA to cancel it. For now, it didn't look promising: Steve, one of Oregon's best weapons, was down and, most likely, out.

Steve fought. To his credit, he kept walking and soaking. With those stitches, it was like sticking a needle in his foot. Steve jogged some, which encouraged Bowerman. It was anathema to Steve to consider quitting. He'd find a way to compete. A young man from Coos Bay raised on toughness didn't quit.

Dellinger, too, assessed the situation. It looked bad, despite Bowerman saying it was nothing serious. Few things were more important to a runner than the health of their feet. Dellinger called Hal Cowan, the sports information director for the University of Oregon, and broke the news, a "killing blow" delivered to Oregon. Steve was tough, but this was something altogether different. In a few years, he'd tell runners he mentored that you can run hurt, but not injured. Here, in 1970, he was *injured*. For now, as of Tuesday, June 16, and the three-mile trials in little more than forty-eight hours, he was doubtful.

Bowerman said Steve "has a sore foot, that's all. It's no great tragedy. But I wish it hadn't happened." They reached the consensus that Steve would run the prelim regardless of how his foot was healing. Dellinger *wanted* a prelim to give Steve a workout since he'd been keeping pressure off the foot and keeping it from getting infected. Dellinger said Steve had been like a "panther laying on that bed all week." Dellinger would rather have Steve grind it out than rest him, a sign of the times where rest was just as often seen as weakness.

Meanwhile, Steve held court with the press from the balcony of his motel room. He reclined in a chair and elevated his bare, right foot on the railing. If he couldn't exercise his body, he'd exercise his voice. He rested his elbows on the armrests and cocked his head to the side. Steve equated distance running to football in that there was offense and defense. But what few football coaches would ever do before the big game was unilaterally tip their hand as to what they'd do. Part of Steve's psychology was his candor, the brashness to be forthright with his plan to hold himself accountable. "I usually play offense, take the pace," he said. "What the opponents do depends on what I do. But I'll probably run a defensive race here and get those guys to wondering what I'm doing." It was one thing to tell his teammates what he planned on doing, but to tell the press—and by extension his competition—was a mistake he'd make on more than one occasion. Despite the foot, he felt confident he could sprint with anybody in the three-mile. "All I'm thinking about is coming across that finish line first."

Looking at Steve's foot, the odds were not in his favor. Bowerman continued to smoke screen. "He has a sore foot, nothing more, nothing less." With every foot strike under normal walking pressure, the skin stretches and pinches. At speed, every foot strike adds hundreds of pounds of pressure to the forefoot, which put ever more strain on those six stitches and the tiny stretch of skin between his toes. It was asking a lot of the freshman and calling it merely a sore foot was a callous dismissal, or perhaps misdirection, on Bowerman's part. But he expected his tiger ready, to "run like hell."

On Tuesday, just two days before the three-mile prelim, Steve laced up his shoes for a little jog. He told Bowerman, "I can't even feel it." Relief . . . for now, however brief.

The week progressed, and tornado warnings alerted the throngs of people in southern Iowa to the regional danger. A storm loomed. It rained all Tuesday night, which only fueled the stifling, 90-degree heat and humidity of the next day. Thunderstorms boomed throughout Wednesday afternoon.

During the storms, the coaches attended scratch meetings and, so far, with twenty-five entries in the three-mile, the NCAA committee promised a three-mile trial. If there were twenty or fewer entries, the committee might wave it, an extra two days for Steve to mend. Steve likely had one race on that bum wheel, not two.

On the eve of the championship prelims, coaches, publicists, and reporters milled around the Hotel Savery ballroom. Coaches leaned in close, looking for that extra piece of information, "whispering in ears . . . sipping their drinks and gleaning what they could . . ." There were rumors that Steve would be scratched, but as of Thursday morning, he was a go. Talk of foot lacerations brought to memory the great Australian miler John Landy, the Buzz Aldrin of sub-four-minute milers.

In the year 1954, the British Empire Games in Vancouver, B.C., billed a duel between Roger Bannister, who had just become the first person to break four minutes in the mile, and Landy, who at one point was fast on his heels to becoming the first himself. A witness peeked into the dressing room where Landy was prepping. He lay supine on a table, receiving treatment for a cut on his foot. Landy had stepped on a camera flash bulb the night before and suffered a significant gash on his heel. Not wanting to worry the public or cast doubt on the race or, for that matter, make excuses, Landy stayed mum. Doctors stitched his heel. In his signature style, Landy set a fast pace. Bannister, in his signature style, sat behind Landy and later outsprinted him. Both broke four minutes that day. If Landy could race exceptionally well on a hurt foot, perhaps Steve could, too. But that was Landy's heel, not his forefoot, and when the running gets serious, all runners are up on their forefoot. Plus, Landy only had to run one mile, not three—four laps, not twelve.

That Thursday morning, the day of the prelims, Steve was doubtful for the race. Word was, though, that the number of entries in the three-mile dropped from twenty-five to twenty-two. There would be two eleven-man heats with five eliminated from each to set up a gold-medal run of twelve.

As it turned out, when the forty-ninth NCAA championships at last got under way, news broke that two runners—Mel Campbell of Nebraska and Merie Valotto of Virginia Tech—didn't arrive before the starting time of the race. This knocked the three-mile field down to twenty, and thus the three-mile prelims scheduled for 7:05 p.m. were eliminated. There would just be the final on Saturday evening. Call it the "luck of the Ducks."

Bowerman and Dellinger had decided Steve was fine to run in the prelims, so the cancellation was a bit of a disappointment. They wanted to test Steve, but Bowerman figured the extra two days would be good for Steve nevertheless. Dellinger had wanted to put Steve through the mill in the prelims, but now, at the very least, they could control his workout and monitor him. Steve, fit from a thousand miles, likely didn't need the work.

In the absence of an elimination round, Bowerman and Dellinger turned Steve loose on the track and definitively sent a message: one mile jog, four 110s, four 220s, and another set of four 110s, followed by another easy one-mile jog around the oval: three miles. Steve pounded out "32s" in the 220s, which had Dellinger nodding that Steve was going to be just fine. "If it were going to hurt he would have felt it on those 32s," he said.

When he finally was allowed clearance to get back on the track, boy, did it feel good to be running again, even in Iowa's suffocating humidity. The air rushing over his skin and the spring of every step was invigorating. Not to mention the quickness of breath and pulse that every runner, on some level, craves. After that training session, he realized it would take more than a little pain to stop him.

As a team, Oregon faltered and hopes of a team championship were quickly dashed by sub-par results from Mac Wilkins in the javelin, Steve Savage in the steeplechase, and Roscoe Divine in the mile. Which left Steve in the second-to-last event to salvage whatever he could for Oregon. The foot was heavily padded and taped. How he fit into that ballet slipper of a track spike was anyone's guess, but he only needed it to last for twelve laps and a little more than thirteen minutes. He was more concerned about the tape wadding up under the ball of his foot than the cut itself. Steve didn't come out to Iowa merely to sit in a motel room. He was here to run, pain be damned. Given the circumstances, he figured it best to run to win and not worry about the clock. It was not a day for records. Secure the ten points.

The start of the race was tepid. The nineteen other runners all knew Steve's playbook. They all wanted him to take the lead and maybe tear up his foot. Bowerman watched with incredulity. Everyone knew what had happened to Steve and not a single runner forced the issue and made him really drive off his foot. They let him lead and control the pace of that lead. Instead, a baffled Bowerman watched as they let Steve—a wounded freshman—take command and run his own race.

Steve's original plan was to follow for six laps—half the race—and then strike the front. But when he got a glimpse of the 4:32 first mile, he sensed they were waiting—baiting him—to take the lead . . . "So, I did."

He went to the front on cue, but still coasted at a relatively benign 70-second-per-lap pace. Steve toyed with Bjorklund and Villanova's Dick Buerkle. The slower pace invited Buerkle to pass with only a quarter-mile remaining. For the entirety of the race, Steve was of the mind to play with their expectations. *Keep 'em guessing. Why take off and outrun them when I can hold on and outsprint them?*

When Buerkle passed Steve, for a moment it appeared that Steve had reached the end of his luck. Steve then sprinted and the fans roared as he surged by Buerkle and extended his lead, running a 55-second final lap. It wasn't until midway through the final turn that his foot began to bother him, damp with sweat and blood. By then, the finish was so close and his lead sizable enough that he plowed ahead to win his first individual NCAA championship in a time of 13:22 flat, a record eleven seconds better than Gerry Lindgren's NCAA championship mark in 1966. He crossed the finish line with his hands up, his head thrown back in exhaustion.

As the adrenaline wore off, and with a slight hitch in his gait, he was terrified to take his shoe off and look at the carnage within. He pulled the shoe off, then the tape, and with it, two stitches and blood.

The University of California, Berkley Golden Bears were the surprise victor of the meet with just 40 points. Oregon finished in a three-way tie for second with 35. Come January 1971, though, Cal would be stripped of the title for having used an ineligible sprinter. Oregon, along with Brigham Young University and the University of Kansas, were granted a three-way share of the title, Bowerman's fourth and final of his illustrious career. The 1970 Oregon track team would be inducted into the University of Oregon Hall of Fame, and they owe it, in part, to Steve securing first-place points on a bandaged and bloody right foot.

Since Jim Ryun had gone into exile, Steve assumed the mantle as the face and voice of track and field. With his penchant for pithy quotes and movie-star charisma, he was a flavor people craved, refreshing and down-right fun to watch. Ron Clarke, the Aussie who happened to be wrapping up his career with a tour of the United States, admired Steve's running and his style. "Prefontaine has the confidence, the cockiness and he's prepared to gamble. He's got the courage to go out there and set the pace and dare his competitors to catch him." Steve's ascension was beautifully timed: it was announced that in just more than two years, Oregon would host the 1972 Olympic Trials.

Steve was just getting started, becoming the avatar for a new generation of athlete: as bold and brash on the track as off. As one writer said in a moment of accidental prescience, "Only tragedy can stop the nineteen-year-old."

CHAPTER 7

BURNOUT

FOLLOWING NCAAS, THE school year since wrapped up, Steve Prefontaine limped back home to Coos Bay, tired and broken down. Waiting for him was an unblemished copy of *Sports Illustrated*. The June 15, 1970, issue practically glowed. Steve, like a "three-year-old opening a Christmas present when he saw the magazine," opened it to page 28 and there it was: "The Freshman and the Great Guru." Steve said, "This oughta help Oregon's recruiting." And also, "What's a guru?"

He stared intently at the article. There, on the cover, it said, "America's distance prodigy: Freshman Steve Prefontaine." He was too young to know in the moment, but earning a cover on the preeminent sporting publication of the era elevated his profile in ways—and the expectations to be great—he likely never saw coming. This degree of notoriety always comes at a cost.

Earlier in the week, Steve also was featured in a full-page spread in the *Sporting News* with the headline, "Next Jim Ryun? Oregon frosh Steve Prefontaine." That comparison, in a matter of speaking, was apropos. Copies of the latter were as "rare as hen's teeth . . . In fact, for Coos Bay, both magazines will become collectors' items." How prophetic that would be.

The attention thrown Steve's way wasn't without criticism. A novice track-and-field fan might think Steve was the first person to ever run fast. No doubt drive-by track fans got a full serving of Steve in *Sports Illustrated*. Harry Missildine of the *Spokesman-Review* out of Spokane, Washington—Gerry Lindgren country—took issue not with the story (he thought it "excellently executed"), but, he asked, "one wonders inevitably where *SI* was when Gerry Lindgren was prodigal? In fact, one wonders where *SI* has been since he's matured."

A fair point, but the media—and especially sports media—have a way of chasing the new flavor, the allure of unbounded potential vs. a long, respectable body of work. Steve's star burned so bright that it was easy to see how someone of Lindgren's stature could be overlooked. Steve had the looks of a heartthrob, sexy, with the bronzed complexion of a career surfer, and was, by virtue of this, undeniably popular with women. For a distance runner, he was muscular, not wraith-like, and he had an electric style of running that made any event he ran a must-see. Add to that that he possessed something altogether intangible and unteachable, something that scores of people would attest to over the years: charisma. When Steve walked into a room, he had what one friend called "It." Others, too, would revel in his charisma. Ralph Mann, a close friend and the 1972 silver medalist in the 400-meter hurdles, said the only other person he met whose charisma matched Steve's was Robert F. Kennedy. People wanted to be around Steve; people wanted to be him. One admirer said, "You know, I was never interested in track or cross-country until HE came along." He made you feel special, even when he was young. Steve had a glaring, hardened intensity, but also an inviting warmth. He'd throw his arm around you or give you a hug. He wasn't afraid of touch, and he quickened the pulse of everyone in a room. He was a star, others merely runners. Because of this stardom, he was in demand, as Ryun was before him. The *SI* cover proved it, rocketing him onto the national scene and bringing the burden of Olympic expectations to the fore. It was one thing to be recognized in track circles, but to be a name of national import was something few could prepare for and fewer could relish.

In the early 1970s, as in generations before, the college season gave way to the AAU track-and-field championships with the potential for international meets in Europe or South America. There was little downtime for the college athlete after a brutal season that started in March (earlier if you count a few indoor meets in January and February) and ended in June. Post-collegiate runners were just ramping up their training however they could find time for it outside their day jobs. Many became teachers because they could run in the morning before school and the afternoons after classes. But the college athlete—tires balding, tank empty—moved right into the summer campaign. With a scarred foot, Steve had no rest and shipped to Bakersfield, California, for AAU nationals in late June 1970. His foot was still tender and sore. He had, at this point, nothing to prove and could only do further damage to his foot, maybe even his body as he compensated for the pain. But Steve's toughness, along with the masochism inherent to running, pushed him to compete. He was too young to understand that he needed to take time away from the rigors of distance running. If he was counseled otherwise, he rebuffed it.

Everywhere Steve looked in this three-mile field on Bakersfield's clay track was awash in talent, many names new, many old. Lindgren, Frank Shorter, Rick Riley, and Jack Bacheler of the older guard were all there. Once the pistol blasted, it was evident that Steve didn't have his usual buoyancy. Steve was, for the first time in a long time, losing ground. His shins barked at him and his bandaged and bloodied foot hurt—it had only been a week since NCAAs. He was forced to run on the outside of his right foot to protect the injury. In so doing, it strained his leg, his knee, his arches, his tendons. Steve had been favoring his bad leg and didn't practice all week. Toward the end of the race, he was sitting back in fourth place. Leading the pack was Shorter. One stride ahead of Steve was Lindgren. After a year beating up on college athletes, Steve was, just as he did a year before at the AAUs coming out of high school, stepping up in class to a new level of runner. Only this time he was of the class and expected to vie for the win.

The pace was tepid, and Steve wished it would have been faster. When two miles went by in 9:05, he knew he was in trouble. He knew he should have stepped up the pace, but he was boxed in and hurting. With 440 to go, Lindgren sprinted to the front, breaking up the huddle of runners. Steve gave chase, but when he went to kick, he felt like "someone had hit me with an ax." Shorter pulled ahead and won over a late-charging Riley and Lindgren. Steve finished fifth.

Lindgren and Steve took off their spikes and walked around the dusty, clay track together in their stocking feet. Lindgren told Steve, "It's tough to come back after a great win like you had at the NCAA."

"I need a rest," Steve said. "I just couldn't sprint."

The AAU race drained him physically, and mentally it destroyed him. Like he said, he needed a rest. Perhaps what he needed most was for someone to tell him to rest and nobody—be it Bowerman, Dellinger, and certainly not the greedy AAU—was about to pull him off the track and protect him from himself. Raising his hand and telling them he needed a break was a sign of weakness and nobody coming of age in Coos Bay could show weakness. It was a time when there was no such thing as "load management" or an era where athletes were given grace and permission to decompress.

Despite licking his wounds, Steve was, for all his intensity and maniacal desire to win, in good humor. "I'm doing great. Last year as a high school senior I finished fourth. How's that for progress?"

For Steve, losing was a relief. Had he finished in the top two, he would have been pressured to join the U.S. team in Europe. Had he qualified, he considered not going anyway. It simplified matters for him. He felt like he was running on a broken leg for the last half mile. No Europe. No problem.

But Steve was too big a draw, too big an asset. Despite his performance at the AAUs, he was selected to go to Europe and Russia. He still wasn't sure if he'd go or not, but he had no summer job, so he accepted, this despite knowing he had little to give. It must have been a sense of obligation, even guilt, that forced his hand and made him comply. Steve couldn't really say "no" to the AAU, a cartel trafficking in athletes. In a reference to the movie *The Godfather*, Frank Shorter would recall, they were the Mafia. The implication if you told the AAU "no" was, "How do you like horse heads?" They ran; and Steve ran against his better instincts.

Steve was set to fly to New York City on Thursday, July 2, 1970, and then off to Paris with the hopes of being back by the first of August or sooner. He grabbed his bag, gave his mother a kiss on the cheek, and hit the road.

WHILE IN EUROPE, Steve ran what he considered to be a light load, fifty to sixty miles a week. After having run on the side of his right foot in the NCAAs and the AAUs, his leg started to rebound, and the volume wasn't causing him extra problems.

Steve let the people of Coos Bay know that he would keep them informed as to what he was up to. Not just the wire services, but from the desk of Steve Roland Prefontaine. In a letter, he said, "There is really a lot of great guys on this team. I have made a few more friendships, which is a very important thing in a man's life, and that's what a lot of track and field is about. My roommate is Rick Riley from Washington State."

Riley noticed something right away about Steve: he was a joy to be around. In low-key settings, he wasn't intimidating or awash in bravado like he was in the papers, just another guy. But to the press he was bombastic, almost as if he knew to put on a show for them. Riley said, "You'd see him talking to a guy from the press or whatever and you go, 'Oh my God, what's he going to say?' and kind of chuckle a little bit." The connection Riley had with Steve went back to the Pacific Northwest: Riley from Washington, Steve from Oregon; Riley the previous national two-mile prep record holder, Steve the current (as of 1970). Riley grew up blue collar, as did Steve, so Riley understood the toughness, the masculinity of it all. "He pissed us off at times, but he was certainly part of a brotherhood."

When they overlapped, it was a slightly more innocent time in track and field. There was no periodization. The grind was simple: a runner rose before daylight and ran. Then did, as Riley recounted, "the same damn thing in the afternoon, seven days a week, over and over." It didn't matter the weather. Steve did that. They all did that.

When they traveled to Europe in the summer of 1970, Riley socialized with Steve every day for nearly a month: bars, sightseeing. Together they flew on planes, ate meals, and attended post-race banquets.

In Paris, France, Michel Jazy introduced himself. Outside of track circles, Jazy meant little, but to them, it would be like young football quarterbacks of the day meeting Joe Namath. Jazy was the Olympic silver medalist in the 1,500 meters in 1960. He held world records in the mile, 2,000 meters, 3,000 meters, and the two-mile. Riley said, "He was a French hero. Well, he came and picked us up."

Jazy took the cohort of runners to the National Institute of Sport in Paris. Wooded trails weaved through the entire property, providing shade and soft ground underfoot. Steve, Shorter, and Riley ran with Jazy, who maintained he wasn't that fit, "But I'll tell you what," remembered Riley, "on this 2,000-meter loop that we were running, we would run 800 meters between two minutes and 2:04, let's say. We did about six of those."

Light running and sightseeing were just about the only things Steve did while in Paris. Steve jogged around the French stadium with Steve Savage, his Oregon teammate. The sun shone bright and the two were in lockstep, shirtless, skin pulled tight. Still healing, Steve didn't compete, which was just as well for someone who was equivocal about the trip in the first place. He saw most of Paris on tours and zipping around the city on the Metro. He wrote home, "Paris is everything a person hears about—and probably a little more."

Though he didn't compete in Paris, his training mileage increased to seventy-five to eighty-five miles a week, and he felt ready for the first time in weeks, "feeling reasonably good." He planned on running the 5,000 meters in Germany, and also against Russia. "Russia is our last stop, and I hope I like it as much as the other places. I'll be glad to get home, though; I just hope I can find a job."

The sense was that Steve longed for home. Dating back to the start of the school year, it was his first prolonged period away. The life of an athlete could be monastic and isolating, even lonely. Steve wanted to unwind, relax. He needed rest. "I really want to spend some time at the beaches and the lakes, water skiing, if possible—for that's what I really miss." At home, he could blend in a little. People would, by and large, give him space. With obligations to the press, a new sense of celebrity, not to mention a wounded foot and the incessant pounding of the roads for well over a year, he was reaching a critical point where it was growing too much to bear. Jim Ryun was all go, go, go, and now he vanished.

The overtones of a Russia vs. United States track meet were always a bit too on the nose. The whole Democracy vs. Communism theme was everpresent. Given that Russia was aiding the North Vietnamese in the quagmire in Vietnam, the meet was particularly grim. Too bad the team couldn't have ended in Paris instead of in Leningrad, but, alas, here they were. *Sports Illustrated* described Leningrad as "awful. When it is raining, which seems often, the city is cold and gray, with matching people. It's easy to understand why Russians suck up vodka by the gallon."

During the downtime, of which there was always a surplus in dual meets,

Shorter, Kenny Moore, and Jere Van Dyk all relaxed together on the in-field grass of the Leningrad stadium. Two native Pac Northwesterners, two U of O alums . . . and Shorter, the East Coast Ivy Leaguer. Seeing them in the grass, Steve came over and lay down beside them. He didn't say a word, merely listened as the veterans talked about their plans for the future. Steve gave off the aura of a little boy thrown into the midst of the big time, and so quickly, too. At the time, Steve looked so young, like an Eagle Scout, still clean-shaven with his hair neatly parted.

For all the machismo, all the posturing, Steve craved mentorship, an older brother—something like sophomore Tom Huggins pulling him away from the smokers his freshman year of high school and showing him the way. As Steve's abilities grew stronger and his body more powerful, it didn't change who he was at his core: he still desired counsel and the leadership of those who had run the path before him, especially as all the newfound atten-tion only isolated him further from his peers. Van Dyk felt Steve was seeking something. "I was grateful and pleased that he was there, and it gave me a sense of a brother," Van Dyk said. "I was his big brother there."

The bond between Steve and Van Dyk had actually begun a few weeks earlier. While at the AAU nationals at the end of June 1970, Van Dyk heard a knock on his motel door and found Steve standing in the intense Bakersfield heat.

Van Dyk, an Oregon grad and a miler, had heard of Steve, but this was the first time they met. Van Dyk recalled it was just the pair of them, Steve on the rise, Van Dyk just a few years older already at the end of his track career. Steve merely wanted to sit with Van Dyk and talk. To Van Dyk, Steve wasn't the brash construct of the media, but a gentle young boy searching for the wisdom of someone older, somebody whom he could trust, someone who had walked the road.

It could be that Steve was starting to feel the weight of the spotlight. Again, a *Sports Illustrated* cover was a heavy crown for any head. As he gave more of himself to the world, his world also began contracting. Van Dyk was struck by Steve's innocence. He ran like a wolf, but he was still a pup.

Things were changing underfoot. Steve, for a time, embodied an innocence—certainly in track and field—that was rightfully challenged and changing. The waters had become brackish from the old-world amateurism and the rumors of something professional, where athletes started realizing they had more power. Van Dyk's impression of Steve, beyond his boyishness, was that of Hank Stamper, the protagonist of Ken Kesey's *Sometimes a Great Notion*, "a very clearly working-class guy who represented what Oregon saw in itself. . . . He represented innocence to me and when I look back on it, just a dying time in America and especially in track and field."

The pair spent hours together watching television and talking. Van Dyk saw in Steve why people related to him: the working-class roots, the blue-collar pugilism. But Van Dyk saw beyond the veneer to the tenderness and sweetness that belied Steve's signature intensity. "Nobody ever saw him, in my mind, as a sweet, innocent boy. That's what I saw. That's what I've held onto my entire life."

In the end, like so many of these international trips, the Russia meet proved a learning opportunity for Steve both on and off the track. The Soviets won the meet, 200–173. Steve, to his credit, finished second in the 5,000 behind Rashid Sharafetdinov, leading the way through 3,500 meters, fading, then rebounding.

After the meet, Van Dyk carried the American flag for Team USA as they entered the stadium to march in as a group for closing ceremonies. He has a photograph that was taken by a *Sports Illustrated* photographer, but it never ran in print. Roughly ten feet behind Van Dyk—and the only person looking at the camera—is Steve Prefontaine, in his Team USA AAU tracksuit, his hair growing out a bit longer, holding a duffel bag in his left hand, looking like the innocent boy Van Dyk remembers.

JUST LIKE THE previous summer, the AAU created more resentment among athletes. A reason the team was one of the most inexperienced teams ever was because many of the seasoned athletes couldn't afford to go; they couldn't miss work to run for free.

On returning to Coos Bay, Steve found a job as a DJ for KBBR, the local radio station, even if it was for just a few weeks before starting his sophomore year at the University of Oregon. He sold advertisements to subsidize his program on the coastal airwaves.

Steve said, "The AAU is going to have to start subsidizing if we are going to have top athletes much longer. It's difficult to ask a man like (shot-putter) Randy Matson, who has a wife and baby, to take three months off from work to compete for his country and then come home broke." Steve absorbed these insights by osmosis with the more seasoned travelers, but it did little to stay quiet about it. He wanted to bring these greater injustices to light. That, too, revealed a self-awareness that his growing celebrity afforded.

Steve heard, but it was unclear if he was being coy, "that a lot of track athletes are paid under the table to compete. No one has offered me anything. I don't know if I'd accept it, if they did." Foreign race promoters—understanding the absurdity of American amateurism—would, in time, pay Steve, and myriad other athletes, under the table, a wink-wink secret.

Steve began thinking of the AAU's utility. What good was it doing? Who was it serving? For him, it was no longer abstract but a concrete reality. At the time, so enmeshed was the AAU with the Olympics that it was the only way to qualify for the Olympic Games. As long as it had that degree of leverage over every track athlete's dream, every athlete had to bow down and kiss the ring. "Whether I still run with the AAU in the years to come depends . . . When they start telling everyone what to do, where to go, when to run and not to run I'll go on my own." The AAU strong-armed him into competing during a summer where he desperately needed rest, for his foot, for his mind. It didn't care about his well-being, that he wasn't his best and was running on "reserve strength." Athletes were indentured servants, and it cared little that Steve needed time to recover. As far as the AAU was concerned, there'd always be fresh meat coming up the pipeline.

Before he injured his foot and the subsequent fallout from that, Steve and Bowerman spoke of taking the long view to avoid the burnout so endemic to amateur runners: see Ryun. Bowerman wanted Steve to progress at a rate of 10 percent improvement per year over ten years. They could move faster, but, as Bowerman said, "by the time he got out of school he'd probably be sick of it and quit. That's what happens to most of our runners. Steve's in no hurry." Steve concurred, even adding, "I don't want to be like Jim Ryun. No doubt he'll come back, and when he does he'll again be the greatest, but I don't want to go through what he did, all that tremendous pressure when he was so young. It came so quickly. World records at nineteen. I don't want that. Later, yes, but it won't be my first love." And yet, despite the awareness that he would need rest, he was forced into running for the AAU to great physical harm and mental fatigue. He was cooked. How ironic, him saying "I don't want to go through what he did" for an *SI* cover story that would invite the very pressure and cautionary tale he hoped to avoid.

Now, after his time in Europe, a new college season loomed, another cigarette lit by the burning embers of the last. As Steve ramped up his mileage, he noticed his foot was bothering him again. He missed practice, sometimes a day or two at a time.

Thinking back to his time in Europe, when he lost in Germany and Russia, he got real down. He lost interest. Or, more accurately, he started to find interest in things beyond running, likely a product of traveling and the influence of older, worldlier teammates. The early 1970s were such a turbulent time, and he started noticing things like politics, ecology, even "finding oneself." Blasphemous as it sounded, he got to thinking that running wasn't everything. It cut into his personal life, or was so demanding that he had no real personal life at all. He wanted to do and try different things. There had to be more to life than running in circles. Every once in a while, he asked himself why he was out there running, "busting myself up." Life could be easier, more leisurely. He looked at other students in college and they were out having fun, doing the things that college boys do. *Why not me?* Steve wondered. He said he never stayed up later than midnight. Campus life started after midnight, he thought, and he'd been in bed for three hours by that point.

It was evident that Steve was burned out: senior year of high school moved into a rigorous summer, then college cross-country, the indoor meets, the spring duals, NCAAs, AAUs, Europe again, the hounding media. He grew fed up with the grind of it all when he could be doing much more enjoyable things. He wanted to read other books, not just the textbooks associated with being a communications major. He simply had no extra time. When the mornings arrived and it was cold and rainy, he asked himself if it was worth it.

Under the weight of it all, he told Tom McGuire of his hometown newspaper, *The World,* that he considered quitting, that if his discipline had flagged, "I wouldn't have come back."

It was likely lip service, but the fact that he voiced it was an illustration of just how tired he was.

In the end, he laced up for cross-country season much as he was expected to. He might have been burned out and questioning whether there was more to life than running, but he was still a competitor. What kept him focused, what brought him back from the brink, was the 1972 Olympics just on the horizon. It gave purpose to his training and extinguished his angst over a fear of missing out on college life. He leaned on his habits, the discipline, the practice of being a runner, the everyday routine of going about the work in the face of unwanting. Discipline, Steve thought, made the difference between an elite runner and a regular runner.

Back home in Coos Bay before the start of his sophomore year at Oregon, he sought the guidance of Walt McClure and Phil Pursian, his beloved high school coaches. Pursian saw that Steve needed to "get away" from the university and the Eugene environment, work out, relax. His freshman year was, to put it mildly, long. That said, being who he was, he wasn't going to sit around. At times, he ran into old classmates back from Vietnam. They took great pleasure in Steve jogging beside them for a few hundred yards or so. Never too busy to slow down and trot with a familiar face from Coos Bay, he'd run the old cross-country trails, along the beaches, and flee, however briefly, the pressures of his burgeoning celebrity that were becoming increasingly inescapable.

CHAPTER 8

PEERLESS

AT THE FALL 1970 NCAA cross-country championships on November 22, Steve was awash in nerves, even scared. He had no real reason to be, especially after making such quick work in the Northern Division and Pac-8 cross-country meets early in the season. Steve was, at last, healthy and by all accounts recovered from his malaise.

Yet Ken Popejoy, running for Michigan State, had a plan. He, like Steve, was a college sophomore in the fall of 1970. It wasn't that long ago—June 1969 at the end of their high school careers—when he had finished a hard-charging second to Steve in the mile at the Golden West Invitational. Prior to that race, Popejoy had stuck his hand out to shake Steve's, but Steve rebuffed him and walked away. It was only after Popejoy ran a brilliant race that Steve relented and said, "Now you deserve to shake my hand. That was a great race."

So here for the cross-country championships, Popejoy lined up at the front of the field. The course was flat and the opening 520 yards—where there promised to be a stampede of runners shooting for the white flag marking the one-lane road through the woods—was wide open. Popejoy confided in Dave, a fellow teammate, that *Track & Field News* always sent a photographer, and they always took a giant photograph at the mass start and plastered it on the cover. "When the gun goes off," Popejoy said, "let's take off and lead this thing. We're gonna get on the cover of *Track & Field News*!"

Several hundred runners, and a brave few dozen who knew they'd shoot for the lead, all leaned forward at the waist as silence fell over the field. The gun blasted and Popejoy and Dave sprinted as if they were running one mile—not six—leading the thundering herd. Lots of puffs and breaths, coughs, sniffles, spit, snot rockets. That many runners was like riding a giant wave, hanging on for dear life lest you get swallowed by the onslaught. They neared the one-lane road, a quarter-mile away, running a 53-55 seconds quarters, a comically ridiculous pace.

In that first hundred yards of the chaotic championship race, Steve was helplessly pinned behind four or five runners bending around an early turn at the start. As the field neared this first turn, someone driving a station wagon—likely as a prank—sped onto the course and up a hill. It cut in front of the field and around the bend, skidding through the mud and shooting a "rooster tail" of muck.

They reached the canopy of the woods and, by now, should have seen a photographer. Dave, huffing, calling into question Popejoy's leadership, said, "I didn't see a photographer, Pope, where's the photographer?"

"Hang in there. He's gonna be here," Popejoy said, still charging. "We're leading nationals!"

They stormed on, very much strangers in a foreign land on the lead in this field, as they approached the half-mile mark. Popejoy and Dave didn't belong here, and they soon heard footsteps charging up on them.

Steve Prefontaine sidled up to Popejoy, right on his elbow, and said, "The fuck you doin', Popejoy?"

"We're getting on the cover of *Track & Field News*," he said, panting.

Steve belted out a few curse words and hit the afterburners, leaving Dave and Popejoy behind, sweat pouring down his face.

"Pre was always up in the hunt," Popejoy said, ". . . he *was* the hunt." Dave and Popejoy ran through the first mile in 4:18 and by now Popejoy realized there was no photographer on the course; there was never going to be a photographer on the course; they were never, ever, ever, ever going to make the cover of *Track & Field News* . . . but they were still in the lead pack, and if a runner finished in the top twenty-five at nationals, you were automatically named an All-American. "Hang in there, Dave," Popejoy said. "We're up front in nationals for God's sake!"

Under the pines of the College of William & Mary's Kingsmill Planta-tion course in Williamsburg, Virginia, Steve settled in, reminded of home in Oregon. It was cool and windy, but, thankfully, no rain. He developed an ache in his right side and grabbed it several times, but it worked itself out. He had charged into the lead by the second mile of the race—past an unlikely set of leaders, merry pranksters, so to speak—and coasted up a hill by the third. Steve relished a good hill, knew the strength he had forged from the punishing streets of Coos Bay, and poured it on.

With the runners behind him strung out, he seized on their "resting for the finish" by throttling up, daring them to stay with him, demoralizing them with his seemingly bottomless reserves. With two-and-a-half miles to go, he was alone in the lead but growing tired. Onward through three, four, and five miles, the final mile a heavy burden where he expected someone to surge up and clip him.

Steve shot out of the woods and down the final chute, "his shaggy hair whipped by a brisk wind and his body lathered in sweat." With people cheering this sophomore sensation, he let loose what he could. He drove hard, eyes closed, head swaying side to side. By now his lemon-yellow singlet had come untucked and swished around his hips. His arms flailed, his mouth a maw. His head tilted to the left, eyes lifeless and blank, and he looked like he might fall right there in the leaf litter at the finish. 28:08, a course record and thirty yards clear of second place.

After the race, Steve was effusive, signing autographs in his left-handed script for admirers, many of whom ran track or cross-country for the local high school. He was asked whether it bothered him, signing all these autographs. "Not at all. I like people," he said. Steve attributed this win to running less, not more, a Bowermanism that it was better to be undertrained than overtrained. There was a residue of the burnout he suffered toward the end of the summer. "What I do in practice is make sure whatever I do, I do well."

As for Popejoy, he and Dave weaved through the course until Dave fell off. Gone. Done. Popejoy, though, was still in the top slice of this field, and he willed himself to carry on. Finally, the bear caught him, with his final mile going in 5:15, and he fell back to twentieth and finished there. In doing so, Popejoy's folly made him an All-American.

"The worst part of that whole story? It's the first year *Track & Field News* did not put the start on the panoramic cover of the magazine," Popejoy said.

———

FOR SOME, BEING the leader of the pack was a joke; for Steve, already peerless as a sophomore, the only joke was the competition. He had further isolated himself. But this was the path.

Steve wrestled with what all distance runners confront: the loneliness wrought not by seclusion but by the surplus of talent. He wrote about it in his letters to Bill Dellinger when he was in high school. Just a few months into his second year of college, he was already experiencing something similar. It wasn't just about being alone on a run, but it's also the monastic life of a high-level athlete. Track was his world and sometimes he grew tired of it and wondered why he punished his body. He routinely asked himself: is it worth it? But people like Steve were wired differently.

Whereas his formative years were devoted to finding his place, belonging; his great motivation now turned to the frontier of his interiority, and to the limits, or the lack thereof, of heretofore unexplored speed. Yes, he felt the weight and burden of expectation, but he was of a mind that it ultimately would, in fact, be worth it. This despite the mornings arriving hours before his peers, greeted by the cold and rain, surrendering to the master plan. Thoughts of Munich always reoriented his compass. He had visions of Munich—the site of the 1972 Olympics—and, fueled by this, knew that was his "why." To win a medal. To be the best, perhaps, as Bowerman teased, the greatest.

Adding to the loneliness was that he was just too damn fast. To push himself where he needed to go required athletes on, or at least near, his level. By and large, as a sophomore, there were none. Bowerman and Dellinger cooked up variations to break up the monotony of Steve's training. Much of his confidence he owed to Bowerman because Bowerman told him what to do and Steve blindly believed him.

In addition to loneliness, pain was and is inevitable; where do you put the pain? Could you even thrive on it, invite it as the throat dried up and the legs were on fire. Steve courted the pain as a mistress; the more tired he got, the better he ran; it was the whetstone that sharpened his will, which came down to the mind as much as the body. Confidence, to Steve, was paramount. He convinced himself that he could do it. When he did that, he usually could. He rarely just thought it; he often said the quiet part out loud, thus drawing ire from rivals, even coaches who thought he should shut his yap. But he often delivered. Frank Shorter recalled why Steve, at times, was fully transparent about his workouts: Steve knew that if you tried to train like him, you'd kill yourself and leave yourself vulnerable to his punishing style of racing.

In the meantime, Steve loped along to eighty-five to one hundred miles per week, powering down to sixty during a competition week. He ran up Birch Lane and Skyline Boulevard, past a rock wall embankment, through Hendricks Park, or around Skinner Butte Park or Spencer Butte, up and down the hills and through the woods. He could run these roads blindfolded.

It was now 1971, early in the track season and even with consistent training he was a long way from his peak. Contrary to what many athletes do, Steve was paging ahead in the calendar year. He figured he wasn't about to spend big efforts until "the big competition" over the summer. He knew that college competition wasn't quite up to his level anymore. Steve, now twenty years old, thought little of his college peers. "You won't have to run that fast to win the NCAA, but the AAU could be different. . . . There's a tough race the week after the NCAA meet and I don't want to finish fifth as I did last year." To boot, this coming summer, the AAU track-and-field championships would be in Eugene.

To seek higher speed—a weakness of sorts for Steve—he sought it in unconventional ways. One afternoon following a long run, he saw the familiar face of Vincent Buford out on the track at Hayward Field. Buford, small in stature and a masterful 220 runner, emerged as one of the premier sprinters in the Pac-8 for Oregon. The mark of any great athlete was the work they did when nobody was watching, and so Buford walked over to Hayward. He had the entire stadium to himself, except for a couple in the stands likely looking for a little privacy. He strided and sprinted, a leisurely workout, when Steve jogged in. "Vince!" Steve said. "I've been having trouble breaking twenty-four seconds for a 220. Do you think you can help me do that?"

"I don't know," Buford said. "But I have an idea of something we can try to see if it works."

"I don't care, let's just do it."

"But you've got to make me a promise that you got to help me break five minutes in a mile."

"Okay, you're on," Steve said.

They started jogging, nice and light, the only sound the bounding of their feet. "I want you to watch me run, a light, smooth 220." Buford took off at the top of the turn, leaning hard to the left, straightened out, and crossed the finish in an easy twenty-five, maybe twenty-six seconds. Buford met back up with Steve. "Watch how quickly I recover after that," Buford said.

"I can do that," Steve said. "Can I run right behind you?"

"Are you ready? Are you ready to go a little faster than this?"

"Absolutely," he said.

Buford started slow. He paced Steve through the first 220s in 25.3, 25.2. Felt good. After a short rest, they ran a little faster, 24.5. Another, 24.2. Steve desperately wanted to break twenty-four seconds and Buford had him right on the precipice. "All right, Pre, we're gonna drop down. Hang right on my heels, dude."

Buford broke and Steve stuck right to Buford's heels, a contrast in talents. Around the turn, and then like a slingshot down the straightway. Buford was right on pace and Steve, as he was told, glued himself to Buford's heels. They stepped across the line, Buford within himself, Steve gassed: 23.4. Steve wrapped Buford up in a giant bear hug and lifted him up off the ground. "He was ecstatic!" Buford recalled. "Just being able to help him break twenty-four seconds was a super milestone for him."

Steve held up his end of the deal, too. Not that day, but sometime later, Steve paced Buford, who had never broken five minutes, through a 4:25 mile.

When the two first ran the 220s under Buford's guidance, save for the couple in the grandstands, there were no cameras, no crowds. This was Vince Buford and Steve Prefontaine alone on the track, brother to brother. "Just the two of us, man, on the track all by ourselves. Guess who else saw it?" And Buford lowered his voice to a whisper, "Nobody."

AS THE TRACK season progressed, UCLA easily beat Oregon, 86–59. Steve watched as UCLA's Wayne Collett, the super athlete and future silver medalist in the 400 meters at the 1972 Olympics, won one event, placed second in another, and anchored two winning relays in the afternoon. Steve ran only the mile in 3:59.1, his second-fastest and second career sub-four mile. There was no need to double Steve back because UCLA had so thoroughly walloped Oregon.

Steve, looking at Collett, shook his head. UCLA had clinched the meet. Why was Collett out there running in a pointless endeavor to anchor the mile relay? Steve thought Jim Bush, UCLA's coach, should know better and not run his athletes ragged. "What's wrong with Bush running Collett like that?" Steve told a reporter. Steve added, "Our coach doesn't USE his athletes. Look at Collett, he could hardly stand up after running the intermediates."

Steve then found UCLA's champion John Smith at the end of the meet and congratulated him. "We'll get you in the Pacific-8 meet," Steve ribbed. Newspaper scribes at the time wrote headlines like, "Prefontaine warns UCLA," referring to his saying to Smith that his team will get them in the Pac-8s, an innocuous statement between rivals.

Regarding Bush's use of Collett, other papers fanned the flames of Steve's criticism, whether or not it was Steve's business (it wasn't). The comments reached Bush and, like Steve, he didn't back down. "Prefontaine's mouth is now running faster than his legs. He's only a sophomore, and when he starts rapping coaches, it's a little hard to take. I can take it, but my athletes were very upset. I don't think I've ever 'used' an athlete. I'd rather lose a meet." Bush put some of the blame on the press, why print Steve's comments? "This is a youngster. He's always popping off. What we're trying to do is build up track and field. There were lots of great marks out there Saturday, and they didn't get the play they deserved."

Even as a twenty year old, Steve always made for good copy, and it wasn't his nature to spout "coach speak" or the vapid comments common to athletes then as now. Few people were as colorful in front of the media the way he was, certainly among distance runners. Despite having a tender-sounding voice, his words in print lacerated, and it was beginning to rub some people raw.

One anonymous local runner in Washington, referring to Steve complaining about not feeling good after a recent best-ever mile and three-mile double against the University of Washington, said, "Didn't feel good! That's something to say after running the best double ever. Who's he trying to impress?" Another anonymous runner said, "Pre says some things that just don't go down right. Maybe he doesn't realize it. But after he ran that 3:57.2 [sic, actually 3:57.4] mile in Eugene last year he said something like, 'Now I can outkick any three-miler in the world. . . . Well, three weeks later four guys outkicked him in the AAU three-mile. And then in Germany, he gets outkicked by Harald Norpoth in a 5,000 and loses badly in Russia, too. After the Norpoth race, [Steve] said, 'I don't have any respect for a runner who'd let a kid do all the work and then go by at the end.' I hope maybe he was trying to be funny, but I don't think so. . . . I wish he'd run some of those super times outside of Eugene, too."

As much adulation that came Steve's way, people also started to interrogate the worthiness, his deservedness of the attention. He was good, but not great; he was great but not yet the greatest. Once outside the bubble of Oregon, more people were willing to take aim at Steve. In track and field, certainly among distance runners, Steve was a new beast, a personality above a person, someone lauded by the press and then equally shamed for the attention rained on him. Decades later, runners said no one felt jealous of his attention, but comments of peers from the early 1970s belie that. There was a degree of resentment when you read between the lines. Finer, more nuanced degrees of isolation.

If it bothered him, he didn't show it. Talk as he might, he walked the walk.

And for an encore to last year's scintillating Twilight Mile—won by Divine and featuring five sub-four milers—Jim Ryun, still the world record holder in the mile, at 3:51.1, was coming to Eugene as part of his comeback. Back at the end of 1970, Steve was asked about Ryun and said that he'd love to face Ryun and he expected him to gear up for maybe one last Olympics. Steve never shied from competition, and he almost unilaterally never showed weakness or fear. He reserved that for Ryun. "I'd rather go down and get clobbered in the mile than have him come up and clobber me in the three-mile. . . . Ryun's been one of my idols. I'd like a crack at Ryun."

Now in 1971, race organizers said it was a done deal and Steve had his strategy. "I'm going to try to run the first three laps in 2:54. Then we'll see what happens."

Ryun looked like a less muscular Clark Kent and just as invisible. Like the fictional Kent, Ryun was a journalist, a photojournalist to be precise, and one of the most unassuming world record holders you ever laid eyes on. Ryun went into a self-imposed exile in his native Kansas after the 1969 AAU championships in Miami, the race where he faded and quit on the second lap, walking off the track not to be seen in competition for nearly two years. At the start of 1971, he admitted that he never "learned how to lose," had ballooned up to 195 pounds, but was back down to his racing weight of 155. He leaned into his career and his young family, while ramping up his mileage to as many as twenty-one miles a day and one hundred miles per week.

Ryun was a cautionary tale in burnout, an avatar of the psychological burden of running with great expectations. It didn't matter that he was the world record holder in the sport's premiere event; if Ryun failed to break four minutes in the mile every time he raced, it was seen as a letdown. For him, the joy of running was gone. He needed to extricate himself from track; he needed to get as far away from it as possible to sense just how strong its gravity was. He remembered being unable to say "no," be it to his university team or the constant nagging from race promoters who wanted to leverage his name on the marquee. After he left track, Ryun received hate mail, saying "you quit" and "quitter."

His wife, Anne, still saw what Ryun had lost. The couple played paddle ball, tennis, and golf, and Ryun took twenty hours worth of classes. Anne was his source of motivation. He said, "I had lost my enthusiasm, but she hadn't." That brought him back. Ryun laced up his trainers and committed to the idea of another Olympic run.

Now twenty-four years old in 1971, he bid farewell to his native Kansas and headed to Oregon to restore his powers, leaving the Topeka newspaper but keeping the camera, shooting for a big lumber company's internal trade magazine. Like all post-collegiate amateur athletes, he needed a job unrelated to his sport, lest the AAU strip him of his amateur status and drive a stake through the heart of his Olympic redemption. The Eugene climate appealed to him. It was far milder than the Midwest, and he didn't mind the rain at all. He began racing again, and now, running twice a day in Eugene, he was finding what he had long lost. "Motivation is what gets you started. Habit is what keeps you going."

For now, having spent more than a year away from track and out of the limelight, he ran fifteen miles a day and corresponded with his old college coach, Bob Timmons. He also trained with Bowerman's team, which put him in direct overlap with Steve. A reporter twisted Steve's statement about running three-quarters in 2:54 into a more antagonistic phrasing, saying, "Prefontaine has said he hopes, in effect, to run Ryun into the ground by going 2:54 in the first three-quarters of a mile." To which Ryun said, "That's fine." Steve never said he'd run Ryun into the ground.

Ryun's tenor was always gentlemanly, even demure. He let his actions speak for him, good or bad; but the sporting climate of the time was changing. Ryun was ill-equipped to deal with all the attention that met him after first breaking the world record. In 1966, at age nineteen, Ryun made a face that looked like he stepped in gum on one cover of *Sports Illustrated*, this after being named Sportsman of the Year. A modern athlete needed to be a personality as lofty as his physical prowess. But Ryun still embodied an outmoded old-world amateurism that was quickly giving way to something altogether new.

Come spring 1971, Ryun was sick of the hoopla. In a highly anticipated rematch, he had fiercely dueled Liquori in what was called the "Dream Mile" at Franklin Field in Philadelphia. It was even called the "Mile of the Century," then the "Super Mile." "Super Mile?" Ryun said. "Gee, just once I'd like to see them call it The Mile for a change." Liquori won again and photographers caught Ryun walking away, head hanging low.

Luckily the hype train would slow down, and Ryun would keep going. Meanwhile, Steve waited like a panther in the bush, having just come off several sizzling college races. The upcoming Twilight Mile had the makings of another classic, a new guard vs. old guard. On top of that there'd be as many as four other sub-four milers for the Twilight Meet.

Ryun looked at Steve and, from what he saw, said Steve's best days are ahead of him. "Don't get me wrong, though. He's real tough now." Reading deeper into what Ryun said, he likely mourned a bit of his own career to date: the brilliant young talent flaming out too early, wilting below burden. Ryun may have seen a similar fire in Steve and an equally hot spotlight and wanted more for Steve, or for Steve to merely have an awareness of the forthcoming heat. If Steve could heed that instinctive warning, maybe he'd be better off, to know when to throttle up or down, to say no instead of yes.

For Steve's part, even he was humbled by the thought of racing his idol. "He's one of the best," Steve told a reporter in 1971. "He's going to get a lot faster, a lot stronger."

Ryun trained, and Steve and the Oregon Ducks reached the end of their 1971 spring season. Steve exited the Pac-8s on May 22, 1971, a winner in the mile and the three-mile. Having won the mile, Steve was cooked, as dead as can be in the three-mile. Steve won the race, though he felt as weak and vulnerable as he ever had on the track. Luckily for Steve, Stanford's Don Kardong did not, in Steve's words, "play it smart." If Kardong had taken off with three laps remaining, he would have won. "I was just dead, just running on pure guts," Steve said.

While Steve punished himself in the race, he wondered—again—if it was worth it, all this fight. That day, he conceded it wasn't, since his team had lost. His feet were badly blistered from the newly rubberized track at the University of Washington—maybe 120–130 degrees of "road smell, melting-tar smell"—and raked the skin off his sockless feet. Throughout the entire race, like a mantra, Steve kept asking himself, *Is it worth it? Is it worth it? Is it worth it?* That age-old question long-distance runners have always asked themselves. On some level, through all the pain, the answer was un-equivocally yes, it was worth it for the rush, for the cheers, for outlasting the person behind you, for the simple satisfaction of a long, anonymous training run—the great majority of all miles.

The Twilight Meet had more or less been an "Oregon family" affair, but since Ryun was here and he was in the midst of a comeback, he was an unofficial stepson of the Oregon family tree. He'd be meeting eleven half-brothers in the mile, where upwards of 15,000 people planned on watching.

Aside from reminding people that he, too, was a force to be reckoned with, Steve was uncharacteristically subdued a few days ahead of the race. He had just gotten over a cold he couldn't shake through much of the spring.

When goaded for a prediction, Steve wisely brushed it off. Despite mentioning his goal to run three-quarters in 2:54 a few weeks earlier, now he kept his strategy close to his chest. "I'm not going to say anything about my plans. I'm just going to run hard and not predict anything. . . . For me to beat somebody like that you have to do something. It's been proven that it's pretty hard to outkick him."

It was being billed as Pre vs. Ryun, but there were ten other contenders, including Oregon alum Arne Kvalheim, and Ryun could walk off the track again. Steve thought he might finish third or fourth behind Ryun and the group. The way Bowerman saw it, Steve was the best of the young milers and Ryun was the best of the previous generation of college milers. "You aren't going to beat him unless you overpower him. . . . I'm sure Pre knows what his opponents' strengths are, and I'm sure Ryun and the others know what Pre's strengths are." Dellinger, too, added, "Everybody in the race knows he must beat Ryun on strength, not speed. It has to be extremely fast all the way to make it more equivalent when they get to that last 110 yards." Therein lurked the power of the front runner who has intra-race strength, the kind Steve had.

Steve felt the pressure, and he experienced first-hand the hype around Ryun, what Ryun must have shouldered before he walked off the track in Miami in the spring of 1969. Steve had known pressure, but this was different, perhaps his first true title bout, his first on-track encounter with a world-record holder. "Half the town of Coos Bay is coming up for the meet, I understand," he said. If he lost, he said, "It's not going to be the end of the world." As with anything of this nature, the sense from everyone involved was impatience to get it over with.

On the night of the race, June 6, 1971, the pollen was thick, most of all for Ryun. The only question Ryun asked Bowerman during his entire stay in Eugene was, "How do I avoid the pollen?"

Late spring in the Willamette Valley brings with it suffocating allergens for the uninitiated. Bowerman had run tests and figured it was best for Ryun to head twenty miles east up the McKenzie River. "But he went fifty miles," Bowerman later said. Bowerman figured it would be no issue at all for Ryun to swoop in for the race.

Three days before the race, Ryun received an allergy shot and retreated to the mountains. He felt good . . . until the day of the race. The hay fever gave him problems, but he didn't want to let on. Ever since Ryun toured Australia and New Zealand in the early spring of 1971, he failed to reestablish his series of allergy shots. When he finally secured regular appointments, he had to wait an entire month and didn't begin treatment until early May. It was not enough time for the medicine to take effect. If he were to perform well in the Olympic Trials a year from now, he'd better get used to the pollen. But despite being fifty miles to the east where the air blowing off the McKenzie River was cool like menthol, the pollen choked Ryun. Getting into the mountains was supposed to help him, get him out from under the blanket of suffocating air so he could parachute in as fresh as possible. Other runners noticed he was sick, and he probably should have withdrawn. This was insider information that Kvalheim tucked away.

Ryun, wheezing, and the eleven other runners lined up for the main event in front of the demanding crowd. Oregon's Nils Emilsson, a half-miler and the rabbit for this race, was tasked with a 1:58 pace. The gun popped and Emilsson toured the oval and pulled the field along. He was a second too slow on each lap and the time through the half-mile was 2:00. Steve was miffed by the pace. *Must I do everything myself. Someone like me who's not a miler can't pussyfoot around the first two laps*. Thoughts of a sub-3:55 mile were gone. Steve trashed the playbook and knew it was up to him to do all the heavy lifting. A crowd of more than 11,000 roared as Steve seized the lead.

If he were to win this race, it would be his mid-race strength that squeezed Ryun's tyrannical kick. Steve now hoped for 2:57 at three-quarters, "then go to work." People lined the track, some standing atop the fence to get a better view, as the field cruised around the turn. Kvalheim glued himself to Steve, but where was Ryun? It was time for him to start moving up through the field. Everyone was looking over their shoulders. When would he strike? While Steve and Kvalheim headed the pack and put ever more distance between them and the field, Ryun was sixth . . . and fading.

On the bell lap, Kvalheim peeked back and, knowing that Ryun was suffering going into the race, figured he was cooked. Kvalheim turned his focus to Steve, who, from Kvalheim's vantage point, started to tire. Steve had no idea Ryun had faded. In his mind, the boogeyman could spring at any moment.

Kvalheim didn't want to jump too soon. He had to time it perfectly, but that could be hard with thousands of people screaming, and perhaps that meant someone—Ryun—was making a surge from the back. He knew how great Ryun was when he wasn't sick, and he would not count Ryun out until the end. Kvalheim didn't want to "blow the whole thing." Coming off the final turn, Kvalheim, at last, poured it on, passing Steve down the deafening straightway as the West Stands violently vibrated. Kvalheim, securing the win, eased up and waved to the crowd. He finished in 3:56.3, just a tenth of a second off the meet record, set by his best friend, Roscoe Divine, in the previous year's meet. Steve took a valiant second, in 3:57.4, identical to his 1970 Twilight Mile. Ryun finished a distant tenth.

Down in the dressing room after the race, Kvalheim told Steve, "If Jim had been there I would have helped you with the pace but he wasn't so I saw no reason to help you."

Steve laughed. "Damn Europeans."

Ryun, coughing by his locker, and not wanting to face an onslaught of questions, briefly entertained the media and quickly left.

Bowerman dubbed the Twilight Meet yet another fantastic renewal. How could he not? But as the people filed out and the stands were once again empty, Bowerman felt sorry for Ryun. The pollen was his kryptonite and, "He was not Jim Ryun the Runner." Ryun, for now, was confronted with the flagging of his own abilities in a post-collegiate climate where a runner lost his structure, his schedule, and, in this case, the greatest weapon of all, his confidence.

As Bowerman had recently mentioned, Ryun was the best of the previous generation of milers with Steve the best of the next generation. But the writing on the walls could not have been any bolder: if Steve didn't heed the warnings laid bare by Ryun's career to date, Steve would likely suffer a similar fate—the burdens, both mental and physical, of running fast were too great to ignore. Few athletes could extricate themselves from the riptide of expectation, or the insatiability of competition. Ryun ran himself too hard and for too many masters, grinding himself to dust. Ryun's diminishing sense of invincibility should have been the distant—though approaching—foghorn, warning Steve of his blind spots, of what happens when you get pegged as the next big thing and keep pushing anyway. Steve did know better, saying as much a year earlier in *Sports Illustrated*. Steve didn't want to be Ryun or suffer Ryun's fate; Ryun was a cautionary tale. And Steve thought simply knowing Ryun's story would prevent it from becoming his as well.

HEAT REIGNED A week later at the NCAA championships, which like the Pac-8s were held at the University of Washington in Seattle, yet Steve's mind was further in the distance. *Next week.*

Part of Steve's distraction was the track. Though Steve was leading his field in the three-mile, he was unhappy with the surface. The black color just radiated the heat. His feet killed him—he wished they had watered the track. Steve's concentration wavered and he almost experienced a calamitous accident. An oblivious photographer ran onto the track on his way to the infield to reach the award stand as Steve drove hard down the track. Feet aflame and blistering, Steve narrowly avoided a collision as the crowd let out a gasp of relief.

Steve paced the field through seven laps in the three-mile, before drifting out into Lane 2 and inviting Penn State's Greg Fredericks to take the lead. But then Steve thought the pace unsatisfactory and frustratingly took it back. Someone had told Steve that Fredericks had a good kick, so Steve tossed in some fast laps to chew away at Fredericks. By the final lap, Steve had amassed a 60-yard lead and shifted into cruise control down the stretch, waving to the fans as he crossed the finish. His time was a meet record, 13:20.1, though his team finished third behind the winning UCLA Bruins.

As Steve easily won, he thought *next week, next week, next week.* Even the night before this race it was *next week.*

"Next week" was the AAU championships on his home track at Hayward Field. Most athletes are so conditioned to be in the moment and to think of the opponent at hand, the trope of take it "one game at a time," "be where your feet are," but Steve now thought so little of his college competition that he was only thinking of the bigger, more challenging, more prestigious meet that lay ahead. The fact that his head wasn't wholly invested in the NCAAs and he still smoked the field spoke to the degree of separation he had created between himself and others. For most runners in the race, the NCAA championship was, understandably, their pinnacle.

Not for Steve, and he all but spit in the face of his rivals. "I got nothing more than just a good, hard workout. I wasn't psyched up about this race. This victory rates way down the list in my book." At least at this moment, Steve went beyond mere trash talk and self-confidence to outright disrespect and arrogance. This overstep spoke to his profound immaturity—not to mention it was downright mean. When people spoke of how Steve Prefontaine might, on occasion, rub them the wrong way, it was this brazen dismissal of quality runners that irked them. What Steve likely was posturing for, what he was signaling by so callously insulting his college peers, was that beating elite college runners was, in his mind, junior varsity, and he wanted everyone to know that if he could win so thoroughly with so little focus and so little regard for his competition, just *imagine* what he could do when he put the full force of his focus into a race. People would soon find out.

To date, the AAU championships had been a thorn in Steve's side. As a graduating high school senior, he'd surprised everyone by finishing fourth in Miami. At Bakersfield in 1970, still ailing from having cut his foot on a protruding bolt, he finished fifth. This year, he had a not-so-secret ace up his sleeve. "Other guys may have strength and maturity going for them in that race but I figure I've got an edge. I'll have Eugene and my hometown, Coos Bay, going for me."

That said, Steve faced the sense of obligation to give his fans something they'd never forget. He always put more pressure on himself to perform in front of the hometown fans, as if he owed it to them. Unable to shake that 1970 performance, Steve had been pointing to the AAU championships ever since the year before, and now he was counting down the days. "There'll be 15,000 people behind me whether I win or lose. And I just hope I don't disappoint them," he said.

Marty Liquori, fresh off yet another NCAA gold-medal mile, said of the AAU field, "This is going to be the best three-mile ever in America, and I think the American record should go." Gerry Lindgren, the current American three-mile record holder at 12:53 flat (the world record at the time was 12:50.4), would be in the field. Frank Shorter, too. Unfortunately, George Young, the thirty-three-year-old schoolteacher from Arizona and a three-time Olympian, would not be running due to an AAU clerical blunder. He never received his entry form, or word about expenses. "This is typical of AAU organization . . . this is why they're in trouble all the time," he said. Leave it to the AAU to prevent a talented runner from toeing the line because of paperwork.

In his paranoia, Steve said, "I'm still not counting him out of the race. Those old veterans are crafty and have read a lot of books. I read one where Herb Elliott said he wasn't going to run in a mile. Then he warmed up on another field, showed up in his street clothes and at the last second changed to his tracksuit. It blew everybody's mind. So until the race starts and Young isn't in it, I'm not counting him out."

Steve, "the smug young man," sideburns striping his face, hoped that third time's the charm when the gun blasted on what was a perfectly sunny afternoon in Eugene. Strangely, Steve was feeling mildly down. Though he had expected to be all jumpy, he was totally calm.

For his part, Shorter's head space was not optimized for this race, the "kind of nervousness you only go through two or three times a year. It's something you can't control. It creeps up on you." Shorter had raced all over the country and all over Europe, but said, "I'm in limbo. Maybe it's because I'm apprehensive about running against Prefontaine in his hometown. Also, my sense of fair play is coming in. If he goes out, should I try and share the lead with him? Or should I lay back and leech off him? Then I think, I've run most of my races in front, so why not? I'm primed to go, but it's like when you step on the gas. It either goes cha-clunk, cha-clunk, cha-clunk or it goes off like a 427 'vette. What kind of race is this for me anyway? Here's Prefontaine. They say he has the best cardio-vascular system in the sport . . . What am I? Just the world's fastest ectomorph."

It was hard not to overlay Shorter's Ivy League–ness over this sentiment. Nobody short of an exercise physiologist could define ectomorph, subtly hilarious as that comment was. Meanwhile, Steve spoke with an everyman quality and pre-fight histrionics that made him all the more relatable, approachable, and far more attractive to the average fan, and especially the Oregonian, who saw something of themselves reflected in Steve's countenance.

Streets are littered with the roadkill of great athletes who couldn't get out of their own heads. Shorter tied himself in knots. Steve Stageberg, a Eugene native, thought, "God does have a divine plan for some people. Running is God's plan for me." Lindgren, now twenty-five with his star dimming, had started schilling cosmetics distributorships, in what could be described as a pyramid scheme, for Glenn W. Turner, a Florida millionaire, with the motto "DARE TO BE GREAT."

Lindgren, in his high-pitched voice, had talked about having a "positive mental attitude," how his high school coach's attitude rubbed off on him to great success. But then, come college, Lindgren's circle of influence became more negative, he developed a "doozie" of an ulcer, almost died. He attributed his failures over the past few years to the negative people in his life. He dispatched them. He began thinking that even if a man had trouble walking, his mind could will him to run a fast three-mile. "Take me. All I am is a little runt who can run," he said.

The three-mile field started to sound like something out of Monty Python. In response to this band of misfits—be it Lindgren's PMA or Stageberg's Holy Ghost—Steve said, "All those things are fine. I have a positive mental attitude, and I think *I'm* divine, but I also think it takes a heck of a lot of blood, sweat, and tears." And, well, there it was: a joke in self-awareness followed shortly thereafter by the blue-collar ethic that endeared him to people.

The meet was running long, and while the three-mile field waited, they were sent back to the dressing room. Amidst the undercurrent of the post-collegiate amateur runner, Lindgren, two years on his own by now in 1971, and Steve warmed up a bit more. Steve later recalled, "And what does Gerry do? He tries to sell me a cosmetic distributorship. Here's the big race coming up and he's making a sales pitch."

Funny as the moment was, as a metaphor it was equally cruel: the runner still benefiting from the structures of college running (meals, housing, coaching, teammates) perplexed by the post-collegiate runner whose focus could no longer solely be about his sport. At the time, this was Lindgren's day job. Without sponsorships or institutional support of any kind to allow an elite runner the freedom to train unencumbered, Lindgren lived in the delicate balance between making a living and making a podium. This was the amateur system of the day for America's best athletic talent. If you still had ability after graduating from college and still had Olympic dreams, you likely coached yourself, or, perhaps, your former college coach drew up some workouts in his spare time, but you didn't want to burden him because he had a team to focus on. You paid for your travel, your food, your gear. What so often happened was the post-collegiate runner's life naturally evolved; he got married, started a family, had to make money, and the casualty of that evolution was any dream of athletic greatness, often when they were still in their physical primes. They were forced into retirement not by injury or erosion of skill, but for reasons baked into the American amateur system. Many former athletes from that era spoken to for this book fantasized about what their careers could have been had they benefited from the sponsorships, coaching, and structure that exists in the current day. They all had the ability. What they needed was help. And the AAU unilaterally ensured that they didn't get it. Nevertheless, it didn't stop some of them from trying.

Back at AAU nationals at Hayward Field, "Go Pre" banners unfurled in the stands. The field gathered and tiptoed to the starting line. Steve cleared his head, the gun popped, and he jumped off the line at the start.

From the outset, Steve was either on the lead or an arm's length away. Lindgren dared to be great and struck the front momentarily early in the race, but soon surrendered to Steve and Shorter, the pair trading the lead like a tennis rally. Late in the race, four were in contention—Steve, Stageberg, Shorter, and Lindgren. By the start of the eleventh lap—just two to go and the crowd bellowing—Steve shot to the lead with Shorter hanging just off his shoulder waiting for the right moment to pounce. At this point, Shorter's concentration waned, and he didn't want to win badly enough. It was, in his words, all over.

Stageberg moved past Shorter and into second. With eleven laps down, the tension mounting, and the cheers escalating, Steve and Stageberg swept into the final lap. Two native Oregonians, one-two, into the bell lap. By this point, Steve knew the crowd wanted it; he did too. He knew the full weight of inherent disappointment, so instead of shouldering that pressure, he turned it into a tailwind. Perhaps greater than Steve's immense physical gifts was his mental approach. If Shorter didn't want it enough this day, Steve always wanted it. And the people loved it. Stageberg, still in Steve's wake, said, "All the way down the backstretch all I could hear was the din . . . it came in waves. It was deafening . . . an extremely surrealistic feeling."

Around the turn, Steve looked over his shoulder and he locked eyes, for the briefest moment, with Stageberg. Steve let up for mere seconds coming off the turn. In that glimpse, Stageberg thought *maybe he's worried*. But Stageberg soon hit the wall and Steve found that extra bit of something down in his gut. He squeezed his eyes closed as his head careened to the side. Two hundred yards to go and he widened his lead and the fans erupted, "losing their minds," as one broadcaster said. Steve ran blind down the stretch as the wire neared; his lead grew from a few strides to twenty yards.

The strain on Steve's face as he surged down the stretch was nothing new among distance runners. He wasn't the first runner to show discomfort, far from the first to experience it. However, he might have been the first to show signs of apocalyptic distress, but upon hearing the roars of the people, he found another gear that transcended consciousness. He rarely raced to merely win; he raced to make a statement, and the crowd felt complicit. He gave, they gave, and they saw him respond. The way he ran, at times, was far from elegant. At five foot nine, he didn't benefit from long-legged grace. Steve often looked like a misplaced running back who might charge through a brick wall rather than glide like a deer, which endeared him even more to the people. It still looked like effort when he cocked his head to the left, brow forever furrowed; and to an audience no stranger to hard work, this display of effort was precisely what made watching Steve perform in Eugene so special. It didn't matter how big his lead was—he never made it look easy. The drama wasn't in the finish; it was in watching Steve pour every bit of himself into the performance, four hundred meters at a time.

Steve crossed the finish, threw his head back, and wobbled as if he'd fall over, a three-mile performance in under thirteen minutes, 12:58.6. Stageberg finished a strong second in 13:00.3, Shorter third, and Lindgren fourth. A swarm of photographers surrounded Steve. Someone had to hold Steve up from falling.

Steve found Bowerman after the race and, feeling so high from this win, lobbied to run in Saturday's mile. Bowerman leveled his gaze at Steve and said, "I think you proved your point."

"That means 'no,'" Steve said. "But I feel so strong. The longer the race went, the stronger I felt."

Once the clock stopped, Steve took off his spikes and showed his bleached-white feet for his signature victory laps, with an "s." He held his spikes in his left hand while waving with his right. He donned a white T-shirt with USA emblazoned on the left breast, "Run for Fun" diagonally across the chest. He waved to the stands, thanking them. When people remember Steve Prefontaine, it is often this exchange that comes to mind. They recall the noise unlike any noise they'd ever heard. They think of the strain on his face when they thought that maybe he'd get caught and they cheered just a bit louder, and they'd see him find more at their behest.

"Did I look tough?" Steve grinned.

Hard as it was to believe looking at him, he thought he had a lot left in the tank. The track, he said, was beautiful. "Those people are fantastic. They're my people, man. How can you lose with 12,000 people behind you," he said, though there were just over 8,000 in attendance, but it sounded like 12,000. Though he had always wanted to perform for the fans, he had never referred to them as his "people." And so, on June 25, 1971, Steve strengthened the bond: Pre's People.

Once his heart rate leveled and his breath came back to normal, he was asked what was on his mind. He thought for a moment, grinned, then said:

"Who's next?"

CHAPTER 9

ASSERTION

ON THE HEELS of his first national AAU championship, Steve Prefontaine won 5,000-meter races in international competition in Berkeley, California, against the Russians where he set an American record; in Durham, North Carolina, in the United States vs. Africa meet; and in Cali, Columbia, for the Pan Am Games, this with nearly a year to go before the Olympic Trials in Eugene. Winning 5,000-meter races made the Olympics in Munich in a year's time feel even more real. Each race was an opportunity to assert himself beyond the borders of his own country. He wanted the world to hear his footsteps.

But literally getting to the Olympics was its own challenge. In the early 1970s, making and competing on an Olympic team was an out-of-pocket expense, where an athlete panhandled to afford such a distinction. The United States did not pay for athletes' travel to the Olympic Trials or the Olympic Games; they had to earn the money themselves. Coos Bay wanted to help their star. When Steve returned to Oregon from the Pan Am Games, organizers in Coos Bay hosted an Olympic fund track meet at Pirate Stadium. The community rallied around its athletes with James H. Whitty of Coos Bay penning a letter to the editor. He wrote that despite organizers planning to raise funds, "There is no substitute for personal donations of cold, hard cash for a cause such as this." He carried on, "Some of the countries that will give us the greatest competition in the Olympics provide all of the money needed for their athletes out of government appropriations. . . . So, each and every one of us, if he or she loves their country, must dig down and provide the funds to make it possible for us to be well represented."

In response, Steve wrote a heartfelt thank-you and published it in *The World* for all of Coos Bay to see. However, the community had raised only $1,000, just over $7,500 in today's dollars. This sum raised the hackles of Caroline McVay, a former Coos Bay resident living in Junction City just north of Eugene. She wrote, "I was shocked when I read in this morning's paper that only 556 people attended the benefit track meet. . . . Who in your one-horse town has put Coos Bay on the map all over the world beside Prefontaine?"

Come fall 1971, he won the individual NCAA cross-country championships in Knoxville, Tennessee, while leading the Ducks to a team national championship. He seemed unstoppable and by all accounts looked unbeatable.

In spring 1972, the NCAA track-and-field championships and the Olympic Trials would be set in Eugene, and the Olympic team would be coached by none other than Bill Bowerman, the very definition of stars aligning for Steve. "Eugene's—and the Ducks'—reputation for being the Notre Dame of track just gets bigger," wrote *The Daily Emerald*. "I look on the Trials as the American Games," Bowerman said. "Every track athlete has a goal to represent his country. I know that the greatest thing that has happened to me is to represent my country as a coach."

Meanwhile in the winter of 1971–72, Steve regularly donned a green hoodie and pulled it over his head as he charged up the steep and winding roads to Hendricks Park in Eugene by Skyline Boulevard and Birch Lane. The rain had an icy bite and dripped off the canopy of towering firs. He ran with Kenny Moore, Oregon alum and Olympic marathon hopeful. Steve spoke in a cheerful lilt as they ran five miles through the woods. It was, at long last, the Olympic Year, and Steve's mind raced as much as his body. By April, he wanted to run six miles in 27:00. By May, a 3:54 mile. And then let those Europeans "wonder what I can do in between." He visualized how the 5,000-meter Olympic final would unfold: 8:25 through two miles and a 4:05 final mile for the gold. At this thought, his pace quickened.

He mentally handicapped the Olympic 5,000-meter final—still seven months away. Steve thought about Great Britain's Dave Bedford (a brash front runner) and West Germany's Harald Norpoth and how there was no way in hell any of them (himself included) could outsprint the European champion from Finland, Juha Väätäinen. What Steve wanted, above anything else, was a race that came down to who's toughest, as he said, "the kind of exhaustion where running is unnatural, where you have to whip yourself to go on. . . . It's going to be a mad race."

As Steve saw it, his youth and inexperience were his secret weapon, not a weakness: they knew little about him (even less if he'd stop talking), but he knew much about them. To boot, he grew tired of hearing how a distance runner didn't reach his peak until he reached his mid- to late twenties. To him, no big difference. After all, he figured, "records, theories, hypotheses—they're all there to be challenged." He swatted away comments about runners like Väätäinen's electric kick. "What if I ran my first mile in 4:08? Let's see then how fast their last laps would be. . . . I'm the dark horse. Who knows, I may have something up my sleeve."

By now, Steve mostly came across as brash, even arrogant, and he fully embraced his role as the dominant voice of track, for himself and others, no matter the attention it drew, good or bad. With every quote, with every performance, he was, in effect, removing any mystery about who he was and what he planned on doing. In the college ranks, he was so superior he could get away with spouting off because he was, by and large, the only one capable of that degree of execution and performance. His grand mistake—and proof positive of his naivete—was failing to recognize that on a global scale, his abilities were not as entirely unique as they were domestically. By 1972, running against international competition was nothing new to Steve. Why the lesson didn't stick was a mystery. West Germany's Norpoth, for example, routinely waited and outkicked Steve, as did others. It could be that after his record-setting 1971 summer, where he defeated the Russians and Ethiopians, he was hubristically awash in his own ability. Like a power pitcher in baseball, Steve likely thought: *here's what I do, come and get me.* In due time, he'd learn; but for now he sought to further assert his dominance and burgeoning sense of self on the track at home, while also deluding himself into thinking he was mysterious.

—

ON JANUARY 29, 1972, the Oregon Indoor Invitational at Memorial Stadium in Portland, the annual spectacle where some of Oregon's best athletes tuned up for their spring season, was, for Steve, a chance to play tiger.

Jim Ryun, "once great and now rebounding," was still attempting his comeback for one last crack at the 1,500 meters in the Olympics. He returned to Oregon, this time for the indoor two-mile race against a fiery field that included Steve vying for his third consecutive two-mile win. Steve now faced the sturdiest field to date. Besides Ryun (a fish out of water in this race), there were the other elder statesmen in Lindgren, Frank Shorter, Mike Manley, and Kerry Pearce. A year ago, Steve spoke of running against Ryun, preferring to go down to the mile and get clobbered than have Ryun come up to his distance and clobber him there, the latter being far more bruising to his ego.

Ryun no longer lived in Oregon. The grass and tree pollen ran him out of town. University of Kansas coach Bob Timmons, who was overseeing Ryun's training, told Bowerman that Ryun wanted to run against Steve in the two-mile. Ryun had said he wasn't out for revenge after losing in the Twilight Mile in the spring of 1971, more redemption for himself and the people of Oregon. Bowerman told Timmons, "Your runner better be ready. Pre won't be out there to play patsy. He's ready to run. . . . If Ryun isn't, he is going to be embarrassed," which was quite a pronouncement from the usually taciturn Bowerman badgering, of all people, a world record holder. This added to the allure of the Oregon Indoor, which, during an Olympic year, felt more meaningful. Olympic hopes started now.

Steve disrobed to his singlet and shorts and tightened the laces on his spikes, shaking out his legs and drawing deep breaths. Lining up against Ryun again made the event a spectacle for the 10,066 fans packed into Portland's Memorial Coliseum. It was touted as the best two-mile field in the history of the meet, but it was sold as a Prefontaine-Ryun rematch. And with no grass or tree pollen for Ryun to deal with, the crowd and the competitors were thinking this could be an epic showdown. Ryun felt he owed Oregonians a good race after sputtering in last year's Twilight Mile outdoors.

Twenty-two laps, 160 yards to a lap, banked turns.

Steve, on cue, sprinted right for the front to jockey for the best position, out of traffic. Pearce went right with him . . . sort of. Throughout the first mile, with Steve working hard on the inside, he eased out a bit, inviting Pearce to share some of the pacesetting, but Pearce wouldn't partake in the pace. Steve shut down the lane and ran angry, closing the door on a 4:16 opening mile. Steve hoped someone would help, but the help wasn't coming.

Through six of those first eleven laps, Ryun stalked. If this two-mile played out like his mile, he was waiting for a final blast in the last one to two laps. Ryun started slipping, swallowed by the tide of the field. Onward Steve relentlessly pressed as the crowd surged with him. With just a half-mile remaining, he looked around for Ryun, whose head was bobbing and weaving a half-lap—eighty yards—behind. Steve had led every lap so far: twenty down, two to go and Steve saw Ryun up ahead ready to be lapped. There was a glint in Steve's eye and the crowd stood to watch as Steve throttled up to Ryun's flank. Ryun moved out into Lane 2 and Steve lapped Ryun with a fierce, man-possessed look in his eyes, blowing by the old guard. It was a move that was as literal as it was figurative: American track—and specifically distance running—was Steve Prefontaine's world now; Ryun's era had passed.

Ryun dug in, but Steve was gone, into the final lap and there was nobody catching him as he was in a full drive to the finish, carried on by the frenzied thousands for 8:26.6, a full wire-to-wire win and a new American collegiate indoor record. All stood as Steve jogged two victory laps.

By the time Steve had gathered his breath, he knew he could have run faster had someone shared the lead with him. He was, admittedly, disappointed in Ryun. Oregon loved its own and didn't take kindly to invaders. The *Oregon Journal* wrote, "At Eugene, heroes are reared—like Prefontaines—not imported. And those who do come from faraway places come to learn."

Steve set out to make a statement. And, in a different way, Ryun made a statement, too.

When it was all done, Steve found Gerry Lindgren, who finished a well-beaten second, and they walked around the bend with their arms around each other, Steve having slayed another titan of the previous generation.

Steve then ran in another pre-college-track-season meet, this a two-mile race in the L.A. Times Indoor in Los Angeles, set for Friday, February 11, 1972. Of particular note was the entry of Belgium's Emiel Puttemans, a 5,000-meter hopeful come Munich. Steve won impressively, and this gave him more confidence, yes, but it also served to send a message, a shot across the bow, that Steve was looking to assault Europe and Europe's best. It gave Steve the real sense that he was among the world's best—not just the best in college, or America, for that matter.

Entering the spring, Steve ranked tenth in the world in the 5,000 and he was fine with that, right on schedule, Steve thought. It's all just part of a plan to be in Munich in September. At this time, his outward motivation was, of course, targeting the Olympics and winning a gold medal. Inwardly, he explored where his limits might be, a continued expansion of the inner map. This wasn't a new concept, per se, but Steve, when prodded, would talk about it, where he saw himself, where he saw others, all in service of physical enlightenment. One coach said, "Cocky? Well, I don't know about that. He's confident. But I think that's what a trackman needs. I like a guy who says he can do something then does it."

That was the difference between other great runners of the day and Steve. Most people thought what Steve articulated. And in vocalizing it, he gave himself nowhere to hide. Others were already saying he was the United States' greatest distance runner, that betting against him in Munich was foolish, that he could cope with on-track challenges better than any runner in history.

The same brashness that could be lauded, just as often could be a point of contention. At the start of his 1972 junior outdoor track season for Oregon, this after winning the two-mile with a murderous headwind, over an archaic surface at Ratcliffe Stadium against Fresno State, Steve said, "That's the last time I'll ever run in this hole." Eddie Lopez of the *Fresno Bee* wrote that Steve "showed a good deal of immaturity." When Lopez wanted to speak with Steve, Steve dashed away and called over his shoulder, "I'm jogging." Lopez later called him "arrogant."

Depending on the mood of the reporter, Steve's confidence could be seen as a natural extension of ability. But some—like Lopez, after he was turned down for an interview—called Steve arrogant, and there was some truth to it.

In late March 1972, he ran the third fastest six-mile for an American, partly as a psychological ploy to strike fear in the hearts of Europeans, a tactic he spoke about openly. In a time when athletes' interactions with the media were almost entirely based on instinct, Steve had a hard time balancing a desire to be forthright with being strategic. His contemporaries thought, sure, share your intentions with your friends and teammates, but don't tell the competition. Though he'd been a media darling since his junior year of high school, he had never prepared for a competition like the Olympics. Unwittingly, Steve was making himself—and how he planned to run—the worst kept secret in the world of track and field.

STEVE LEFT LITTLE to the imagination toward the end of April, ahead of the annual Twilight Meet at Hayward Field. It was scheduled several weeks ahead of its normal running, which had to do with the NCAA schedule and the Olympic Trials coming to Eugene. Bowerman didn't expect anything sensational.

On April 23, 1972, Steve won in an astonishing 3:56.7 Twilight Mile, crossing the finish and holding his arms above his head. "I needed that," Steve said. The past few weeks, it had been difficult to run, mentally challenging. It could have been that the looming presence of the Olympics being so close yet so far away made it difficult to stay grounded in the moment. Mentally, he hadn't been ready to run. Looking too far down the calendar, Steve at times would lose sight of what was right in front of him. Each race in 1972 served a greater purpose than merely winning. It became an exhibition in peacocking, in messaging. He wanted those paying attention to fear the pain he promised to inflict. Steve's winning mile fired yet another "psychological rocket," but not necessarily at the Europeans.

Just up I-5 in Corvallis, a brisk miler at Oregon State University named Hailu Ebba, an Ethiopian, had recently run a 3:59.3 mile in a different meet. And when runners started to trespass on Steve's turf, he flexed. Hungry to compete and to find a worthy rival, Steve hoped to meet Ebba on the track at Hayward Field. As Steve ran off to the showers, he'd soon get his wish. His head was back in the game.

And so it was: Ebba vs. Steve. "Sings a song by itself. It ripples like Ricardo Montalban-Sophie Loren or Abercombie and Fitch," as one newspaper said.

If anyone would relish such a challenge it was Steve. That year, he was asked to reflect on why he ran. "There's a lot of factors that make me run," he said. "The biggest one is that I enjoy it, or I acquired an enjoyment for it after so many years of running. It's part of my life. The other part is the Olympic Games and trying for a gold medal. And the third thing would have to be competition. I love to compete." Nobody asks a baseball player, a football player, or a basketball player why they play those sports, and yet, distance running always invited this degree of inquiry and introspection. Running in other sports was punishment, so to be a runner made you a special kind of freak.

Oregon State coach Berny Wagner fretted that running Ebba in the mile might be too physical for the young man. Steve made running aggressive, turned it into a brawl. This worried Wagner. Running against Steve was taxing. Not just the running of it, but the full-contact nature that Wagner accused Duck runners of. "We feel Hailu might get hustled and I'll be very disturbed if that happens."

If people (including Steve) hoped for Steve and Ebba to face each other, Wagner wanted nothing of it. He entered Ebba in the half-mile, instead of the 1,500—the metric mile, it being an Olympic year, colleges amended their distances to reflect the forthcoming Olympiads. "Pre was the best high school distance runner in the country," Wagner said, "now he's the best collegiate distance runner, and he's going to be the best distance man in the world. Hailu's just a freshman with little competitive experience." Wagner hinted that the pressure would be too much for Ebba.

The day of the meet, Saturday, May 6, 1972, the forecast called for "not a drop in sight," low clouds in the morning then a shimmering sun and blue skies. More than 9,000 fans arrived at Hayward Field, all in T-shirts and jeans, skin exposed with highs in the 70s. Partway through the meet, Wagner needed to stop the Ducks somehow. The Ducks kept winning, winning,

winning. Where could he stop this dam from bursting? He knew Steve was entered in the 1,500. The only runner in Wagner's stable capable of running with Steve was Ebba. All week, Ebba had been taking tranquilizers to assuage the pressure he was feeling. That said, Ebba wanted to run against Steve, pressure be damned. Wagner and Ebba agreed: they would challenge Steve.

When Ebba surfaced from the corral and the announcer broadcast the bout, the crowd roared. They had heard about how swift Ebba was, and now they'd get to see a true headlining event amidst what was proving to be a landslide. Steve, in what would make him such a magnetic presence and altogether difference species, said he, "wanted the race to be a question of who had the most guts, not who had the most speed." Translation: Ebba had the speed, Steve had something borne of his upbringing—toughness, grit. Bowerman was caught off guard by the entry of Ebba. Bowerman grabbed Dellinger. "Tell Ritchie to give Pre a hell of a first lap. That's the only way Pre can run with the half-miler."

Rick Ritchie took the directive. At the gun, Ritchie sprinted for the lead and blazed an opening quarter in fifty-seven seconds. Ebba kept his gaze wide-eyed and fixed on Steve's back; Steve's brow was furrowed, lips pressed tightly to his teeth. Ritchie gave all he could—a sixty-second second lap—so Steve took command of the race through a half-mile in 1:57. The field cruised around like a flock, as one, with Ritchie peeling off.

After three laps, at last, Ebba struck as fast as he could. The people hoped for this moment. Steve, for his part, could feel Ebba, the presence of him moving up to challenge. Steve thought, *instead of giving him his race, I'm making him run mine.* Steve parried, knowing that if Ebba didn't power past with 300 yards to go, there was no way Ebba would pass him if it came down to sheer will. Down the backstretch, the pair matched strides. In races this short, Steve, at times, struggled to bury his competitor. His mid-race strength couldn't grind the superior speed of his rivals. Ebba wasn't fading. He had the speed, but Steve had the people.

There was a sense among the crowd that perhaps Steve had met his match, and then, as if on cue, Pre's People roared, full force. Past the East Stands, Steve edged ever so slightly out into Lane 2, then Lane 3, which pushed Ebba wider. An OSU assistant coach saw what Steve was doing and admired it,

"Hailu didn't know enough to hold his ground and be bumped." Steve's plan was to strand Ebba, make him run farther. This upset Ebba. "His strategy was outrageous . . . this is running not fighting." Oh, but to Steve Prefontaine, running *was* fighting. Ebba maintained there was a foul; the officials said no. There was no "sudden lurch" to the outside, rather a subtle drifting on the turn that caused the least experienced of the two to suffer more ground. Steve rarely resorted to such tactics as he was, more often than not, alone on the lead. But here he began to show some experience gleaned from running against international competition—that a race, at times, required more than just footspeed and endurance; Steve would call it guts.

Kenny Moore witnessed it and said Steve "did it like a master. Pre's tactics are not unusual. I thought Hailu's biggest mistake was not trying to pass Pre with a quick, decisive move. I don't think Pre would have gotten back around if he had."

Dan Fouts, the former Oregon quarterback and NFL Hall of Famer, was at that meet and remembered, "Pre held him off that last corner, three or four lanes on the track. The crowd saw that and went absolutely crazy and broke the kid's spirit. Hailu was a real miler and he was fast and Pre was not, so it took Pre everything he had to beat him. He never disappointed."

Around the turn and down the stretch, Steve's determination prevailed, as he wobbled and winced to the finish three strides ahead of Ebba in a slugfest that brought everyone to their feet—3:39.8 to 3:40.4. At the line, Steve glanced up at the scoreboard and saw his time. He wanted a guts race; he got a guts race.

The sun beat down on the pair, both slight in stature, all bone and skin, Ebba grimacing slightly; he knew that if he had passed Steve there was no catching him. Ebba pulled on a pair of black track pants and joined Steve as they jogged around the track together. Steve made a habit of trotting around Hayward with a rival by his side. He'd wave, they'd chit chat. Steve and Ebba appeared to be having a nice conversation after one of the most thrilling duels Steve had ever been a part of. Even in defeat, Ebba etched himself into the lore of Hayward Field, proving that he, too, had the guts, but as the *Register-Guard* put it, "Steve Prefontaine reached back for more intestines than one man's stomach should hold in repelling the inspired challenge of Hailu."

And in a photograph of Steve and Ebba following the race, down on Steve's feet were a pair of flat trainers—not a three-stripe Adidas or the interwoven matrix of Tigers that Steve often wore. These shoes were white with a dark—what might you call it?—a . . . swoosh? They appeared to be the Nike Cortez, a Bill Bowerman design, and if it's not the first photograph of Steve in Nikes, it's certainly one of the first.

Going back six years, in 1966, Bowerman noticed that Tiger's Spring Up shoe model had a lousy outer sole that "melted like butter." It's midsole held up. The Limber Up model had a superior outer sole. An increase in recreational runners needed a road shoe with more heal-to-toe shock absorption. "That was the purpose of the Cortez," Knight recalled in *Bowerman and the Men of Oregon*. "When we put that together, Bill and I sent over the components and said here, make this. [Onitsuka] were kind of reluctant, but they finally did it. That was about 1967. That was the first innovation for the American market."

Because Blue Ribbon Sports had been around since 1964 importing Tigers from Japan, their presence in the running shoe business was nothing new. What *was* new was the fact that now they were designing their own shoes. In designing the Cortez, Bowerman had created "the ultimate distance training shoe" that he and Knight wanted to name the Aztec. Adidas claimed that name, so Bowerman asked Knight, "Who was the guy who kicked the shit out of the Aztecs?"

"Cortez," Knight said.

"Okay. Let's call it the Cortez."

After several years of distributing Tiger shoes, Onitsuka sought greater market share and greater reach than other U.S.-based companies could offer, certainly more than the roguish Blue Ribbon Sports team. After a meeting with an Onitsuka executive, Knight, stealing a folder out of the executive's briefcase, learned that Onitsuka planned on vetting other distributors.*

---

* For a greater, more detailed blow-by-blow history, read Phil Knight's memoir *Shoe Dog*.

It confirmed Knight's instincts, despite such a nefarious means of reconnaissance, that Onitsuka planned on reneging on its deal with Blue Ribbon Sports for a more robust partner. It became clear to Knight, as well as Bowerman, that they'd be better off making their own products, not merely being a middleman for someone else's. Then, as 1971 gave way to 1972, through its legal travails and breaches of contract with Onitsuka—the manufacturer of the Tiger shoes that Knight distributed—Blue Ribbon Sports became Nike.

For a new brand, they'd need a new look. Knight found an artist—Carolyn Davidson—and commissioned her to draw up a logo for this new shoe company. Knight wanted to name it Dimension Six. He was quickly overruled and settled at the last minute on "Nike"—the Greek goddess of victory—literally dreamt up by one of Knight's earliest employees, Jeff Johnson. The logo, they said, looked like "a wing," "a whoosh of air," and "like something a runner might leave in his or her wake." They called it a swoosh.

Always thinking and tinkering, Bowerman noticed there was little by way of advancement for a shoe's outsole—the uppers, sure, but not what contacted the ground. Bowerman mulled this idea in his head and famously borrowed Mrs. Bowerman's waffle iron and ruined it by pouring urethane onto the appliance. Without a chemical releasing agent, the iron sealed shut. He bought another waffle iron and instead made a plaster mold from the iron's square nubs. Bowerman took the mold to the Oregon Rubber Company and paid them to pour liquid rubber onto it. The ensuing product proved too brittle. Lastly, Bowerman, eschewing the waffle iron but maintaining the idea of it, punched holes in a sheet of stainless-steel, creating a "waffle-like surface." The mold created from this steel sheet was workable. Bowerman shaped and sewed the shoes, then shod one of his Ducks. The runner could not be caught. They were on to something wholly innovative.

In 1972, Knight debuted his Nike line (alongside Tigers as well) at the National Sporting Goods Association Show in Chicago. In bright orange boxes with "nike" in lowercase, the products themselves weren't great, not yet, but salesmen had trusted the people from Blue Ribbon Sports, and they'd trust them now. These salesmen pointed to Davidson's logo, and they asked them what it was. Knight told them it was a swoosh. "It's the sound of someone going past you."

Soon Onitsuka got wind of their distributor making their own products as a new brand. This ignited a legal fight that would take a couple years to settle. As Nike ramped up production, it outfitted a Notre Dame quarterback and the entire 1972 Ducks football team with its football shoe, and a Romanian tennis star, Ilie Năstase, in a pair of Nike Match Points. Though Nike dabbled in athletic shoes for other sports, at its core it was a running shoe company, and it needed a *runner*. Knight, naturally, had his eyes on Steve Prefontaine. Knight later wrote in *Shoe Dog*, "Pre was unlike any athlete this country had ever seen, though it's hard to say exactly why. I'd spend a lot of time studying him, admiring him, puzzling about his appeal. I'd asked myself, time and again, what it was about Pre that triggered such visceral responses from so many people, including myself. I never did come up with a totally satisfactory answer."

Though Steve wouldn't compete in Nike track spikes until 1973, Knight had plans to outfit Steve in their burgeoning product line. He had the look, he had the moxie, he had the speed. "We were certain," Knight wrote, "he'd be a Nike athlete, and perhaps the paradigmatic Nike athlete."

CHAPTER 10

ASCENSION

AFTER WINNING PAC-8 and his third NCAA championship in the 5,000 meters, Steve headed home to Coos Bay. Hardly ready to focus on the Olympic Trials, he had a sore throat, diarrhea. He pointed to his head. "It's here, too."

Bill Bruns and Rich Clarkson of *Life* magazine shadowed Steve around his hometown, Bruns interviewing and filling up his notebook, Clarkson snapping photos. They were working on a profile for Olympic purposes. Steve hadn't made the team yet, but they were banking on it. Steve stood with them as he watched his old high school coach, Walt McClure, receive a "rousing sendoff" after twenty years of coaching and teaching at Marshfield High School. Rob Brandon of the Coos Bay Quarterback Club presented McClure with a brand-new color television, "to watch Pre run." McClure also was lauded for his work as a biology teacher and "for relating so well with the kids." For his part, Steve called McClure his "second father," a sentiment multiple former athletes had of McClure, especially given the often-tumultuous upbringings many suffered.

Steve laced up his tri-striped Adidas flats and donned a full tracksuit. He jogged on the dunes at Horsfall Beach. Closer to the ocean, the sand was packed down from the tide. The Pacific Ocean was gray-blue with foamy waves. Steve had the slightest mustache growing and sideburns down past his ears. The breeze blew back his lion's-mane hair. The ocean behind him made him look small, insignificant, almost as if the fury of the ocean could swallow him whole. He began to see himself in equally poetic terms, "I'm an artist, a performer. I want people to appreciate the way I run." Where once he ran to excel and belong, his purpose was evolving, with running becoming a gift for others to enjoy, as performative as it was driven by results.

This shift wasn't just rhetorical—Steve's friends witnessed his attitude changing as well. Back near the U of O, Steve now lived off campus in a single-wide trailer at the River Bank Trailer Park in Glenwood, a speck of a town between Eugene and Springfield. He lived there with his roommate and close friend, Pat Tyson. In the four years since Tyson had first met Steve at the 1968 pre-Olympic meet that Dellinger invited them to, Tyson had noticed a greater sense of maturity in Steve he hadn't originally seen. Tyson heard a more articulate person, measured, better dressed. He was aware of how he projected himself. Steve began to understand that he was or could be the face of something, both figuratively and literally. To that end, Tyson and Steve had a mustache-growing contest to see who could grow the best one. "His was a little more awesome than mine," Tyson said.

Be it the mustache, the longer hair, or the alarming lack of body fat on Steve's body, he looked older than his twenty-one years. Heavy browed, prominent cheekbones while running; the mask suited him. Gone was the cherubic face on the cover of *Sports Illustrated*.

Most of all, Tyson noticed what a beautiful summer it was, blue skies, 80–85 degrees almost every day. *Is this real? Everything's right here.* With the rigors of the Olympic Trials forthcoming, there was no shortage of media showing up at the trailer to see, speak, or photograph Steve. Yet Tyson never noticed Steve getting moody or sensed that the pressure bothered him. Still, he wanted to stay out of Steve's way. He never wanted to pry.

Steve planned on running seventy-five miles in the week leading up to the Trials while also trying to keep from getting sick. Dellinger was, as always, keeping a watchful eye on Steve's training, reveling in the young man's confidence. Steve was reaching a peak, mentally and physically, as they began to cut his mileage down.

The pressure was substantial. People expected Steve to not only make the Olympic team, some even predicted he'd win the gold medal. The fact that the Trials were on his home turf—though an advantage—only added to the pressure. Upwards of 15,000 people would pack into Hayward Field to watch the 5,000-meter final—should he make it there. The final was scheduled as the last event of the week-long festival, the "American Games," as Bowerman once called them.

To date, many runners attempted to shoehorn some altitude training into their regimen. Frank Shorter and Jack Bacheler trained in Vail, Colorado, living in the home of a ski-boot manufacturer. Steve dismissed the idea, didn't think it had much merit. That is, unless you'd started training at altitude four years before.

George Young, Steve's primary competitor, and the one who gave Steve the most anxiety, arrived in Eugene three days early. Nobody had seen him in public, and his whereabouts had been a mystery, which suited his temperament.

And like a king lording over his domain in the days leading up to the 5,000-meter prelims, Steve signed autographs, sat shirtless in the sun, jogged and strutted when the track was clear—all a part of his psychological strategy, to be seen. "I don't want to give away all my secrets, but sure, I want them to know I'm around. It's a psyche."

Finally, the Trials arrived. For all his confidence, Steve was harboring doubts. He hadn't raced 5,000 meters since the NCAAs. His last competitive race was the 3,000 meters at the Rose Festival in Gresham, Oregon, on June 24, 1972. For his opening heat at the 5,000-meter trials, it was nice to be lauded as 12,500 fans cheered his name as he stepped onto the track. For his people, he grasped "this emotional power that they are throwing out. They're wanting it just as much as I am. For me to be able to give it to them is a satisfying thing."

As one scribe wrote, "The Prefontaine mystique was as thick as the pollen count in this verdant valley when the great moment came." Steve took the lead for a good two miles into his heat, untucking his shirt and unleashing a measured, winning kick. Steve won his heat easily in 13:51.2 without breathing hard. He could have hammered that final mile but thought better of it. He eased in the final fifty meters then turned and waited at the finish for his competitors. He felt so strong that he thought he could have gone out ten minutes after his heat and run faster than the winner of the second heat of the 5,000. He thought that he'd run workouts twice as hard as he had raced that evening, but that's what made racing enjoyable: pain in practice, pleasure in the race. Despite the easy win, he didn't want to talk to reporters. Now that the Trials had begun he was on edge, in ways that he had never been before. "I get upset easily. Somebody will ask a dumb question and I'll blow up and I just don't want something like that to happen now." The job wasn't done and he wanted to maintain his focus. The final was the most important race of his career. The weight of it was palpable. "If I win then, I'll talk as long as anyone wants to talk. I don't have much to say until I win—if I win."

If I win.

That wasn't exactly the one-note brashness that people painted him with. Steve had been so nervous in the run-up to this race. He couldn't think straight or sleep. He was still a mess. After a workout, his coaches took one look at him and told him to cool it, drink a few beers, just relax. "And that's what I did. Went down and had a few too many," Steve said.

He had rested four to five days before his heat and began to wonder if he'd lost a step. The race, if nothing else, was a "psychological factor." He didn't know if he could measure up with the best in the country. This race helped quell those doubts.

The following day, in the dressing room beneath McArthur Court, Steve drew a comb through his hair. "How fast will I run? . . . Faster than George Young would want to run, I hope," an impish grin curling on his face like the Grinch.

Just yesterday, before Young's preliminary heat, Bob Steiner, the public address announcer, introduced Young as America's most versatile distance runner. Young had won a bronze medal in the steeplechase at the 1968 Olympics, finished sixteenth in the marathon, and was, at one point, the American record holder of the 5,000 meters. He aimed for a record fourth Olympic team. Young found the announcement "quite embarrassing. It's not a good thing to hear when you're trying to get ready for a race. But if that's what the people like to hear then that's all right, too."

Few people wrote off Young, least of all Steve, but many people had already anointed Steve the victor. However, if Young thought Steve was unbeatable, he wouldn't be here. And, he reasoned, if Steve beat him in Eugene, he'd try again in Munich, the top three finishers earning a spot on Team USA.

The sense going into the final was that the pace would be hot. Steve, always posturing, said, "I imagine I'll end up taking the lead. Young is another of those guys who lets everybody else do the work." Steve kept a close eye on Young's heat and thought that Young ran a smart race, that he was in good shape.

Gerry Lindgren also found himself back in good shape, competitive shape, at least. Two weeks before the Trials, Lindgren was hit by a car. He said he used cryotherapy to nurse his leg back to health. "When Bowerman found out I needed ice, all ice disappeared in Eugene," Lindgren said. He said the university ice machine broke and the ice machines at the fast-food joints did as well. Lindgren planned on running the 5,000 and 10,000 meters. As for the 5K, he figured the winning time might be 13:20. "The last mile will be murder, the last quarter will be something else. I'm most concerned about being in the top three. I want to get back into top form. If I make it to Munich, that would give me the time. Doggone it, I'm optimistic." He looked around Hayward Field and saw so many of "Pre's People" wearing "Go Pre" T-shirts. "I got to get hold of a 'Go Pre' T-shirt. It's the neatest thing I've ever seen."

"Sure, I'd like to beat Pre," said Sid Sink, another finalist. "Everybody would. He's kinda cocky . . . which is great for him, but it also makes all the rest of us want to beat him."

While Lindgren nursed his knee, he pulled Steve aside and let him know he had a practical joke planned ahead of the final. Nothing serious, just something to lighten the mood. Lindgren didn't want to "freak Pre out." Nothing likely could have freaked Steve out, so it came as no surprise to him when Lindgren jogged around Hayward Field wearing a bright white T-shirt with a red stop sign lettered "Stop Pre" to counter the ocean of green and yellow "Go Pre" shirts. "Now Gerry knows how the Christians felt in the Coliseum," wrote *Track & Field News*.

Bob Hersh, a New York City attorney, and Dick Drake, *Track & Field News*' managing editor, hatched the idea as a fun "answer to the 'Go Pre' shirts and the partisan crowd here." They found a silk screen and the basement of a willing Eugene resident, Tom Gillespie, who helped make twenty-six shirts. John Gillespie, Tom's brother, said, "We're Pre fans. In fact, my brother wouldn't wear one during the race because he's such a fan. We go to all the dual meets and everything."

At last, it was the culmination of a week-long festival, twenty-two events coming to a head. More than 15,000 people jammed into Hayward Field to get a glimpse of Steve in his element, at his premier distance. There was too much anticipation, too much to bear. The race itself was a relief. At some point an athlete just wants to compete. Enough with the ceremony.

The runners lined up. The moment was here, but he was scared and he doubted himself. The gun blasted.

Steve ceded the lead pack to Lindgren and found an easy cruising speed. Now that he was in it, his focus shifted to the plan at hand. The work was done and now it was time to see who had the strength to make the Olympic team. Dellinger was pleased to see that Steve wouldn't have to shoulder the lead on his own. Lindgren graciously paced the field through the first three laps. Around they went, four laps; a mile gone. Eight laps; two miles gone. Steve peeked at the clock, dismayed: 8:46. He had hoped for 8:42, the precision of that hope. With a mile left, Steve felt Young moving up on his shoulder. Now was the time to go. He had to see what he had left, not what anyone else had. *If he burns me, he burns me.*

Len Hilton, the only other runner close to Steve and Young, retreated as Steve led them through the next quarter mile in 64.6, and the following in 64.5. It left just the two at the point of the spear. For Dellinger, it was part of the plan. They wanted to break Young before the final quarter with Steve picking up from 65 to 63 to 61. Both similar in stature and a contrast in style; twenty-one vs. thirty-four; potentially first Olympic team vs. fourth; 70s counterculture vs. 60s straight edge. Steve, his golden hair blowing back, cut a hole in the wind with Young coasting behind him. Coming to the top of the homestretch, with just over two laps remaining, Steve found a higher gear still, brow creased, mouth open, fingers loose, and legs high-kneed and churning. Young started to tire. "Pre's People" could see it on his face, but he had been here before, though he had never heard anything like the jet-engine roar of the fans in the West Stands. Like Steve Stageberg once said, "If you're running here against somebody like Prefontaine, the only thing you can do is pretend the cheers are for you."

The surge from "Pre's People" carried Steve farther, faster. With slightly more than two laps to go, Steve clipped off a 60.5-second lap and still no sign of tiring. Steve tore around the track in his Oregon colors, a haymaker 58.2 swung at Young and this lap broke "the old man," and he slipped back. The fans at Hayward were in a frenzy. Just one more lap remained and Steve, by now, must have known he had made the team and delivered on a promise. He need only stay upright and not get complacent. By the East Stands for the final time, homegrown power, and, at this point, paranoid. With 180 yards remaining between Steve and a spot on the team, he looked around for Young. Steve caught a spike on the track and stumbled. He didn't fall and gathered his composure around the final turn, slowing down just a touch. All alone, fifty yards clear of Young, Steve grinded down the straightway with the fans in the West Stands pushing him to the finish in what would be a new American record: 13:22.8, a time that would be a Hayward Field Olympic Trials record for forty years.

Steve knew he let up psychologically once the win was secured. After Steve hit the tape, he whipped his body around to see the vast distance between him and Young, some eighty yards back; nearly one hundred yards behind Young was Hilton, who would finish third.

Steve was swamped by fans seeking his autograph. He gave his parents a sweaty hug. Steve also gave his older, half-sister Neta—his caretaker and protector from when he was just a baby—a hug. The back of her shirt read: "Munich here comes 'PRE.'" After two victory laps—one with Young, picture Achilles dragging the body of Hector—Steve looked into the stands and found somebody wearing a "Stop Pre" shirt. "Hey, that's cool. I think I'll wear it," Steve said to the fan, who happened to be John Gillespie. "I can have this?"

"Do you want it?" Gillespie said.

"For sure."

He grabbed a shirt from its creator and pulled it over his head. It hung on him like a gown. He took two more victory laps with an army of children dogging him for autographs, or near him just to feel the shimmering light of their hero. They wouldn't have known it based on his performance, but the pressure Steve shouldered was unlike anything he had ever experienced. His old high school coach, Walt McClure, once told him that the path he was on would create more expectation and Steve would have to find a way to metabolize the pressure and perform. "I feel like a big gunnysack of boulders is off my shoulders," he said.

To those who witnessed, they saw that "the weight of the world had been lifted." There was a moment, caught by photographer Bob Kasper, after Steve's victory where Steve wore the countenance of the thousand-yard stare. His hair was tousled and strands of it were glued to his forehead with sweat. He showed no smile, eyes soft and vacant. Pat Tyson, his roommate from the trailer, said, "Everybody was around him, looking at him, but he wasn't aware of them. . . . He was in another world."

Steve found Bowerman, smiled at his coach, and said, "Hey, Bill, I'm on the team."

Bowerman grinned at the rube, the Oregon tiger.

There came a time in most races when Steve wondered if it was all worth it, when he asked himself *Why am I here? Why am I doing this? Why run this hard?* Running at Hayward, all he had to do was listen and surrender.

STEVE SPENT THE week after the Trials decompressing with light jogging, nothing strenuous. After the Trials, he developed a cold and went home to Coos Bay for one day. It was likely his body coming down off the adrenaline and stress. With a Team USA tracksuit on, he went for a six-and-a-half-mile run in the morning and a six-and-a-half-mile run in the evening on the streets of his boyhood neighborhood.

But the boulder off Steve's back was replaced by another burden. Now that he had made the team—to run for the ol' red, white, and blue—and had done so in record-fashion, he proclaimed how ready he was for Munich and that he would run ten seconds faster. He had to wrestle with a new set of expectations. People couldn't imagine him losing. He gave them that impression. In fact, the only two races he lost on American soil since track season as a freshman in the spring of 1970 were two Twilight Mile races to Roscoe Divine and Arne Kvalheim.

Back in Eugene, but before leaving with the Olympic team, Steve grabbed beers with his roommate Pat Tyson. Tyson was never one to prod or talk about Steve's running or the pressure Steve was under. He gave Steve the respite he needed, saw Steve for something other than a runner and beyond the phenomenon he'd become. They headed over to the Paddock Tavern—Steve's favorite bar—and knocked back a few beers, played pool, Pong, maybe some air hockey. He needed moments like this to feel like the regular, twenty-one-year-old young man he was, not just this great American hope to win a gold medal.

In a quiet moment in the nook of his trailer, Steve penned a letter for the people of Coos Bay. He wrote, "I would like to take this time to thank all the people who have backed me over the past years. You have given me the breaks I needed to get where I am now. You are my friends and my best fans. I hope I can live up to all your expectations. I'll be leaving in a few days so thanks a lot." Steve loved the pen and compulsively wrote letters and postcards to friends and family, even the community at large, namely his hometown of Coos Bay. He had long leveraged *The World* almost as a proto–social media "posting" to the newspaper, either in the form of a letter to the editor or as a travel dispatch, as he once did during summer campaigns to let his fans know what he was up to, how he was doing, and how grateful he was for their support. Rather than forgetting his roots, he actively cultivated them, thus creating a deeper bond.

Steve packed his bags and along with Tyson and Steve's girlfriend, Mary Marckx, drove to the Eugene airport. Given the antiquated security of the day, they walked up the ramp of the plane before boarding. Steve hugged the two of them tightly and didn't let go. It was the kind of embrace that almost begged them to pull him back. "It wasn't like, 'I wish I wasn't going,' but it was almost like that," Tyson recalled. "'I'd prefer to stay home. I don't really want to go.' I don't know if frightened is the word, but he's going to miss 'Pre's People.' He's going to miss Eugene."

The plane taxied from the terminal, gained speed down the runway, and took flight. Steve looked out the window as the plane climbed away from the place that gave him the most comfort. He flew all the way to Brunswick, Maine, where head coach Bill Bowerman convened the team before they would eventually ship off to Europe.

By the time Steve acclimated to Maine, he wrote back home to Tyson, letting him know how much Maine reminded him of Oregon, with a twinge of homesickness. He already expressed how eager he was to get back to Eugene so they could grill some food, throw some parties, and be college kids again. Steve also made a note to Tyson not to overtrain.

Steve ran eight miles his final morning in Maine, got on a plane for Queens, New York, and ran another six miles. He was bouncy, bubbling with confidence. If anything, he thought, he might be putting in too many miles before he boarded yet another plane for Oslo, Norway, the site of a pre-Olympic meet. Never known as a kicker, Steve's workouts were geared toward squeezing out his rivals' kicks: a series of three three-quarter miles in 3:11, 3:07, and 3:01; shag; then nine 330-yard sprints, then four 110s. Despite the cold he endured before he left the States, he felt great. Bowerman kept a close eye on Steve and acknowledged that any way you looked at it, Steve was the exception to the rule, young and capable. "I've stopped trying to figure out what Pre will do. He's not putting in all this work for nothing."

While in Oslo, some runners looked to stay sharp, or, in the case of Steve's Norwegian friend Arne Kvalheim, still needed to post a qualifying time for the Munich Games. Steve did a favor for Kvalheim, that old Oregon Duck who once helped recruit Steve to Oregon. Kvalheim needed a brisk pace in a 1,500-meter race in Oslo, and Steve wrapped this gift to his friend. It was Steve's first race since the Trials. After settling in fifth in the early goings, he soon took over the lead for the bulk of the race in a navy-blue Team USA uniform. Finland's Pekka Vasala sprinted ahead with about 300 meters to go. Steve battled Italy's Gianni Del Buono by inching him wider and wider into the middle of the track. It was the difference between second and third, and he earned the fastest 1,500 of his career in 3:39.4. Kvalheim finished sixth and qualified for the Norwegian team. "I was just running to get the carbon out of my system," Steve said.

The following night, Kvalheim, holding up his end of the bargain in a 3,000-meter race, blitzed to the front and edged ahead of Steve to set a swift pace. Steve drafted behind Kvalheim. At the halfway point, Kvalheim pulled out into Lane 2. As Steve eased into first, Kvalheim patted Steve on the back. Steve was on pace for an American record. He extended his lead to 15 yards and the announcer said, "The thing I admire about Prefontaine is that he says he's going to do something and he has the courage to do it." At the bell, he had a 30-yard lead. The fans loved what they saw. The lead grew, he was all by himself, and he secured a new American record of 7:44.2.

After the race, while wearing a blue USA sweatshirt with his spikes under his arm, he appeared to be squeezing his blue singlet into a ball as he spoke. Chuckling, he said of Kvalheim, "We'd like to see each other over in Munich. He asked me if I'd help him in the 1,500 and I asked him if he'd help me in the 3,000. It kinda worked out very nice. . . . I'm not even tired now."

Elsewhere, Belgium's Emiel Puttemans and Finland's Lasse Virén raced in Sweden with Virén breaking the world record in the two-mile in 8:14. Many runners Steve would face—Great Britain's Ian Stewart and David Bedford, along with Virén and Puttemans—all ran in this race in 8:28.2 or faster.

The 5,000 would be a race for the ages.

CHAPTER 11

SHIELD

HARALD NORPOTH, THE twenty-nine-year-old West German 5,000-meter runner, said the conditions for the new Olympic stadium were the worst of his long career, this after a trial race a month ahead of opening ceremonies in Munich. Eighty-thousand people could sit in this stadium, what some called "Germany's biggest frying pan." Some athletes considered the environment suffocating. Scoreboard malfunctions, cramped living conditions in the Olympic Village, not to mention the solar-magnifying power of the steel and spunglass roof ($52 million in 1972); long jumpers dealing with crosswinds and hammer throwers narrowly missing a runner on the track; 95-degree field temps softening the track surface, according to sprinters. This was what $612 million—four times more than the Mexico City Games (nearly $4.5 billion in today's dollars)—had secured for the XX Olympiad. That said, it looked magnificent. "The grass surface was so well manicured that it looks like a billiard table and the track the color of continually watered brick," said marathoner Kenny Moore.

Thanks to Team USA's gold and bronze medalists Tommie Smith and John Carlos having raised their fists and bowed their heads atop the podium in silent protest for human rights in the 1968 Mexico City Olympics, the Olympics were no longer seen as a celebration of apolitical amateur athletics. Maybe they never were. Go back to Hitler's Olympics in 1936 and try to make the case that the Olympics were just about athletics. A mere twenty-seven years since the end of World War II, and here they were, back in Germany. For fear of over-militarizing, security was soft, more of an honor system than a strict set of rules. Upon arrival, the lack of security in the village put Bowerman on edge. He wrote a letter to Clifford Buck, president of the American Olympic Committee, and told him, "We should secure the whole village" from "pickpockets, thieves, women of the street," but he didn't have much sway. An illustration of just how loose it was around the Olympic Village, Stan McSwain of Coos Bay, who made the trip to Munich and also had "Go Pre" license plates for his car back home, easily found Steve and told him, "Now listen to me kid and I'll tell you how to win the 5,000-meter race. Just remember and do all that Coach Walt McClure told you and you'll be a lead-pipe cinch for that gold medal." Steve kindly posed for a photograph with McSwain.

As the games neared, and as much as IOC president Avery Brundage would have loved for the Olympics to be solely the purview of brawn—no politics allowed—the games were forever changed. And when Rhodesia—now modern-day Zimbabwe, and a country formerly under the colonial dominion of the United Kingdom, this "white supremacist nation tucked beneath black Africa"—was invited to the games by the IOC, many Black American athletes were willing to sacrifice their eligibility in protest. Lee Evans, the 400-meter world record holder, issued a group statement that said, "In light of the Rhodesian acceptance into the Games, the United States black athletes now in Olympic Park believe it imperative to take a stand concerning the issue. We denounce Rhodesia's participation and if they are allowed to compete, we will take a united stand with our African brothers."

A spokesman for Rhodesia said the nation was given standards for entering the Olympic Games. "We met them. It was agreed upon and we are staying here."

Such was the backdrop heading into the Munich Olympics.

Steve granted many interviews. His reputation for good copy made him the most coveted person to cover. He was the requisite media darling of these Olympics. About the youth—the team at large and him—he said, "Yeah, I've heard all that junk, and I may get beat by some thirty-year-old Russian, but only if he's faster, not because he's older." True . . . but like a senior in high school defeating a freshman, speed often came with age and tactical instincts with maturity.

Steve had been out of the United States for several weeks and hadn't raced in quite some time. He was noticeably antsy and grew fatigued with interviews and talking to reporters. After all, what more could he say that hadn't already been said? Nevertheless, he rarely, if ever, said no to meeting with reporters, especially his Oregon correspondents. A week before his first Munich race—the 5,000 preliminaries—he stood outside the fourteen-floor U.S. team compound in the Olympic Village eating an ice cream sundae when the Eugene *Register-Guard*'s Blaine Newnham found him. Steve cast his eyes at the surrounding buildings. Steve's sideburns had thickened, as had his mustache, and his hair was longer; he had the air of someone who has been through three Olympic Games, not at the beginning of his first. Steve wanted to break out. He felt caged. "I'll go crazy here. Waiting is the only problem."

The 5,000-meter preliminaries would include sixty-one total runners, five heats where the top two finishers of each heat and the next four fastest runners from any heat would qualify for the final. This week—the whole month, really—gave him too much time to think about his competition and how the race would play out in his head. He was eager to watch the 10,000 meters as many of his 5,000-meter rivals would be running in that race, too. Steve wasn't worried about runners trying to double in the five and ten— Lasse Virén, Mohammed Gammoudi, David Bedford, Emiel Puttemans, among others—because, "When I make my move in the 5,000 it will be *wooosh*. And the guys who have already run 10,000 meters twice will feel like they've hit a stone wall." This was where Steve made a grave miscalculation; several of the 10,000-meter runners would play a major factor in the 5,000. In his defense, Steve's logic made sense. He figured he would be coming into the 5,000 far fresher, and his training under Bowerman's watchful eye had been going so well, he knew his tank would be fuller than the 10K runners.

Echoing Steve's impatience over having to wait so long to run his event, Dellinger, who recently touched down in Germany, said, "It's a matter of waiting out the days. The hours go by pretty slowly before the competition. You feel you can't do certain things because you might get hurt. So, you sit around, watch television, think about the race. I suppose by now every runner over there has run his race 200,000 times."

As much as Steve was labeled as cocky, or brash, he could be equally doubtful. Or, if not doubtful, desperate for his fans to pump the brakes a bit. It's as if he sensed it before he departed for Europe at the Eugene airport when he tightly hugged his girlfriend, Mary Marckx, and his roommate, Pat Tyson, that extra second longer than usual, that he knew, despite his belief in himself, that this was an altogether different departure, an intimidating maiden voyage of a frontier he had previously only visualized but that was now becoming all too real. "It's the expectations back home that they don't know they're puttin' on me," he said. "I haven't even got the best time. I've got the fourth fastest time. Just because I beat everybody in America doesn't mean I'm going to beat everybody here. The people back home think I'm a shoo-in. But the competition here is four times better." During Steve's entire time in Munich, he was just as likely to say the gold medal was his to lose before becoming more grounded and hedging people's expectations. His mind volleyed around so frequently; it was likely a side effect of boredom given that his last formal race was on August 2 in Oslo. Aside from workouts and a two-mile time trial, Steve would have no official races for more than a month when the preliminaries for the 5,000 would start on September 6.

To stay sharp, Steve snuck away to the nearby training track. Running under the shadow of the Olympic Tower, Steve couldn't believe how his body was responding. If his mind had grown weary, his body was sharp. Wearing a white USA T-shirt, he moved briskly over the practice track adjacent to the main stadium. He was doing things he never thought possible, and it gave him tremendous confidence. He ran 3:59s in practice to his own internal clock. He hoped it kept up. He handicapped his rivals, like Finland's Virén, who had been setting records all season. To this, Steve figured Virén must level off while he himself was still on the way up. "Right now, I feel so good I don't know how fast I can go and it scares me a little thinking I have that much inside of me."

Dave Wottle, the eventual 800-meter gold medalist in these Games, watched from the stands of the nearby practice track. Steve on the track, Bowerman in the middle of the field calling out splits. Wottle watched Steve pace himself to a four-minute mile, "Just boom, boom, boom, 60, 2:01, 3:01, 4 minutes, and then he did a ladder," Wottle recalled. "It just blew my mind.

People asked me, 'Was he ready to go in the 5,000?' Heck, yeah, he was ready to go."

Of all the runners in the field, he was undeniably the most consistent, which was something you could always say about the record of Steve Prefontaine: he almost never ran a clunker of a race or eased if he was winning or losing. He said he hadn't run a bad race in two years, and he was correct. Steve stopped far short of guaranteeing victory. "I'm just saying—no bad races."

He allowed that he'd be disappointed if he didn't finish in the top three. He smiled. "But I'm not thinking about silver or bronze, only gold." If he kept posturing like a gold medalist, he might will it into being, might make his competitors wilt, or at least doubt their abilities. The glut of time Steve had on his hands allowed his mind to factor in all possibilities. The *New York Times* noted that Steve was "trying to sound typically confident without being cocky," this in reference to someone like Virén, who, to Steve's estimation, had been laying all his "cards on the table" by setting records. Speaking of laying too many cards on the table, when asked how fast he thought he could run the final mile of the 5,000 meters, he said with a Huck Finn grin, "I haven't been running those 3:59 miles in workouts for nothing." Indeed, and he did it just as much to show his toughness. He soon told *Sports Illustrated*, "A lot of people run a race to see who is fastest. I run to see who has the most guts, who can punish himself into an exhausting pace and then at the end who can punish himself even more. Nobody is going to win the gold medal after running an easy *first two miles* [emphasis added]. Not with me. If I lose forcing the pace all the way, well, at least I can live with myself. But if it's a slow pace, and I get beaten by a kicker who leaches off the front, then I'll always wonder, 'What if . . . ?' Right now, I'd say we'd go out in world-record pace and for the first couple of miles—and then I'll turn it on, start destroying people. If anybody wants to beat me, let them run a world record." In the pantheon of Steve's boldest proclamations, this stood tallest. A step further: delusional; but it could just as likely be something *he* needed to hear himself say.

There was a shoot-for-the-stars-land-on-the-moon quality to his vision. Years ago he had taken a photograph of this very site and put a pin in that photograph where he figured the podium would be. Of course he won the gold. He could see it in his mind's eye, but he was, indeed, tired of waiting and of all the buildup, not to mention he had developed a cold, likely on account of being in close quarters with so many people, be it on airplanes or the dorms. Steve was sniffling and had been on penicillin for a week.

The time continued to pass slowly, and Steve remained, it would seem, equal parts nervous, upset, and confident. People continued to pester him about the race, and he was so sick of it. He couldn't talk about it any longer, but he would because the media loved him and what else was he going to do? He'd give them good copy one way or another, swing from one extreme to another. He was, after all, only twenty-one years old, young, immature, and in the deepest waters he had ever been in. So within a week of saying he would start "destroying people," he then added, "The average person doesn't realize that it's not only being good or being the best—it's being good on that day." He thought he might not even make the finals. And two days before the heats were scheduled to start, he was all the more agitated, "Everybody is expecting so much from me, and why talk if I don't know what's going to happen out there?" Steve never underestimated himself, but he allowed for some of that. This was the longest stretch without an actual race in years. Sure, his training was going well. His physical body was as good as ever, but his head wasn't all there. Like a fit Thoroughbred horse cooped up too long in its stall, Steve needed the heat of competition, he needed it done. He was looking forward to a long vacation when this was all over. "I'm sick of track and field. I just want to get the dang thing over with." More than likely, he was tired of talking about it. By now, it was just a few days away.

On September 3, via TV from the Olympic Village, Steve watched the 10,000-meter finals and saw Finland's Virén not only trip and fall on the twelfth lap (which also brought down Gammoudi, who would not recover in that race), but also get back up, win the race, *and* break the world record in 27:38.35. Steve was very impressed. Virén would have to bounce back on short rest for the 5,000-meter heats and finals. "That's a lot of running," Steve said. "Anytime you run under 28 minutes twice, you're going to feel it. Maybe Virén is Superman, but I don't think so."

Dellinger saw live what Steve saw on TV and said, "Lasse Virén is going to be the guy Steve Prefontaine has to beat in the 5,000 meters." He couldn't imagine a man falling and still breaking a world record, the toughest of all distance records, in his opinion. He saw how easy Virén looked, long, tall, graceful.

The Games were waning and Steve had been away from Oregon for nearly six weeks. It was lonely in Europe, despite being there with friends and peers. Steve even said, "If I really fall flat on my face, I might retire from track. But as long as I satisfy myself, that's all that counts." On another note of Steve's vacillating moods in his prolonged time in Germany, Kenny Moore wrote in *Bowerman and the Men of Oregon* that Steve said, "I'm going to win that gold medal. Silver is crap. Bronze is crap. God, if I only got a bronze I could never go home to Oregon again! I'm going to win that gold medal." Whatever the outcome, and whatever his mood, he was quick to quote Bowerman that he could come back on his shield or bearing his shield.

"I'd like to come home bearing my shield," Steve said.

ON SEPTEMBER 5, FRANK Shorter, the eventual Olympic marathon champion, noticed the courtyard to their Olympic Village apartment complex was empty. As he would recount in his memoir *My Marathon*, "something was off; something was wrong." He went inside where his roommates and a few other athletes, including Steve, huddled around a tiny black-and-white TV set. Steve, having grown up speaking German, translated the news, relaying what Shorter said was "too shocking to believe."

In the pre-dawn hours on Tuesday, September 5, 1972, one day before the 5,000-meter preliminaries and the day Steve's parents were arriving in Munich, "Arab commandos seeking to free fellow guerrillas held in Israel took over that country's quarters, loosed a burst of gunfire fatal to two of the Jewish contingent and took nine persons hostage." Due to the lax security that so troubled Bowerman in the first place, the attackers snuck into the Village and commandeered the Israeli dorms.

The Olympics were suspended.

Tensions were high and the Village on lockdown. By now, Dellinger knew he needed to break Steve out of the Village. Once Dellinger contacted Steve, he told him to climb the fence to break free. Dellinger sought an old friend from Springfield, Wayne Sabin, now teaching in Bonn, Germany. Dellinger shared an apartment "off campus" with Sabin and Max Truex, another friend. Few people knew Steve better than Dellinger, and he thought it best to get Steve away from the Village. Dellinger didn't break any other athlete out of Olympic Village, only Steve, Oregon's own. Steve had wanted to get into the mountains to clear his head, get away from the onslaught of media, but this was altogether worse. He needed time and space to process what had happened.

They took Sabin's car and drove into Austria. Steve and Dellinger forgot their passports, so they figured they were in for trouble at the Austrian border. The border patrol officer recognized Steve's face and seemed to know Dellinger's name. Sabin had remembered his passport, so they were waved through provided they return to Germany in two hours. Steve moved in with Dellinger for the rest of the Olympics. There was a park nearby, so Steve could train without burden.

Few found it hard to focus after eleven Israelis, five Palestinians, and one German police officer had died during the attack and its aftermath. Steve likely wasn't alone in wanting to pack up and go home. Others were more defiant. Dellinger lobbied Steve to get his head back in the game. Those runners you were expecting to be burned out from the 10,000? They just got an extra day's rest. No use pouting.

As much as Steve wanted to put the tragedy behind him, sweep it away and myopically focus on his one and only task, it deeply troubled him. "If they loaded us all into a plane right now to take us home, I'd go," Steve said. In fact, Steve would later admit that it took him a full year to get over "the Israeli thing. A full year." Steve was a sensitive person, admittedly so. Compound that with his immaturity and he "just couldn't take it."

Steve's mental preparation had always been important to him, even vital. When asked how important, Steve would say, "It is probably 80 percent of your preparation. Even if your body is ready, you must have it upstairs or it just won't go." His results were mixed when he was thrown off his routine. One early incident took place during his senior year of high school. It was a

Saturday, May 24, 1969. On the bus ride to Silke Field in Springfield, as was customary for any bus trip Walt McClure oversaw, he wanted his athletes to focus on their events when they were about forty-five minutes from their destination. Quiet and contemplative, Steve would have been visualizing his attempts at doubling in the mile and two-mile.

At 11:30 a.m., on the opposite, southbound side, a passing vehicle "cut sharply" in front of a station wagon being driven by forty-five-year-old Fred Stafford. After being cut off, he stomped the brakes and lost control of the car.

Across the divide, the bus full of athletes saw the car when the accident started. Those kids in the first few rows of the bus witnessed the accident unfold. The station wagon slid into a ditch and flipped, throwing Stafford from the car. He landed, unsettlingly, on his back, where he lay motionless. The car rolled up and over, clearing Stafford, and came to rest several yards from where he lay.

The bus pulled over. McClure told everyone to remain seated as he crossed the interstate and the median to check on Stafford. The boys on the bus watched. Few on the bus had experienced such a thing, few had witnessed such kinetic violence, how a momentary lack of control of a vehicle, no matter the speed, could leave a man far-flung and at the mercy of machines. Soon, as more people gathered to help, McClure walked back to the bus. He and his team couldn't wait any longer. The mood on the bus was understandably somber.

Sitting at the front of the bus—wasn't he always in front?—was Steve. According to Steve's close friend Ron Apling, Steve was rattled by what he saw out his window, for what he could likely never unsee. Steve would have to put the image of a man being thrown from his car behind him and find a way to perform.

Steve won the mile and two-mile that day, but the mile race was far closer than any previous race he had experienced that season—significant for someone who had dominated every race for the last two years of high school.

Now at the 1972 Olympics, with the greatest mental challenge of all, he'd need to find a way to compartmentalize the attack, silo it away, and try his best to perform for his country, for Oregon. Given his swinging commentary from brazen overconfidence to tempered enthusiasm and back with little more distraction than extra time on his hands, the deaths of the athletes were proving difficult for him to brush off like a blip in the weather.

Delayed a day by the attack and run on September 7, 1972, Dellinger liked what he saw from Steve in his qualifying heat. Steve ran toward the front of the field the entire heat, often trading the lead with Puttemans or Spain's Javier Álvarez Salgado. When Puttemans swiped the lead from Steve on the final turn, Steve turned his attention to looking over both shoulders, content to finish second. That secured the pair a spot in the final. It was, in Dellinger's eyes, "easy for him."

Given all the waiting and the pall hanging over the Olympics, it was a relief to just compete. Steve took off his spikes and walked barefoot on the track, trying to warm down after running 13:32.6. This not being Hayward Field, he was quickly restrained by the Olympic security. Steve looked up into the stands to the people screaming "Go Pre." His people found him. He was relieved.

Now that he qualified for the final, maybe now he could just *run*, run as he never had before, despite all that had happened. The game plan would be to set a hard pace and then run a four-minute mile to kick. Steve shared with John Dixon of *The Independent* that he felt no one would be able to stay with him over the final five laps, which he planned to run an average of 60 seconds a lap: a four-minute closing mile. Tony Benson of Australia said, "If anybody can run a four-minute mile at the end of 5,000 meters, he can have the bloody gold medal."

Steve couldn't keep his strategy—as great as it was—to himself. As with much of his posturing, he likely thought that saying he was capable of a four-minute mile so late in an Olympic final race would intimidate his competition. For all the public trumpeting to the media of a final mile in four minutes, Steve made it sound as if he was the only one capable of such a thing. It was a grave miscalculation on his part. Ian Stewart of Great Britain knew there were four or five in the race who could. Including himself. But mum's the word.

—

ON THE AFTERNOON of Sunday, September 10, 1972, when the 5,000 meters was set to go, it was muggy in Munich. Given the hot conditions in the stadium, the runners would not find any relief. All thirteen runners took their place at the top of the backstretch, the starting line for the 5,000 meters. Steve, the youngest in the race by two years, stood beside Puttemans toward the outside of the field, bib No. 1005. He kicked his feet, pulled his trunks up, then shuffled and kicked his feet. He was fidgety and visually nervous, but so was everyone else. Ralph Mann, who had won the silver medal in the 400-meter hurdles and would become a close friend of Steve's, had noticed that Steve looked rather gaunt, sunken. Stewart would start on the far outside, Virén and Gammoudi, the defending 5,000-meter champion, toward the middle. Gammoudi toppled over Virén in the 10,000-meter final and did not finish, so he entered the 5,000 meters far fresher than he otherwise would have had he finished the 10,000.

The stadium was packed, and flags waved. There were yellow shirts freckling the crowd, many of which read "Go Pre." Steve's girlfriend sat in the stands, along with Steve's parents, who had spent the previous weeks visiting some of Elfriede's family from her native Germany.

At last, it was time. Steve had summoned the strength through qualifying and here he was, at the starting line, and . . . he lost his motivation to run. After all the years, all the work . . . it wasn't there. Running seemed so pointless, what with the death of fellow athletes. When they were called to the starting line, he thought to himself, *God, it's almost over. This whole thing is almost over.* The gun was about to pop off for the biggest race of his life, and he was absent in mind. He wasn't himself. *This isn't me about to run this race.* In his own words, the tragedy had stripped him of his desire and, worst of all, his identity. He was a ghost of himself, and if he was going to win— or even medal—there were factors at play as strong or stronger than the twelve other men in the field.

Yet here he was, looking stricken, his ribs, even his sternum, visible through his skin. Alas, he shook his legs out one more time, approached the line, and took his mark. The starter raised his pistol into the air. A calm settled over the field and—pop—they were off.

Ian McCafferty and Ian Stewart cleared the field to establish better position as the field bent around the first turn. Steve settled in mid-pack, amidst a flurry of traffic, where someone stepped on his foot and tore his shoe. Just a shoe, not his foot. David Bedford of Great Britain was predicted to set the pace—a suicidal one, perhaps—but he loped toward the back of the field early on. Bedford had set a blistering sub-60 first lap in the 10,000 final a few days before and ultimately finished sixth. What he was waiting for in the 5,000 was anyone's guess. When it came to pushing the pace, "he must be the first one to make a move," David Coleman, the TV race announcer, said in his brilliant British accent. . . . "This is very slow, in fact, they've jogged half a lap."

There was no urgency, only runners anticipating who would make the first mistake. Steve coasted in seventh past the finish for the first of twelve times. Coleman was borderline insulted at the tepid nature of the pace, and, one surmises, so too was Steve as he moved up to fifth on the outside as they neared the first full lap. *I kept wondering why one of those guys wouldn't take it. They were just setting it up for Virén*, Steve thought. Coleman noted that if they kept this pace up, Ron Clarke's long standing 5,000-meter world record of 13:16.6 from 1966 would not be in jeopardy. After ninety seconds, the Russian Nikolay Sviridov throttled up, to which Coleman said, "And the nonsense has stopped, and the racing has started."

Steve dropped back to ninth, running along the inside and drafting behind the leaders. Granted it was early in the race, but he wasn't following his natural instincts. Finland's Juha Väätäinen, the European champion, who had a "blistering kick," according to Coleman, sat behind Steve four back from the rear. Virén ran last of them all. Two full passes by the finish—600 meters—went in a lethargic 1:41, following a 71-second quarter mile. The first of the five kilometers ticked by in 2:46. Sensing little urgency, Steve, along with Bedford, quickly rose through the field to chase down the Russian, still in front. Beyond that, Coleman added, "There's not much action out there at the moment, but there's a great deal of thinking. These athletes puzzling out what to do about this."

Coleman, ever measured, said, "Prefontaine can't leave it to a short finish. He's got to push from a lap and a half to two laps out." Coleman pegged it, but Steve couldn't give himself over to it yet, fully surrender to who he was in the biggest race on the biggest stage of his young life. He had said that if it's a slow pace and he lost to a kicker who leached off the front, then he'd always wonder "What if . . . ?"

Still, the pace crawled. Steve, back to seventh and having run just under four minutes of the race, coasted to the outside of Lane 1, still beside Bedford, these two front runners trapped mid-pack. Down the backstretch again, Steve's arms swung casually. He was a stride ahead of Bedford. "One suspects that they're all waiting for David Bedford," Coleman said. Just as the field completed four laps, Bedford tripped on Steve, and Steve flailed, but regained his rhythm. He would suffer a hole in his left leg an inch-and-a-half long and an eighth of an inch deep. Back around the turn and straightening down the homestretch again, Steve peeked over his left shoulder at Gammoudi and then targeted Puttemans, who was just ahead. Steve momentarily brushed shoulders with Puttemans and angled to get near Stewart, who had been in third by himself behind McCafferty and Sviridov. Steve came into full view, that rounded chest thrust forward in stark contrast to the plywood-pectorals of just about every other wraith, 4:52 into the race, "Real burly for a middle-distance runner, cocky American, he believes in himself utterly," Coleman said. At this point, Virén shot like a bullet up into the lead pack as Steve whipped a quick "holy-shit" look over his right shoulder. Gammoudi, as if pulled on a string, followed Virén, who by now had struck the lead five minutes into the race. Stewart threw his weight and pushed Gammoudi away so he could draft behind Virén with nine laps left and just over five minutes lapsed. As quickly as Steve had moved into the top three, he slipped right back to seventh. Steve now strung out wide in Lane 2 to avoid traffic, but taking on more distance than Virén, who hugged the inside as if painted there, as were Stewart and Gammoudi. In a comic twist, Steve ran right beside West Germany's Norpoth, who once coasted off Steve's shoulder for eleven laps in a 1971 race and then blew Steve off the track in a brutal, lasting kick. The entire field bunched into a ten-meter cluster, Virén still leading, Steve again accelerating up into fourth alongside Gammoudi, having just run 2,000 meters in 5:32.6.

At this moment, far, far later than anyone had predicted, Bedford all but sprinted to the spearhead of the pack. "The inevitable happens; they were all waiting for this," called Coleman, "Bedford goes in front." Gammoudi wiped his brow and Virén kept a watchful eye on Bedford's feet, so close to tangling with his own. Almost a curse, Steve was back in seventh and in traffic, a terrible and dangerous place to be pinned. The pace did not quicken despite Bedford's surge and the field remained bunched. Steve, again on the turn, swung out four runners wide into the middle of Lane 2, covering ever more ground as the race neared its halfway point. As if feeling the danger of all that extra distance, Steve sped up and moved into third place with Stewart to his left. "All of them still playing wait and see," Coleman said as the Spaniard Javier Álvarez Salgado took his share of the lead. Anyone who knew Steve as a runner, knew his style, could sense his growing impatience. The race wasn't supposed to be this slow for this long. Much of that banked on Bedford, but also much of it rested on the reputation—the very nature—of Steve himself. What was he waiting for?

A year and a half earlier, on March 20, 1971, an early track meet for the Ducks in Steve's sophomore season, Dellinger wanted Steve not to run too hard, follow the leader through the first mile, then have at it the second mile. It caught everyone off guard. The *Register-Guard* wrote, "He looked like Steve Prefontaine. He ran like Steve Prefontaine. He even watched the scoreboard clock the way Steve Prefontaine watches it. But heck, it couldn't be Steve Prefontaine. As every track nut worth his salt knows, Steve Prefontaine doesn't sit back and let someone else set the pace." But that one time in 1971 and again here at the Olympics, he was running counter to his style and to how he'd learned to run and dominate for the better part of the last five years.

A surge from McCafferty shuffled Bedford back several spots all while Virén skimmed the inner lane not taking an inch of extra distance. Steve, still in third, bent around the turn while they straightened out. Coming up on 2,500 meters complete, Steve maintained his advantage in third to the outside with no foot traffic before him. He quickly shot a look down at his feet as if maybe he took a spike, but it mattered little. The 80,000 people roared, flags waved. The tension grew and Steve casually sidled up to McCafferty and closed the gap on Álvarez Salgado, who had led for the past lap or more. Coleman said, "Still the race hasn't really started."

Down the stretch again, Steve snuck a look over his right shoulder, his brow deeply furrowed. Five laps remaining, Puttemans charged past Steve and, along the inside, there was Virén lengthening his stride, tucking in beside Steve's swinging left arm. Väätäinen, trying to snake his way through on the inside, tapped Bedford to move aside. Bedford shrugged him off and Väätäinen flailed his arm in frustration. "And surely, somewhere, someone, must go," Coleman said, imploring a runner to have the courage to break it wide open. Steve, again, was swallowed by traffic down on the inside in fifth place. They passed 3,000 meters in 8:20; for perspective, a month before, Steve set an American record in the 3,000 in Oslo in 7:44. Here, the race's color commentator said, "The suspense must be appalling among those who haven't total confidence in their sprinting ability." When Steve saw two miles flash in 8:52, he knew he was in trouble. Not long ago, Steve had said, *Nobody is going to win the gold medal after running an easy first two miles. Not with me. If I lose forcing the pace all the way, well, at least I can live with myself.* On American soil, Steve never would have waited this long to assert himself, to make the race his own and bend the others to his will, win or lose. He was disillusioned that other runners wouldn't take charge. The moment, to this point, had subsumed him, stolen his identity. But not any longer. Which meant only one thing . . .

Just shy of four laps remaining, Steve, at long last, made the move. Out in the middle of Lane 2, for the first time, with the assuredness they had all expected, Steve Prefontaine struck the front for the first time in the 5,000-meter final of the XX Olympiad at 9:23. "This is sure being left to the faster miler and Prefontaine believes it's him," Coleman said. "The American now committed."

Those "3:59s" he'd been running, this was why. Steve briskly pushed the pace and the field that was once bunched into a 10-meter box strung out by 20. "The American in front, almost a cult of the United States. He's sort of an athletic Beatle." Coleman noted that all around the stadium American fans wore T-shirts saying "Go Pre." Stewart stayed tight with Steve with an ailing Bedford in third while Steve breathed the clean air from the front. "The Europeans say that he hasn't really been in a war yet, but this boy's got utter belief in himself and he's inexperienced enough in many ways not to know how good the others are," Coleman said.

"Go Pre" signs and yellow shirts freckled the crowd. Their guy was in front, leading the Olympics. Virén moved out from the rail and began a hard charge toward Steve so as not to let him go unchallenged in this final mile. All runners looked as if they were standing still when Virén uncorked some of that beautiful stride, "states his intention now," with three laps remaining.

Steve still led with Virén drafting. Stewart traveled in fourth with Gammoudi behind him and the field strung out ever more. At last, a clear lead pack of five established itself as the class of the world: Steve, Virén, Puttemans, Stewart, Gammoudi.

Virén ran collected and calm, and Steve started to show his signature strain, still flying, still in charge, chest-thrust and plowing, a style that had so endeared him to his "people" back home. "And suddenly it's starting to happen and runners are losing touch," called Coleman. Steve leaned hard into the turn with that head ever cocked to the side. Steve took a one-stride lead down the straightway with Virén taking a swift peek over his right shoulder where he saw Puttemans, Gammoudi, and Stewart, in that order.

Nearing two laps to go, Virén whooshed into the lead and Gammoudi—his strategy all too obvious—followed, leaving Steve in third. Puttemans gave chase, as did Stewart. "These five are clear," Coleman said. A lap and three-quarters left and, "They really have left this one to the fastest finisher."

Steve ebbed to fourth into Gammoudi's slipstream. 600 meters to go. At that moment, Steve laid his belly down and thrust by Gammoudi into third, second, and back in front, a mad dash for gold. Steve put some daylight between him and Virén, about whom, Coleman said, "there's almost a certainty about [Virén's] running in the past six weeks that's almost made winning seem inevitable." Steve in front and down the straight for the next-to-last time, the arms pumped harder, the bear climbing on, these five well clear. Steve, in command, straightened down the stretch. "The chunky American driving for home!" Coleman said. Virén, sticking to Steve like a tick, kicked into another gear and turned over his superior foot speed, his elegant length, to pull even with Steve 50 meters from the bell. Gammoudi, too, would not let Virén and Steve run free, breezing past Puttemans—who hit the wall—leaving Stewart to ration speed and save ground in fourth, stalking.

Steve was nearly in a full charge with 400 meters remaining. Virén, in a drive, passed Steve on the outside 15 meters from the finish on the second-to-last lap. By now, Gammoudi was shoulder to shoulder with Steve. Virén hit the line in front. "This time the bell!"

Virén charged on while Gammoudi climbed up into second, Steve in third down on the inside. The crowd was riotous in its collective fervor; the runners could barely hear their own breath or the sounds of foot strikes. Round the bend and Steve shot a look over his left shoulder. If he saw anything at all, it was Stewart about five meters back. Perhaps sensing that Stewart was cooked back in fourth, perhaps thinking that no matter what, the medals belonged to Virén, Gammoudi, and himself in an unknown order, Steve made a decision. With 300 meters to go, Steve swept to the outside of Gammoudi and let loose a monstrous sprint, "The American attacks on the outside!"

Parrying, Gammoudi cut Steve off, blocked his momentum, and zipped ahead of Virén by a stride. These three, so close, too close. At 12:52.5, Steve laid it all out in what would be a move his peers would question for decades. So many would say, you have one move at that time in the race, when the body is so desperately in oxygen debt that you can no longer overdraw, what they saw next hurt them as much as it was, no question, hurting Steve in the moment. His head wavering and his arms pumping so hard, Steve attacked Gammoudi *again*, this time 180 meters from the finish. Gammoudi veered over to block, which played right into Virén's scheme. Though Gammoudi looked wounded by the battle, he had a bit more than Steve. All the while Virén watched and waited as did Stewart some 7 to 8 meters back, surveying the theater before him. "These are the medal men!" called Coleman.

Into the turn with roughly 150 meters remaining, Gammoudi moved ahead with "The Finn and the American gearing up for the final attack!"

Virén waited no more: he uncorked an impeccably timed kick. Steve again looked over his shoulder knowing that by now he had no chance at defeating the Tunisian and the Finn.

Steve tried on the final corner, he poured forth, but it was like Virén was dropped in at the top of the stretch. He burst in front of Steve and exploded past Gammoudi. In the replay, you see the moment when Steve knew he couldn't keep up, that Virén was in another league. Immediately Steve looked behind him for new worries. At this moment, 110–120 meters or so from the finish, there was undeniably a sense of panic.

The crowd roared for Virén, chasing his second gold medal of the games. Gammoudi seemed to be practically standing still, so was Steve, and Stewart charged like a locomotive from the rear. "Virén goes for home! Gammoudi is bankrupt, so too is Prefontaine!"

By now Steve ran on dread, willing the finish to find him. His arms were no longer part of his body. He looked over his left shoulder, his right shoulder. Steve was never a kicker, not in the class of these great closers, but he knew the feeling of a runner gaining on him. Rare was it that he lost in the United States, but there were the few times in the mile when he felt the looming presence of the long striding Arne Kvalheim in 1971 or Roscoe Divine in 1970; when he knew in his bones he was clipped after leading for most, if not all the way. And here, in the final mile, Steve did what he could and had been swallowed by Virén and Gammoudi. The finish was just a few meters away . . .

"Stewart with a late run!"

Eyes wide, a peek over Steve's right shoulder, the head wobbling, his body no longer collected, his feet turning over as if running up a dune. And there in his eyes was the fear of prey surrendering to the teeth of the hunter. One look, two, and Stewart at last pulled even with Steve 15 meters from the finish and, in a delicate mercy, passed him. Steve gave over to gravity. In that moment, he was closer to death than life, so gassed and tired, wasted. All that carried Steve across the finish line was momentum and the instinct to stay upright. "Prefontaine dies in the final strides! . . . The American bows his head desperately."

It was over.

Virén had won in 13:26.4, Gammoudi second, Stewart third; Steve, fourth, in 13:28.4, .8 seconds behind Stewart.

Steve pushed a finger onto his nostril and blew his nose. He hung his head low and he walked a wobbly line. He whipped the hair out of his eyes. He stared at the ground and soon took off his spikes to free his feet, pale as ghosts, from burden. Steve, his skin the color of the medal he just missed, walked across the track and onto the grass.

When he looked up, he saw the "Go Pre" banners still slung over the fences. What he appreciated, above all, was that they left them up even after he lost. If he was coming home on his shield, his people would carry him.

PART III

CHAPTER 12

BROKEN

"I'VE GOT NOTHING to say," said a crushed, crestfallen Steve Prefontaine.

Blaine Newnham, who had covered Steve so thoroughly for the *Register-Guard* before and during the Olympics, couldn't let Steve go. Steve started to march away from Newnham, having already spoken with him so much in the lead up to the 5,000-meter final.

Newnham, soft spoken, a fine writer, far from combative, worked up the courage and said, "Wait a minute. Look, you gotta talk to me."

"I don't have to talk to you," Steve said.

"What about all those people back in Eugene?"

"What do you mean?"

It was two months since he won the 5,000 at the Olympic Trials. Steve said on that day of those same people back in Eugene, "I'll tell you one thing. I love every one of them . . . but there is a breaking point in each race when you wonder if all the sacrifice is really worth it. You think 'Why should I do this? I don't have to run this hard.' But that's when I think about them. They keep me going. They appreciate what I am doing. I realize that my running is something I can share with them. I run as much for them as I run for myself."

In the moments after the Olympic 5,000, Newnham kept pleading, "The people at Hayward Field. Pre's People. They've lived this race with you. They can understand what happened. We've got to talk."

"Well, I don't know what to say."

"Let's talk about the race. . . . How bad did you do? How old are you?" Newnham's mind raced because he knew he had to keep Steve on the hook because he might break bait and walk away and there was no way Newnham could catch him.

"Twenty-one."

"And so you finished fourth in the world at that age. How bad's that?"

"It's not too bad."

"Did you run for third or second? No, you ran to win. You took the lead with a mile to go. You ran your butt off and you finished fourth. How bad's that?"

"It wasn't that bad."

Steve softened at all of this. He knew what it meant to let people down when they expected so much of him. But what Newnham reiterated was that nobody was disappointed in him. Steve needed someone to, effectively, give him a hug, to tell him Pre's People understood. Newnham, almost like a hostage negotiator, brought Steve back to himself.

Around this time, when Steve was being interviewed, David Bedford, Britain's own brash front runner who finished a disappointing twelfth in the 5,000, walked by. Steve yelled over to him, "I'll see you in Montreal and I'll kick your butt." Steve planned on meeting Bedford, among others, to drink a lot of beer because, after all he'd been through, "Isn't that what the Olympic Games are all about?"

Within an hour of the finish, Newnham noted how low Steve was, but "in the moments that followed, he regained his bravado, his zest for life, his unflagging confidence."

Steve said, "I know I'm better than fourth in the world, I'm just fourth best in the world today. . . . In four more years I'm going to be a helluva lot tougher than that Finn. He'd better watch out."

Steve emptied himself onto that track in Munich and Virén and Gammoudi galloped away from him. Something else happened in that race. Steve realized there were limits to bravado. Steve had to know, on some level, that he had a lot of growing up to do. That would take time, and nobody who suffers heartbreak cares to hear that time heals all wounds. His thoughts bandied about; high one second, low another. With time, though, he'd come to realize there was so much more to look forward to, a new Steve for a new era.

Newnham called Steve's race his "greatest defeat and his greatest achievement." It was that dichotomy, those seemingly disparate poles, that Steve had been wrestling with for the better part of a month. Within an hour after the race, still abuzz from it, Steve was in the throes of processing it in real time. He said, on the one hand, that he had nothing to talk about and that it simply wasn't his day, almost with a shrug. This was the first race where his trash talk and his brazen transparency betrayed him, the only time to date he couldn't bend the race to his will while leaving his competition in ruins; in this rare moment he was the wreckage. Make no mistake, he shaped the nature of the race's final phase. "I didn't have anything left the last fifty meters and that means I ran a hard mile. I made those sons-of-a-guns run that last mile. Maybe I could have run a faster time if I'd have held back, but I was running to win."

Yes, he ran to win, and yet . . . Steve didn't run the race he was supposed to. Or, more accurately, once the race unfolded in a manner that didn't align with his expectations for the first two miles, he failed to adapt. He respected his competition too much. From the outset, he wanted to wait and to push that final mile. To his credit, he did. He wanted to run a four-minute final mile and he ran 4:06; Lasse Virén ran roughly a 4:01 by one account, 4:04 to 4:02 in another, which made more sense, given that Virén won by two seconds, and they were neck and neck going into the bell lap. But before that last mile Steve wasn't true to his racing instincts. Steve hated to be mid-pack, or back of the pack, but the Olympics proved too big for him mentally. At Hayward Field, no way would Steve let two miles crawl in 8:52 like that. At the worst time, on the biggest stage, Steve did not dictate the terms of the race until it was too late.

Steve's girlfriend at the time wondered after the race, *Would he kill himself?* But any runner would tell you that you learn more from a bad race than a good one. Bill Bowerman, ever mindful of perspective, said, "He couldn't have done any better. He's young. He's got a lot of races ahead. He'll be fine. Believe me, he'll be fine."

The Olympics wasn't the first time Steve had lost a race, but it was the most public of defeats. He wasn't necessarily equipped to metabolize and process what was, to him, a disaster (on and off the track). At the start of Jim Ryun's comeback in 1971, he had mentioned that he hadn't learned how to lose, and now Steve would have to confront that same quandary and turn it into his greatest teacher. There would be no redemption for another four years—the thought of that alone was paralyzing.

Post race, he also said, "A medal would have been nice, but it doesn't make that much difference." This was categorically false: it made all the difference. It was all he thought about. It was the forever-answer to his constant burning question *Is it worth it?* But what he couldn't know was that losing the race—and the Olympic experience en masse—fundamentally changed him.

Post-Olympics, Steve was invited to run in a few meets—hush, hush—to make some money, as many American runners did at the time. Other runners close to Steve were invited to, say, set the pace in a race for $100. They'd meet the race organizer at the hotel and he'd say, "How much did we agree on?" Then hand over an envelope with cash, a violation of the amateur rules.

A few days after the Olympics, Steve ran second in a 5,000 in Rome and toward the end of the race, he just quit and waved the guy past him. It was something Steve had never done, he didn't care, he didn't have the spirit, and, "It started me to thinking." Once the race was over, he admitted that it deeply bothered him that he quit with 50 yards to go. Something inside of Steve was broken.

Bill Dellinger, for his part, figured Steve would move on soon enough. No sense in dwelling on the past. Dellinger provided a postmortem on Steve's experience in Munich. He wrote, "After a couple of days, he'll realize that 1972 made him tougher and that it will pay off for him in 1976 and later if he wants." Dellinger ran in three Olympics, so could Steve. "I think Steve is very glad to have it all over."

Back in Eugene, Pat Tyson had woken early on the morning of Steve's 5,000-meter Olympic final. He recalled that it was a beautiful Sunday morning. He had already gone for his morning run. The race was set to go off just after 7 a.m. local time. The only thing open at that time on a Sunday was church. Tyson turned on one of the many televisions Steve owned in the trailer, prizes from races he'd won. Tyson watched it by himself. "I don't know if I used the word disbelief, but every time I watch that race, even today, [I think] he's gonna win. You know he's going to win when he takes the lead even with 250 to go. That was a sad, quiet moment in Eugene," he said.

Tyson did what any good roommate would do. He gathered up all the newspapers he had collected since Steve left for Europe, so they'd be waiting for him when he returned. Come Monday, he grabbed a fresh *Register-Guard* and flipped to the sports page: "Pre's warning for 1976: 'He'd better be ready.'" Tyson must have smiled at the sight of it. Tyson set the *Register-Guard* newspaper on the pile he saved and waited for Steve to come home.

For Steve, it was a matter of motivation. For the past four years, the 1972 Olympics was all he thought about. It all built to that moment, and it was *that* close. He had thought about the Olympics every day since 1968. Two seconds separated him from Virén, him from gold. Two seconds on paper, but it was a crushing defeat in real time. The thought of having to do this all over again for the next four years was an unbearable, overwhelming thought. "If I can keep up my interest in track and field and find a job that allows me to stay in Eugene and train, then I'll win the gold medal in Montreal. They were better than me today, but the race didn't hurt my confidence. It just wasn't my day, but I had nothing to be ashamed of."

PRIOR TO THE Olympics, Steve had decided to take off the 1972 cross-country season of his senior year at the University of Oregon. He had run a savage campaign, and he needed the rest physically and mentally. He had made the mistake in the past of not giving his mind and body rest. In the fall of 1972, he took the time he needed. As a result, he had extra time on his hands, so he bartended at the Paddock to earn money to pay his parents the $1,000 he borrowed for a caravan. The Pad was Steve's favorite watering hole, so he combined work with play.

"Relief is just a swallow away, at the nearest beer parlor," wrote Charles Maher of the *Los Angeles Times*. Steve made no secret that beer was an integral part of his life, his training, even his livelihood at the Paddock. At his relatively young age, he had been drinking beer for "many, many years." One time, when Steve complained about keeping his weight down, a friend said, "Stop drinking beer." Steve replied, "I'd just as soon stop breathing."

The Paddock, down on the Amazon Parkway, looked more like a fallout shelter from the outside. Locals frequented the tavern, as did University of

Oregon athletes. They played pool, Pong, or air hockey. It was off campus, but not that far. The Pad was dimly lit and when you entered the bar, Pong was immediately to the right. Tables and lounge chairs lined the perimeter. Thirty or so feet inside was the bar. The floor was carpeted, stained with spillage. "A good place to drink really cheap beer," Pete Shmock, a former U of O shot-putter said. Georgia Pope, a server there and a friend of Steve's, said, "It was a red-type carpet. Oh, it was gross. I can't believe I used to get on the floor and search for money."

Shmock was not only on the same track team as Steve, but the same beer drinking team at the Paddock. "We won often," he said. Four guys lined up on one side of a table and the other four lined up opposite. Steve was the anchor leg. He might not have had a kick on the racetrack, but he was the closer in beer relays. "He had one of those unusual gifts, which was he could open his epiglottis and didn't have to chug. He just opened up and threw the beer down. Needless to say we won a lot of beer drinking contests [over the years]. Pre was a badass and came through in the end," Shmock said. "It made me gag to watch," Craig Blackman, a sprinter and teammate, recalled. "He could just open his throat." "If you were at the tavern before a game, he could out-drink anyone and he guzzled a pitcher faster than anybody else," Harvey Winn, U of O's backup quarterback to Dan Fouts, said. "He could party with the best of them. He'd be shit-faced at two o'clock in the morning and at six o'clock he'd be running on the streets."

That he chose to party like this after his return from Munich was not entirely surprising. Despite his devotion to training, Steve had been a partier from the moment he stepped on the Oregon campus, once staying up past closing time drinking beer by the pitcher at the Cooler, then projectile vomiting the following morning while running fartleks at Hayward Field. By 1975, when Steve owned his own house, he installed a crude keg-o-rater because he couldn't be bothered with returning dozens of empties, Oregon being the first state in the Union charging a deposit. Beer was in his blood.

The cheap beer would be enough to satisfy the college student, but talk to anyone from that time and Aunt Bea, the cook at the Pad, was the star they flocked to. She was soft spoken, a little roly-poly with a white bun tightly balled atop her head. She loved the athletes like they were her own children. "We have this person who's going to take care of us," Blackman said. She would make anything for anyone to whatever specs they desired. Her Reuben sandwiches and burgers were the stuff of legend, as were the onion rings. "The best burgers and fries in town," Vince Buford, a sprinter on the team, said. "Aunt Bea, my God, she loved when that group of athletes came in. It seemed to be something special when the track guys came in. We huddled around her, we gave her hugs and she was still inside the window trying to cook the burgers."

And, of course, "Pre was her favorite," Doug Chapman, a sprinter at U of O, remembered. Blackman added, "Steve was her baby. 'Get the hell out of the way! Step aside, step aside!'"

"That was a big competition with Bea," Pope said. "But, see, it all depended on the season." Fouts, Hall of Fame NFL quarterback and the quarterback for the Ducks at the time, took issue with Steve being Aunt Bea's favorite. "*I* was her favorite," he said. "The first time I met her, the first day I was working there, we closed together. I was driving home, and she was in front of me. She hit the curb and lost the hubcap. I stopped, got the hubcap, brought her home, and put the hubcap back on her car. From that moment on, she said I was her favorite. So there you go."

Steve was a draw, too, when he was bartending. Everyone wanted a piece of Oregon's favorite son. Winn often bartended with Steve . . . sort of. "He had to take a break every time a girl he was dating came in," Winn said. "He had to take a fifteen-minute break at least to go talk to them. He left us hanging out to dry because he was always talking to chicks. You had to work your ass off because he had too many girls coming in to see him. He was a chick magnet. They couldn't get enough of him."

In the moments when he might not hop the bar to meet a girl, he said, "I like sitting behind the bar and talking to people. Very relaxing."

Bowerman and Dellinger recommended beer to their athletes. "Well maybe not as much as I put away sometimes, but beer is very relaxing," Steve said. He considered it good, like after the Olympics when he went out with David Bedford for not just "regimen drinking; it was serious drinking. . . . I think it's good, especially in the spring and summer after you've gone out and lost five or six pounds, to be able to sit down with the guys you ran with and have a nice cold beer. It's much better for you than a soft drink. Beer has some natural things in it, like salts and stuff that can replenish the salts you burn up."

But in the fall of 1972, Steve wasn't rebounding—this was something else. Whether by design or not, Steve was largely invisible following the Olympics. It could be that he was tired of the circus surrounding him and he actively avoided attention. There wasn't a race on the calendar to shift his focus. People close to him found him moody, "hopping from emotion to emotion," and he began "partying and drinking much more than he used to."

Amidst such turmoil, Steve returned to Coos Bay on September 30, 1972, for a meet-and-greet at the Bay Area Athletic Supply on 163 No. 2nd Street. Free door prizes! Fifteen "Go Pre" sweatshirts. He wasn't the conquering hero he had hoped to be, but he put on a brave face for the people who revered him. Children turned out for autographs with the chance of winning one of those sweatshirts. Coos Bay mayor Wendell Pynch presented Steve with a key to the city, two commendations from the Coos Bay City Council, and a "Prefontaine Way" street sign. Later that night, there would be a banquet in his honor at the Timber Inn.

Steve wore the mask of someone happy with himself and content, but he was beaten down and broken.

"He was crushed," Steve Bence, a friend and former teammate recalled. "Sometimes I tell people that you don't have a weakness you need to work on, you're overusing some of your strengths. That's what I saw in Pre. That event forced him to come down a bit to Earth."

Steve, at last, met the limit for what his candor could bring. Dating back to his days as a cub runner for his high school team, he talked a big game, but he had always backed it up. Intimidation, sure, but it was just as likely a means of personal accountability. But now he felt he had failed. Where there had been unassailable confidence, now doubt existed. At twenty-one years old, fourth best in the world, a quarter-life crisis.

According to Gerry Lindgren, Steve, "was very depressed. He talked of suicide, said he wanted to go out while he was on top. I told him his best years would come AFTER he couldn't race . . . He was COURAGEOUS. From the starting gun until the finishing tape he raced. He made everyone race. He could be beaten, but you had to race him every step of the way." Other peers of Steve said, yeah, sure, he was bothered by the race, but he was already learning from it and charting a course that would land him on the podium. His emotions would swing from revenge to futility. Four years was so far away.

Steve reached a point where he again questioned the utility of it all. It was something of a pattern by now: he'd leave for Europe and return shaken, unmotivated, burned out. It could be that facing his most difficult competition during a time on the calendar when his tires had lost their tread extinguished whatever fire he had. Mark Feig, a former teammate, remembered how depressed Steve was. "When he came back from Munich, he was devastated. He was like, 'I'm gonna quit. I don't want to do this anymore. It's not worth it.' We're like, 'You're not done. You lost. You got fourth. It was a gutsy effort. In '76, you're gonna win.' He said, 'Gosh, that's so far away.'" Even when the going was good, he often asked himself if it was worth it. He was talking about the pain during a race; but of the pain afterward, the pain that lingered unresolved after a disappointing race, he said precious little.

His cousin, Ray Arndt, saw Steve not as a runner, not as a media darling, not as "Pre," but as a young man trying to find his footing. Arndt saw the degree to which Steve suffered disappointment. "He would go into depression. . . . When he came back [from Munich] a lot of his so-called fans ignored him, disowned him."

When Steve returned to his trailer, he saw the mountain of newspapers that Tyson had saved, someone who definitely did not abandon Steve. Tyson knew not to prod about the race or his future. He left Steve alone. Steve never talked about the race, nor did Tyson ask about it.

As the weeks and months passed, Tyson noticed a sense of joviality from Steve. Maybe with everything behind him, he felt lighter and could slip into a relative degree of anonymity. He seemed more mature, more clear-eyed. He went to the dog pound and adopted a six-month-old German shepherd/ Doberman pinscher mix and named him Lobo. Lobo ran with Steve, a willing companion, the first dog Steve ever had. Tyson said, "He started training the dog and maybe there's a little metaphor there about the dog doesn't care what place you got."

Arndt saw the ups and downs of Steve's moods, too. Arndt was never one to fawn over Steve; he wanted to know what was happening below the surface; how was Steve, not Pre. "Not once did I ever go to a track meet and then run down to the field and pick him up and give him accolades about being the greatest thing since apple pie and Chevrolet," he said. He'd meet him at the Paddock Tavern, or maybe they'd run into each other in Coos Bay. Away from the circus, "Basically all I did, all I wanted to do was tell him, 'You did really well. How are you feeling?' And a lot of times he would tell me to shut up and say, 'I don't want to talk about my feelings.' And that was a true message to me because when somebody doesn't want to talk about their feelings, they're usually trying to cover up something. He had a lot of issues that he buried because my cousin learned how to be tough from the get-go. Who likes to be strapped by their dad?"

Arndt might get on his motorcycle and find Steve at the Paddock. After the Olympics, Arndt deduced that Steve never got "un-depressed," that perhaps he needed professional help. Steve was so far ahead of his time in terms of sports psychology: visualization, goal setting, trash talk. His rigid sense of toughness forged by his upbringing precluded his ability to seek a trained ear and work through his depression, the softer things. The loss in the Olympics challenged his very sense of self.

Athletes today—be it Simone Biles or Naomi Osaka—have evolved to remove themselves from competition for the purposes of mental health, the ultimate sign of strength. Instead, with little awareness given to headspace, Steve self-medicated, hid in public, put on the mask. But Arndt wanted to do his best to extricate Steve from the spotlight, so he'd take him to biker bars around town. Arndt wasn't into the Hell's Angels, fighting, or crank, but he found these bars more real, more, in his words, "human." Arndt said, "Let's play pool. Let's forget about who you are. You're not a runner. You're not famous. Just be yourself." They'd get drunk, and laugh, and talk. "I didn't spend a lot of time being his fan. I tried to be his cousin who cared about him for the short life he had," he said.

Steve's future, at least for now, felt uncertain, aimless, and drifting. "I'm kind of floating along," Steve said. "I don't have any goals."

The words were jarring, showing the dire nature of his state more clearly than anything else. All Steve had ever thought about were goals: a time, an American record, a championship, a medal. From September through October 1972, Steve didn't do much at all. Sure, he ran six or seven miles a day, gained a bit of weight, played with his dog, drank. The running was more out of habit than anything. Seeking company, he visited Dellinger in his office on campus. Steve asked if he wouldn't mind going out for a four-mile run. There was more bounce in Steve's steps. The four-mile run turned into a nine-miler and all Steve talked about the whole way was how he was going to run in the Montreal Olympics in four years. At that point, once the miles crept above four, Dellinger figured Steve had at least to some extent metabolized what had been his most public failure and was looking forward instead of backward.

The residue of the attacks and what was, to him, an Olympic failure, would never fully wash away. He would tell a reporter in 1974, "I couldn't take it. I'm a very sensitive person. I react. It took me a year to get over the Israeli thing. A full year." But in late 1972, after a few months passed, he was ready to honor his commitments to his school, to Bowerman, to Pre's People. No, he wasn't over the Olympics. That would take more time. He was greatly humbled, which would prove formative in the ensuing years. There was a new world ahead of him, borne of new experiences that would usher in a new way of thinking, a new way of showing up, not just on the track, but off, for there was so much more to living than running. His brazenness had gotten him to a point and upon reflection it didn't lift him to the medal stand. He was prepared to look outward as well as inward, to serve others while leveraging the full force of his personality and celebrity. From his vantage point, with clear eyes and perhaps a greater sense of purpose, the best was yet to come. For now, at least, he lifted his chin and aimed his gaze at what lay ahead.

CHAPTER 13

REBUILT

STEVE PREFONTAINE WASN'T the only Oregonian who came home from the Olympics dejected. Bowerman, too, returned from Munich lacking his usual resolve. Kenny Moore noticed Bowerman was "exhausted and discouraged." Phil Knight drove to Eugene to see Bowerman and thought he looked like he hadn't slept in decades. Bowerman told Knight, as they overlooked the McKenzie River, that the 1972 Olympics was the nadir of his life. Knight had never seen Bowerman look defeated before, but that's what he saw sitting before him.

It should have been the greatest honor of his storied coaching career—leading the American track contingent in Munich—but he had become more of an administrator, not a coach. He knew on paper it was a great honor, but still he was "disappointed I took the job." Bowerman was peer-pressured into accepting it, was told by Yale University track coach (and a former Olympic team head coach) Bob Giegengack, that Bowerman owed it to his country and to track and field. Bowerman added, "Friends in Eugene said I owed it to my state and to the University of Oregon." Instead of coaching, Bowerman was tangled in red tape, like how many toothbrushes or pairs of track shorts his team needed, waiting for the team's track gear to arrive in Germany (far too late), and dealing without "toilet articles" for an entire week. In the end, Bowerman said, "Really, I've failed. Where have I succeeded?"

Back in Oregon, Bowerman thought about his future. The decision was as easy as it was abrupt: prior to the start of the 1973 track season, without warning, after twenty-five years, at the age of sixty-two, Bowerman "suddenly, dramatically, unexpectedly, conclusively," retired as the Oregon Ducks track-and-field coach, with Bill Dellinger succeeding.

Bowerman wasn't going anywhere and wasn't about to fade into the background, though. The West Stands at Hayward Field were no longer up to code, no longer "patchable," according to the city of Eugene fire marshal. The stomping, the "demanding crowd," as Bowerman called them, had rendered those beleaguered benches unsafe. If Oregon ever wanted to host a major track meet again on the level of the Olympic Trials, they would need to be torn down and replaced. It could be that Bowerman looked on those West Stands and saw something of himself: worn down, in need of replacing. It gave him renewed purpose: "My last and best contribution I can give the University of Oregon is to put all my energies into getting a facility for the athletes, students, and community." The university lacked the funds to rebuild them. The money would have to be raised, and there were few better than Bowerman to rally the community around its treasure. He figured it impossible to fundraise and coach to the fullest of his abilities. As the saying goes, it was better to whole-ass one thing than half-ass two.

He was as busy as ever with the $600,000 fundraising project for the grandstands, while also developing the waffle outsole—and the Waffle Trainer—that would soon become one of Nike's greatest and most iconic products.

The retirement of Bowerman didn't have much of an effect on Steve, if any. Steve could always seek Bowerman's counsel on campus, on the phone, or at Bowerman's house up the McKenzie River where he once posed for the cover of *Sports Illustrated*. Dellinger had drawn up most of Steve's workouts anyway, and Bowerman would always keep a close eye on Steve.

Steve's return to competition after nearly five months away was the two-mile at the Sunkist Indoor in Los Angeles. Lasse Virén, the Olympic 5,000- and 10,000-meter champion, was in town, but he was experiencing stomach problems. Steve was also having his own problems. Once he committed to a spirited return to track, he had ramped up his training too fast and his knee was bothering him. This race would be a test as to whether he would run this year or not.

On January 19, 1973, Steve was smashing, winning the two-mile in 8:27.4, a meet and arena record just 1.2 seconds off the American record. It disappointed Steve that Virén, who finished last, wasn't in top form due to illness. The win over Virén was cheapened and didn't feel wholly deserved, a hollow redemption. On the flip side, it appeared Steve's knee wouldn't be an issue. The crowd roared for Steve. He was, in his words, "self-satisfied because it's the motivational factor I've needed since the Olympics." He then said, "If I had run 8:50 and finished third I would have walked out of this place and never run another track meet in my life."

Steve next won the mile at the L.A. Times Indoor meet against Marty Liquori, then the country's best miler, himself making a comeback from injury. Steve blew away the field all while leading from the front. He was the only runner in this race to break four minutes.

After the race and wearing a maroon track jacket with stripes down the side, he was seated in the crowd and was approached by commentator Adrian Metcalfe, who asked, "Was it a tactical plan to go out from the front?"

"Well, I think everybody knew my plan. For me to win a race against competition of that nature I have to go out hard and just about lead from the start. The runners in that field are all runners that hang on and then outkick you at the last. My tactic was just to go strong and run the first three-quarters of a mile hard and then just hang on the last quarter."

"You didn't seem to be hanging on. It seemed like you could have gone about three more laps."

Steve laughed, "I could have maybe gone *one* more lap," as he leaned in toward Metcalfe, "but I don't know about three more." He laughed again.

"Does it give you a thrill as a long-distance runner to come and beat the milers at their own game?"

"Yeah, you might say that. I wish I could beat some of the *three milers* at their own game," Steve said with another big laugh, leaning in again with his signature warmth.

This self-mocking tone was a big departure from the bravado that had long defined him before the Olympics, and it spoke to bigger shifts within him. The Olympics were a great educator. The race itself, yes, but the killing of the athletes appeared to reorient his sense of meaning, maybe even his

place in the world as something of a greater ambassador, equal parts intro-
spective and extroverted. His brazenness had taken him as far as it could. As
Steve Bence said, later recounting Steve prior to the Olympics, "Pre was so
sure of himself that he was cocky. When he got knocked down, he had to pull
himself back up. I don't think people called him cocky after [the Olympics]."

In mid-April 1973 at Hayward Field, as Steve marched toward the end
of the collegiate outdoor season, he ran what was considered, at the time,
to be the best double in the history of track and field: a mile in 3:56.8
and running back in the three in 13:06.4. After the mile, Steve put his arm
around underclassman Scott Daggatt, one of the swifter milers on the team.
Daggatt looked a little goofy with his large glasses and floppy hair. He was
far more into music than athletics and most of his friends were hippies, not
jocks.

In 1971, Daggatt was still in high school and he wanted to attend Oregon
to see just how good of a miler he could be. He attended a meet specifically
to speak to some Oregon runners. Daggatt saw someone wearing dark sun-
glasses in the stands, all by himself. Daggatt approached him and asked, "Are
you Steve Prefontaine?"

"No, no I'm not," he said.

"Oh, well, that's okay. I see that you're an Oregon runner and I don't care
who I talk to. I'm interested in going to the school."

"Oh, yeah, I'm Steve Prefontaine," he said. And he shared his thoughts
about the school, that it was the place to go if you wanted to be a great
runner. Steve introduced Daggatt to Bowerman. Daggatt remembered Steve
being nice, conversational. Daggatt would later walk on to the team and be
on full scholarship by his sophomore year. He proved to be a quality miler
and one of the few runners on the team who could keep pace with Steve in
workouts and push Steve to his limits, one of the few runners, according to a
peer, who scared Steve. Daggatt recalled, "I didn't run the races Prefontaine
did, but the point is I could work out with Pre, and he liked that."

The double took a lot of starch out of Steve and he did the previously un-
thinkable: he took a week off from competing and would skip the next meet
in Pullman, Washington. He saved his energy—and dealt with a pinched
nerve in his back—for Pac-8s and the annual spring Twilight Meet, where

Dellinger touted as many as five or six guys who might break four with a dozen under 4:07. It would be Steve's fourth Twilight Mile. He lost to Roscoe Divine in 1970, lost to Arne Kvalheim in 1971; but finally won a Twilighter in 1972, which set the table for his final one as a senior. Dellinger wanted to see Daggatt lead the first lap in 59 seconds, Todd Lathers take over the second lap in 60 seconds, Steve command the third in a total of three minutes to that point in the race, with the fourth lap "Up for grabs."

On a chilly night, 46 degrees with a ripping wind, Steve twice approached Dellinger and said his legs were "dead," still reeling from that mile/three-mile double. Steve didn't want to run. His back was nagging him, too.

"Look at all those people," Dellinger said, pointing to the stands, some 6,000 people all bundled up, puffs of breath in the air. "They came to see you run." Such urging was all Steve needed to hear. In Steve's defense, if his body was telling him he was cooked, then his coach should not have guilt-tripped him into running in the exhibition Twilight Meet. Knowing the burnout Steve had experienced in the past, this was, to put it mildly, questionable coaching on Dellinger's part. But there they were: "Pre's People" had turned out. They always turned out. Steve warmed up.

With the temperatures dropping and a near-freezing windchill, Daggatt rabbited a 57-second lap, two seconds faster than planned. Lathers was supposed to command the second lap, but his lap was lacking, so Steve took charge with Knut Kvalheim—Arne's younger brother—drafting behind Steve in a half-mile time of 1:58, then three-quarters in 2:58. Kvalheim was breathing down Steve's neck.

Steve showed them the meaning of haste.

When he hit the tape, he did a double take at the scoreboard to make sure the time was right: 3:55.0. The fastest mile in U of O history, run in Nike spikes with the signature swoosh. As Phil Knight wrote in *Shoe Dog*, "Bowerman finally had [Pre] wearing our shoes." Steve had long worn Adidas spikes in competition, even through the Olympics. But as Nike leaned into the development of its own line of trainers and spikes, the models became more and more to Steve's liking. By the spring of 1973, as Knight wrote, "our shoes were finally worthy of Pre. It was a perfect symbolic match. He was generating thousands of dollars of publicity, making our brand a symbol of rebellion and iconoclasm—and we were helping his recovery [from the Olympics]." And recover he did. Roughly nine months past Munich, Steve was in the throes of his usual dominance. He was nearly a year closer to Montreal. Steve was back on the path and by all accounts stronger than ever before.

Just a few weeks later, on May 17, 1973, no doubt a result of Steve setting a blistering time in Nike spikes, his likeness was allegedly used in promotional materials in Europe. Bowerman, none too pleased with Knight, his Nike cofounder and former athlete, wrote: "Dear Mr. Knight: I have been advised that you used a picture of Steve Prefontaine in some material that you sent out advertising Nike shoes. I am aware that some of the German, Swedish and other foreign manufacturers and their sales representatives have used pictures of world-class athletes in their advertising and claims. While I have given you designs that I have innovated, at no time did I give you permission to use any athlete's name or picture in your sales promotion. It will be necessary for me to be in communication not only with the NCAA but, also, with the Amateur Athletic Union, advising them of what may be an infringement on the privacy and the rights of this young man. Violations by other producers are not, in my opinion, a license for any of our athletes or myself to follow a similar course. While we do like your product, we cannot make any kind of endorsement. I hope you understand."

Bowerman's language in this letter was impersonal (treating Knight not as a colleague and former athlete but as some distant third party) and bizarre: Nike products were ostensibly Bowerman's products, certainly whatever appeared on Steve's feet, the most important feet this side of Michael Jordan Nike ever shod. Yet despite their professional and personal connections, Bowerman and Knight had a relationship that was forever coach and athlete. They were never chummy, and the nearly thirty-year gap in age between Nike cofounders assured it would always be more father-and-son, coach-and-athlete—never as brothers. Bowerman had insisted early on in their partnership that Knight have a controlling interest in their venture, from Blue Ribbon Sports to Nike. Bowerman was never shy to voice his concerns; he wasn't in the shoe business for world domination. But he drew a strong line as it related to his Oregon Tiger in Steve Prefontaine.

With amateurism still reigning in track and field, shoe advertisements never featured an athlete, as that would be a violation of the amateur code and would threaten their status as amateur athletes. Here, Steve had no say, and his name, image, and likeness were used without his or Bowerman's knowledge. Some fifty years later, college athletes sought to leverage their own likenesses for personal gain, seeing as throughout collegiate history, colleges and universities, not to mention TV networks, raked in billions of dollars a year while the athletes got, at most, a college scholarship. As college sports became big business, you saw the "buying" of top-rated recruits primarily in football and basketball, but rarely, if ever, track and field. But in the 1970s, for perhaps the very first time in college track and field, a shoe company had sought to use the premier athlete of the day to bring heightened awareness to its latest line of competitive footwear.

Nike was all too eager to forefront its footwear on the most popular distance runner in the land. Though Nike put out football, basketball, and tennis shoes, the company was, first and foremost, a running-shoe company—its DNA was running. It could barely wait to slap the swoosh on Steve's feet for the world to see. Bowerman was right to call out Knight for threatening Steve's amateur status. The AAU had proved ruthless in denying an athlete eligibility (see Wes Santee) and could have rendered Steve a professional, and thus his Olympic redemption and dream could have ended right there in 1973.

It never came to that, though, and that sizzling mile time kept Steve occupied about Ryun's world record of 3:51.1, or Belgium's Emiel Putteman's three-mile record of 12:47.8. Like anyone at that age when there was more time in front than behind, anything seemed within reach.

STEVE SKIPPED THE Northern Division meet and flirted with skipping Pac-8s. His back was screaming. Dellinger said, "Pre is in pain." They'd wait and see how quickly it healed, if it healed. They thought it was a muscle pull and that heat would fix it. But it got worse and he couldn't log his Sunday run. Up until 1973, Steve was freakishly durable. He had the cut on his foot ahead of the 1970 NCAA championships, and he got the occasional head cold, but just about everyone living in Eugene got sick during the wet winters and springs, Oregon crud as it's called. Now Steve was under doctors' orders to go light and take his medicine. Jogging was painful and Pac-8s—at Hayward Field, competing in his final track meet before his people *as an Oregon Duck*—seemed doubtful, according to Steve's doctor. With extra rest and medicine, Steve would be sure to perform for his people.

On May 20, 1973, it would end: Steve's final collegiate race at Hayward Field. It wouldn't be his final race ever at Hayward, but it was still the end of something that began when he ran (and lost) on the Hayward cinders in the summer of 1968 as a soon-to-be high school senior, all the way through to the current day. Gone was the cherubic face of a young man on the cover of *Sports Illustrated*. In its place was a man with hair down over his nape, his sideburns turning to chops, and the mustache giving him the swashbuckling look of Wyatt Earp. While in full drive, and his hair blowing back, you could see the hints of a receding hairline. Even at the age of twenty-two, he looked older, and his body, too, had begun to chip and crack. That wasn't to say he was slowing down. If anything, he was better than ever, surer of himself though more understated. In a word, mature.

Eugene mayor Les Anderson—father of Jon Anderson, who, on Patriots Day 1973, won the Boston Marathon—said, "Pre penetrates the track and into the crowd. Some athletes win a race and afterward they're poker-faced. Pre's expression is, 'You helped me win it.'"

During his final three-mile as an Oregon Duck at Hayward Field, this for the Pac-8 championships, Steve's back was, indeed, bothering him. Nevertheless, he wanted to do something special for the fans—11,000 people came to see this final chapter. Ideally, he would have doubled in the mile and the three, but his body wouldn't allow it. The Kenyan John Ngeno from Washington State University was Steve's chief rival in the three. Throughout the race, Steve limped, winced, groaned, moaned, and grunted his way to the front of the field one last time in Oregon yellow, to make it seem like he was hurting more than he was, playing mind games. He had never resorted to theatrics in the past. Finally, Steve quit the mind games and eventually built a 50-yard lead down the stretch. The fans cheered, "Go, Pre!" again and again. He looked up into the crowd and a lot of races went through his mind, almost like a slideshow. His final three-mile as a Duck went in 13:10.4.

He never lost a collegiate track race (Twilight Meet races were exhibitions) at Hayward Field. Wendy Ray, from his usual perch up high in the Hayward Field broadcast booth, called out, "Thanks for the good times, Pre."

After the race, Steve was momentarily melancholic. *Sports Illustrated* called it a "suitably happy ending to a long love affair." Steve wasn't leaving them for good. This would always be his home, but no matter how many more times he would run at Hayward Field—hopefully through the entire decade of the 1970s—it was the end of his college outdoor track career, the one that made him more than a runner: a bonified star. Steve turned to the stands and put up one finger and raised it high. "They've given me a lot and I hope I've given them a lot in the last four years. But time goes and you've got to go with it," Steve said.

THE HEAT AND humidity were stifling. It was June 1973, and Steve was in Baton Rouge, Louisiana, for the NCAA championships. Like any meet on location, there was more downtime than anything. Steve grabbed his camera, sophomore Mark Feig, and rented a car.

Feig grew up in Eugene and watched all the great Oregon milers. He saw himself as one of them one day. As Feig grew to know Steve, he always saw him as a big brother. Steve, likewise, embraced the role of elder statesman, similar to when he was a cub in 1969 and 1970 and the likes of Jere Van Dyk and Kenny Moore offered him mentorship when his eyes were wide as golf balls. Steve and Feig connected because they were homegrown. The insular community of runners born and raised in Oregon set them apart from the transplants. Coming out of South Eugene High School, Feig was the best high school miler in the country, not unlike Steve a few years back. He never quite lived up to the billing, but by 1973, Feig had come so very close to breaking four minutes, within just four tenths in the 1973 Twilight Mile, that it finally gave him confidence that soon he could do it. "Steve never told me what to do in a race," Feig recalled. "You just run your best race, which is kind of cool that he wasn't trying to guide me that much. It was more, 'Let's just go hang out or go have a beer.'"

But this day down by the bayou, with the windows down, they drove out into the countryside where Steve eventually pulled the car over. He saw flowers he thought were beautiful and took out his camera and snapped a few photographs, a relaxing pastime divorced from the rigors of running. It allowed him to look inward, and maybe he grew more comfortable not broadcasting to the world his feelings and intentions. Steve built a darkroom outside his trailer and developed his own photographs.

Ahead of the NCAAs in June 1973, Steve had decided it was best to keep his cards close to the chest. "A football coach doesn't tell you what plays he's going to run. I might run the last mile in under four minutes, or I might run the last 440 yards in 51 seconds." Why should he tell them what he's "going to put in the cake"? After Munich, he'd learned his lesson, somewhat, that he didn't have to be so publicly forthright with his intentions. Steve had previously worn his racing on his sleeve but was more content, of late, to let his racing do the talking. But he was far from reticent. He placated the media after he won his preliminary heat in an NCAA record time for the three-mile where he raced, of all places, in the back of the pack through the "early part of the race." He hated it. Too much pushing and shoving. "I almost decided to punch out a few guys' lights . . . but I didn't."

Come Saturday, Steve would be running in his final track-and-field meet as a Duck. It was three years before that he nursed his right foot to relative health after that pool incident. Steve was bursting out of his skin trying to make sure he raced, injury be damned. These days, he gave way to a more easygoing assuredness, a surrendering to the conditions, that even *he* couldn't bend the arc of the universe to his will. "I might get up Saturday morning feeling bad and finish fifth or sixth. That's what racing is all about." It is hard to imagine him saying such a thing before the Olympics. He was, as one writer said, "the voluble Oregonian," but has since "mellowed with an Olympics-worth of maturity."

On Saturday, June 9, 1973—the same day the great racehorse Secretariat ran to a Prefontaine-esque 31-length win in the Belmont Stakes to win the Triple Crown—Steve finished his college track career undefeated as he won the three-mile. Steve had made it look laughably easy, closing out his career as the only runner to win four consecutive NCAA titles at three miles (he benefited from being in the first enrolling class that allowed freshmen to compete on varsity). Steve had done something no other runner had done, which gave him a "warm feeling."

With his singlet untucked (and eventually cast off altogether) and barefoot, Steve jogged a victory lap around the stadium. The scoreboard listed the top five three-mile results from the schools. MANH for Manhattan College (fifth); W. ST for Washington State (fourth); back-to-back COLOs for Colorado (third and second); and, atop the list not OREG for Oregon, but PRE, 13:05.3.

WITH STEVE'S OUTDOOR college track-and-field career over (he would have one more redshirt semester in the fall of 1973 at Oregon to run cross-country), he had to consider what post-collegiate running looked like for him. He would remain an amateur, but he had the wherewithal to know he was an attraction and that he had leverage. With the right degree of savvy—or redirecting the brashness he had historically reserved for his rivals toward the Amateur Athletic Union—he was testing the limits of amateur racing as it was currently structured. He planned on breaking new trail, which was something athletes did not do back then. Everyone else merely got in line and dealt with the necessary evil that was the amateur system.

A week after NCAA championships, on June 16, 1973, after having initially balked at going to Bakersfield for the three-day AAU championships, Steve came within .4 seconds of breaking the American three-mile record in a time of 12:53.4. He was playing a game of chicken with the AAU. Steve thought its draconian authority over where and when an athlete could run was deeply un-American, this from an institution that purportedly gave the athlete full freedom to pick and choose. Steve had every intention of running in Europe under his own banner on his own time and dime, not the AAU's, a declaration of independence. "I've run five years for my country on a team. Now I want to run for me." Still, by running in the AAU championships, Steve was throwing the AAU a bone. In return, Steve hoped for a travel permit from the AAU.

He wanted to travel on his own schedule and run against those he deemed worthy. Even make some money under the table. Steve began to realize that he and his peers had more power than they realized. "If the athletes don't take the initiative in this, who will? We know the AAU and the American Olympic Committee won't. I hate to sound critical, but to me the AAU is just a bunch of old men taking medication so they can stay alive for another four years to hassle us. Right now I'm being hassled. I don't need it, really."

The real question would be if Steve would race in the Restoration Meet at Hayward Field scheduled for June 20, 1973, another exhibition meet— just like the Twilight Meets—to raise money for renovations. The West Stands were dilapidated and held together with spit and prayer. Bowerman was still spearheading the fundraising, and he had a headliner in Steve that could draw people out, the proceeds going into the Hayward Field coffers. Steve and 1972 800-meter gold medalist Dave Wottle were supposed to leave for Europe on June 19. While in Bakersfield, Steve hatched an idea. Steve knew Dave Wottle was going to Europe with him. "Hey, why don't you just come up to Eugene in a couple of days. They're trying to raise money to restore the stadium. We'll go after the world record in the mile. I'll bring you through in 2:56 for three-quarters."

Wottle had an apocalyptic kick. It was how he won his gold medal in Munich. *Steve Prefontaine willing to be a rabbit? Why not?* Steve knew Wottle was the superior miler and Steve figured that the pair of them could team up for a special headlining event. Here, Steve was willing to sacrifice himself. He couldn't expect to win, but he knew his star power combined with Wottle's kick might break Jim Ryun's long-standing world record . . . and raise a lot of money for Hayward Field.

The pair were stark opposites. Wottle was tall, pale as a sheet, ran with a golf cap. He raced no longer than the mile and saved his energy for the end. He was soft-spoken, even bashful. Steve was shorter and would never cover that glorious mane of hair; he led from the front, muttonchops and dark mustache. Steve was also soft-spoken, but he carried a heavy fist. Wottle was more shy and didn't socialize much; though Steve appreciated the quieter moments, he was just as comfortable being the center of attention. Wottle never drank. Steve made a sport of it.

Dave Wottle was the NCAA mile champion, but he had never run faster than 3:57. Steve, to his credit, had run 3:55 earlier in the year in blustery conditions, call it the Hayward magic. Deep down Wottle knew he needed a better mile time if he was going to tell people the mile, and not the 800 meters, was his best event. Wottle had always wanted to run against Steve, and if that were to happen Steve would have to drop down and set the pace. "I know his plan; he'll try to take me out and break me early," Wottle said. How close they got to that world record depended on Steve. He would sell out for Wottle, for Hayward Field.

The day could not have been better, on the eve of summer, balmy and windless. Wearing a "Nike" track-and-field T-shirt and Nike trainers, Steve checked in with a clerk shortly before his event was set to go. The stands were flush with 12,000 people. Wottle, who had just been commissioned as a second lieutenant in the Air Force Reserves, had been tabbed to run in the Air Force colors instead of his usual Bowling Green University kit. While in Eugene, a captain for the Air Force gave Wottle his uniform. Wottle wanted to focus on the race, and he wasn't sure if he was supposed to be saluting or calling him sir or not. Eventually and unceremoniously, Wottle slipped away to warm up. The plan was simple: stay with Steve. Steve said he was going to pull them through in 2:56. His gift to Wottle. Wottle thought, *Pre's the best rabbit you can have, except he's the type of rabbit who usually wins.*

Wottle was feeling good. He had slept ten hours the night before and logged an easy two-mile morning run. As race time neared, he jogged two-and-a-half miles as the stands swelled to the brim, hip to hip. The last time Wottle raced at Hayward Field was the Olympic Trials a year before. After he tied the world record in winning the 800 meters, he went across the street to McDonald's and treated himself to a Big Mac meal. He wasn't much for ceremony or theatrics. And when he was called to the starting line for the "Super Mile," the people screamed and Wottle began to tingle. Then he heard the screams for Steve.

Whoa.

The race went off and just like Steve told Wottle, he paced him through three-quarters of a mile in 2:56, Steve hugging the inside lane and Wottle coasting to the outside of Steve's right shoulder. Wottle had never gone faster than 3:01 for three-quarters. Steve's legs felt heavy and, at this point, he wanted to explode. He had run four three-mile races in 13:20 or below in ten days. The acceleration wasn't there. He had no *snap*. Wottle was told by his Bowling Green coach that his best races would come off a fast pace and right there before him on a platter was about as fast as he'd ever experienced. Steve put the world record in Wottle's sights; all Wottle had to do was take it. Steve rushed by the East Stands with 220 yards to go. Fans knew the book on Wottle and, right on cue, Wottle surged 10 yards clear of Steve.

There would be no catching Wottle, but Steve chased after him not only to keep up with the clock, but to give his people in the rickety West Stands reason to cheer. Maybe the roar would push Wottle past the point of reason, past Ryun. By the time Wottle struck the tape, the time was 3:53.3, the third fastest mile ever. Wottle winced at the finish. Steve finished a few yards behind Wottle and gave his people all that remained, what would be his career best mile, 3:54.6. A little girl screamed, "That's okay, Pre! Don't worry about it!"

Years later, Wottle looked back at this race with a rare pang of regret. So much of his mindset was geared toward winning the race, not the clock. Time was secondary. He never wanted to sell out too soon. "Instead of going for it and laying it all out on the track and say, 'Hey, you know, if I can run a 55-second last lap, I can get a world record,' I was holding back because I was afraid of tightening up down the home stretch. Steve being the strong runner he was, I thought he could beat me. . . . I regret that, truthfully. I regret that he brought me through such a great race and a great time, and I didn't lay it all out there on the track. That's a weakness I had."

Wottle also didn't want to like who he was running against, the better to flog them. He wanted to run angry. And after the race, with the fans still clapping and cheering, Wottle began his victory lap. Steve jogged up beside Wottle and grabbed his arm and raised them together above their heads. Wottle thought, *What are you doing running with me? This is my victory lap.* "How stingy," Wottle remembered. "How stingy of me. Steve was endorsing me to the fans at Hayward Field. He was also saying, 'You did that because of me,' and he was absolutely right."

Ernie Cunliffe, who was the coach for the Air Force working with Wottle, found Steve and told him, "It was a best-of-life for seven [other] guys [in the race] and you made it possible. You set it up for them." Steve often made it possible for others to level up, his gift to them. The few who beat him also ran out of their shoes. Wottle bettered his best time by nearly four full seconds to win this night, the fastest mile ever run at Hayward Field, this in the temple of milers.

Wottle recalled, "If he had not brought me through in 2:56, there's no way I could have run that fast. It was a valuable lesson for me to learn back then. I did reflect on it afterwards thinking, 'No one's on an island. You have a family, you have coaches, you have teammates, you have competitors. All that together is what makes runners achieve their goals.' Steve helped me learn that lesson. I was always grateful for that."

The Restoration Meet was a beautiful illustration of Steve's evolution as a person. He started to see his rivals as peers, even if it meant falling on his sword to lift others up, all to give back to his community, these people, those stands.

After the race, Steve was swarmed by children seeking autographs. He signed them attentively. One of Steve's older fans brandished a bottle of champagne in a paper bag. The fan offered Steve the bag and Steve, appreciatively, took a swig.

CHAPTER 14

GALVANIZED

DAVE WOTTLE BOARDED his plane for Helsinki, Finland, intent on meeting Steve. Wottle figured someone would pick him up. He touched down in Finland, no ride. Steve didn't give Wottle a phone number or information about where they were staying. He walked all over Helsinki to find a cheap place to stay. It was close enough to the stadium so he thought that if he hung out long enough, surely Steve would show up for workouts.

The first day, no Steve. Second, third, nothing. Wottle sat in the stands at the stadium getting angry. There was only so much running a person could do, and he didn't drink, so he couldn't merely pass the time drinking with the locals. Wottle finally saw Steve enter the stadium. Why he was late was anyone's guess. Wottle stormed down and cursed Steve out. What the hell?! You bring me over here! Steve just laughed. Eventually, Wottle cooled off when Steve pulled a pair of shoes out of his bag. They sat down and Steve handed Wottle a pair of spikes: Nike Pre Montreals. A red, white, and blue prototype that Steve planned on using for the 1976 Olympics in Montreal. They were beautiful. Steve said, "You mind wearing these?" Wottle loved them and gave Steve some feedback so he could report back to Bowerman at Nike.

Those Nikes in hand were the key for Steve, for his future. Phil Knight worried about Steve. To save Steve the shame of "going around with a begging bowl," Knight, at the behest of Bowerman, hired Steve to work for Nike. In his memoir *Shoe Dog*, Knight wrote, "In 1973, we gave him a 'job,' a modest salary of five thousand dollars a year . . . We also gave him a business card that said National Director of Public Affairs. People often narrowed their eyes and asked me what that meant. I narrowed my eyes right back. 'It means he can run fast.'" According to Kenny Moore in his book *Bowerman and the Men of Oregon*, Steve's salary was in violation of the AAU rules "against enrichment from sport." There was a loophole: This was merely a job. It just so happened to be a shoe company. How serendipitous.

Up until then, Steve would take under-the-table money by wedging in extra races in Europe (which greatly aggravated his back), or by driving Datsun 240-Zs from southern California north to Portland. But working for Nike under an official sounding title gave him cover for what he really was: a celebrity endorser of Nike shoes.

In a few months from now, in 1974, when Steve would officially graduate from the U of O, he would work for Nike doing outreach in the community, meeting with local high school athletes to teach them about mental toughness and effort. It helped sell shoes. He wasn't an official sponsored athlete, not like Ilie Năstase, the Romanian tennis star Nike was outfitting at the time, but unofficially that's essentially what Steve was. It was a brilliant maneuver that allowed Steve to maintain his amateur status, train, and not have to worry about money the way generations of young track-and-field athletes had in the past. After all, he worked in "public affairs," not as a sponsored athlete. Steve would, along with Geoff Hollister and Jeff Bannister, tour local schools hosting clinics and answer questions from young people . . . and sell shoes. Steve would tell the teenagers, "To give anything less than your best is to sacrifice the gift," sometimes with his shirt off, lying in the grass with dozens of eyes glued on him, a rapt audience of boys who so desperately wanted to be him. Somewhere nearby would be Hollister opening the trunk of his VW pickup van showcasing and selling beautiful pairs of waffle spikes. Here was this Oregon company founded by Oregonians; shoes designed by an Oregonian and modeled by the most popular Oregonian of the day.

Nike was still a fledgling company in 1973 and into 1974, but through timing and coincidence, Nike and Steve interwove together from Nike's founding. Steve embodied the rebellious spirit of early Nike; it was almost as if Nike and Steve were fraternal twins born seconds apart. "Whenever people saw Pre going at his breakneck pace . . . I wanted them to see Nike. And when they bought a pair of Nikes, I wanted them to see Pre," Knight would write.

Breakneck speed happened in fits and starts during Steve's European sojourn during that summer of 1973. In his first few races, Steve finished second in the 1,500 and second in the 5,000, then eleventh in the 1,500 but only 3.5 seconds behind the winner, Filbert Bayi, in a blanket finish. Steve laughed; he felt great with 110 yards to go; he looked up and "there must have been 10,000 people ahead of me." In Helsinki, Steve set the American record in the 5,000 meters (13:22.4) by finishing a spirited second to Emiel Puttemans while also defeating Lasse Virén. Steve finally won a 5,000-meter race, in Oulu, Finland, over the Kenyan Paul Mose in a walk, 13:40.6.

As much as this summer tour was about running some international meets—for Team USA and the AAU and some other boutique meets—it was more about using running as an excuse to travel and be among friends. Besides his job at Nike, Steve could also pocket some under-the-table money. A cohort of runners—Wottle, Steve, Ralph Mann—were staying north of Helsinki at a training camp where Steve posed for a photo with his hands in his pockets, boots, bell bottoms. Mann, who just turned twenty-four, joined Steve in the photograph. That same trip, Steve and Mann posed atop a ski jump overlooking Finland's vibrant evergreens. From high above, the landscape looked like Oregon.

Steve loved the time they spent in Finland, where Jaakko Tuominen hosted them and took them to the lake. Tuominen, a prominent leader in Finnish track and field, a coach, and a friend of Mann's, had arranged for these top-flight Americans to compete, but also to see the beauty of Finland and beyond. While kicking back drinks, Steve picked Tuominen's brain about organizing boutique track meets like the ones he operated in Finland. Steve said he'd like to do that in the United States one day, take the power back from the AAU, break new trail for American track and field.

The Tuominens had a sauna by the dock, and Steve loved nothing more than a good sauna. A wood-burning fireplace created the heat, and all it took was a cool bucket of glacial lake water to steam up the room. At one point, Wottle and Steve bathed in the steam, but it was thinning out. Steve got up and grabbed a bucket of water. He dumped the water then bolted out of the sauna and locked the door from the outside so Wottle couldn't escape. The steam quickly swallowed Wottle. Wottle looked out the window and he screamed at Steve to let him out. He was getting steamed alive like a crab. Steve laughed and laughed. He underestimated how much heat he threw at Wottle, but he didn't care. At last, Steve flipped the lock on the door and ran. Wottle burst out of the sauna yelling, "I'm gonna kick your ass!" Steve, not to be out-kicked this time, jumped in the lake. Wottle stopped at the end of the dock watching Steve tread water. "How is it?" Wottle asked.

"It's fine," Steve said.

Wottle then jumped in and gasped, just about having a heart attack the water was so cold, extinguishing Wottle's fire. "I tell people I don't have any eyebrows because Prefontaine burned them off my head."

Tuominen toured Wottle, Mann, and Steve around the lake in his speedboat. They went water skiing completely naked, with Tuominen trying to make them crash as he whipped the boat, slinging them through the boat's wake. It was a great time, but soon, they needed to head south for other obligations.

Wottle and Steve posed for a photograph while standing in the parking lot in front of the Astoria Restaurant in Leuven, Belgium. Steve wore a T-shirt and jeans, his feet exposed in sandals befitting Woodstock. Soon, returning to the site of Steve's greatest and most public defeat—Munich— Wottle and Steve, wearing AAU USA tracksuits, stood beside each other for another photo, Wottle looking bashful, Steve trying to look tough but unable to keep a straight face. While in Germany, Steve helped Wottle pick out a quality Minolta camera.

Steve, by now, had moved on from Munich in the sense that he didn't dwell on it. He said he didn't think of the Olympics any longer. He thought they were too political. But of course he thought about the Olympics. How could he not when he set foot on that track where, a year before, he was so deep in oxygen debt that he nearly fell over at the finish when Great Britain's Ian Stewart surged past him in the final strides? More accurately, he had moved past the defeat and treated it like a data point.

While racing in Munich, throwing salt in his front-running wounds, was none other than West Germany's Harald Norpoth, now thirty years old, who leeched then outkicked Steve at the finish to win the 5,000 with Steve finishing second. "Anybody but him," Steve said. Steve was disappointed and his back still bothered him. His coaches saw him tightening up. He wanted to step up the pace but . . . couldn't. He wasn't tired but his body had nothing to give. For this brief moment, he lost his fastball.

AAU officials told Steve and Wottle to reconnect with the AAU team for a meet in Italy, but they were dragging their feet and didn't want to be pressured by bureaucrats. Steve said, well, maybe we'll try to get down there if we can. The AAU chewed Steve out. Wottle was always one to do as he was told, but Steve was hellbent on flaunting his independence and wanted to make the AAU sweat. Eventually, Steve and Wottle hired a cab to drive them from Munich to Milan. The fare was obscene, but if the AAU was so desperate for them to be at the meet, it could pay for their fares. AAU officials were furious with Wottle and Steve, and by the time they arrived, the team was eating in the cafeteria. In walked Wottle (against his character) and Steve, defiant, insubordinate. Wottle said, "My chest was all puffed out because here we are in direct violation of the AAU and Pre was, of course, leading the way."

Because of his back pain, and having lost seven of eight races, Steve figured it best to cut his trip short. He thought fondly of those times as he boarded a plane back to Oregon having not run as well as he wanted. He wasn't at his best in Europe, at least from a racing perspective. AAU doctors were no help, so he packed his bags and left, further grist for his growing list of resentments. Steve was upset he didn't get to run in Russia. Without "weapons," he couldn't win. Since he paid his own way, he didn't feel beholden to anyone. Steve likened the trip to a scouting mission, as if he needed more reports. "It will make me a better runner and a better person," he said.

Once he touched down in Eugene, glad to be home, Steve walked with a slight limp. He waved to a reporter and told him that his back continued to nag him. "But it's funny. I've got a good mental outlook. I know I've learned a lot, and I'm looking forward to running next year. I feel so much better than I did last year after the Olympic Games," he said. Next year, 1974, he wouldn't have to contend with the rigors of college meets and he could train toward the European tour schedule, which didn't ramp up until the summer. However, he also would be on his own for the first time and thrust into the world of post-collegiate running, where a runner had to figure it out on his own, where he wouldn't necessarily have coaching at his beck and call. Luckily, Nike had him covered with a steady salary that afforded him the time he needed to train.

For now, Steve planned on swimming, no running. He needed to get well.

TIME PASSED. STEVE gutted out a third and final NCAA cross-country championship over Western Kentucky's Nick Rose in the fall of 1973. Shortly thereafter, he graduated from the University of Oregon with a degree in communications. In the winter of 1974, he ran a few indoor races and of course competed in the Twilight Meet in April, where he set two American records in the same race—six miles in 26:51.8 and 10,000 meters in 27:43.6. As an amateur runner no longer running in college and now competing under the banner of the Oregon Track Club, he was proving to be every bit as powerful on American soil, ready to take on world records. He had his commitments with Nike and he was running upwards of 140 miles per week. He skipped the AAU championships and instead ran in Europe. Wins were sparing, but he was breaking many American records, including the 3,000 meters, the two-mile, and the 5,000 meters. By July 1974, Steve owned a "clean sweep" of all U.S. outdoor distance records from 3,000 meters to 10,000 meters. Despite not having the classic structures he'd had in his life since he started running track in 1965, Steve was performing remarkably well against the clock, even if he wasn't winning races overseas. In what little downtime he had, he still found moments to hang out with runners.

Musicians hang out in music shops. Writers hang out in bookstores. Runners hang out in running shoe stores. At times, he frequented the Athletic Department, the Nike shoe store, that was about the size of a shoe box. He liked to pop in and talk to his friends. The people who worked there, namely young women like Maryl Barker and Debra Roth, talented runners themselves, thought nothing of Steve; meaning he was just . . . Steve, another person. At twenty-three, he was barely older than they were and never gave off a pompous air to them.

On the road with Geoff Hollister and Jeff Bannister, Steve loved to talk to and inspire kids. At a clinic in late August 1973, Bannister, a decathlete, talked about weight training for runners. Hollister talked about injury prevention. But it was Steve who always stole the show. He shared his secrets, knowledge, and experience. He talked about racing techniques, psychology, training methods—everything about what it takes to master the art and craft of running.

Hollister then displayed for the kids the Nike "Finland Blue," a model of running shoe for $14.30. They hung up colorful warmups, travel bags, T-shirts, and other apparel. Steve told a reporter that, no, he wasn't there to sell shoes, annoyed by the implication. But . . . well . . . of course he was the show pony to make the shoes a must-have. "Be like Pre" could have been the slogan, if such a thing was allowed by amateur rules of the day. "I'm here to talk about running. They don't have to come up here and do this. They sell enough shoes without leaving the store. They're doing it because they want to."

Someone asked him that if he liked kids so much, why didn't he coach them. "It's too much responsibility, especially with the younger kids. It's so easy to ruin them. You really have to understand individuals." Also, coaching for money was still a violation of the amateur rules.

That said, Steve proved he could, in fact, understand individuals. He already was coaching Roth, and Barker needed a new coach late summer and into the fall of 1974. Steve was happy to help.

To Barker, Steve was an easygoing guy, positive, no arrogance. She remembered meeting him by the East Stands at Hayward Field for her first workout. He told her, "This is what your times will be for your mile for next year. Your splits will be 70, 70, 70, 70."

"Really?" Barker said. A 4:40?

"Even if you come close, look what you will have accomplished." He made her feel what was possible. He knew the wonder of personal discovery through running. He wanted to give that feeling away.

Steve differed from her first coach, who basically told her she needed to look like a skin-wrapped skeleton to make the national team. As a result, she climbed on the scale multiple times a day, running more than she should have while eating less. Steve never expressed concern for how much Barker weighed or how she looked. His mantra: do the work. But also, "don't think about how far you have to run during the race. Think about what you're going to be doing. Instead of going, 'Oh, my gosh, I've got six more laps to go.' It's like, 'Okay, I'm going to be doing this at this point.' I was sorry that I didn't get to have him coach me sooner."

A sample week that Steve scribbled on Athletic Department stationery looked like this:

Maryl,

If your [sic] ready, I want a test [sic] you the rest of the week.

> *Thurs.*
> *20x220 38–40 220 rest*
> *3 mile run*
>
> *Fri. AM 4–6*
> *PM 4–6*
>
> *Sat. 12x440 78–80*
> *220 rest*
> *4 mile run*
> *6x220 2 in 40, 2 in 38, 2 in 36*
>
> *8 mile run Sun.*

P.S. I'll talk to you Mon. about it.

Barker had a nagging knee injury, a combination of overtraining, excessive pronation, and poor nutrition on account of her previous coach body shaming her. Steve taught her that she can run with pain, but not with injury. He drew up workouts for her in pencil, on graph paper, in the hard-easy fashion of his mentors and coaches—Walt McClure, Phil Pursian, Bill Dellinger, and Bill Bowerman, who always said, "In every case, I would prefer to undertrain a runner rather than overtrain him." Steve's hard workouts for her were track repeats with goal times for the workout. "Easy" days were usually a morning run of four to six miles, and an evening or afternoon run of four to six miles. He told her to run on soft surfaces, and on Saturday, September 28, 1974, a three-mile time trial. She dreaded the test run.

Coach Steve didn't want to burn her out or aggravate her knees. He worried about overworking her as he worried about what he saw happening in southern California with fifteen-year-old Mary Decker. She was a running prodigy. Steve said, "She's the greatest female 800-meter runner in the world right now at fifteen and she can be the greatest for quite a few years, but she's not going to make it if she keeps going like she is now. She's going to be . . . burned out before she gets to what should be her best years."

Steve offered the best counsel he could, be it from afar, in the case of Decker, or those right in front of him. In Roth's workout sheet, Steve wrote, "Deb, your mileage needs to increase," and four to six miles on the "rode." Steve and Roth had the same size feet, so he would give her his old red-white-and-blue spikes and she noticed how he wore a characteristic hole in the upper of the shoe. "God knows what I did with those," she said.

The *Register-Guard* got wind of Steve's coaching and drew up a small profile on Barker. She posed for a picture with Steve. He wore a denim jacket, jeans, T-shirt tucked in, and hands on his hips with a big smile, a natural. Barker wasn't even looking at the camera. In the article, she said, "You have to know how to run hills; that makes the difference," and "He told me to be concerned about being in a certain position at a certain time in the race. And you should never think about how much farther you have to run!"

Listening to Coach Steve gave her confidence, not just in herself, but for women running in general. Steve thought that women belonged in and among the men training at Hayward Field. "I remember Debbie and I were running, doing our workout and it was raining," Barker said. "We were soaked and the guys weren't out there and we're just like, 'We're *tough*. We're just as good as they are.' It felt so free."

Helping runners had healing properties for Steve, as he continued to mend his mind after the Olympics. By now, it was just more than two years until the next Olympics. He could strike with the full force of his body, his learning, his maturing sense of self as he crested into his mid-twenties, where most runners began hitting their peak. He'd spent high school and college focused solely on his races, but increasingly it was the running of others that was giving him purpose.

In Coos Bay, there was another young woman who was, in a sense, on the same level with Steve. Her name was Fran Auer Sichting—Fran Worthen in the current day—and she was an elite sprinter and a gravity-defying long jumper. Her name started surfacing in 1973 as a headline grabber. Most stories that mentioned her also mentioned Steve. "She's the greatest sprinter to ever come out of Oregon right now. It's difficult for a sprinter to train in Coos Bay with the rain and the bad weather," Steve said.

"I remember when he was just a skinny little kid running around Coos Bay," Fran said.

"You know, I remember when she was just a skinny little kid running at Marshfield but now she's one of the finest sprinters in the world," said Steve.

Back when she started sprinting, the general thought was, in her words, that "girls trying sports was a passing fad." But as she saw Steve excelling, "I was building my own dreams."

Worthen competed in track meets close to home. When Steve saw Fran, he made sure to encourage her while she was warming up. "I'll be rooting for you," he said, words a "scared, little kid from Coos Bay" needed to hear.

On his trips back to Coos Bay, he'd frequently call and ask to get dinner, or they'd go for a run on the beach. Fran's idea of a long run topped out around 400 meters, but they jogged along and spoke as friends. She'd huff and puff, and he'd be chatting away. He was the only person she knew who understood the at-times-unbearable weight of talent. He'd express his growing discontent with the treatment of athletes, and not just men—women, too.

In 1973, Fran broke Wilma Rudolph's 100-yard-dash record by covering the distance in 10.5 seconds. "It was fast enough to make the nation sit up and take notice of the pretty brunette," wrote *The World*, such was how sports journalism treated just about every woman at the time. Rare was the article that involved a woman that didn't comment on her looks. *Sports Illustrated* led a story on Fran that began, "Anyone feeling sorry for himself should consider the plight of Francine Auer Sichting, a 5'9", 19-year-old freckled lovely . . ."

In an AAU meet in late June 1973, in the semifinal heat, she set a new

American record of 23.2 in the 220, but it wouldn't be ratified because AAU officials started her in Lane 9 (international rules only recognize records broken from Lanes 1 through 8, as Lane 9 has virtually no curve).

Though the AAU wouldn't allow her record to stand, in her heart she knew she ran 220 yards faster than any American woman ever had. She, like Steve Prefontaine, thought little of the AAU. "It has a way of screwing up an athlete's career. All they want us to do is go out and run and keep our mouths shut."

Steve had now been critical of the AAU for six years, dating all the way back to his first summer abroad, and he had seen, heard, and experienced enough. He grew more vocal with his distaste of the AAU and its treatment of track-and-field athletes. He experienced, for example, the squalor of living conditions—cramped quarters, clogged toilets, incessant after-hours noise, swarms of mosquitoes—at the Pan Am Games in Cali, Columbia, in 1971. Meanwhile, the officials were staying in "plush hotels." This was a frequent complaint shared among the athletes.

As a twenty-three-year-old, Steve's commentary became more global, more pointed at the greater establishment, not so focused on how he planned to mount heads on his wall. "Be an athlete, they tell you. Get out there and bust a gut, but you're not going to get anything for it. That's what they tell athletes in the United States." Steve lamented that he couldn't even coach distance runners. "Who around is more qualified to coach distance men than I am?"

In the spring of 1973, Senator Marlow Cook from Kentucky authored a proposal that would put the athletes under the purview of a federal sports commission and out of the hands of the AAU. Steve was all in favor. "We are the ones that have been getting the raw deals for years. If it weren't for us, those guys on the AAU board wouldn't have any jobs." This sentiment echoed—and was evidence of—conversations Steve had with Bowerman. Referring to his angst over the 1972 Olympics, Bowerman said, "The aristocracies of the world became unpopular after 1918, but that's exactly what we have here [with the AAU] . . . a group of old men perpetuating an idea for themselves."

It seemed clear to Steve that he needed to see the power structure of

American track and field burned down and rebuilt. "We're supposed to be goodwill ambassadors when we go abroad, but it's hard to do when you are representing your country and worrying about how you are going to be able to pay your bills when you get back home. It doesn't seem quite fair to me."

That fact, the having-to-waste-time-on-a-menial-job fact, made it unfair for U.S. athletes "to compete against people from Finland and the USSR. Their people have the best facilities, medical care, housing, and food allowances . . . Here I sit doing my best to keep it together and living on food stamps . . . American athletes have to pay their own way to Olympic Trials and I've seen them standing around eating hot dogs for a week just so they can compete to go and represent the most powerful country in the world. Anybody knows that you can't be at your best when your training table is the corner hot dog stand."

Amidst this backdrop, an enticing option surfaced as a competitor to the AAU in the form of professional track.

BY THE TIME the 1972 Olympics arrived, the AAU had been organizing American track-and-field events for the entire century. It had a monopoly on the athletes, their schedules, their races, and their careers. So perhaps it shouldn't have been a surprise when someone came along with an eye to challenge the AAU's hegemony. What was a surprise was that Steve wanted no part of it.

Immediately following the Munich Olympics, a man named Michael O'Hara had announced the formation of the International Track Association (ITA). Professional track and field had arrived. O'Hara said the ITA would offer "a chance for dedicated athletes to live like human beings, by getting monetary rewards for performing." The trade-off for athletes who signed with this upstart league was loss of amateur eligibility and thus no more Olympic teams. It was a big ask at the time and it proved just how much influence the AAU—and the Olympics as an idea—still wielded.

O'Hara, a former college volleyball player, studied business at UCLA and earned a master's in business administration from Southern California. He grew enamored with the "minor sports," track among them. While competing on the U.S. volleyball team for the 1963 Pan Am Games, he ingratiated himself with the track-and-field athletes of the time where he learned of "the sacrifices trackmen have to make, and it was then the germ of an idea began to manifest itself in my mind."

O'Hara started a consulting firm in L.A. called O'Hara Management Entertainment and taught management and marketing for Santa Monica College. After watching his friends found leagues like the American Basketball Association and the World Hockey Association, he grew confident that perhaps track and field needed its own league so they could enjoy wealth and fame, not just the personal pride peddled by the amateur establishment. O'Hara didn't want to trespass on the Munich Olympics, so he had been researching, developing, and planning for more than two years prior to Munich. He surrounded himself with track experts and set out to bring professional track and field to the forefront.

For decades, it was athletes who got strung along and exploited by a myth: amateurism. The ITA's mission was to bring over the table what was once under. The power brokers of amateurism fought an archaic war and were increasingly proving to be a constitutional monarch withering below a rusty crown.

At a press conference featuring the first cohort of professional ITA athletes, in mid-November 1972, Jim Ryun told the room he was a "professional jock." The people in the room laughed and Ryun smiled.

The arc of Ryun's career had reached the end game. After literally falling down in the 1,500-meter semifinals in the Munich Olympics (and thus failing to qualify for the finals), after what was a years-long journey to reclaim the magic of his 1967 world record in the mile, Ryun's final chapter was signed on the bottom line. He was done being an amateur, and so were many others. There was potential for him to earn anywhere from $18,000 to $25,000 ($125,800 to $174,733 in 2024 dollars) as a miler in the 1973 season—more from commercial endorsements—something previously and categorically off the table for a track-and-field athlete still wishing to compete in the Olympics, "no longer a slave to the Olympic code," as the *New York Times* reported.

While on the "shamateur" circuit, Ryun often was labeled the "Boy Scout" for not taking advantage of the under-the-table payments many other athletes gladly took just to make ends meet—Steve Prefontaine among them. As a world-record holder, Ryun could have made a mint on races, nor did he ever take advantage of the double-plane-fare trick, where an athlete could take their extra plane ticket, return it at the counter, and pocket the cash. Ryun failed to recognize, or at least ignored, that taking the pay exposed the AAU and amateurism for the frauds they were, call it a tax on its hypocrisy.

Starting a life or being a world-class athlete were untenable for most athletes. Many had to make the simple—though difficult—choice between a life and running; many chose a life even when it robbed them of time in their athletic prime. So many runners spoken to for this book retired from track in their mid-20s because they had to make a living. They look at runners of today—with awe and a tinge of jealousy—and how it's routine for many to run in two, three, sometimes four Olympic cycles because the structures are in place for them to fully maximize the finite power of their bodies. Ryun said, "I won't have to work eight hours a day and train two hours more . . . I knew at Munich after I fell, I was through. But now my motivation is greater than it ever was. I'm not running for a watch, or a trophy, or a medal, I'm running for my livelihood."

"But won't the fans put pressure on you to win?" someone asked.

Smiling, knowing the pressure he'd been under for more than five years, the burnout, how he had walked off the track in 1969, his beleaguered comeback, how he never dominated again, he said, "If you don't think they haven't . . ."

An anonymous runner not wanting to poke the AAU bear said, "Track's been an art that has stagnated because of its amateur status. The AAU would say, 'Hey, Michelangelo, you're a hell of a sculptor but you can only work at it three hours a day.' In the pros a guy can train eight hours a day if he wants to, and maybe bring the mile record down to 3:45 or something." As Tom Von Ruden, a middle-distance runner, said, "I was tired of the hypocrisy of amateur track. I was tired of the constant hassle of trying to deal with the different organizations."

When news of the ITA reached Bill Bowerman, he said, "Athletes signing with the professional track circuit have dollar signs in their eyes and mush in their heads." Bowerman elaborated, "These people promoting professional track are looking out first for themselves. I have no objections with Ryun or anyone else signing if they can put their talent to work, but I think it's a very limited number who can make any money out of it." He worried that it could dry up the amateur ranks. At that time, there was no turning back. You became a pro; you were done as an amateur. Bowerman looked at the signees and deemed them over the hill, anyway. Like the AAU, the power was still from on high, though the floor the athletes were on was at least a few stories higher.

However, as the ITA got underway in the spring of 1973, Steve Prefontaine held out, retaining the amateur ideal because he had unfinished business with the Olympics. He wasn't interested in turning pro . . . yet. Steve said, "Maybe in a couple of years if things go."

Steve had watched Ryun appear on NBC's *Today Show*, where he said that a track athlete has other obligations, finances. An amateur in the United States cannot equal the Europeans, who often granted their athletes stipends and/or jobs so they could train, pay for their travel, and their medical care. Remove the stress of money and time, and it freed them to train free from burden. For Steve, who for a time had been on food stamps, it clearly weighed on him. "A runner can only go poor for so long," Steve said. "If you can make money with your talents, why not? Right now, pro track sounds a lot better than the Olympic Games, the way they are now."

Though he wasn't joining the pro ranks, Steve could see the negotiating power that the ITA represented. The simple existence of professional track would give the athlete leverage and possibly pressure the amateur establishment to make staying in the amateur ranks more alluring. "The dollar is a mighty strong bargaining point," Steve said. So, too, were the Olympics as an idea.

In an ideal world, amateurs and professionals could compete together. The pros run for money, the amateurs don't—this way the best were always brought to the field, not, as it would seem, runners past their prime running on reputation. It would ensure a compelling product, but for now, that violated amateur rules. In the meantime, Steve planned on sitting back from the pro scene, watching from the sidelines, and not putting any limit on his future.

Steve looked at other foreign athletes, like Olympic champion Lasse Virén, who could train in Brazil for the winter (summer in the southern hemisphere). "The government takes care of them," Steve said. Steve rightfully questioned why the United States didn't grant similar support to its athletes. After years and one Olympic cycle, Steve had seen the light, and he now had the cultural heft, even celebrity, to take the lead. "Our program is lacking. We are going to make a lot of adjustments and get rid of a lot of archaic methods if we are going to be competitive at world class. We can't go on natural talent any longer. We must have facilities and we must get more competition against European runners. We live in our own world." And that world was terribly lacking. Steve wanted to see training camps, medical attention, coaching clinics, rule changes that would allow a runner to coach runners. "Who knows more about track than a competitor? There are too many coaches who haven't experienced competition and coach from a book."

Even if pro track came knocking, "I'm not going cheap," he said. One look at Steve and you saw he had all the markings of a new wave, a marketable, modern athlete. If Ryun, past his prime, earned upward of $25,000, Steve, in his prime and awash in moxie, could likely earn four times that, maybe more. The longer Steve held off, the more he hoped that dollar number would climb, as long as the ITA remained solvent, and he remained relevant.

Meanwhile, in March 1973, the first unofficial ITA meet—call it a dress rehearsal—took over Pocatello, Idaho. The meet attracted 10,480 people to see Ryun, among others. The ITA had inked a deal with the great, though aging (a theme with the ITA), Kip Keino, the versatile Kenyan who won two gold medals and two silver medals in his career (most notably the 1,500-meter gold medal over Ryun in 1968), but he wouldn't be running in Idaho in the mile against Ryun. Instead, what fans saw was Ryun running against blinking light bulbs pacing him around the track (now standard in Diamond League meets). The lights were set to 62-second quarters while Ryun ran a solo 1,500 meters, so when he outpaced the lights, people assumed he was running at world-record pace. Instead, it was a "poky" 3:50.3.

The ITA had to teach the athletes the finer points of showmanship. People were turning out to see recognizable names. The operation manual called for athletes to be responsive to the fans, wave during introductions, smile, turn to all sides of the arena. "Many USA athletes act glum, as if they are about to be shot the next minute . . . keep in mind that we are entertainers also and a bit of 'show biz' will be appreciated by your fans. . . . All should be prepared to take a victory lap if requested and wave during that time . . . Act happy that you won, don't be embarrassed. There is a bit of ham in all of us."

O'Hara wisely geared the ITA meet experience toward the sports fan, not the track-and-field fan. "If we can educate him, stimulate him and interest him, we think we can make ITA." There were gimmicky relays that pitted a set of high jumpers, long jumpers, female sprinters, and hurdlers against one another. Another heat, of sorts, were between shot-putters, vaulters, hurdlers, and sprinters.

The first official meet would be in Los Angeles, but Idaho proved there just might be a hunger for this kind of spectacle and that it wasn't merely a novelty act bound to fail once people grew bored. What the ITA needed were not just big names of the formerly great, but big names of someone in his prime, at the height of his powers, still on the way up the mountain.

It needed Steve Prefontaine.

In the spring of 1973, Steve—then in his final track season with the Oregon Ducks—went down to California for their usual spring break training trip, this time to Bakersfield. Steve ran the six-mile in 27:09.4, setting a new American record. Race officials awarded him a transistor radio as the top athlete of the meet. He then departed early for Los Angeles to watch the first official professional track meet—Kip Keino's debut—and he said, "I've been running for my country a long time. Now I run for Kip." More than 12,000 people showed up for the meet, but they might have been underwhelmed by the highly touted duel between Ryun and Keino. Keino won by a full second over Ryun in 4:06 to Ryun's 4:07.1. Fans saw a competitive race, but not a world-record-breaking race. Perhaps track fans enjoyed the race, but the general sports fan O'Hara so desperately wanted to win over? Not so much. Steve ran 4:06 in high school.

Steve took it all in. "Yes, I definitely would be interested in it for the right offer, but so far there doesn't seem to be enough money. It will take more than $25,000 to buy my amateurism. I know I have to get more than what they're giving Kip Keino." That said, he also thought the competition left a lot to be desired. He was faster than everyone in the ITA circuit by a long shot. Steve wanted money, but he craved competition.

While Steve was in Los Angeles, he met with Southern California track writers and for his time earned the title "talkative." Though he would run in AAU meets in the forthcoming summer once his NCAA commitments were through, he still took the time to rib the AAU, saying, "The AAU just uses athletes and I've had enough of that."

In years past, though Steve often spoke his mind, his scope was far narrower, usually on himself and his competition. He often sought the friendship and mentorship of runners a few years older than he. Now he became the elder statesman. He had earned a certain measure of gravitas, and he wasn't afraid to wield it. He was, by far, the most outspoken athlete criticizing the AAU at the time.

As the ITA traveled to Portland, Oregon, for an indoor meet, Ryun signed programs and scraps of paper. There was a horde around the still-world-record holder. As the throng thinned, there stood a young man with golden hair and a dark mustache, too old for an autograph. Ryun cuffed a program around the young man's head, almost like he was tousling his hair, as he would a young boy.

"Hey, hot dog, how are ya?" Ryun said.

"Just fine, Jim." Steve smiled.

This much was obvious. Steve was keeping a close eye on professional track. Once Ryun extricated himself from the herd, he said, "We have to have Prefontaine. If we have him we get the larger crowds."

At the next ITA meet, some 7,435 people packed Portland's Memorial Coliseum. The *Register-Guard* said this number might have been more out of curiosity than anything. Steve scouted it out. The problem, if you could label it so in the early goings of ITA meets, was a lack of competition. Ryun vs. Keino could not be the only feature for the fans, even for Ryun and Keino. O'Hara said the ITA hadn't "reached Mecca yet." Through the early going, the ITA lacked bodies. O'Hara once cited golf as a model in that nobody necessarily cared if you shot 10-under or 4-under par to win; they cared about the money won and the competition. But golf had full fields of dozens of golfers, a cut, and even if there were familiar faces, at least there was the off chance that someone could creep into the picture. Track was different. It mattered if a miler could break four minutes. Keino defeating Ryun by one second and being well over four minutes felt like the junior varsity. The ITA essentially was having a weekly match race between Ryun and Keino; or Brian Oldfield hurling the shot. Soon enough, that would be . . . boring. "They have to wait for more bodies," Steve said. Strong, deeper fields would drive those winning times down. The ITA was a brilliant concept—it's what we see in the current day with the Diamond League and Athlos—but as long as the best athletes chased the Olympics, the ITA would get the rest and that, in the long term, under these current conditions, was untenable.

Someone asked Steve if he had decided about turning pro after college or remaining an amateur a bit longer. "Not yet," Steve said.

"What would it take?"

"Zeroes . . . lots of 'em."

To its credit, the ITA was growing. It would add meets, money, and bodies after its first full-fledged season. For 1974, it planned on eighteen meets, including one in Tokyo. Lee Evans was 1973's top money winner, with $13,900. ABC, who broadcasted just one meet in 1973, planned on airing three in the 1974 season. Post Cereals added $10,000 toward a shot-put prize, and Persona, a subsidiary of Philip Morris, spent $10,000 toward a grand prix pole vault prize. Far ahead of its time and super progressive, the ITA had offered equal prize money for women. The only issue, if sprinter Lacey O'Neal had one, was there weren't enough events for women and there weren't enough women in general to increase the competition.

The first year wasn't all "roses and lollipops," as the *New York Times* reported. A starter fired his pistol for the gun lap a lap too soon; confusion over rules created controversy (heads crossing the finish—not torsos like in international competition—mark the winner); there were rumors of bribes to throw a race, to which O'Hara said he "didn't anticipate this kind of pressure so soon, in our first year." He placed calls to the FBI and Pete Rozelle, commissioner of the NFL.

But Ryun, Bob Seagren, and Evans still believed in professional track. Evans, maven of the 400 meters, said, "After a world-class athlete finishes college, I think he should jump to join the pro tour—the AAU should have turned him against amateur track by the time he is a senior."

Pro track only stood a chance if it had the fastest runners, the longest and highest jumpers, and the best throwers, period. "The star quality to outshine all the others, of course, rests in the charismatic countenance of Oregon's Steve Prefontaine," wrote Robert Fachet. "He has America's fastest 1973 times at every distance from one mile to six, and he seems to make headlines every time he opens his mouth."

For this reason, Steve was the ideal mold for pro track. The ITA's best shot at securing a talent like Steve was shortly after one Olympic cycle, but not so close to the next one that the athlete felt it best to hold off just a little longer. As Steve graduated from college in late 1973, he had a decision to make as the calendar paged to 1974. He no longer had a team, a locker, or a steady coach as he entered what would be the physical prime of his career. The clock was ticking on that "prime," and would he "waste" it by signing with pro track for the sake of money? Or could he hold out a few more years and one more Olympics? O'Hara said, "He's a fine young man and we'd love to have him since he handles himself so well on and off the track. I'm very hopeful we can obtain his services for next year. We are negotiating with him right now and the jury is still out."

In the meantime, Steve kept running as an amateur, in indoor meets, and, when spring arrived, smashing performances in Twilight Meets at Hayward Field, all with eyes toward a summer campaign in Europe.

Through the fall of 1974, the ITA had been in touch with Steve, trying to put a number on Steve's amateurism. On October 11, 1974, Steve wrote to his old roommate Pat Tyson, "I'm back to hard training again but I don't know why. This running has to go somewhere. I just turned $75,000 down for ITA but then what's money..."

This running has to go somewhere... In a few months, Steve would turn twenty-four. He looked around him and everybody was gone. Most of the guys he ran with had moved on from track and field and started careers, families. They didn't have Olympic-level talent, or if they did, they could no longer afford to pursue the dream. That left Steve alone. He, too, was eager to start a life that maybe didn't revolve around running, but a life that integrated it and leveraged his profile. He knew he was running out of time. So many of the runners who were his idols and mentors just five years before were gone from the sport, pushed out in their prime by the structures of amateurism. Steve was the old man now. He didn't want to waste his time chasing his tail any longer. The Olympics were still two years away. Steve reasoned he could hang on for that.

The feeling was he had reaped all there was to sow from amateurism (except an Olympic medal). There was always a what if? He had been labeled a "lion in Eugene and a lamb in Europe." Steve earned a salary from Nike as the "national director of public affairs," which was basically a shadow sponsorship deal, "intentionally imprecise," as Phil Knight noted, that afforded him the basics so that he didn't have to beg for money or otherwise waste his time better spent on or near the track where he could be wearing Nike shirts and shoes.

When pro track arrived in Eugene several months later, mid-May 1975, Steve had allegedly been offered $200,000—$1.15 million in today's dollars—at the start of 1975 to sign with the ITA. By this time in the ITA's lifespan—its third season—the ITA was late on checks. The writing was on the walls. One wondered if the ITA had $200,000 to offer one athlete. Steve turned it down. "What would I do with all that money?" he said.

For someone who complained incessantly about finances, of being on food stamps, of wanting to open a bar, there were innumerable things he could have done with that money. But that would fly in the face of the image he created for himself. When offered the throne, he chose to walk among the masses. Perhaps there were some who were insulted that he didn't take the money. Here he was, sitting on a winning lottery ticket and he wouldn't cash it. Maybe it just felt good to be coveted. It was proof positive how important an Olympic medal was to him, that it was unfinished business. Through it all, perhaps, he figured there was another option, and that's what he sought to prove.

In the years following the Olympics, he had emerged out of the ashes, fully feathered. In 1974, he had run better than he ever had with six American distance records between 3,000 meters and 10,000 meters, even coming within five seconds of Ron Clarke's world record in the six-mile.

Going from 1974 and into 1975, what Steve had in mind was an entirely new paradigm for amateur track and field. Something out from under the thumb of the aging despots, but not treading into the full professionalism put on display by the International Track Association; a third estate where the athlete had agency, where they were the power brokers. New possibilities for a new era.

And Steve Prefontaine would be its leader.

CHAPTER 15

ROGUE

BACK IN THE summer of 1973, when Steve Prefontaine traveled to Europe—specifically Finland, Steve hatched an idea to host a series of small track meets primarily in Oregon. In Finland, he had grown close to Jaakko Tuominen, the Finn coach and organizer. What Steve loved was being a tourist in between track meets. He loved how Tuominen showed him the local fare, toured him around the countryside. Steve, proud of his Oregon roots, knew he could do something similar. Sure, the AAU would throw a fit since Steve's venture would be outside its purview, and bringing over foreign athletes was something historically only the AAU could approve. But Steve was at the height of his popularity and the apex of influence—if he wanted to bring a cohort of athletes over to the United States, he would ask for forgiveness, never permission. Steve did, in fact, file the proper paperwork, but before the AAU could deny him, he had already mailed out his invitations to the Finnish athletes, Lasse Virén among them. Ollan Cassell, the AAU track-and-field administrator, when "presented with this *fait accompli*," as Kenny Moore wrote in *Bowerman and the Men of Oregon*, "and Pre's popularity, Cassell had no choice but to grant the AAU sanction."

He had a map that would take him to and through the 1976 Olympics. He felt confident about the trajectory of his life through track and field and beyond. He would be twenty-five in 1976, and while still objectively young, he knew the end was on the horizon. He gave thought to what that might look like as a figurehead, a potential Olympic medalist, a spokesman for Nike—hell, even the owner of a sports bar, the Sub-Four.

For now, on February 7, 1975, two weeks after his twenty-fourth birthday, Steve announced that his major gamble had paid off: he confirmed that in just three months' time, a small group of Finnish track-and-field athletes were coming to Oregon for a series of track meets that would start in Madras, Oregon. From there they'd head to Coos Bay; Vancouver, British Columbia; Tacoma, Washington; and end in the shadow of "Pre's People" at Hayward Field on Thursday, May 29, 1975.

Just after the 1975 New Year, Steve had called his old high school coach, Walt McClure. Steve expressed his grand plan of organizing these boutique meets, and McClure said Steve confirmed that the Finns were a go. "Right now, six men and two women want to come to Oregon. I wondered about Madras, but Steve said he has a friend there who is willing to pay for the entire meet, if necessary."

Madras wasn't near any major cities. It was difficult to get to. It was quite possibly the worst location to launch an international series of track meets, but size didn't matter; it was scope, the vision that something of this nature could, in fact, be executed from the ground up, by, for, and of the athletes. Madras is a pushpin in the middle of Jefferson County, central Oregon. High desert country, it's nearly 2,000 feet higher in elevation than the coast, which was one of the reasons Steve enjoyed it so much. And with a population of barely 2,000 people, the relative anonymity he enjoyed there had its own powerful appeal.

And so, Steve, a notoriously wild driver, would hop into his butterscotch MGB, put the top down, his long hair blowing back, and speed to the middle of nowhere to see his close friends, Bud and Maxine Gauthier. He'd first met the Gauthiers a few years prior after a race in Portland. Steve had been swarmed by autograph seekers, mainly children—he'd sign autographs all day for kids. So, with a pen in his left hand, Steve signed a young boy's program and turned his back and signed more autographs. Steve then rotated back around and there was the same boy . . . again . . . with something new to sign.

Wait a minute? Didn't I already see you?

The kid wasn't being greedy; he was the emissary for his sixteen-year-old sister, standing a bit in the distance. Steve motioned her over, and that was how he met Desiree Gauthier, a fine sprinter herself, from Madras High School, and her youngest brother, Danny. Their parents, Dr. Bud Gauthier and Maxine Gauthier, social butterflies, soon shook hands with Steve, and they hit it off.

The Gauthiers were *the* family in Madras. Bud was a dentist, and the family also owned a bar in town, the Meet Market. They were rabid track-and-field fans with three children who were exceptionally talented runners. Though Steve grew closer over the years to his mother Elfriede, his father Ray, his younger sister Linda, and his older half-sister Neta, the Gauthiers were a surrogate family for him—maybe not the family he never had, but a different family, one he might have longed for: lighthearted, boisterous, jovial, affluent.

Steve took a shine to Danny, and one morning, after Steve had stayed the night, Danny placed a model down on the table, a project for school, and it was a mess. He spooned a bowl of cereal and munched away. Steve looked down at Danny and eyed the model. "What's that?" Steve asked.

"I have to take a model to school today," Danny said, "and I had to rush it."

"Why are you taking it?"

"It's due today."

"Yeah . . . listen . . . if you're not going to do the best job you can, it's not worth doing at all," Steve said. Danny thought about this. He was concerned with merely finishing the job; he knew it wasn't good and he merely wanted it done. Steve continued, "You just gotta manage your time better so next time you don't have to rush it, and you can do your best work."

Danny took it to heart, these little morsels of wisdom from the mind of someone he revered. Steve had always believed in giving your whole heart over to something—the Olympics, a school project. Don't leave behind a legacy of mediocrity, go for broke. "He was very passionate about hard work and effort," Danny recalled. "His magic was that he would put in more effort than anyone else. You have more guts and effort than everybody else, you might not be the fastest, might not be the best, but he could do those things and those would make the difference."

Other times, Steve took Danny and Danny's best friend, Greg Kemper, running. They would take off at a sprint trying to be faster than the one and only Steve Prefontaine. Steve labored behind them, dramatically breathing heavy. "Within 100 yards, we were dead and gone, and he would make us keep going," Kemper said.

Perhaps another reason he got along so well with Bud Gauthier was Bud's love of fast cars. He raced them, even owned a Porsche. Steve's friends never liked riding with him in his MGB. One friend said he was crazy and wouldn't get in the car with him. Another, who often rode with him, recalled the worry he felt at the risks Steve took darting in and out of traffic. If Steve had too much to drink, only Ralph Mann successfully took Steve's keys, as Steve never let anyone drive his precious car. "That damn MGB," Mann recalled. Steve drove like he raced and raced like he drove: full speed or nothing. Steve confided in Bud that if he ever died young, it would be because of a car accident.

Steve and the Gauthiers would often talk on the phone, and when Steve made the drive to Madras, he sat around the dinner table and talked, spiritedly, about the state of track and field. "Steve was a real activist," Desiree Kelly, Bud and Maxine's middle child, remembered. "He saw what was going on in Europe and how the athletes were supported. They didn't have to work extra jobs." Conversations around the table always turned toward the AAU and Steve's feuds with its army of bureaucrats telling him when and where to race, boarding athletes in hotels with "walls made of paper."

Steve sat at the head of the Gauthiers' dinner table with a glass of wine in hand, holding court with Bud and Maxine. Steve, brimming with his signature energy, thought it'd be cool to bring some European athletes over. And why not take them around the Pacific Northwest, not just New York or Los Angeles? Steve wanted to show off his little slice of America, his beloved Oregon. Show them the Deschutes River. Go horseback riding. Go crabbing on the coast. Jog up the emerald hills near Hendricks Park in Eugene with the rhododendrons in full bloom, up the impossibly steep, winding, hairpin turns at the intersection of Birch Lane and Skyline Boulevard.

The past few summers, it had been Steve who traveled to Europe to challenge the best middle-distance runners in the world. He grew tired of always going to them on their turf. Steve worked the phones and called many of his friends and colleagues to get this Pacific Northwest series of meets off the ground. Mike Manley—who ran for Team USA in the steeple-chase in the 1972 Olympics, and who was also a member of the Oregon Track Club and a high school teacher in Eugene—agreed to run the 3,000 with Steve in Madras. Leveraging his relationship with Bill Dellinger, several University of Oregon runners and throwers would fill out the card for the Madras meet, as well as a handful of post-graduate athletes from the Oregon Track Club and Seattle. This created a draw for the European athletes to come over to the United States.

The Finn Tour represented power: power for the individual, power for the athlete. But this first iteration was also a chance for Steve to attempt revenge, the cherry on top. Just two and a half years before at the 1972 Olympics, Lasse Virén won the gold medal in Steve's event, the 5,000 meters. Steve had only run against Virén outdoors in Europe (beating him in Helsinki in 1973) and he wanted to see what he was capable of in the United States, in Eugene, at Hayward Field with perhaps 12,000 people screaming Steve's name. Steve had been a road dog and now he wanted to harness the full power of the home-field advantage.

While organizing the tour, for the first time in his life, he spent the winter and early spring outside of Oregon. The loneliness of the long-distance runner applied not just to the rote mileage alone on the road, it was also about lacking peers, even coaching. A runner with enough time and money had to seek out the others. So Steve sought his rival Frank Shorter, who proved to be a great training partner for Steve, as Shorter was always willing—in an unspoken way—to share the training load, take his share of the lead. Shorter liked to think that his candor with Steve and his sense of fair play was why Steve elected to join Shorter in Colorado that winter. They performed "overdistance work," twenty miles a day at a six-minute clip, some intervals, at altitude. They trained so well together because there was honor in trading off load during a workout. Shorter could lead a set of 800s and, with a nod, Steve would lead the next set, never missing a stride. The altitude would help and being outside the bubble of Oregon might have been re-freshing for Steve. He traded rain for snow. Steve and Shorter ran during freezing temperatures, the wind sharp and pointed like broken glass. Their lungs burned and Steve pissed and moaned. As Shorter recounted in his memoir *My Marathon*, "He could bitch with the best of them." Steve kept complaining and Shorter chimed in, "Steve, no other runner in the world is working as hard or suffering as much as you and I are right now." Steve shut up, no small feat.

Word got out that Steve Prefontaine was in Colorado, so he sat down with Mike Monroe of the *Denver Post*. The story started, "Steve Prefontaine isn't a Communist. Hasn't burned his draft card. Probably loves apple pie. But he says he is fed up with the manner in which America treats its amateur athletes and would change his citizenship tomorrow if he could." A few paragraphs later, Monroe wrote, Steve "*is kidding on the level about changing his citizenship* (emphasis added). He is an intense individualist and classifies himself as an 'internationalist.' He's not un-American, just pro-Pre."

Steve told Monroe, "People say I should be running for a gold medal for the old red, white, and blue and that bull, but it's not gonna be that way. I'm the one who has made all the sacrifice. Those are my American records, not the country's. I compete for myself. To hell with love of country." He wasn't bitter about the treatment of himself and other amateur athletes but "outraged." He said distance runners were at a disadvantage, expected to live by all the rules—like not being allowed to coach—but still train and make a living. "I'll tell you, if I decide to compete at Montreal, I'll be a poor man."

Steve was working on what it would take to not be a poor man. He still drew a $5,000-a-year salary from Nike, which afforded him a car and a house in Eugene. He also was hard at work trying to open a bar called the Sub-Four in Eugene. He knew what a life after running looked like. He could see the end coming and wanted to be ready for it. He *was* ready for it, just not yet. Whether it was an actual want ad or a tongue-in-cheek one posed by Monroe (more than likely the latter), this ran atop the *Denver Post* story:

"WANTED: Country that cares about its amateur athletes to provide home for one of world's best distance runners. Will provide limitless talent, willingness to work hard, renewed enthusiasm. REPLY: Steve Prefontaine, Sub-Four Bar, Eugene, Ore."

This story hit the AP wire. In modern-day parlance, it went viral. And not in a good way.

Dwight Stones, the brilliant high jumper, was asked about Steve's blast at the United States. He said, "I think Steve put his foot in his mouth. I can say that because nobody has put his foot in his mouth more than me. He went a little too far. I've had my differences with the AAU, but I'm proud to be an American. I hope Steve makes a retraction or expands on what he meant. Maybe there were some things taken out of context."

Bingo.

The country at large didn't get wind of that context for a long time. There was no ESPN or twenty-four-hour sports or news networks, no social media, for an athlete to clarify, offer context, and put people at ease within hours. As a result, the lag between print and context could take days or weeks and people's reactions took place in that liminal time.

In a letter to the editor in the *Democrat-Herald*, a reader wrote, "As an American citizen, I resent the article you printed on Steve Prefontaine. I, for one, would rather not have an athlete run for this country who feels so strong against it. I feel this is the best country in the world and wouldn't leave for any reason. I can respect a distance runner as I have run the mile myself. I also feel Steve Prefontaine should follow through with leaving or withdraw his statement. I for one hope he doesn't run for the United States of America feeling the way he does."

When the *Capital Journal*, an Oregon newspaper out of Salem, which can be a representation for literally hundreds of papers across the country, ran the AP version, the lede read, "To hell with love of country . . . I compete for myself." Followed by "Prefontaine said he's so fed up with the treatment of American athletes that he'd change his citizenship tomorrow if given the chance." To those who thought Steve was universally beloved, they found out Steve had his detractors, too.

The *Oregon Journal* drew up an editorial titled "Prefontaine misses the point." It was on one hand empathetic, understanding Steve's frustrations. The *Oregon Journal's* problem with Steve was, in a sense, logical: Steve conflated the AAU with the USA. "Many a young man who served in the armed forces came out with an abiding dislike for the military," the board wrote. The country was not the AAU, it is mom and apple pie. And here was where just about every other news outlet erred and proliferated with every newspaper inch: Prefontaine said he would change his citizenship tomorrow if given the chance. Steve cringed at seeing his words in print.

Newspapers who picked up the story failed to note that the writer of the story *explicitly* said Steve was kidding. For the *Denver Post* reporter's part, at least he said so. The same couldn't be said for the rest of the country, and suddenly people were calling for Steve's head on a pike. How quickly he went from fan favorite to pariah.

For damage control, Steve turned to Oregon.

April 20, 1975, nearly a month to the day when the *Denver Post* story ran, Blaine Newnham of the *Register-Guard* called Steve. Steve said he was embarrassed, that people had a right to be upset, but, "Really, the Associated Press owes me an apology. I don't want to have to justify something that was taken out of context."

Steve said he loved America, would have cut his hair and gone into the Army had he been drafted. "I do like apple pie. I wasn't an anti-war demonstrator when I was a student. I wasn't a hell raiser. I've got a diploma. The Associated Press version of that story didn't differentiate between the American government, and the American sports structure. If you asked me if I would give up my American citizenship, I would say never. But if you asked me if I'd trade our sports program for a Finnish sports program or a Russian program, I'd say darn right."

In little more than two weeks, Steve would put it behind him. He had meets to run (both managing and literally running in them), the first of the five, in Madras, punching the American running culture into a corner.

PICTURE THIS: SEVERAL Olympians, future Olympians, borderline Olympians, and Division I athletes converged at Madras High School in early May 1975.

It had a circus-like feel. These athletes, with Steve Prefontaine as the P.T. Barnum, barnstormed the town, set up shop, put on a show, and would move on to the next city. Steve's responsibilities were threefold: organize, promote, and be the headliner of the meets. He endured tremendous stress and it showed. Steve had always felt the pressure to perform. He still had to train while ensuring that athletes had accommodations and entertainment. The pressure here was unlike anything he'd encountered. This tour represented a new future for Steve, one with more agency over his career as an athlete. If he continued down this path, he might outsource some of the more granular specifics, the better to put his face—and the faces of others—on the marquee. The Finns who came over boasted twelve national records, three Olympic gold medals, three world records, two European championships, and two bronze medals. All eight members of the team who planned on competing had, at one point or another, been in the top ten in the world in their respective events.

The experience, so far, had only lit a larger fire to continue to organize stuff of this nature. If track fans couldn't travel to Portland, New York, Miami, Los Angeles, or even Eugene, Steve wanted to bring the meets to them. "It all depends on how successful it is." Steve could barely contain his glee over what was to come. "This weekend, this will probably be the best track meet in the country," he said. It was but a first step, and what a step it was. The possibilities were invigorating. There was a new way forward.

Here in Madras, Steve was set to run the 3,000 meters, sometimes called the metric two-mile. Finland's Rune Holmén would be Steve's main competition, as well as Eugene's Mike Manley. Lasse Virén was still in Finland but planned on coming to the United States in the next week or two. He was recovering from an injury he suffered during a sixty-mile road race in Finland. But Jaakko Tuominen, the tour leader for the Finns, said, "Virén is coming here in quite good shape." Steve must have been salivating.

Finns were his kind of people: hard drinking, hard playing, ruthless competitors. When they arrived in Oregon, Steve wanted to give them a taste of his home state, so he took them to Round Butte Dam along the Deschutes River, Hay Creek Ranch for horseback riding, and to Warm Springs Indian Reservation. He was proud of where he came from. Track was his passport to the greater world, and he sought to return the favor.

A rain squall emptied the skies thirty minutes before the start of Steve Prefontaine's Northwest Tour with the Finns. On top of the rain, it was cold and blustery, the kind of air that chilled skin pink. According to the *Oregon Journal*, only 426 paying customers showed up. Some other accounts would say closer to 600. Steve had hoped for 2,000 people. Really, he was hopeful his meet this Sunday would be the best in the country (it might have been the only one). He had run all over the world, but never in this region of Oregon. Steve had hoped for a mellow afternoon, some good times, some good performances.

Out on the discus field, Pentti Kahma beat former Oregon Duck Mac Wilkins by three feet. The year before, in 1974, Kahma was the best discus thrower in the world. In one year's time, Wilkins would win the gold medal in the Montreal Olympics and break the world record in the discus. But here on the high desert, both had modest throws in far-from-pristine conditions.

For Steve, it was time to warm up for his main event. Robert Gauthier, the eldest of the three Gauthier children and a gifted distance runner, stood beside Steve. Robert wasn't competing, but as he was something of Madras royalty, he was going to warm up a bit with Steve beforehand. Steve dipped into his bag and pulled out his Team USA singlet from the 1972 Olympics. Steve said, "Go ahead, put this on."

Robert took that priceless uniform and slipped it over his head and pulled it down over his torso. That singlet represented Steve's greatest disappointment, his most public defeat. Yet that was nearly three years before—little about Steve on the inside or out was the same. Jogging around the stadium and onto part of the high school cross-country course, there was an ease about him that made it obvious: Steve was no longer the same runner who had been defeated in that singlet.

The people had endured the weather, and it was time for the main event: Steve Prefontaine in the 3,000 meters. Steve wore an Oregon Track Club T-shirt, shorts, and spikes to claw over this old cinder track. The race kicked off and Holmén and Manley led through the early part of the race in a "cat and mouse game." Halfway through the race, Steve took command, but he wasn't going all out, not yet. He felt mildly flat. At last, Steve built an "unshakeable lead" by the time they reached the midway point of the race. He was never one to throw in a dud, so he kept pushing. Around the far turn and heading for home, he extended his lead over Holmén and Manley and grabbed at the tape a winner.

"For an old man," Steve said, all of twenty-four years old, "it was not too bad."

After the meet, all the athletes and local luminaries celebrated at the Gauthiers' house, toasting, laughing. The Finns could drink. The first meet was done and out of the way. Sure, the weather was garbage, and the crowd was small but passionate, but Steve nevertheless stuck the landing.

In five days, the second meet was taking shape in Coos Bay.

Steve was going home.

THE TRIP TO Coos Bay had the makings of a high school reunion. At a party, Steve ran into Bruce Laird, a Marshfield High School graduate and former fraternity brother at the University of Oregon. One of Laird's lasting memories of Steve—and one that would foreshadow the kind of man he'd become—took place in the hallways of Marshfield High.

Steve, then a scrawny freshman, walked the hallways and found someone, hard as it is to imagine, smaller than him, being picked on by, as Laird recalled, some "toughies." The kid was bullied by thicker, taller, meaner upperclassmen. The physically unassuming Steve saw this and, without hesitation, stepped in front and backed the bullies down. "He always had a forceful personality," said Laird. "You look at his career where he was trying to make a stand on certain things he thought were right or wrong, and he wasn't going to stand by. That was just who he was."

Laird saw the kid getting pushed around and did nothing. He played football and could've thrown his weight around, but there was Steve doing the work. "And it was a wake-up moment for me. Here's this guy who's smaller than me, walks up to these pretty solid thugs and backs them down. It says a lot about a person's character, who they are."

There could only be one hometown. Eugene liked to claim Steve as its own, but Coos Bay could say it was the crucible through which he forged an identity, where he grew up, faced challenges, weathered parental beatings, developed that signature intensity and pugilistic nature on the track and trails.

In the same way he leaned on the Gauthiers in Madras, he leaned on Walt McClure to help with logistics to organize the second meet of the Finn Tour, this at Marshfield High School, a "shitty high school track," as Matt Centrowitz, an Oregon transfer and native New Yorker sitting out a year of college eligibility, said (back then transfers had to sit out a year).

It would be nice to make a happy buck from the meet, but McClure's main goal was to "put on a great track meet." If they broke even, all the better. It was a happy return for McClure, back to the site of so many practices and track meets. He had left coaching and teaching a couple years before to sell insurance. Now, he'd be helping Steve host a track meet at Pirate Stadium. The Euros beat Steve in Europe, but wouldn't in his backyard.

Thankfully, the weather was far more cooperative in Coos Bay than it had been in Madras, and not surprisingly, people turned out on May 9, 1975. Two thousand people were on hand to watch Steve run the 2,000 meters, an odd distance, but one with an American record ripe for the picking. It would give Steve all seven American records from 2,000 meters to 10,000 meters. Motivation would not be an issue, not in front of this crowd at this stadium, which was not even a mile away from his childhood home.

Though time and distance separated them, Steve always remained close with his half-sister Neta. Steve had since moved out of his trailer and owned a house in Eugene. It had a few bedrooms, a vegetable garden out back. He rented out a couple rooms to pay for the mortgage, but he reserved the apartment upstairs—just in case—for Neta, who was married with two young children and entering her mid-thirties. Since leaving their home in Coos Bay when Steve was a child, life had been challenging for Neta. An abusive childhood attracted that as an adult, and Steve made sure she knew he could provide sanctuary. He always kept that photograph of her tucked in his wallet, an ever-present reminder that she was his protector. Steve opened his house to her, but she needed to make sure her children finished school first. Then she'd likely leave her husband. He told her, "If you need a place to come, you come here." It was perhaps the most thoughtful gesture anyone had ever made for her, and she'd never forget it.

A few days before the race, Steve told Neta that he would gun for the 2,000-meter American record and dedicate it to her son Michael as a gift for his ninth birthday. It wouldn't be easy. "I've been working too hard and been under too much emotional strain to do anything like that," Steve prefaced. But he would try. On Steve's radar were times like France's Michel Jazy's 2,000-meter world record of 4:56.2, Belgium's Emiel Puttemans 4:59.8, and the U.S.'s Marty Liquori's 5:02.2.

By the time Steve was set to run, he spoke with U of O's Lars Kaupang about setting a swift pace, something for Steve to draft off. He agreed, and as the gun popped, Kaupang opened with laps of 60 and 62 seconds. It was a spectacular sight; such collective speed had never graced this track.

Steve took the lead from Kaupang and the people cheered. It must have felt wild running on this track he once called home, back when they still had cinders underfoot. "Well, it's MY track. I know the turns are too tight and it's not too level and all that, but I learned to run on it, so I'm not going to complain about it," he said. He powered around the oval in 60 seconds, again in 60 seconds, and one last final push of 59.4 to break the American record in 5:01.4.

After the race, Neta told Michael, "You better go talk to your uncle." Michael, a shy boy, with a little autograph book in his hands, walked with his head down in and among the throng of children circling Steve looking for an autograph. Steve spotted him and said, "There's my birthday boy!" If you were a kid plucked out of the crowd it was enough to make you feel lighter than air and special beyond words, like "a million dollars," Michael would recall. Steve hoisted Michael onto his lap like he was a mop-haired, mutton-chopped, mustachioed, skinny-as-all-get-out Santa Claus, took Michael's autograph book and wrote, "Happy birthday" and signed it "Uncle Steve," an American record *just for him*.

McClure, who, back in the late 1960s, often winced at Steve's inability to control his pace on this very track, put his arm around Steve, smiling so wide his eyes were practically closed, and said, "The little guy came through."

Naturally, Steve wasn't happy with his final lap because he hadn't done any speedwork. But, like always, he ran the way he felt and, at the moment, he felt strong and powerful, ready for a good three-mile or 5,000 meters. "I knew after the first three-quarters of a mile I could have the American record if I wanted it. But Jazy's (world record) time is a pretty outstanding record."

In the moments just after a win, it was easy to be buoyed by the jubilation, the phalanx of children surrounding him. He signed every autograph on programs, hands, arms, anything the kids could think of. Soon, it would be time to toast and celebrate and move on. One way or another though, Steve would be back. "It's nice to be home," he said.

FRANK SHORTER WAS supposed to attend the third meet in Vancouver, British Columbia, on May 15, 1975. He was supposed to give Steve a challenge in the 5,000, but he dropped out with an illness. Steve was disappointed and it showed in the race. Steve was flat in winning the 5,000 in 13:46.4. Jon Anderson, the 1973 winner of the Boston Marathon and son of Eugene mayor Les Anderson, replaced Shorter, but he was no match. Neither was Finland's Rune Holmén, who finished, yet again, a distant second to Steve. Steve said, "There aren't too many people who can push me on this continent, or for that matter on other continents, too." Not 100 percent true, he lost more races than he won abroad, but Steve was cresting into the full height of his power as a runner, as a leader, and the thought of unleashing his power would usher in the life he most wanted for himself and others.

Steve quite enjoyed running in front of the Canadians, but it was time to head south. Tacoma, Washington, the site of the fourth meet, had fallen through due to mismanagement on the part of the local organizers, so it was onto the Modesto Relays in California where the competition would be stiffer and Steve would be one race nearer to his big finale in Eugene, never one to ever get too far from his people for too long. However, they would be disappointed: Lasse Virén would not be coming to the United States to challenge Steve at Hayward Field.

Steve received a telegram from Finland that Virén's injury would, in fact, preclude him from coming to Hayward Field for the highly touted rematch. Steve confided to friends how incensed he was. He was furious. He didn't know what was going on. Steve planned on sending a telegram to learn what happened, get more details. Steve said, "Apparently he ran a race last week and strained a muscle and is not working out."

Virén's withdrawal probably had more to do with Steve's bragging about how strong he felt. Prior to the Finns' arrival, Steve had run a brilliant 10,000 meters in an April 1975 Twilight Meet. Bowerman would later recall, "I told him that sounding off about how strong he was had been a mistake, that if he wanted to get those runners over here to his lair, he had to be more sly. But that was hard for him. He didn't look beyond races. Hell, he didn't look beyond laps." Though he had learned a valuable lesson from his pre-Olympic bravado, this proved old habits die hard. He loved letting people know how great he was feeling, even if that tipped his hand. He was categorically the worst bluffer and, in this case, Virén figured it best to fold and ante up another day.

Steve would also say, "Losing him makes everything I've done worthless, but I understand. There were meets in Europe when I didn't show up to run against him." But losing Virén did *not* make the Finn Tour worthless. It had the effect of undermining the influence of the AAU (and the ITA); it showed that change was imminent.

The other six athletes Steve brought over were great, no denying it. But they weren't the reigning 5,000- and 10,000-meter Olympic champion. They weren't the ones who trounced Steve in Munich in 1972. Virén, and runners like Virén, routinely beat Steve in Europe. Virén was the case study to prove that perhaps Europeans were lambs when they left the borders of Europe. Steve had already beaten Virén in the indoor two-mile in Los Angeles in 1973, but Virén had had a stomach bug, so it felt cheap. But at Hayward Field? That would be the test of Steve's great experiment. Also, Virén gave Steve's project a greater sense of legitimacy. If he could bring more athletes to the States of Virén's caliber, it would cement Steve's influence as a power-broker athlete. Nobody was more disappointed than Steve. "It would have been nice having him here to kick some European butt. But I'll be prepared no matter what."

CHAPTER 16

FIRE

ON THE FLIGHT from San Francisco to Eugene, Steve squirmed in his seat. He had taken a quick break from the Finn Tour to run a disappointing two-mile race at the Modesto Relays, and now he was heading back for the final Finn meet at Hayward Field. He tried sleeping. He snapped his window shade shut, banged his head against the wall. He closed his eyes for less than a minute. He still stewed over how poorly he ran at Modesto. Steve never thought he ran good enough. He felt lethargic. He again wanted to quit training. Done running. Maybe not though. He had come too far. Steve was just getting started. The Olympics were just a year away.

He had spent so much of his life to that point focusing on that single event. Time marched on. He wrestled with doubt. He found his footing and a greater vision beyond himself, and it pulled him back from the cliff's edge. When he looked out at the horizon, there was bounty. Steve knew the end was near, and he was no longer "just floating along," as he once was. Whereas running was once a means for him to find belonging, he now wanted to find ways to expand that sense of advocacy for others. On the cusp of the final chapter of the Finn Tour, he was at the height of his celebrity and named the most popular athlete by *Track & Field News*.

While at the Modesto Relays, Steve talked with his fellow athletes about the AAU and the moratorium rule. Kenny Moore, writing for *Sports Illustrated*, said, "An athlete who declined a spot on the national team or who did not run in the national AAU meet would be suspended for one year if he or she competed abroad during certain moratorium periods before the AAU championships and the international meets."

The very fact that the Finn Tour existed at all was proof positive that the AAU's once-draconian stranglehold on the sport was loosening its grip. This was something Shorter attested to about the forthcoming meet in Eugene. "That meet was the watershed. It never dawned on me that my [amateur] status might be in question. It finally reached the point where it was like, 'Okay, enough's enough.' We're all trying to progress and grow and we had this instinct of staying in the sport, and working with the sport, it was to help professionalize it, so that other people could do the same thing. You realize, yes, there's an individual benefit to it. That really isn't your goal. It's more like to love being there, you love doing it, so you want to stay involved in it. A statement was being made and I was helping to reinforce his statement."

Steve was powerful on the day of the last meet, Thursday, May 29, 1975, a spectacular day for Steve to close out the Finn Tour. No Virén, no problem. "Pre's People" turned out. Steve had done it. He had, with the help of the communities, brought international talent to the United States outside the influence of the AAU. Steve proved himself a capable organizer, a leader on the track and a front runner off the track as well.

Steve revved the engine of his 1973 MGB and sped down Eugene's High Street. Roscoe Divine, Steve's former teammate and friend, was walking down High Street when he heard the engine of Steve's car. Steve downshifted and yelled out to Divine, "C'mon, I'll give you a ride."

"I'm not riding with you! You drive crazy," Divine said.

"Suit yourself," and Steve zipped off, always zipping off.

Shorter arrived in Eugene to run against Steve in the 5,000 meters. He no longer had the flu, which had kept him from running against Steve in Vancouver. Shorter's plan was to stay in Eugene and run in the Bill Bowerman Classic on June 7, then stay through the AAU championships on June 20-21, also at Hayward Field.

By the end of the Finn Tour, athletes everywhere were getting more brazen with their distaste of the AAU, no doubt a result of Steve's candor and the very existence of this series of track meets. Shorter said there was talk among athletes that during the forthcoming AAU meet, maybe a 440 runner suddenly cramps up at the end, or athletes run odd events, thus fulfilling the obligation to compete in an AAU meet so a runner could still earn his or her travel permit to go abroad and not be beholden to the AAU to compete in international dual meets. The AAU lorded these travel permits over the athletes as leverage. Shorter said, "You talk to a lawyer and they look at you kind of weird and say, 'they can't do that to you.' If the United States government can't keep schoolteachers from going to North Vietnam, then how can the AAU tell you [that] you can't compete in Europe? Basically, it's a constitutional violation." Voices like Shorter's, with his law background, would be instrumental in the ultimate dismantling of the AAU. Steve had the charisma of a figurehead; Shorter was a chief of staff.

Meanwhile, Steve told Steve Bence, Mark Feig, and Matt Centrowitz—two current and one red shirting Duck—to meet him at his house. The four sat around Steve's coffee table and played spades. "Pre was always hyper before a race and needed the distraction of playing cards to settle him," wrote Bence in his short memoir, *1972: Pre, UO track, Nike shoes, and my life with them all.* They played cards for three hours, which, Feig recalled, Steve just needed several hours to rest.

Steve was fidgety, expressing annoyance that Virén had dropped out, that the AAU was threatening retribution over the Finn Tour, and that he'd sunk much of his own money into these meets. It was a lot to handle, but it would all be over soon. The AAU was likely bluffing. Any track meet without Steve Prefontaine was like a rock festival without a headliner.

For his race that day, Steve donned a black Norditalia singlet, pulled it down over his tight, lithe body. He never wore black. Always Duck yellow, a Team USA singlet, or an Oregon Track Club singlet, never black. He pulled a tracksuit over it. Ralph and Mary Batey, friends of Steve's from Tacoma, Washington, gave Steve a ride to Hayward Field ahead of the meet. He was in a good mood. They told him they'd see him after the meet. As he exited the car, he told them he was going to "throw one damned good drunk after all this is over."

He jogged around Hayward Field and met up with Shorter. They relaxed on the infield together, both lying on their stomachs, hanging out, two of the premier distance runners in the United States. The U of O's Paul Geis was supposed to run in the 5,000, but Bill Dellinger didn't want Geis locking horns with Steve given NCAA championships were the following week in Provo, Utah. That's why this meet was named the "NCAA Preparation Meet." Dellinger didn't see a scenario where Steve lost the race, and Steve and Shorter planned on sharing the pace-setting duties. For Shorter, he said, "The pressure isn't on me."

As Steve ran out of the corral, he blew a snot rocket in the direction of several reporters and jogged to the track, where he looked up and saw that 7,000 people had turned out for the crown jewel of his unprecedented Finn Tour. He waved and warmed up. So many miles on this track. The runners eased up to the starting line and took their positions. This was it.

Geis and Terry Williams blitzed to the early pace through the first mile, a picture-perfect evening with people packing the East and West Stands. They carried Steve and Shorter through an opening mile of 4:17. They still held strong, coasting along at modest 66-second laps through the second mile. By now the tension was ramping up for what should be a match race between Shorter and Steve. Who needed Virén? Steve once said, "How can you lose with people like this?" They were forever his tailwind.

Shorter struck the front in the third mile with a benign 68-second lap. By now Pre's People could sense the tension developing on the track. Steve thought the pace insulting and threw in something fast, took off on his own at a 63-second clip. The unbearable weight of the past month, really the year to date, had grated on him. The controversy around his "to hell with love of country," the challenge of these meets, all that stress bottled up in his body. This was just his second year removed from college, still adjusting to being fully on his own. He felt sluggish, but he wanted to shake this race out of complacency. Doing the math, Steve had given up on the idea of breaking his own American record, let alone a world record. But, swelled by the people in the stands, he extended his lead. At three miles, Steve was a full eight seconds ahead of Shorter, maybe 50 yards. By now, Shorter waved the white flag, took in the full experience of the rabid homestretch. In a final, lasting drive to the finish, Steve crossed the tape as the second fastest American at 5,000 meters (second to himself) in 13:23.8. He whipped his head back to see just how much distance he had between him and Shorter, a distance of at least 50 meters, maybe more. Shorter, the 1972 Olympic marathon champion, finished with a lifetime best 5,000 in 13:32.2. Steve threw his head in the air the way he always had. He untucked his singlet and rolled it up his torso to let the cool air breeze over him. His chest heaved.

After the race, a pristine evening in Eugene, Steve was surrounded by his parents and several reporters who kept a respectable distance. His mother asked Steve, "What are you going to do next?"

"I'll probably run a mile in the Bowerman Classic and then we'll see." Reporters closed in around him. "C'mon over here you guys, I'm just talking to my parents. There is no reason you can't listen in."

To Steve, people had doubted his ability to pull off the Finn Tour. It was a lot of work, but worth it, Steve thought. Maybe he had a future as a promoter? It was good for the Finns and track and field in the United States. But it was so much of a hassle. His training suffered. He needed sponsors "if there's a next time." No athlete outside the purview of the AAU had executed such a feat. Where before a post-collegiate runner felt the futility of their pursuit and the crunch of time, Steve showed a new way, a new path where he might be able to keep racing, as long as he loved it, as long as his body gave him permission. He might just be able to make a living and run, race, and end his career on *his* terms, nobody else's. Where before, it was the bureaucracies that held an athlete's career in its hands and wielded the tired ideal of amateurism like a tattered flag. Steve proved otherwise: if they believed hard enough, they had the power all along. What they needed was a charismatic leader. What they needed was Steve Prefontaine.

THE ANNUAL UNIVERSITY of Oregon track-and-field banquet was held immediately following the meet at the Black Angus Restaurant on Franklin Street. Steve, with his girlfriend, Nancy Allman, snuck into the banquet and sat beside senior miler Scott Daggatt. "You're going to get honored tonight and I think that's great," Steve told Daggatt. Daggatt received the Hull-Bristow Award as Oregon's outstanding senior trackman. Making the awards more meaningful was the fact that it was voted on by his teammates. Steve and Daggatt chatted some. It meant the world to Daggatt that Steve showed up to see him. Daggatt, not much of a partier, had an early night ahead of him because he had a 10 a.m. business law class the following morning.

Steve stayed at the banquet for ten minutes or so, but he found a moment to speak with Dellinger about training for the mile in the Bowerman Classic the next week. He told Dellinger he was on his way to a farewell party for the Finns at Geoff Hollister's house in south Eugene. But first he wanted to stop by the Paddock "for a couple of beers."

Harvey Winn, a former quarterback for Oregon, was at the Paddock after the track meet. In came Steve and there were some of the Finnish athletes with him. "He was having a ball," Winn said. "When the track meet was over, he'd always be willing to party."

Steve was drawn, tired, likely dehydrated. But as was custom, he drank a few cold beers at the Pad. Beer was always his recovery drink. After some time at the Paddock, Steve drove to Hollister's party, sometime between 11 p.m. and midnight. The party was already underway, a big send-off for the Finns, who were letting loose.

The entire Gauthier family was there—Bud and Maxine, Robert, Desiree, and even little Danny. The Gauthiers' cousin Rick Bailey was there, too. Robert remembered Mac Wilkins, the great discus thrower, who had finally defeated Pentti Kahma that night, in the kitchen drinking vodka, face-to-face with each other, the competitive juices extending beyond the discus ring in this jovial atmosphere. The Finns were drinking vodka like water in the kitchen out of tall glasses. Robert already had quite a bit to drink and was, in his own words, "super drunk." He tried dancing with the Finnish long jumper, the one woman who traveled with the team.

Steve and Hollister toasted to everyone there, about what they had accomplished, how great the experience was. In the back of the room near a large cake stood Bailey. Frank Shorter stood beside Bailey, and Shorter dipped his finger in the frosting and licked his finger clean. "Enticing, isn't it?" Shorter said. Bailey, a track super fan, couldn't believe he was there among all these athletes and that Shorter—a gold medalist!—spoke to *him*. There was Wilkins and Kahma; a Finnish pole vaulter wildly dancing; and there was his poor cousin Robert getting suckered into pounding a giant glass of vodka. This could be trouble.

Desiree was eighteen and not drinking. She saw how celebratory everyone was, the relief on their faces. Very festive, not raucous, lots of laughter, buoyant, hopeful. Steve found Desiree and said he planned on coming to Madras in a couple of weeks. In fact, Steve had plans to build an A-frame house in Madras so he had a training base at altitude.

Beer flowed, sandwiches circulated. Jon Anderson was talking about AAU frustrations. Steve, tired from the day—from the month, even the year—interjected, "Where is the talent that I competed with when I started in 1969? The shortage is of guys who are out of school and can still figure ways to train and find competition. I'm twenty-four years old and Frank is twenty-seven, and we're veterans. That's the shake. That's what's wrong with the American system."

People at the party said Steve wasn't there very long, maybe forty-five minutes. It was getting on past midnight, now May 30, 1975. Bud and Maxine, along with Desiree and Danny, were leaving. Steve begged Bud three times not to drive all the way back to Madras. Steve worried they were too tired to make the three-hour drive. Robert saw Steve talking with Bud out on the deck. Robert noticed that Steve looked heavy-lidded and super tired himself. It made sense to Robert; Shorter had given Steve a pretty good challenge and it was the last of these meets. Steve was understandably worn out. Steve shook hands with Bud and parted. Shorter was ready to leave, so Steve walked down to his car with Shorter, as Steve said he'd give him a ride back to Kenny Moore's house up the windy hills near Hendricks Park in east Eugene. Steve's former high school coach, Walt McClure, was at the Hollister party, as were Steve's parents. As they readied to leave for the long drive back to Coos Bay, Steve told them to drive safe.

Robert ran down the steep driveway to see Steve. Robert didn't know if Steve was leaving for good, so he wanted to shake Steve's hand and say good-bye. Bailey was there too, and Steve looked lucid, certainly not intoxicated, by their recollection, but Robert had had quite a lot to drink that night. He had seen Steve drink maybe two beers that evening, but Steve also had a few beers at the Paddock before arriving at Hollister's. Other witnesses admitted that Steve had had three or four beers at the party—and he wasn't at the party long.

Steve planned on dropping Allman off at her car at the U of O ticket office, where she had earlier left it, then Steve would drive Shorter up to

Moore's house, then he'd be back at the party. Shorter, in his memoir *My Marathon*, wrote, "Pre wasn't drunk. There was no way I would have gotten in the car with him. I wouldn't have let him get behind the wheel if he'd been loaded. I had been with him at a lot of parties and bars and knew the signs of drunkenness." But in a story that ran on May 30, 1975, Shorter was asked how much Steve had had to drink. Shorter declined to specify how much (which was in and of itself a damning admission), telling the *Register-Guard* only, "enough to affect his driving." After dropping his girlfriend off at her car, Steve's MGB groaned up the steep pitches, roads he labored up on foot dozens of times, if not more, over the years. He pulled the car up to Moore's house on Prospect Drive atop the Judkins Point Hill. The hill overlooks the Willamette River and a giant field that would one day be threaded with miles of wood-chip running trails, aptly named Pre's Trail, inspired by the pillowy trails he loved running on in Europe.

Steve cut the engine outside Moore's house where he and Shorter talked for two or three minutes. They spoke of their greater mission of taking down the AAU for good, of athlete rights and empowerment. They agreed to meet first thing in the morning for a ten-mile tempo run, up and around these hills Steve knew better than anyone. He was clear-eyed and engaged; tired, yes, but excited for the challenges that lay ahead. There were rumors of "sandbagging" races to stick it to the AAU, but that wasn't in their DNA. They would run hard; they would fight hard. This fight chose them. "Let's go over that tomorrow, when our heads are clear," Steve said.

Shorter slammed the passenger door closed. Steve sped away.

SKYLINE BOULEVARD IS about as steep and narrow a road as there is in Eugene. The road can barely fit two cars side by side and the steep rock faces, vegetation, and parked cars can make for a claustrophobic, thread-the-needle drive. It was a clear night, or early morning, as Steve drove down the boulevard from Moore's house. The road was dry as chalk.

Steve's MGB's headlights illuminated the road before him, casting shadows beyond the steep and imposing rock face to Steve's right. The engine revved in first to second gear as Steve stepped on the clutch and grabbed hold of the gear shifter. The steering wheel was right in his lap and he had a confident hold on the wheel, his seat belt unattached. He eased his little sports car around the corner as he hugged closely to the edge of his right lane.

Coming toward him, more than likely in his lane, was another MGB roadster, headlights blinding, heading straight for Steve's bumper. His eyes widened and he panicked, cutting the wheel sharply to the left and into the opposite lane, still heading downhill on Skyline. His car's left front wheel slammed into the curb, traveling about four feet in the earth before hitting a rock wall embankment of volcanic basalt. The car careened off the rock face with a distinct "thump," flipped, and landed upside down. There it came to rest.

The car's fluids leaked in distinct patterns, running in streams down the hill toward the intersection at Birch Lane. The area was lit by a streetlight 100 feet away. Broken glass scattered on the road. The car pinned Steve beneath it, resting atop that massive chest, and he was, for a short time, fighting to breathe.

At 12:30 a.m., Bill Alvarado was preparing for bed at his home on 2415 Skyline Boulevard, roughly 250 feet by road to where he heard, according to the police report, "the squeal of tires, a loud thump, and then silence" at 12:39 a.m. It being so quiet atop Judkins Point, he "felt an accident had occurred" and "rapidly dressed." Alvarado hurried out to the road to locate the accident. He saw a light-colored sports car hardtop speeding away past him at a "high rate of speed" up the hill traveling south toward Kona Street. Alvarado waved his arms and hollered at the driver to stop, but the car shot past him. Alvarado ran back inside, grabbed his keys, started his car, and drove in the direction of the fleeing sports car. He drove the Skyline loop and did not find the sports car that sped by him. Turning left back onto Skyline from Birch Lane, he found the overturned car that had flipped minutes before. By himself, he raced back up to his house and told his wife to call an ambulance and the police department. Alvarado told his sixteen-year-old son, Arne, to stay put. But Arne, who had seen two sets of headlights nearly collide from his upstairs window, ran down the hill to the scene where he saw a person pinned beneath the car "gasping," "choking." Arne apologized to the man that he could not lift the car, though he tried. Arne's father also tried.

They were quickly running out of time, if they hadn't already. Alvarado's back would ache well into the next day from trying to lift the car that he had recognized as Steve's, hoping he was wrong, hoping it wasn't him.

Sgt. Richard Loveall arrived at the crash scene. Several minutes had passed and, by now, it must have been clear that the driver had been killed. Loveall found no pulse. A neighbor, Dr. Leonard Jacobson, confirmed it. Later, Dr. Edward Wilson, assistant medical examiner for Lane County, listed the official cause of death as "traumatic asphyxiation," a form of suffocation brought about by the weight of the car on Steve's chest. He would say, under these conditions, Steve could not have lived for more than a minute. There were no other injuries that contributed to his death.

At 1 a.m. on May 30, Officer Rex D. Ballenger responded to the fatal car accident. When Ballenger exited his cruiser, which he parked at the foot of the hill on Birch Lane, he said he could smell alcohol in the air a half-block away. It was more than likely the acrid scent of "vomitus," but there likely was some alcohol mixed in.

Ballenger surveyed the scene, the car, the driver, whom he had not yet identified. He noted that there were no skid marks leading to the rock embankment. The *Register-Guard* story that published later that day reported that there were 40 feet of skid marks from the center line to the curb. There were scuff marks on the road leading to the point of impact left by a forward rotating tire sliding sideways, according to the police report. Other officers rooted around the nearby bushes to ensure there hadn't been any other passengers flung from the car. On the road lay a tape cassette of John Denver's "Back Home Again." Perhaps the driver took his eyes off the road to insert the cassette into the tape deck.

One officer found the driver's wallet: Steve Prefontaine.

Ballenger followed Bill Alvarado back up to his house where Alvarado relayed everything he had experienced, what he saw, who he saw, what he heard.

Loveall told Officer Raynor to search the area for the car that matched the description Alvarado gave. They found it at 1770 Kona Street, about 1,000 feet away from the crash scene, the Bylund residence.

Karl Lee Bylund, twenty years old, had been, according to the police report, the driver of the car that sped away. He said that when he turned onto Skyline, Steve's car was already flipped over. He said he exited his vehicle and saw that the driver was injured. Bylund got back in his car and motored up Skyline past the waving Alvarado to contact his father, who was a doctor. Bylund called the police and reported what he saw. He was "shook up." Bylund later agreed to a lie detector test, and it was determined that he was telling the truth, but Bylund's truth contradicted what Arne Alvarado swore he saw from his window, of two cars heading toward each other.

Raynor and Ballenger examined Bylund's car. It showed no signs of being involved in an accident. Ballenger drove back down to the crash site where lab technician James E. Porch was photographing the scene. Soon, the fire department arrived so that photographs could be taken from a ladder truck. Al's Towing arrived and lifted the car off Steve's body. The car was uprighted and transported to their lot.

Steve was then placed in a call car and driven to England's Funeral Home. At 4:15 a.m., Porch drew a vial of blood that was later determined to have a BAC of .16 percent, the legal limit being .10 percent and impaired .15 percent or above.

THE NEWS TRAVELED quickly. Steve's next of kin were notified of his death at 4:30 a.m. by Lt. Cutler. From there, phones rang and the reports on television and radio hit the airwaves. "The impact is unbelievable and the shroud is over the whole nation," said Norv Ritchey, the University of Oregon's athletic director. But no two places were more affected than Eugene and Coos Bay.

People from New York, Los Angeles, and Seattle called Bill Dellinger. He could offer little. He was in shock like the rest of the community. He said, "The fact that people thought of him as a superhuman makes it a lot tougher to accept. I don't think most people looked at him in an ordinary sense."

Bill Huggins, a Coos Bay insurance salesman and father of Tom, Steve's high school running partner, said, "I just chatted with him briefly and told him to stop by the house next time he was home. I'm just sick, and you can imagine the feeling of the community here. He's a part of a lot of people's lives in this community and people are numb. It's a personal loss to a lot of people." Another Coos Bay resident said, "Gosh, he was our boy."

Doug Crooks, Steve's high school rival, working in Washington, D.C., editing a publication for Ralph Nader at the time, heard the news and started crying. Ralph Mann, the 1972 silver medalist in the 400-meter hurdles, later recalled how "He drove too fast. He never wore a seat belt. Pre was a party guy. There's a lot of what ifs in that situation." Mann would have been at the meet and at the Hollister party had he not been in the throes of his PhD exams that weekend at Washington State University. "What would have happened if I would have been there? Would I have told him to put his seat belt on? Would I have driven? I did that before when he had too much. I always wondered what would have happened if my exams weren't the same week as that meet." Shorter also exhibited his own survivor's guilt, exacerbated by being the last to see Steve before the accident. "If we had talked for thirty seconds more or thirty seconds less, five seconds more or five seconds less . . ."

The Gauthiers had arrived safely at home in Madras. They were barely home before Bud received the call from Geoff Hollister, phones ringing all over Oregon. It was maybe 6:30 in the morning when he heard that Steve had died. He woke up Desiree. He was sobbing. "He jumped on top of me . . . I had never seen my dad like that," she said. Their bond was strong. Just a year before, Steve had written them a letter saying, "Hello, Just a short note to say thank you so very much for the two wonderful days you let me share with you. I wish the whole world would be filled with individuals just like you two, then we would have a world with love and peace. Hopefully I'll see you soon. Take care, Steve."

Bud soon told the *Register-Guard*, "Last night my little boy was playing around with Pre. How do I wake him up and tell him this? Pre was going to come to my house Monday."

The shockwaves kept spreading. Since Steve had changed addresses, his invitation to travel with the United States team to China earlier in the month had likely gotten lost. He was preoccupied with organizing and headlining his Finn Tour, so he likely would have turned it down anyway. Pete Shmock, a former Oregon shot-putter and teammate of Steve's for three years, made the three-week trip, as did Mike Manley, a steeplechaser with the Oregon Track Club, and Dick Buerkle, a 5,000-meter runner who had defeated Steve indoors on the east coast in the winter of 1975.

On May 30, 1975, the team was flying back to Seattle. They passed through customs and into the main terminal. Shmock heard someone yell, "Pre's dead!"

This was Steve's community, a tight-knit group of elite track athletes. It had to be wrong. Shmock said, "I remember the silence and the shock of hearing that." The rest of the team knew Steve, but few, if any, were college teammates like Shmock was. Was it already five years—March 1970—since they posed for that photograph in Juarez, Mexico, toasting beers, baby-faced and innocent?

Thousands of people unfolded their *Register-Guard* newspapers and on the front page was a giant, piercing, haunting photograph of Steve's face, those giant eyes, moments before his final race, staring blankly. "Pre's death 'the end of an era,'" read the headline. There was an emptiness, as Pat Tyson, Steve's former roommate, recalled. He was living in Seattle teaching junior high at the time. He was out for his usual morning run when he got an "unexplainable urge to return home." Standing at his door was his landlady. "I've got some bad news," she said. "Real bad, Pre is dead. He died in a car wreck."

"I don't believe that," Tyson said. He thought there was no way. Had to be a mistake. Steve couldn't die. He's too full of life to die.

In Coos Bay, the morning of May 30, after he had heard from Lt. Cutler, Steve's father called Neta, who lived in nearby Coquille, and asked if she'd like to come down to the Eugene Police station with him to collect Steve's belongings, a black duffel bag, his wallet. When Ray Prefontaine opened the wallet he sifted through its contents. "Oh, my God," he said. He removed a photograph and held it up for Neta to see. Neta recalled, "It was the picture of me. He kept it in his wallet all those years."

THERE WAS NO place more appropriate to honor Steve Roland Prefontaine's life than in Coos Bay at Pirate Stadium, where it all began. There would soon be a plaque on the foundation of Pirate Stadium's massive bleachers—where all these thousands came to pay their respects—that read: Steve Prefontaine set his last American record on this track May 9, 1975, running the 2000m in 5:01.4.

On Monday, June 2, 1975, some 2,500 people descended on Marshfield High School. Dozens of cars parked bumper to bumper along Seventh Street as mourners walked to Pirate Stadium. Six pallbearers placed Steve's casket, now covered with yellow chrysanthemums and forest green ferns, before the lectern where Bill Bowerman, sunken and solemn, said, "Pre's legacy to us is that the good things of track and other sports may be freely enjoyed by athletes and spectators, won by truth, honesty, and hard work. With his characteristic courage and persistence, through difficult communication, Pre opened that door. He was able to get that final step in athlete emancipation through our national organization."

Sounding like Marc Antony from Shakespeare's *Julius Caesar*, Walt McClure said, "I am here not to mourn Steve Prefontaine but rather to pay final tribute to an outstanding young American. The characteristic that separated Pre from the rest of the field was his pride. To be the best was his only goal. Limitation was not in Steve's frame of reference. He was continually extending the boundaries of his frontier." And McClure added something that would become, most certainly, prophetic: "the accomplishments of such an individual are often recognized years after the deed, the act."

Reiner Stinius, a Finnish national and graduate student at the U of O, presented the Prefontaines with a wreath made of blue and white flowers arranged in the pattern of the flag of Finland. Pallbearers Frank Shorter, Jon Anderson, Brett and Bob Williams, Jim Seyler, and Geoff Hollister carried the casket to the center of the field near the west goal posts. Though the casket was closed for the service, Steve was dressed in his blue Olympic blazer with the Olympics logo embroidered on the breast pocket. Nearby, the Marshfield High track team wore their purple and gold Pirate colors. Eventually his bronze casket was placed in the light-blue hearse. It traveled around the track, leading a convoy, one last lap before exiting the east gate on the way to the cemetery. The crowd slowly filed out.

Earlier in the thirty-three-minute program, Steve's cousin, Jan Prefontaine, who lived in Washington, D.C., sang a song she wrote about him called "Pre—January 1974." She asked him one time, "Why don't you leave Oregon for bigger and better things?"

"I can't leave my people," he said.

Now the stadium was empty, save for the ground crew picking up the chairs and flowers. Four young girls stepped onto the track and started running. One of the girls was considerably younger and smaller than the other three and trailed them—like Steve Prefontaine was way back when. One of the older girls dropped out, but the younger girl charged ahead in pursuit of the leaders. She didn't hit the line before the other two. She gave her best, got up for third. She never quit.

ON TUESDAY, JUNE 3, 1975, the East Stands at Hayward Field were nearly full for another memorial service. This included Bowerman, Shorter, and Kenny Moore. Steve's body now rested at Sunset Memorial Park in Coos Bay, where in the years to come, people would leave shoes, medals, and coins on his headstone, just as they would at Pre's Rock, the memorial at the site of Steve's accident, a shrine of sorts where people make pilgrimages. Shorter shared, "Just the other day Steve was asked about my running and what he thought my success would be at 10,000 meters both this year and next. His answer was classic Steve. 'If he's having a good day and running the right race, nobody can beat Shorter at 10,000 meters . . . nobody but me.'"

As Bowerman spoke, a man cradled a weeping girl. One boy said he planned on building a frame at school and placing an article about Steve's career in it. It was also announced that the forthcoming Bowerman Classic would henceforth be called the Prefontaine Classic, its namesake to this very day as part of the Diamond League.

The clock on the scoreboard counted up. It stopped at 12:36.2, what would've or could've been a world record in the three-mile for Steve, that coveted record, three consecutive 4:12s. The people in the stands clapped and cheered.

They had to imagine the fire.

A HIGHER STANDARD
THAN VICTORY

ON MAY 25, 2024, people walking along Agate Street in Eugene, Oregon, were abuzz for the Prefontaine Classic, founded forty-nine years earlier, at Hayward Field. As part of the Wanda Diamond League, the Pre Classic attracted the best athletes from around the world, this in an Olympic Year, where Hayward Field would, once again, host the U.S. Olympic Trials—the "American Games," as Bill Bowerman once called them.

Track and field might not arrest the attention of the casual sports fan like it once did when distance runners like Steve Prefontaine, Jim Ryun, and Frank Shorter graced the covers of *Sports Illustrated*. But here in Eugene you wouldn't necessarily know that track and field has long taken a back seat to other mainstream sports. Eugene takes its identity as TrackTown USA very seriously.

On the east side of Hayward Field, along plate-glass windows that line the sidewalk, are images of famous Oregon Duck runners and coaches from the age of Bill Hayward to Bill Bowerman to Bill Dellinger and beyond. Most prominent among the images is, of course, Steve Prefontaine. Cast your gaze up to the brilliant tower structure that looms over the finish line and there's an imposing image of Steve running early in his Oregon career, eyes cast south in the direction of the old finish line in the shadow of the West Stands. It's still a magical place, if a bit airbrushed and modern to the point of corporate, a $270 million structure, the house that Steve Prefontaine built.

In the 2024 renewal of the Bowerman Mile, the world's best milers were on display with Great Britain's Josh Kerr and Norway's Jakob Ingebrigsten—outspoken rivals—waging an all-too-familiar war, with Kerr winning in a fiery 3:45.34, a personal best and world-leading time heading into the Paris Olympics. Though Ingebrigsten didn't win, there's a Prefontaine air to him, a runner with slicked-back coiffed hair, tattoos, self-assuredness bordering on arrogance, and a willingness to strike the front and dare everyone to stay with him. (He would set a ruthless pace in the 1,500-meter final in the Paris Olympics before fading to fourth in the final strides. Four days later he would win the gold in the 5,000 meters in smashing fashion, Steve Prefontaine's signature race. Ingebrigtsen is also a Nike athlete with middle-distance versatility that makes him feel like a modern-day Prefontaine only with more hardware.)

Perhaps there's no crowd on the planet that appreciates that fearlessness—that brashness—than the people of Hayward Field, certainly the silver-haired contingent who at one point called themselves "Pre's People." In many places in Eugene, Steve is larger than life and casts an outsized shadow over Oregon, over American track and field, this from a runner who never won an Olympic medal or held a world record. He has endured, in part, because, as Phil Knight wrote in an email for this book, "In the track and field world Pre is eternal, which comes out of his appearance, running style, and unbelievable will to win."

We can agree that it was altogether *something more,* for there were scores of runners with a will to win, who did just that, but are forgotten in the way a wave washes away a footprint. Bowerman, in his eulogy for Steve at Hayward Field on June 3, 1975, encapsulated the allure of Steve better than anyone ever had, or, quite frankly, ever has, in the fifty years since Steve's death. He said, "Pre, you see, was troubled by knowing that a mediocre effort could win a race, and a magnificent effort can lose one. Winning a race wouldn't necessarily demand that he give it everything he had from start to finish. He never ran any other way. I tried to get him to. God knows I tried. But Pre was stubborn. He insisted on holding himself to a higher standard than victory. A race is a work of art. That's what he said. That's what he believed. And he was out to make it one every step of the way."

Within a week of Steve's passing, he was memorialized with the Prefontaine Classic, a meet that would, in perpetuity, bear his name and court the best track-and-field athletes the country—and eventually the world—offered. No other track meet bears the name of an athlete, and so every year the world gets a perennial celebration of Steve Prefontaine's enduring influence.

Pat Tyson, Steve's close friend and roommate from the Glenwood trailer, said, "Why does Babe Ruth endure today? Why does Mark Twain? Well, there's certainly enough people that are living who have passed his baton on, his memory. Nike certainly has because as Phil would say they needed three of us: Two of us wasn't gonna make Nike. So, Phil has the money to help promote Pre with the statue on campus, a documentary, and the Diamond League, and the best track meet in America—the Pre Classic—to keep his legacy, so there's plenty of enduring memories passed on by those that are living, that are now aging, that I believe can keep it going."

Wade Bell, who ran for Bowerman back in the 1960s and has been a decades-long track official, likened much of Steve's appeal to the small-town boy making it big. Broader still, Steve's ghost remains relevant when we see the Eugene Symphony perform scores inspired by him, or an artist displaying a Prefontaine statue in front of the Fifth Street Market pavilion, a shot put's throw away from the Nike Store, a store bearing giant posters of Steve in breathtaking motion. As the journalist and biographer Howard Bryant has said, "Everybody gets forgotten. The only people who don't get forgotten are the ones we keep telling stories about, the ones we keep repeating."

For fifty years, Steve has endured, but for a time, by the mid-1990s, Steve was fading from the public consciousness. In fact, after Steve's death, some runners, the brilliant miler Marty Liquori among them, began to question the utility of their maniacal pursuit of equity in track and field, saying, "To me the greatest effect that Pre had on American distance running was, when he died, all of us who were putting 100 percent into it, we had the attitude of we're making a lot of sacrifices, we're not making a lot of money, but it's going to pay off. What you do until you're thirty is going to pay off for the next fifty years. When Pre died, we said, 'Oh, wait a minute, you might not get seventy years."

Twenty years after Steve's death, his peers, his classmates, his fans were cresting into their mid-forties. Middle age is a particularly ripe time for nostalgia, and this group of Baby Boomers was delivered a Nike-subsidized documentary in 1995 titled *Fire on the Track*, and it drummed up all the memories and reinspired and reminded people of the special talent and iconoclastic person that was Steve Prefontaine, so vibrant a personality taken all too soon. It was narrated by Oregon's most revered writer, Ken Kesey, and it reignited a fervor around this singular spirit. It also allowed Nike—in the throes of Air Jordan's cultural dominance—to harken back to its roots: distance running. *We may be this now, but we were once Steve Prefontaine.*

It's a fine documentary, if a bit sanitized, in that Steve's peers could reflect and wax poetic about their long-gone friend and rival. It's also hard not to divorce the notion that it's a genius piece of content marketing for a corporate behemoth. In the case of Steve, he became bigger than track . . . and we keep talking about him.

It's no coincidence that, over the years, Nike saw fit to platform personalities of this nature, from Prefontaine to Ingebrigsten. It all started with Steve Prefontaine in Nike's birth sport. He gave Nike the initial lift to gain its ultimate altitude. Nike's roots were running, and Steve was its firstborn. Phil Knight wrote that Steve was the "paradigmatic Nike athlete." Though Nike planned on outfitting Steve head to toe up to and through the 1976 Olympics, concrete plans at the time of his death were impossible based on the rules in the mid-1970s. In an email, Knight wrote, "We knew if and when the rules changed, he would be a great endorsement, but had no specific plans, not knowing when the track-and-field authorities would change the rules." One of the great tragedies of Steve's short life was that his likeness is plastered all over the University of Oregon, and the cities of Eugene and Coos Bay, and, in a sense, is exploited for the gain of others. And yet, he never got to reap the rewards himself. Just like the power brokers who selfishly leveraged the athletes of the 1970s, there's a case that, in death, Steve is still very much used to espouse and celebrate the humble rebellious ethos of a company now worth more than $100 billion. In exchange, as the slogan goes, "Pre lives."

Nike saw the power in platforming and forefronting the athlete and forging living icons, of creating mythology. Its biggest, and most influential, was Steve, totemic in part because he was an athlete who died young, who could be lionized and preserved in amber as the consummate rebel with a purity of spirt unweathered by time. Before Michael Jordan, there was Steve; Steve was the foundation. "There is no Nike without Pre," Pat Tyson said. "They needed some superstar and Michael Jordan wasn't ready. They needed that bridge. They wouldn't have made it." Steve Bence, a former teammate of Steve's and a longtime employee of Nike, said, "Nike wouldn't exist without Pre. . . . Without Pre endorsing the shoe by wearing it in competition, I don't think Nike would have succeeded." In a 1974 Twilight Meet at Hayward Field, Steve debuted the beautiful red, white, and blue "Pre Montreal" track spike and broke the American 10,000-meter record in them. Nike needed Steve and, for the purposes of keeping the flame burning, Steve also needed Nike.

Fire on the Track catalyzed two feature films—by two different sets of creative (and warring) teams, in back-to-back (!) years—*Prefontaine* starring Jared Leto, and *Without Limits* (the far superior of the two) starring Billy Crudup. Thus, a runner who never won an Olympic medal or broke a world record, remains, to this day, an avatar of self-belief, hard work, and determination, a philosopher runner who, as Bowerman noted, sought a higher purpose than winning. Above all, a legend that superseded the man at the heart of the myth. Many people who knew Steve and who were candid in their remembrances of him for this book bristled at the "Pre-ness" of it all. To them, he was just . . . *Steve*. Ralph Mann, Steve's close friend and 1972 silver medalist in the 400-meter hurdles, said, "Eugene has basically deified him. When I first met him, he was a twenty-year-old collegiate runner. He died at twenty-four. That's awfully young for someone to have the qualities they placed on him. He was a good-time guy who loved people, *really* loved women, and had an enormous ability to drink and carouse and make fun of life. It was a thrilling experience to be around him."

These films were screened to innumerable track and cross-country teams across the country, turning teenagers (likely coached by people who remembered watching Steve on ABC's *Wide World of Sports*) into a generation of new people inspired by the courageous front runner. Some of these young athletes would eventually become coaches themselves, and they too would show the movie and admire this long-gone hero who espoused that, "To give anything less than your best is to sacrifice the gift."

"I thought a little bit about that quote," remembered Oregon shot-putter, and former teammate of Steve's, Pete Shmock. "He lived that. He never said anything about that when I was around him when we were drinking beer. We were just . . . drinking beer. He wasn't philosophizing about how one should live their life. He was such a bigger-than-life character. He was open about going forth with this great drive and not sacrificing his gift. That larger-than-life personality, plus all the records he broke, the image of his face when he's grinding through the pain. All of those are examples, especially in track and field, about how one wants to be in one's life. Let's just strive for that."

Yet another aspect that projects Steve into the future was his activism and his spirited case against the dismantling of the AAU. It would take three more years, but in 1978 the AAU was finally, and irrevocably, declawed of its power in track and field. One pictures Steve smiling, and also wondering what the hell took so long? The Amateur Sports Act of 1978, wrote Joseph M. Turrini in *The End of Amateurism in American Track and Field*, "stripped the AAU of all of its international franchises. Each Olympic sport would have its own autonomous national governing body that would be independent but now directly attached to the United States Olympic Committee." And by 1979 the "AAU bowed out of track governance and gave its IAAF franchises to the Athletics Congress, the newly created national governing body for track and field." This new U.S. national governing body's executive board had to be "composed of at least twenty percent active athletes," which echoed a sentiment Steve once had: "If I had thirty athletes behind me, we could form our own federation."

Ken Popejoy, whose open hand was at one point ignored by a smug and immature Steve Prefontaine at the 1969 Golden West Invitational, said, "I respected his advocacy. There's people who have talent, but I've never seen anybody since that has had the advocacy and the passion and the unselfishness as him. That's why his legend has endured because people saw that."

What also can't be denied was the serendipitous timing of Steve's life. Lightning had struck in the early 1970s. So much was changing. Amateurism was dying, professional track was on the rise, shoes were changing, athletes were changing. The confluence of Steve's charisma and look, combined with his talent, his coach, his 1970 appearance on the cover of *Sports Illustrated*, and the rise of an upstart shoe company in Nike created an alchemy that could never be bottled again in track and field. Steve was a showman and saw his running as performance art when others were merely competing.

Which was exactly what professional track—the International Track Association—desperately needed but would never get. Steve's passing might have been the death knell for the upstart professional track league. Steve played hard to get and rejected every offer. Though he hated being a poor man and said that training for the 1976 Olympics would have left him penniless. (How poor? Well, he bought a sports car and a house, so it stands to reason he might have played up the poor-man routine for sympathy; maybe it was a mask, but an honorable one.) He may have hated being poor, but he hated being told what to do even more. Had he accepted the $75,000 offer in 1974 or the $200,000 offer in 1975 he would have been obligated to run in every ITA meet. If the ITA season interfered with the Napoleonic obsession and Sisyphean desire to conquer Europe, he'd have to acquiesce to the ITA. Given enough motivation, maybe he would have torn up his contract and paid them back. Steve once expressed that he never would have wanted running to be a job. He wanted full autonomy. Top-flight athletes made substantial tax-free income under the table. Why take a pay cut? A big incentive to competing in Europe was that that's where the most money was to be made: duty-free cash in a crisp, white envelope.

Steve's passing was a blow to the ITA's capacity to attract a runner at the height of his athletic prowess and the crossover appeal the likes of which track and field had never seen. Jim Ryun populated several covers of *Sports Illustrated*, but he didn't excite people on a carnal level. Unless the AAU would allow amateurs to swim in a pool "contaminated" by runners earning over-the-table money—thus inviting the best athletes and the best competition—fans would get a second- or third-rate product of once-heavyweights living off reputation over ability. Whether or not the ITA even had the money to honor what it offered Steve was up for speculation. It likely borrowed against what it forecasted a Prefontaine signing would bring to the ITA coffers in gate revenue and sponsorships, a futures commodity with a dynamite mustache.

By summer of 1975, this after Steve's death, the ITA was floundering and after the 1976 Montreal Games, when Olympic athletes failed to sign, the ITA folded, ending its four-year-run at a rain-dampened meet in Gresham, Oregon.

In an era before mass proliferation and splintering of media, Steve found ways to connect with his fans. He wrote dispatches from overseas and letters to the editor letting "Pre's People" feel like they too were along for the ride, much in the way parasocial relationships exist in the social media landscape of the modern day. Being so photogenic and endlessly quotable allowed him to leverage the media to create a personal brand before such a thing even existed, much like what we see with Michael Jordan or Aaron Rodgers, Sha'Carri Richardson or Noah Lyles. Steve would often express, especially as his career began to take off, how running was a means of personal discovery.

At Hayward Hall, on the footprint of so many of Steve's brilliant performances, there's a quote from Bill Bowerman's eulogy of Steve saying, "The real purpose of running isn't to win a race. It's to test the limits of the human heart." It's a sentiment that Steve, no doubt, matured into as he crested into his mid-twenties and looked beyond himself and toward the community at large, his people.

In the final strides of Steve's last race, in an image timeless in its beauty and meaning, that community, the "demanding crowd," all stood on their feet, clapping, cheering, and screaming Steve's name. With every stride, his lead grew. The people looked to him, squinting into the day's waning light, then stared in awe at the massive distance between Steve and second place. Down the final straightaway, he was all alone, his spikes clawing at the track. Steve reached out for the tape with his hand, and he whipped his gaze over his shoulder down the long expanse of the home stretch to measure the distance between him and the rest, never losing sight of those left in his wake. As he broke the tape, the people roared once more, and the shadows lengthened over the track, Steve aglow by the setting of the sun.

ACKNOWLEDGMENTS

Over the course of reporting for this book, Dave Wottle, the 1972 gold medalist in the 800 meters, and who, for a time, had run the third fastest mile of all time and the fastest ever mile run at Hayward Field, told me, "No one's on an island. You have a family, you have coaches, you have teammates, you have competitors. All that together is what makes runners achieve their goals. Steve helped me learn that lesson. I was always grateful for that."

And so it is with book writing.

This book came to pass out of luck and serendipity, as many things do in the arts. As a result of starting the *Creative Nonfiction* podcast in early 2013, drip by drip I've built a robust community of fellow tellers of true tales. One, the author Kim H. Cross, who I consider a dear friend now, asked me during peak COVID-19 pandemic times if I had a literary agent. I said that despite my efforts and more than one hundred agent rejections over the years, no, I did not. Kim thought this unacceptable and introduced me to Susan Canavan of the Waxman Literary Agency.

I pitched Susan my dusty baseball memoir, and she said that it was fine and all, but memoirs are a tough sell and you're not famous enough, but are you working on anything more commercial? The question caught me flat-footed. I filibustered, then peeked over at my bookcase and saw the spine of Tom Jordan's slim, decades-old biography *Pre: The Story of America's Greatest Running Legend, Steve Prefontaine*. It being 2022, I told Susan, "I've been saving string on a Steve Prefontaine project because in three years it will mark the fiftieth anniversary of his death." Susan immediately said, "I can sell that on proposal."

And she did! To Matt Harper at HarperCollins. So, a big thank-you to Kim, to Susan for taking me on, and more on Matt in a moment.

Despite being a writer of nonfiction for more than twenty years, I was and, if I'm being honest, still am, something of a nobody. My name, cool as it is, isn't Michael Lewis or Howard Bryant, Susan Orlean or Laura Hillenbrand. Early in the book proposal stage, you rely on people who have no idea who you are to talk to you for a long time, and you can't tell them you have a book deal in place and that things are a go. That comes later . . . you hope. So I must thank the people who were so generous with their time not knowing who I was, who put their faith in Steve's story, who ultimately gave the proposal the acceleration it needed down the runway to give it lift. They are Coos Bay natives and Marshfield High School alumni Darrelyn Coats, Roger Bingham, Ron Apling, and Jay Farr. Thank you for your time and trust so early in the process when things were very much an unknown. Also, a big thanks to Fran Worthen, who drove me around Coos Bay, showed me the old running routes, and brought me to Steve's grave. Fran is a treasure.

I confided in very few people over the course of this book's creation, but the people I spoke to most often, and who sandblasted the varnish of my imposter syndrome and apocalyptic self-doubt from my hull, were Bronwen Dickey, Kim H. Cross, and Ruby McConnell. Heart emojis to you three.

With apologies (the original title of these acknowledgments) to Glenn Stout, who read and edited the RDOAT—roughest draft of all time—ahead of my first deadline: 160,000 words, 500-plus pages of shapeless drivel with a directive of, "We need to cut 50,000 words." I should probably give Glenn a couple more thousand dollars and a gift card to BetterHelp, if such a thing exists. It is no coincidence that his rates increased after working with me. So, thank you, Glenn. Your list of books in which you've been acknowledged numbers somewhere in the thousands by now.

Which brings me to Matt Harper, a seasoned marathoner who makes a wicked mockery of Heartbreak Hill every Patriots' Day for the Boston Marathon. I won the lottery. Every exchange we had was a master class in how to craft a biography. He was so invested in the book and open to ninety-minute Zooms to talk things through. His initial editorial letter, which I sent to the aforementioned Glenn Stout, was the best letter Glenn had ever seen, this from someone who has had his hand in more than one hundred books of his own. I saw fellow writers' eyes turn red with fury and green with jealousy when they heard the extent to which Matt was involved with the shaping of this book and seeing things that I could never see, making conclusions I could never deduce on my own. If you enjoyed *The Front Runner*, it's because of Matt. If you didn't, you need only blame me.

Kudos also go to Michele Soulli, who is an intrepid researcher and genealogist. She helped find some family documents that I otherwise would not have found on my own. She has helped authors like Jeff Pearlman and Jonathan Eig spin incredible biographies. Writers, you should totally hire her.

Hundreds of hours of interviews went into this book and only a few were quoted on the record, but none were wasted. There are too many to mention, but your time and generosity helped build the world and helped me accomplish my goal, which was, to quote an interview Eig did about his Rev. Martin Luther King Jr. biography, "We'd turned him into a monument and a national holiday and lost sight of his humanity. So I really wanted to write a more intimate book." Every conversation rounded out Steve's character and brought us back to the man behind the myth, flaws and all. You helped make Pre, in my eyes, Steve again.

And, of course, all the gratitude to my wife, Melanie, who makes it all possible. Thank you for the health insurance.

NOTES

PROLOGUE

1   *"belongs to the world"*: Dennis Anstine. "A premonition?" *The World,* June 20, 1975, page 8.

2   *twenty-one; and Steve's girlfriend:* "They came to pay Pre final tribute," *The World,* June 3, 1975, page 12.

2   *"Pre is eternal"*: Phil Knight email to author, February 5, 2024.

2   *"keep that door open"*: Carl Cluff. "Pre's people pay tearful tribute to favorite son," *Oregon Journal,* June 3, 1975, pages 17, 20.

3   *"so valuable his time"*: Blaine Newnham. "Pre's last lap back where it began," *Register-Guard,* June 3, 1975, page 1C.

CHAPTER 1: FORGED

7   *"used to jabber incessantly"*: Ray Arndt interview with author, May 18, 2023.

7   *"so did I"*: Ray Arndt interview with author, May 18, 2023.

8   *were always at war:* Ray Arndt interview with author, May 18, 2023.

8   *"ran away from me"*: Ray Arndt interview with author, May 18, 2023.

8   *full custody of Neta:* Ray Prefontaine court record, December 2, 1946.

9   *he was her baby:* Neta Prefontaine interview with author, December 18, 2023.

9   *"was big enough to"*: Neta Prefontaine interview with author, December 18, 2023.

9   *"you to be good"*: Neta Prefontaine interview with author, December 8, 2023.

9   *Steve was an embarrassment:* Ray Arndt interview with author, May 18, 2023.

9   *worried about him constantly:* Neta Prefontaine interview with author, December 8, 2023.

10 *"in front of my eyes"*: Ray Arndt interview with author, May 18, 2023.

10 *"glass the wrong way"*: Bill Dixon. "His absence is felt with sharpness," *The World,* May 29, 1976, page 11.

10 *safekeeping, in his wallet:* Neta Prefontaine interview with author, December 8, 2023.

10 *"with an iron fist"*: John Van Zonneveld interview with author, May 2, 2023.

11 *"stemmed from his childhood"*: John Van Zonneveld interview with author, May 2, 2023.

11 *"switchblade in your pocket"*: Kenny Moore. "What I'd like to do," *Track & Field News,* March 1972, page 3.

12 *"Football was suicide"*: Kenny Moore. "What I'd like to do," *Track & Field News,* March 1972, page 3.

12 *"was a good runner"*: Ray Arndt interview with author, May 18, 2023.

12 *"cheering for him"*: Ray Arndt interview with author, May 18, 2023.

CHAPTER 2: DANGEROUS

13 *second father to him:* Tom McGuire. "In Perspective . . . 'Life' team follows Pre," *The World,* June 16, 1972, page 17.

14 I'll never do that: Walt McClure. "The 'Pre' View," *Coach Magazine,* date unknown, page 21.

14 *sentiment shared by many:* Roger Bingham interview with author, April 12, 2022.

14 *for a fourteen year old:* Howard Kubli interview with author, May 15, 2023.

15 *"the potential to be":* Tom Huggins interview with author, May 10, 2023.

15 *headed for the streets:* Kenny Moore. "What I'd like to do," *Track & Field News,* March 1972, page 3.

15 *"The Blue Course":* Tom Huggins interview with author, May 10, 2023.

16 *"of Steve Prefontaine again":* Roger Bigham interview with author, April 12, 2022.

16 *"team's No. 2 runner":* Kenn Hess. "Bench splinters," October 26, 1965, page 10.

16 *"hard worker this fall":* Kenn Hess. "Bench splinters," *The World,* October 26, 1965, page 10.

17 *saw composure from Steve:* "Pirates' runners qualify for State but lose district title to N. Eugene," *The World,* October 30, 1965, page 10.

17 *"was a good one":* Blaine Newnham. "Steve Prefontaine," *Register-Guard,* June 1, 1975, 1B.

17 *"was born to compete":* Blaine Newnham. "Steve Prefontaine," *Register-Guard,* June 1, 1975, 1B.

18 *"sting like a bee!":* Howard Kubli interview with author, May 15, 2023.

18 *"just kind of him":* Howard Kubli interview with author, May 15, 2023.

18 *"check out what we're doing":* Phil Pursian interview with author, August 29, 2023.

19 *two-mile in 10:54.4:* "MHS frosh spikers win," *The World,* April 14, 1966, page 14.

19 *two-mile in 10:08.6:* Kenn Hess. "Marshfield edges North Bend for Coos track crown," *The World,* May 7, 1966, page 14.

19 *"know who this is?":* Bob Hylton interview with author, June 27, 2023.

20 *hypnotized by Steve's rhythm:* Bob Hylton interview with author, June 27, 2023.

20 *80 or so yards:* "Siuslaw runners win Gold Beach Invitational," *The World,* October 10, 1966, page 11.

20 *following week in Salem:* "Pirates, Bulldogs runners in District 5 meet today," *The World,* October 28, 1966, page 12.

20 *between Eugene and Creswell:* Kenn Hess. "Prefontaine's 'Discovery' on race track," *The World,* May 1, 1969, page 14.

20 *"in purple and gold":* Kenn Hess. "Prefontaine's 'Discovery' on race track," *The World,* May 1, 1969, page 14.

21 *"to call an ambulance":* Bill Keenan interview with author, November 9, 2023.

21 *to Keenan and McNeale:* Bill Keenan interview with author, November 9, 2023.

21 *with McNeale finishing second:* "Pirates capture state cross country berth," *The World,* October 29, 1966, page 13.

21 *"you're gonna be dangerous":* Bill Keenan interview with author, November 9, 2023.

21 *"a giant among runners":* Walt McClure. Essay on Pre's training, "The 'Pre' View," *Coach Magazine,* 1972.

21 he wanted to be: Kenn Hess. "Prefontaine's 'Discovery' on race track," *The World,* May 1, 1969, page 14.

21 *son of a bitch:* Greg Barnett interview with author, May 15, 2023.

22 *the two-mile standard of 9:45:* Kenn Hess. "North Eugene wins District 5 track crown," *The World,* May 19, 1967, page 15.

22 *their letter that year:* "Athletic awards given 85 at Marshfield High," *The World,* May 24, 1967, page 14.

22 *would fall into place:* Dennis Anstine. "A premonition?" *The World,* June 20, 1975, page 8.

23 *"of things to come":* Walt McClure. Essay on Pre's training, "The 'Pre' View," *Coach Magazine,* 1972.

23 *deeply, gnawed at him:* Pat Putnam. "The Freshman and the Great Guru," *Sports Illustrated,* June 15, 1970, page 3.

23 *beaches. Up the hills:* Pat Putnam. "The Freshman and the Great Guru," *Sports Illustrated,* June 15, 1970, page 3.

CHAPTER 3: CHAMPION

24   *losing another race:* Phil Pursian interview with author, August 29, 2023.

24   *ruthlessness to his training:* Phil Pursian interview with author, August 29, 2023.

25   *a typical week of workouts looked like this:* U of O Special Collections.

25   *"exhilarated, not exhausted":* Kenny Moore. *Bowerman and the Men of Oregon.* Rodale Press, 2006, page 91.

26   *"through your bare feet":* Kenny Moore. *Bowerman and the Men of Oregon.* Rodale Press, 2006, page 124.

26   *envy of every rival:* Kenny Moore. *Bowerman and the Men of Oregon.* Rodale Press, 2006, page 125.

26   *marveled at Steve's strength:* "Marshfield's veteran runners open season," *The World,* September 15, 1967, page 16.

27   *hit the road running:* Tom Huggins interview with author, May 10, 2023.

27   *"hard as we do":* Tom Huggins interview with author, May 10, 2023.

27   *"only secret to success":* Ron Clarke. "The Unforgiving Minute," Runner's Tribe Books, 2016, Loc. 2597.

27   *not to lose again:* Kenn Hess. "Prefontaine, Huggins set pace for MHS runners," *The World,* October 25, 1967, page 10.

28   *"Show me something, Prefontaine":* Kenn Hess. "Prefontaine, Huggins set pace for MHS runners," *The World,* October 25, 1967, page 12.

28   *McClure had ever seen:* Kenn Hess. "Prefontaine, Huggins set pace for MHS runners," *The World,* October 25, 1967, page 10.

29   *(meaning high school) history:* "South gets meet nod," *Register-Guard,* October 26, 1967, 2C.

29   *"diminutive bundle of energy":* "Bucs, Prefontaine, breeze to crown," *Register-Guard,* October 28, 1967, 2B.

29   *get back on course:* "Marshfield takes District 5A-1 country crown," *The World,* October 28, 1967, page 13.

29   *out of a pool:* "Bucs, Prefontaine, breeze to crown," *Register-Guard,* October 28, 1967, 2B.

29   *"pleased to do so":* Letter from Bill Bowerman, October 30, 1967, U of O Special Collections.

29   *wishing him luck:* Letter from Bill Dellinger, November 1, 1967, U of O Special Collections.

30   *a 10:45 a.m. gun:* "Prep meet schedule," *Statesman Journal,* November 1, 1967, page 13.

30   *foot traffic was thick:* "State Pre, NWC X-country meets slated here Saturday," *Capital Journal,* November 2, 1967, page 19.

30   *in from the northwest:* Weather Underground, https://www.wunderground.com/history/daily/us /or/salem/KSLE/date/1967-11-4.

30   *by about 100 yards:* Doug Wellman interview with author, September 6, 2023.

30   *best of them all:* "Corvallis tied, Chemawa 2nd," *Statesman Journal,* November 5, 1967, page 26.

31   *"a rewarding outdoor season":* Letter from Bill Dellinger, January 31, 1968, U of O Special Collections.

32   *to his bedroom desk:* Geoff Hollister. "Out of Nowhere," Meyer and Meyer Sport, 2008.

32   *until the late 1970s:* Martin Haggar interview with author, June 20, 2024.

32   *and 142 pounds:* "Steve Prefontaine runs mile in 4:13.8," *The World,* March 25, 1968, page 15.

33   *put him at 4:12:* "Marshfield junior runs 4:13.8 mile," *Register-Guard,* March 24, 1968, 4B.

33   *"we go against USC":* Letter from Bill Dellinger, March 25, 1968, U of O Special Collections.

34   *"it sure does help":* Jerry Urhhammer. "Classy dual meet outshines point outcome," *Register-Guard,* April 14, 1968, 1B, 4B.

35   *grind his competition under:* John Dhulst. "Prep-o-sitions," *Oregon Journal,* March 26, 1967, page 22.

36   *"to Compete Here Friday":* "Top prep distance star to compete here Friday," *Corvallis Gazette-Times,* April 23, 1968, page 14.

36   *62 degrees at 5 p.m.:* https://www.wunderground.com/history/daily/us/or/salem/KSLE /date/1968-4-26.

36   *to break nine minutes:* "Prefontaine's 9:01.3 for 2-mile ranks 9th nationally," *The World,* April 27, 1968, page 13.

37 *of breaking nine minutes:* "Two mile mark set; Sparts win," *Statesman Journal,* April 27, 1968, page 14.

37 *full thirty-six seconds behind:* "Prefontaine clocks fastest Oregon prep two-mile vs. Spartans," *Corvallis Gazette-Times,* April 27, 1968, page 10.

37 *roughly a half-lap:* Jack Rickard. "Prefontaine misses goal," *Corvallis Gazette-Times,* April 29, 1968, page 12.

37 *Steve was keyed up:* Kenn Hess. "Bench Splinters," *The World,* May 7, 1968, page 15.

37 *himself, There she goes:* John Dhulst. "Prep-o-sitions," *Oregon Journal,* May 7, 1968, page 24.

38 *a chain-link fence:* Kenn Hess. "Girt's sparkling hurdles stints keys Pirates' county spike victory," *The World,* May 4, 1968, page 13.

38 *McClure consoled Steve:* Kenn Hess. "Bench Splinters," *The World,* May 7, 1968, page 15.

38 *"his real talent":* "District 5 meet next for Pirates' spikers," *The World,* May 14, 1968, page 15.

38 *"Ya, I'm ready":* Paul Harvey III. "Prefontaine ready for state two-mile," *Register-Guard,* May 19, 1968, 1B.

38 *"money in the bank":* Kenn Hess. "Pirates runner-up to Grant in state A-1 track meet," *The World,* May 27, 1968, page 21.

39 *the final hundred yards:* Kenn Hess. "Pirates runner-up to Grant in state A-1 track meet," *The World,* May 27, 1968, page 21.

39 *"twisted from the strain":* Wayne Faligowiski. "Grant, Central win titles," *Democrat-Herald,* May 27, 1968, page 16.

39 *ahead of Mark Hiefield:* "State prep track results," *Capital Journal,* May 27, 1968, page 28.

39 *"and all the best":* Letter from Bill Bowerman to Walt McClure, U of O Special Collections, May 27, 1968.

39 *stopped running or competing:* Walt McClure. "The 'Pre' View," *Coach Magazine* draft, page 22.

40 *along the beach:* Kenny Moore. *Bowerman and the Men of Oregon.* Rodale Press, 2006, page 112.

40 *to like running alone:* Dick Fox. "Prefontaine leads Oregon to NCAA x-country title," *Daily Press,* November 24, 1970, page 19.

40 *"feel that the only":* Letter from Bill Dellinger to Steve Prefontaine, U of O Special Collections, June 10, 1968, page 1.

40 *"4:05 for the mile":* Letter from Bill Dellinger to Steve Prefontaine, U of O Special Collections, June 10, 1968, page 2.

41 *ramped up his training:* Walt McClure. "The 'Pre' View," *Coach Magazine* draft, page 22.

41 *Your's truly, Steve Prefontaine:* Letter from Steve Prefontaine to Bill Dellinger, U of O Special Collections, July 31, 1968, pages 1 and 2.

41 *For that Pre-Olympic meet:* Letter from Bill Dellinger to Steve Prefontaine, U of O Special Collections, August 6, 1968, pages 1 and 2.

42 *big fish in it:* Pat Tyson interview with author, July 12, 2023.

42 *coach, "become somebody special":* Pat Tyson interview with author, July 12, 2023.

43 *ultimate signifier: your PR:* Pat Tyson interview with author, July 12, 2023.

43 *"of your Tiger shoe":* Kenny Moore. *Bowerman and the Men of Oregon.* Rodale Press, 2006, page 159.

44 *and sipping hot chocolates:* Phil Knight. "Shoe Dog," New York: Scribner, 2016, page 51.

44 *"That's me. I'm Pre":* Pat Tyson interview with author, July 12, 2023.

44 *a seventeen-year-old kid:* Pat Tyson interview with author, July 12, 2023.

45 *"trying to hook up":* Pat Tyson interview with author, July 12, 2023.

45 *"of Hayward Field":* Jerry Uhrhammer. "Moore, Gerry shove 'Big Four' into wings," *Register-Guard,* August 24, 1968, 1B.

45 *"I'll accept that":* Jerry Uhrhammer. "Moore, Gerry shove 'Big Four' into wings," *Register-Guard,* August 24, 1968, 1B.

CHAPTER 4: PREVIOUSLY UNKNOWN SPEED

46 *Gamble, who placed second:* "'Pre' off 'n running for Pirates," *The World,* September 7, 1968, page 13.

46 *pull his teammates along:* Kenn Hess. "Bench splinters," *The World,* September 25, 1968, page 19.

46 *"and into the fall":* Walt McClure essay on Pre's training, "The 'Pre' View," page 22.

46 *The work started now:* Kenn Hess. "Bench splinters," *The World,* September 25, 1968, page 20.

46 *his hair a mess:* "Prefontaine, SE triumph," *Register-Guard,* October 26, 1968, 1B.

47 *behind Steve in second:* "Prefontaine runs away with crown again but Pirates fourth as team," *The World,* October 26, 1968, page 15.

47 *had in high school:* Doug Crooks interview with author, May 8, 2023.

47 *"So do I":* Kenn Hess. "Bench Splinters," *The World,* October 29, 1968, page 17.

47 *"part of his brashness":* Doug Crooks interview with author, May 8, 2023.

48 *"way of reinforcing it":* Martin Hagger interview with author, June 20, 2024.

48 *his heels this year:* "CC meet Saturday," *Capital Journal,* October 31, 1968, page 22.

48 *"Steve is still hungry":* John Dhulst. "A-1 team harrier title up for grabs," *Oregon Journal,* October 31, 1968, page 23.

48 *early in the race:* "Prefontaine repeats as A-1 harrier champ," *The World,* November 4, 1968, page 21.

48 *Doing the math: sub-twelve:* "Prefontaine repeats as A-1 harrier champ," *The World,* November 4, 1968, page 21.

49 *make a game of it:* Doug Crooks interview with author, May 8, 2023.

50 *"to explore the unknown":* Walt McClure essay for *Coach Magazine,* pages 22–23.

50 *"How's that for openers!":* Kenn Hess. "Prefontaine runs fastest-ever Oregon prep mile—4:11.1," *The World,* April 5, 1969, page 8.

50 *Steve felt "dried out":* Kenn Hess. "Prefontaine runs fastest-ever Oregon prep mile—4:11.1," *The World,* April 5, 1969, page 8.

51 *"that national prep record":* John Dhulst. "Prep-o-sitions," *Oregon Journal,* April 8, 1969, page 22.

51 *"might get a 'no'":* Phil Pursian interview with author, September 18, 2023.

51 *him, were too boring:* Phil Pursian interview with author, September 18, 2023.

51 *go beyond yesterday's limits:* Phil Pursian interview with author, September 18, 2023.

52 *"your shoulder, Steve Prefontaine!":* John Dhulst. "Hann challenges 9-minute mark," *Oregon Journal,* April 19, 1969, page 11.

52 *thinking about this one:* Doug Crooks interview with author, May 8, 2023.

52 *Newland told Crooks:* Doug Crooks interview with author, May 8, 2023.

53 *of this "irreverent youngster":* Rick Riley. "One runners' 'tribute' to a departed friend," *Spokesman Review,* June 3, 1975, page 23.

53 seconds? Well, good luck: Rick Riley interview with author, July 19, 2023.

53 *clear of Riley's record:* Kenn Hess. "Bench Splinters," *The World,* April 22, 1969, page 13.

53 *"The Pacesetter Never Wins":* Kenny Moore. "But only on Sunday," *Sports Illustrated,* February 26, 1973, page 40.

54 *"to run himself blind":* Kenny Moore. "But only on Sunday," *Sports Illustrated,* February 26, 1973, page 41.

54 *"there sucking on me":* Kenny Moore. *Bowerman and the Men of Oregon.* Rodale Press, 2006, pages 242–243.

54 *gets in someone's head:* Martin Hagger interview with author, June 20, 2024.

54 *"we're going for it":* Kenn Hess. "Bench Splinters," *The World,* April 22, 1969, page 13.

54 *"way for five weeks":* Kenn Hess. "Prefontaine's national record proud, thrilling accomplishment," *The World,* April 29, 1969, page 11.

54 *dream he ran 8:40:* John Dhulst. "Prefontaine's dream comes true," *Oregon Journal,* April 26, 1969, page 11.

54 the whole thing again: Kenny Moore. "The Pre Chronicles—Part 5, 'What I'd like to do,'" *Track & Field News,* March 1972.

54 *meet of the season:* Reid English. "High Points," *Statesman Journal,* April 23, 1969, page 21.

54 *"be pushed this time":* Chuck Boice. "Prefontaine shoots for national two-mile record here tonight," *Corvallis Gazette-Times,* April 25, 1968, page 10.

55 *coincidental time of 8:40 p.m.:* Chuck Boice. "Prefontaine shoots for national two-mile record here tonight," *Corvallis Gazette-Times,* April 25, 1968, page 10.

55 *Crooks' head.* Beat Crooks: Doug Crooks interview with author, May 8, 2023.

55 *"He was all business":* Phil Pursian interview with author, August 29, 2023.

56 *pace early than late:* "Prefontaine sets national 2-mile record—8:41.5," *The World,* April 26, 1969, page 14.

57 *laps down in 7:40:* "Prefontaine sets national 2-mile record—8:41.5," *The World,* April 26, 1969, page 14.

57 *to go for it:* John Dhulst. "Prefontaine's dream comes true," *Oregon Journal,* April 26, 1969, page 11.

57 *of a confident grin:* Chuck Boice. "Prefontaine loves to run and win," *Capital Journal,* May 6, 1969, page 23.

57 *for the "Marshfield Machine":* John Dhulst. "Prefontaine's dream comes true," *Oregon Journal,* April 26, 1969, page 11.

57 *"there before the reporters":* Phil Pursian interview with author, August 29, 2023.

58 *"must be the Olympics!":* Doug Crooks interview with author, May 11, 2023.

58 *him a standing ovation:* "Prefontaine sets national 2-mile record—8:41.5," *The World,* April 26, 1969, page 13.

58 *right off Steve's shoulder:* Doug Crooks interview with author, May 11, 2023.

58 *"in his effervescent style":* "Prefontaine sets national 2-mile record—8:41.5," *The World,* April 26, 1969, page 13.

59 *"previously unknown speed":* Chuck Boice. "Prefontaine erases two-mile record with 8:41.5 run," *Corvallis Gazette-Times,* April 26, 1969, page 14.

59 *legs knock-kneed and faltering:* John Dhulst. "Prefontaine's dream comes true," *Oregon Journal,* April 26, 1969, page 11.

59 *"two feet of snow":* "Prefontaine may seek more marks," *Corvallis Gazette-Times,* April 28, 1969, page 12.

59 *highlight of his life:* Scott Candland. "Steve Prefontaine: He makes things happen," *The World,* May 28, 1974, page 10.

CHAPTER 5: GRADUATION

60 *"can this kid run?":* "Prefontaine may seek more marks," *Corvallis Gazette-Times,* April 28, 1969, page 12.

60 *The "backwoods sports buffs":* Kenn Hess. "Prefontaine's National Record proud, thrilling accomplishment," *The World,* April 29, 1969, page 11.

60 *"proud of this boy":* Kenn Hess. "Prefontaine's record proud, thrilling accomplishment," *The World,* April 29, 1969, page 11.

60 *"where I am now":* Scott Candland. "Steve Prefontaine: He makes things happen," *The World,* May 28, 1974, page 10.

61 *read through it all:* Pat Putnam. "The Freshman and the Great Guru," *Sports Illustrated,* June 15, 1970, page 30.

61 *Oregon or Oregon State:* "Prefontaine may seek more marks," *Corvallis Gazette-Times,* April 28, 1969, page 12.

61 *"and he hung up":* Kenny Moore. "The Pre Chronicles—Part 5, 'What I'd like to do,'" *Track & Field News,* March 1972, page 4.

61 *regretted breaking the record:* Jerry Uhrhammer. "Runner Steve Prefontaine—What are his limits?" *Register-Guard,* April 30, 1970, page 1C.

61 *[3:59.4] and Martin Liquori [3:59.8]:* Kenn Hess. "Prefontaine's 'discovery' on race track," *The World,* May 1, 1969, page 12.

62 *beat any other option:* Phil Pursian interview with author, August 29, 2023.

63 *"too fast for you?":* Kenny Moore. "The Pre Chronicles—Part 5, 'What I'd like to do,'" *Track & Field News,* March 1972, page 5.

63   *"seventh heaven":* Erich Lyttle (director). *Fire on the Track* documentary, Chambers Productions.

63   *his 3.0 to 3.45 GPA:* Roxanne Johannesen. "12 Marshfield students earn top grade," *The World,* May 1, 1969, page 7.

63   *"Where's the dotted line?":* Pat Putnam. "The Freshman and the Great Guru," *Sports Illustrated,* June 15, 1970, page 30.

63   *"to become a Duck":* "Oregon selected by Prefontaine," *The World,* April 30, 1969, page 16.

63   *just four college runners:* George Pasero. "Pasero says," *Oregon Journal,* May 3, 1969, page 13.

64   *"pitfalls along the way":* Letter from Bill Bowerman to Kenn Hess from May 8, 1969, *The World,* June 3, 1975, page 13.

64   *from shooting for it:* Ed Grosswiler. "Pre to shoot for 'good one' in mile in county meet Friday," *The World,* page 14.

64   *evening at Pirate Stadium:* https://www.wunderground.com/history/daily/us/or/north-bend /KOTH/date/1969-11-1.

64   *"ready to drop sometimes":* Kenn Hess. "Kirk Gamble has his own shadow," *The World,* May 22, 1969, page 19.

65   *record by thirteen seconds:* Kenn Hess. "Keen contests spice CC meet," *The World,* May 10, 1969, page 10.

65   *Gamble, Class of 1969:* Jay Farr interview with author, November 30, 2022.

65   *it was too fast:* John Dhulst. "'Pre' misses sub-four mile bid," *Oregon Journal,* May 10, 1969, page 13.

66   *fastest prep mile ever:* John Dhulst. "'Pre' misses sub-four mile bid," *Oregon Journal,* May 10, 1969, page 13.

66   *"a boy like that?":* Kenn Hess. "Prefontaine mile clocked at 4:06.9," *The World,* May 10, 1969, page 10.

66   *"is willing to pay":* John Dhulst. "Prep-o-sitions," *Oregon Journal,* April 29, 1969, page 18.

67   *"I didn't do it":* Ron Apling interview with author, August 8, 2022.

67   *"began to get ideas":* Kenny Moore. "The Pre Chronicles—Part 5, 'What I'd like to do,'" *Track & Field News,* March 1972, page 3.

67   *"if I'll just double":* Phil Pursian interview with author, September 18, 2023.

68   *"the U.S. travel squad?":* Phil Pursian interview with author, September 18, 2023.

68   *to keep him company:* Phil Pursian interview with author, September 18, 2023.

68   *raised $1,000 for him:* "Prefontaine makes unit," *Capital Journal,* July 9, 1969, page 25.

69   *fine, but physically tired:* "Prefontaine tries AAU track meet," *Gazette-Times,* June 27, 1969, page 10.

69   *Bacheler "like a groupie":* Tom Jordan. *Pre,* Rodale, 1997, page 110.

69   *"heralded rematch":* Tad Bartimus. "Ryun quits; will mull future," *Capital Journal* (Miami AP), June 30, 1969, page 21.

69   *didn't care to talk:* Ray Crawford. "Jim Ryun leaves silently," *Miami Herald,* June 30, 1969, page 71.

69   *He was in tears:* "Ryun off U.S. team," *San Francisco Examiner,* June 30, 1969, page 53.

70   *photographers snapped pictures:* Luther Evans. "Ryun quits, Liquori wins by a mile," *Miami Herald,* June 39, 1969, page 76.

70   *"Nope":* "Ryun off U.S. team," *San Francisco Examiner,* June 30, 1969, page 53.

70   *do some serious thinking:* Tad Bartimus. "Ryun quits; will mull future," *Capital Journal* (Miami AP), June 30, 1969, page 21.

70   *"competition, too much pressure":* Ray Crawford. "Jim Ryun leaves silently," *Miami Herald,* June 30, 1969, page 71.

70   *"want to run anymore":* Ans Dilley. "Jim Ryun: 'Just quit, that's all,'" *Fort Lauderdale News,* June 30, 1969, page 43.

71   *three-mile, Steve was afraid:* "Prefontaine 4th in race," *The World,* June 30, 1969, page 18.

72   *way without giving everything:* Ken Moore. "Our man in Miami . . . Prefontaine runs fourth," *Register-Guard,* June 30, 1969, page C1.

72   *"grin on his face":* Ken Moore. "Our man in Miami . . . Prefontaine runs fourth," *Register-Guard,* June 30, 1969, page C1.

72 *"charging up at them"*: Ken Moore, "Our man in Miami . . . Prefontaine runs fourth," *Register-Guard*, June 30, 1969, page C1.

72 *"watch in the future"*: "Prefontaine 4th in race," *The World*, June 30, 1969, page 17.

73 *"teams like these two"*: Howard B. Thompson. "Letter from Florida notes runner-coach bond," *The World*, July 26, 1969, page 15.

73 *displeasure at finishing fourth:* Steve Savage interview with author, June 16, 2023.

73 *"to be an alternate"*: "Smith bumps Prefontaine," *The World*, July 19, 1969, page 13.

73 *in the L.A. smog:* "Summer's experience spurs Pre," *The World*, August 23, 1969, page 14.

73 *"sufficient for me psychologically"*: "Summer's experience spurs Pre," *The World*, August 23, 1969, page 14.

74 *"soon dropped away"*: Bob Payne. "American girls end Russian domination," *Spokesman Review*, July 20, 1969, page 55.

74 *"wobbled noticeably"*: Ken Moore. "Knoke finishes in fine form," *Register-Guard*, July 20, 1969, 1B.

74 *winner, Rashid Sharafetdinov of the U.S.S.R.:* "U.S. sweeps trackfest," *Honolulu Star-Bulletin*, July 20, 1969, page 53.

74 *the team . . . again . . . momentarily:* "Prefontaine misses trip," *Oregon Journal*, July 22, 1969, page 23.

74 *"has been brought together"*: "Prefontaine cut by track team," *Corvallis Gazette-Times* (New York AP), July 22, 1969, page 11.

75 *meet in Stuttgart, Germany:* "Steve 'upset,'" *Albany Democrat-Herald*, July 22, 1969, page 10.

75 *the very next day:* "'Pre' runs in Europe," *Oregon Journal*, July 23, 1969, page 32.

75 *"Prefontaine is learning fast"*: Kenn Hess. "Prefontaine finds AAU frustrating," *The World*, July 23, 1969, page 15.

75 *"control and athletic freedom"*: Joseph M. Turrini. *The End of Amateurism in American Track and Field*. Chicago: University of Illinois Press, 2010, pages 1–2.

75 *"and caused illegitimate outcomes:* Joseph M. Turrini. *The End of Amateurism in American Track and Field*. Chicago: University of Illinois Press, 2010, page 13.

76 *athlete couldn't even coach:* Joseph M. Turrini. *The End of Amateurism in American Track and Field*. Chicago: University of Illinois Press, 2010, page 14.

76 *"amateur track and field"*: Joseph M. Turrini. *The End of Amateurism in American Track and Field*. Chicago: University of Illinois Press, 2010, page 13.

76 *meets dominated competitive track:* Joseph M. Turrini. *The End of Amateurism in American Track and Field*. Chicago: University of Illinois Press, 2010, page 15.

76 *an athlete's Olympic eligibility:* Joseph M. Turrini. *The End of Amateurism in American Track and Field*. Chicago: University of Illinois Press, 2010, page 16.

76 *"competes under our protection"*: Joseph M. Turrini. *The End of Amateurism in American Track and Field*. Chicago: University of Illinois Press, 2010, page 24.

76 *International Amateur Athletic Federation (IAAF):* Joseph M. Turrini. *The End of Amateurism in American Track and Field*. Chicago: University of Illinois Press, 2010, page 17.

76 *"track franchise in 1913"*: Joseph M. Turrini. *The End of Amateurism in American Track and Field*. Chicago: University of Illinois Press, 2010, page 18.

77 *"think they do either"*: "Track squad returns home; will take protest to Nixon," *Gazette-Times*, August 14, 1969, page 17.

77 *"and three bucks a day"*: Kenny Moore. *Bowerman and the Men of Oregon*. Rodale Press, 2006, page 140.

77 *"religion, preaches higher sentiments"*: Joseph M. Turrini. *The End of Amateurism in American Track and Field*. Chicago: University of Illinois Press, 2010, page 25.

77 *"not compatible with amateurism"*: Joseph M. Turrini. *The End of Amateurism in American Track and Field*. Chicago: University of Illinois Press, 2010, page 34.

77 *"hell they wanted to"*: Joseph M. Turrini. *The End of Amateurism in American Track and Field*. Chicago: University of Illinois Press, 2010, page 37.

78 *"of a totalitarian country"*: Joseph M. Turrini. *The End of Amateurism in American Track and Field*. Chicago: University of Illinois Press, 2010, page 61.

78   *"all the papers, TV"*: Joseph M. Turrini. *The End of Amateurism in American Track and Field.* Chicago: University of Illinois Press, 2010, page 42.

78   *"wreck the all-powerful AAU"*: Tex Maule. "The end of the AAU," *Sports Illustrated,* September 25, 1961, page 20.

78   *"it cannot survive long"*: Tex Maule. "The end of the AAU," *Sports Illustrated,* September 25, 1961, page 22.

79   *"since I can remember"*: Tex Maule. "The end of the AAU," *Sports Illustrated,* September 25, 1961, page 22.

79   *"in the Augsburg meet"*: "Track team backs Bob Beamon," *Register-Guard,* August 5, 1969, page 2B.

79   *pressure on the AAU:* "U.S. athletes back on track," *Register-Guard,* August 6, 1969, page 1D.

79   *ol' red, white, and blue:* Kenny Moore. *Bowerman and the Men of Oregon.* Rodale Press, 2006, page 142.

79   *shot-putter and U of O alum:* "No boycott, but issue's still alive," *Spokesman Review,* August 6, 1969, page 8.

79   *laughing at the absurdity:* "Yanks take track lead," *Spokesman Review,* August 6, 1969, page 8.

80   *interpreter for his teammates:* "Summer's experiences spurs 'Pre,'" *The World,* August 23, 1969, page 14.

80   *"went for a run":* Chuck Russell. "Coos Bay track star anxious to compete," *The World,* July 30, 1969, page 12.

80   *brilliant in an "electrifying":* "European track squad records win over U.S.," *Tri-City Herald,* August 1, 1969, page 24.

80   *some fourteen seconds back:* "Europe wins; Gerry stars," *Spokesman-Review,* August 1, 1969, page 20.

80   *"don't like fourth places":* John Dhulst. "'Pre' beats 'Pre'diction," *Oregon Journal,* August 5, 1969, page 24.

80   *was impressed with Steve:* John Dhulst. "'Pre' beats 'Pre'diction," *Oregon Journal,* August 5, 1969, page 24.

80   *in the 3,000 meters:* "Prefontaine U.S. hope," *The World,* August 5, 1969, page 9.

80   *home, ready to rest:* John Dhulst. "'Pre' beats 'Pre'diction," *Oregon Journal,* August 5, 1969, page 24.

80   *Werner Girke in Augsburg:* "'Pre' finishes 2nd in Germany," *Oregon Journal,* August 6, 1969, page 27.

80   *"you should not do":* "Summer's experiences spurs 'Pre,'" *The World,* August 23, 1969, page 13.

81   *won in "crushing style":* "U.S. keeps record, beats Britain again," *Progress Bulletin,* August 14, 1969, page 22.

81   *He was cooked:* "Summer's experiences spurs 'Pre,'" *The World,* August 23, 1969, page 13.

81   *finished in third place:* "Vollmer hurls discus 196-2; Prefontaine finishes fourth," *Oregon Journal,* August 14, 1969, page 31.

81   *like running at all:* "Pre heads home after 4th place," *The World,* August 14, 1969, page 15.

81   *160 at its end:* "Summer's experience spurs Pre," *The World,* August 23, 1969, page 13.

81   *victory stand to be:* Carl Cluff. "Pre pins his Olympic hops on Munich map," *Oregon Journal,* January 31, 1972, page 20.

CHAPTER 6: LIMITLESS

85   *"to tie his shoelaces":* Harley Tinkham. "UCLA's Bush fears ambush at Oregon," *Los Angeles Times,* April 14, 1970, page 50.

86   *of $30,000, perhaps more:* Joe Matheson. "Volunteers repair Hayward Field," *Register-Guard,* April 12, 1970, page 2B.

86   *urethane, all-weather surface:* Bill Mulflur. "It'll take Duck comeback to level UCLA," *Oregon Journal,* April 15, 1970, page 25.

86   *through town; they waved:* Jerry Uhrhammer. "Runner Steve Prefontaine—What are his limits?" *Register-Guard,* April 30, 1970, page 1C.

86   *"like a new man":* Stan Rotenberg. "Frosh quartet aiming for UCLA meet," *Daily Emerald,* April 15, 1970, page 13.

86 *took a victory lap:* Al Crombie. "Records rebuff track stars' best," *The Columbian,* February 2, 1970, page 19.

86 *"world's next great runner":* Carl Cluff. "'Pre' called 'World's next great runner,'" *Oregon Journal,* February 2, 1970, page 17.

86 *"to go with it":* Carl Cluff. "'Pre' called 'World's next great runner,'" *Oregon Journal,* February 2, 1970, page 17.

87 *"been who he was":* Pat Tyson interview with author, July 12, 2023.

87 *the six-mile was 29:30:* George Pasero. "Pasero says," *Oregon Journal,* February 26, 1970, page 25.

87 *"Okay. Fine. Got it":* Kenny Moore. *Bowerman and the Men of Oregon.* Rodale Press, 2006, page 241.

87 talent comes the temperament: Kenny Moore. *Bowerman and the Men of Oregon.* Rodale Press, 2006, page 239.

88 *"asking, 'Who's boss here?'":* Kenny Moore. *Bowerman and the Men of Oregon.* Rodale Press, 2006, photo insert.

88 *"study in smooth efficiency":* Larry Lavelle. "Easter Relays next for Stanford's track squad," *Palo Alto Times,* March 23, 1970, page 27.

88 *a full seven seconds:* "Oregon U spikers halt Stanford, Fresno State," *Sacramento Bee,* March 22, 1970, page 60.

88 *"he runs pretty good":* Bruce Farris. "Get Ducky exhibition," *Fresno Bee,* March 22, 1970, page 28.

88 *"of beers after training":* Pete Shmock interview with author, May 17, 2023.

88 *"one of the guys":* Stan Rotenberg interview with author, May 22, 2023.

89 *"Well I best go":* Postcard from Steve Prefontaine to Dave Wilborn, March 23, 1970.

89 *dubbed Oregon's best performer:* Ron Reid. "Cal's kiddie corps," *Times,* April 9, 1970, page 30.

89 *did but he relished:* Jerry Uhrhammer. "Cal crowds good fans," *Register-Guard,* April 14, 1970, page 3B.

89 *"to see—real confidence":* "America's Ron Clarke," *Times,* April 21, 1970, page 30.

89 *the Saturday sports section:* Jerry Uhrhammer. "Prefontaine's brilliant run highlights Oregon victory," *Register-Guard,* April 26, 1970, 1B.

89 *hopes weren't too high:* Jerry Uhrhammer. "Runner Steve Prefontaine—What are his limits?" *Register-Guard,* April 30, 1970.

90 *the pressure cook him:* Jerry Uhrhammer. "Prefontaine's brilliant run highlights Oregon victory," *Register-Guard,* April 26, 1970, page 1B.

90 *in his words, ridiculous:* Jerry Uhrhammer. "Runner Steve Prefontaine—What are his limits?" *Register-Guard,* April 30, 1970, page 1C.

90 *This was unexplored territory:* Pat Putnam. "The Freshman and the Great Guru," *Sports Illustrated,* June 15, 1970, page 30.

90 *out and do something:* Jerry Uhrhammer. "Pre says he feels ready for anything,'" *Register-Guard,* April 26, 1970, page 1B.

90 *begun his kick earlier:* Jerry Uhrhammer. "Runner Steve Prefontaine—What are his limits?" *Register-Guard,* April 30, 1970.

90 *secured many laps before:* Jerry Uhrhammer. "Prefontaine's brilliant run highlights Oregon victory," *Register-Guard,* April 26, 1970, page 1B.

90 *"I'm always exploring myself":* Pat Putnam. "The Freshman and the Great Guru," *Sports Illustrated,* June 15, 1970, page 30.

91 *waving to the fans:* "Hair flying at the tape, 'Pre' waves to the crowd afterwards," *Register-Guard,* April 26, 1970, page 1B.

91 *easy Steve was running:* Jerry Uhrhammer. "Runner Steve Prefontaine—What are his limits?" *Register-Guard,* April 30, 1970, page 1C.

91 *the crowd in frenzy:* Steve Savage interview with author, June 15, 2023.

91 has to work hard?: Jerry Uhrhammer. "Pre says he feels ready for anything,'" *Register-Guard,* April 26, 1970, page 1B.

91 *grinned at the thought:* Carl Cluff. "Weather can't stop Prefontaine—can anyone?" *Oregon Journal,* April 27, 1970, page 22.

92   *"a world-class distance runner"*: Mary Dufort Harris. "Pre commands national spotlight," *The World*, April 29, 1970, page 4.

92   *could excel at something:* Pat Putnam. "The Freshman and the Great Guru," *Sports Illustrated*, June 15, 1970, page 29.

92   *"going to be doing"*: Jerry Uhrhammer. "Runner Steve Prefontaine—What are his limits?" *Register-Guard*, April 30, 1970, page 1C.

92   *"trying to hurt you"*: Jerry Uhrhammer. "Runner Steve Prefontaine—What are his limits?" *Register-Guard*, April 30, 1970, page 1C.

92   *"game in a way"*: Jerry Uhrhammer. "Runner Steve Prefontaine—What are his limits?" *Register-Guard*, April 30, 1970, page 1C.

93   *"far out of sight"*: Jerry Uhrhammer. "Runner Steve Prefontaine—What are his limits?" *Register-Guard*, April 30, 1970, page 1C.

93   *championship in the three-mile:* "Duck sophomore has big goals in first season," *Gazette Times*, April 30, 1970, page 14.

93   *He was not joking:* "Duck sophomore has big goals in first season," *Gazette Times*, April 30, 1970, page 14.

94   *"him and his career"*: George Pasero. "Pasero says," *Oregon Journal*, June 8, 1970, page 21.

94   *"do with its idea"*: Jerry Uhrhammer. "Divine raced wrong guy; Pre digs lack of fans," *Register-Guard*, May 19, 1970, page 1C.

94   *"you out that week"*: George Pasero. "Pasero says," *Oregon Journal*, June 8, 1970, page 21.

95   *air calms with it:* Kenny Moore. *Bowerman and the Men of Oregon*. Rodale Press, 2006, page 129.

95   *"had the demanding crowd"*: Kenny Moore. *Bowerman and the Men of Oregon*. Rodale Press, 2006, page 130.

95   *like a pitcher's fastball:* Kenny Moore. *Bowerman and the Men of Oregon*. Rodale Press, 2006, page 241.

95   *"chilly, gusting winds"*: Tom McGuire. "Pre barely misses in sub-four attempt," *The World*, May 4, 1970, page 12.

95   *against a quality field:* "Duck spikers too strong for OSU," *Gazette-Times*, May 4, 1970, page 14.

95   *"heck of a mile"*: Carl Cluff. "Talent-laden festival meet adds Beamon, Carlos," *Oregon Journal*, June 4, 1970, page 23.

96   *had lost the fire:* Jerry Uhrhammer. "Roscoe is back," *Register-Guard*, May 13, 1970, page 1D.

96   *"given me a gun"*: Jerry Uhrhammer. "Roscoe is back," *Register-Guard*, May 13, 1970, page 1D.

96   *care if you lost:* Jerry Uhrhammer. "Roscoe is back," *Register-Guard*, May 13, 1970, page 1D.

97   *"a return to winter"*: Jerry Uhrhammer. "Ducks survive wind to overcome Huskies," *Register-Guard*, April 5, 1970, page 1B.

97   *"take it, I'm hurting"*: Roscoe Divine interview with author, March 22, 2024.

97   *accelerating to outpace Smart:* Carl Cluff. "Duck, UCLA spikers steam toward collision in Eugene," *Oregon Journal*, April 6, 1970, page 22.

97   *to win in 4:03.2:* Jerry Uhrhammer. "Ducks survive wind to overcome Huskies," *Register-Guard*, April 5, 1970, page 1B.

97   *"didn't hold him accountable"*: Roscoe Divine interview with author, August 21, 2023.

98   *"You'll get your chance"*: Roscoe Divine interview with author, August 21, 2023.

98   *"Divine-Pre dual Twilight feature"*: Stan Rotenberg. "Divine-Pre dual Twilight feature," *Daily Emerald*, June 4, 1970, page 16.

98   *Steve was unimpressed:* Phil Pursian interview with author, September 19, 2023, part 2.

99   *"a sub-four-minute mile"*: Jerry Uhrhammer. "Duck runners past and present, challenge mile barrier," *Register-Guard*, June 4, 1970, page 1C.

99   *them at the mile:* Carl Cluff. "Can Pre outshine veteran stars in mile?" *Oregon Journal*, June 5, 1970, page 18.

99   *"things happen"*: Jerry Uhrhammer. "Mile attack features Twilight Meet tonight," *Register-Guard*, June 5, 1970, page 2B.

99   *"attention in his event"*: Kenny Moore. *Bowerman and the Men of Oregon*. Rodale Press, 2006, page 243.

100   *eyes with piercing intensity:* Jerry Uhrhammer. "Ducks do it in style as 5 break barrier," *Register-Guard,* June 6, 1970, page 1B.

100   *run a smashing mile:* Jerry Uhrhammer. "Ducks do it in style as 5 break barrier," *Register-Guard,* June 6, 1970, page 1B.

100   *up by the reaction:* Jerry Uhrhammer. "Ducks do it in style as 5 break barrier," *Register-Guard,* June 6, 1970, page 1B.

100   or walk the walk?: Roscoe Divine interview with author, August 21, 2023.

100   be just as beautiful: Pat Putnam. "The freshman and the great guru," *Sports Illustrated,* June 15, 1970, page 29.

101   *"to WATCH that race":* Jerry Uhrhammer. "Ducks do it in style as 5 break barrier," *Register-Guard,* June 6, 1970, page 1B.

102   *"foot-stomping, screaming throng":* Carl Cluff. "Wow! Divine (3:56.3), 'Pre' (3:57.4)," *Oregon Journal,* June 6, 1970, page 13.

102   *"been from another team":* Jerry Uhrhammer. "Ducks do it in style as 5 break barrier," *Register-Guard,* June 6, 1970, page 1B.

102   *"they both got me":* Carl Cluff. "Wow! Divine (3:56.3), 'Pre' (3:57.4)," *Oregon Journal,* June 6, 1970, page 14.

102   *and his running style:* Carl Cluff. "Wow! Divine (3:56.3), 'Pre' (3:57.4)," *Oregon Journal,* June 6, 1970, page 14.

103   *"the face with noise":* Roscoe Divine interview with author, August 21, 2023.

103   *like a proud father:* Pat Putnam. "The freshman and the great guru," *Sports Illustrated,* 1970, page 29.

103   *"teethed on stopwatches":* Pat Putnam. "The freshman and the great guru," *Sports Illustrated,* June 15, 1970, page 29.

103   *Dame fans bleed football:* Jerry Uhrhammer. "Ducks do it in style as 5 break barrier," *Register-Guard,* June 6, 1970, page 1B.

103   *hand to shake Steve's:* Photo of Roscoe shaking Steve's hand.

103   *leaning on the senior:* Carl Cluff. "Wow! Divine (3:56.3), 'Pre' (3:57.4)," *Oregon Journal,* June 6, 1970, page 13.

103   *magic of that mile:* Kenny Moore. *Bowerman and the Men of Oregon.* Rodale Press, 2006, page 243.

104   *to acclimate his athletes:* "Oregon seeks 1972 track test," *Register-Guard,* June 13, 1970, page 1B.

104   *"not fighting the Spaniards":* Carl Cluff. "Bowerman says Pre's injury 'Not Serious,'" *Oregon Journal,* June 15, 1970, page 25.

104   *of his right foot:* "Prefontaine will still run," *The World,* June 16, 1970, page 11.

104   *That was Bowerman's directive:* Blaine Newnham. "Steve Prefontaine: January 25, 1951–May 30, 1975," *Register-Guard,* page 2B.

104   *"needed six little stitches":* "Prefontaine will still run," *The World,* June 16, 1970, page 11.

104   *title chances were shot:* "Pre suffers foot injury," *Register-Guard,* June 16, 1970, page 2B.

105   *ten to twelve miles:* Tom McGuire. "Prefontaine: The training and the competition," *The World,* September 18, 1970, page 10.

105   *their makeshift motel infirmary:* Jerry Uhrhammer. "Divine's injury kills UO's track chances," *Register-Guard,* June 21, 1970, page 2B.

105   *room calling them "Champs":* Roscoe Divine interview with author, March 22, 2024.

105   *to walk one mile:* "Pre ready to compete," *Register-Guard,* June 19, 1970, page 2B.

105   *test run on Tuesday:* Jim Moackler. "Prefontaine cuts foot—doubtful," *Des Moines Tribune,* June 15, 1970, page 17.

105   *"hobbling Duck out there":* Jerry Uhrhammer. "Ducks one of eight contenders for NCAA track crown," *Register-Guard,* June 17, 1970, page 1D.

105   *entries dropped to twenty-five:* Jerry Uhrhammer. "Ducks one of eight contenders for NCAA track crown," *Register-Guard,* June 17, 1970, page 1D.

105 *"to running two races"*: Blaine Newnham. "Steve Prefontaine: January 25, 1951–May 30, 1975," *Register-Guard,* page 2B.

106 *needle in his foot*: Carl Cluff. "Bowerman says Pre's injury 'Not Serious,'" *Oregon Journal,* June 15, 1970, page 21.

106 *which encouraged Bowerman*: Jerry Uhrhammer. "Ducks one of eight contenders for NCAA track crown," *Register-Guard,* June 17, 1970, page 1D.

106 *it was nothing serious*: Carl Cluff. "Bowerman says Pre's injury 'Not Serious,'" *Oregon Journal,* June 15, 1970, page 21.

106 *news, a "killing blow"*: George Pasero. "Oregan's Prefontaine math miss NCAA 3-mile," *Oregon Journal,* June 15, 1970, page 23.

106 *give Steve a workout*: Carl Cluff. "Bowerman says Pre's injury 'Not Serious,'" *Oregon Journal,* June 15, 1970, page 25.

106 *"that bed all week"*: "Pre ready to compete," *Register-Guard,* June 19, 1970, page 2B.

107 *"run like hell"*: "Clarke, near end of line, hails 'Pre' as great one," *Capital Journal,* June 16, 1970, page 13.

107 *"can't even feel it"*: Carl Cluff. "Pre: 'Can't even feel it,'" *Oregon Journal,* June 17, 1970, page 29.

107 *bum wheel, not two*: Bob Payne. "Wild midwest weather adds to NCAA track tensions," *Spokesman-Review,* June 18, 1970, page 6.

107 *"gleaning what they could"*: Jim Bainbridge. "NCAA track buttonholing like a political convention," *San Francisco Examiner,* June 18, 1970, page 62.

108 *perhaps Steve could, too*: Al Lightner. "Sportslightner," *Statesman-Journal,* June 18, 1970, page 37.

108 *gold-medal run of twelve*: Jerry Uhrhammer. "Less than 50 may win NCAA," *Register-Guard,* June 18, 1970, page 1C.

108 *field down to twenty*: "Dropped baton may prove costly for UCLA," *Sioux City Journal,* June 19, 1970, page 12.

108 *"luck of the Ducks"*: Carl Cluff. "Pre gets 2-day 'rest,'" *Oregon Journal,* June 1970, page 17.

108 *workout and monitor him*: "Pre ready to compete," *Register-Guard,* June 19, 1970, page 2B.

108 *"it on those 32s"*: Carl Cluff. "Pre gets 2-day 'rest,'" *Oregon Journal,* June 1970, page 20.

109 *run his own race*: Carl Cluff. "3 track titles for Ducks? It computes," *Oregon Journal,* June 22, 1970, page 25.

109 *"So, I did"*: Jerry Uhrhammer. "Divine's injury kills UO's track chances," *Register-Guard,* June 21, 1970, page 2B.

110 *55-second final lap*: Jerry Uhrhammer. "Mann, Cal surprise at NCAA track test," *Register-Guard,* June 21, 1970, page 1B.

110 *thrown back in exhaustion*: Photo, *The Columbian,* June 22, 1970, page 16.

110 *at the carnage within*: Ron Maly. "Rain runner Sink wades to steeplechase record," *Des Moines Register,* June 21, 1970, page 29.

110 *two stitches and blood*: Kenny Moore. "The Pre Chronicles, Part 5, What I'd Like to Do," *Track & Field News,* March 1972, page 6.

110 *"competitors to catch him"*: Jim Moackler. "Prefontaine may run defensively at NCAA," *Des Moines Tribune,* June 16, 1970, page 17.

110 *the 1972 Olympic Trials*: "Oregon bid approved," *Register-Guard,* June 17, 1970, page 1D.

110 *"stop the nineteen-year-old"*: Red Hurd. "Pre-view of a star," *Capital Journal,* June 16, 1970, page 12.

CHAPTER 7: BURNOUT

111 *"What's a guru?"*: Tom McGuire. "Prefontaine featured on *Sports Illustrated* cover," *The World,* June 12, 1970, page 10.

111 *"will become collectors' items"*: Tom McGuire. "Prefontaine featured on *Sports Illustrated* cover," *The World,* June 12, 1970, page 10.

112 *"been since he's matured"*: Harry Missildine. "A new cycle? (Seattle hopes so)," *Spokesman-Review,* June 14, 1970, page 4.

112 *"until HE came along"*: Kenn Hess. "Prefontaine the World's SWO Athlete of the Year," *The World*, December 31, 1969, page 15.

113 *his arches, his tendons*: Tom McGuire. "Year has been a long one for Prefontaine," *The World*, September 15, 1970, page 10.

113 *boxed in and hurting*: Jim Bainbridge. "AAU hurdles title to Hill," *San Francisco Examiner*, June 27, 1970, page 27.

113 *"me with an ax"*: Pat Putnam. "No! Not John Smith!" *Sports Illustrated*, July 6, 1970, page 13.

113 *"I just couldn't sprint"*: Carl Cluff. "Bouncy leaps 26-2; Pre: 5th," *Oregon Journal*, June 27, 1970, page 15.

114 *mentally it destroyed him*: Tom McGuire. "Year has been a long one for Prefontaine," *The World*, September 15, 1970, page 10.

114 *"How's that for progress?"*: Pat Putnam. "No! Not John Smith!" *Sports Illustrated*, July 6, 1970, page 13.

114 *No Europe. No problem*: "Bouncy claims AAU crown; laboring Pre finishes fifth," *Register-Guard*, June 27, 1970, page 1B.

114 *had little to give*: Tom McGuire. "Year has been a long one for Prefontaine," *The World*, September 15, 1970, page 10.

114 *"you like horse heads?"*: Frank Shorter interview with author, June 26, 2024.

114 *of August or sooner*: "Prefontaine headed for Europe again," *The World*, July 2, 1970, page 13.

114 *kiss on the cheek*: Photo of Pre kissing mom goodbye, *The World*, page 1.

114 *causing him extra problems*: Tom McGuire. "Year has been a long one for Prefontaine," *The World*, September 15, 1970, page 10.

115 *"Riley from Washington State"*: Steve Prefontaine. "Paris is everything one hears about . . ." *The World*, July 22, 1970, page 10.

115 *"chuckle a little bit"*: Rick Riley interview with author, July 19, 2023.

115 *"part of a brotherhood"*: Rick Riley interview with author, July 19, 2023.

115 *and the two-mile*: https://en.wikipedia.org/wiki/Michel_Jazy#World_records.

116 *"about six of those"*: Rick Riley interview with author, July 19, 2023.

116 *"probably a little more"*: Steve Prefontaine. "Paris is everything one hears about . . ." *The World*, July 22, 1970, page 10.

116 *"feeling reasonably good"*: Steve Prefontaine. "Paris is everything one hears about . . ." *The World*, July 22, 1970, page 10.

116 *"what I really miss"*: Steve Prefontaine. "Paris is everything one hears about . . ." *The World*, July 22, 1970, page 10.

116 *"vodka by the gallon"*: Pat Putnam. "Don't drink the water," *Sports Illustrated*, August 3, 1970, page 8.

117 *his hair neatly parted*: Jere Van Dyk interview with author, December 7, 2023.

117 *"his big brother there"*: Jere Van Dyk interview with author, December 7, 2023.

117 *the intense Bakersfield heat*: Kenny Moore. *Bowerman and the Men of Oregon*. Rodale Press, 2006, page 244.

118 *"onto my entire life"*: Jere Van Dyk interview with author, December 7, 2023.

118 *meters, fading, then rebounding*: "Russian spikers whip U.S.," *Capital-Journal*, July 25, 1970, page 14.

119 *"I'll go on my own"*: Bill Mulflur. "Prefontaine: AAU must subsidize athletes," *Oregon Journal*, August 14, 1970, page 34.

119 *running on "reserve strength"*: Tom McGuire. "Year has been a long one for Prefontaine," *The World*, September 15, 1970, page 10.

120 *than running in circles*: Tom McGuire. "Year has been a long one for Prefontaine," *The World*, September 15, 1970, page 10.

120 *hours by that point*: Pat Putnam. "The Freshman and the Great Guru," *Sports Illustrated*, June 15, 1970, page 30.

121 *it was worth it*: Arne Kvalheim. "Story of a long distance runner—work," *Daily Emerald*, December 4, 1970, page 10.

121 *"wouldn't have come back"*: Tom McGuire. "Year has been a long one for Prefontaine," *The World*, September 15, 1970, page 10.

121 *were becoming increasingly inescapable:* Phil Pursian interview with author, March 7, 2024.

CHAPTER 8: PEERLESS

122 *in nerves, even scared:* Arne Kvalheim. "Story of a long distance runner—work," *Daily Emerald*, December 4, 1970, page 10.

122 *road through the woods:* Ray Brown. "Famed runners go in x-country," *Daily Press*, November 23, 1970, page 14.

123 *leading the thundering herd:* Ken Popejoy interview with author, May 20, 2023.

123 *turn at the start:* Dick Fox. "Prefontaine leads Oregon to NCAA x-country title," *Daily Press*, November 24, 1970, page 19 (photo).

123 *"rooster tail" of muck:* Jerry Lindquist. "At random," *Times Dispatch*, November 24, 1970, page 38.

124 *of home in Oregon:* Dick Fox. "Prefontaine leads Oregon to NCAA x-country title," *Daily Press*, November 24, 1970, page 20.

124 *but, thankfully, no rain:* "Harriers tenth; Martin makes All-American," *Virginia Gazette*, November 27, 1970, page 37.

124 *poured it on:* "Oregon wins cross country," *News and Observer*, November 24, 1970, page 15.

124 *him strung out:* "Ducks' Prefontaine wins NCAA cross country title," *Oregon Journal*, November 23, 1970, page 29.

124 *"resting for the finish":* Dick Fox. "Prefontaine leads Oregon to NCAA x-country title," *Daily Press*, November 24, 1970, page 19.

124 *up and clip him:* "UO unofficial victor; Pre individual winner," *Register-Guard*, November 23, 1970, page 1C.

124 *"body lathered in sweat":* "Oregon survives protest, wins cross country title," *Enterprise Record*, November 24, 1970, page 9.

124 *swished around his hips:* Carl Lynn (photo). *Times Dispatch*, November 24, 1970, page 38.

124 *litter at the finish:* "Pre his finish," *Spokesman Review* (AP photo), November 24, 1970, page 14.

124 *28:08, a course record:* "Prefontaine wins race," *Capital Journal*, November 23, 1970, page 42.

124 *thirty yards clear:* "Ducks win NCAA meet," *San Bernardino County Sun*, November 24, 1970, page 31.

124 *"I do, I do well":* Dick Fox. "Prefontaine leads Oregon to NCAA x-country title," *Daily Press*, November 24, 1970, page 20.

124 *"cover of the magazine":* Ken Popejoy interview with author, May 20, 2023.

126 *would be in Eugene:* Carl Cluff. "Pre lops along awaiting big competition," *Oregon Journal*, April 9, 1971, page 20.

127 *to a whisper, "Nobody":* Vince Buford interview with author, July 31, 2023.

128 *so thoroughly walloped Oregon:* "Bruin thinclads dump Ducks 86-59," *Statesman Journal*, April 25, 1971, page 19.

128 *run his athletes ragged:* Harley Tinkham. "Prefontaine's mouth runs faster than legs—Bush," *Los Angeles Times*, April 27, 1971, page 36.

128 *"running Collett like that?":* Carl Cluff. "Pre scorches mile, Bruin coach," *Oregon Journal*, April 26, 1971, page 22.

128 *"after running the intermediates":* Harley Tinkham. "Collett busiest runner as Bruins breeze to 86-59 win over Ducks," *Los Angeles Times*, April 25, 1971, page 43.

128 *"Pacific-8 meet," Steve ribbed:* "Prefontaine warns UCLA," *Argus*, April 27, 1971, page 11.

128 *"the play they deserved":* Harley Tinkham. "Prefontaine's mouth runs faster than legs—Bush," *Los Angeles Times*, April 27, 1971, page 36.

129 *"outside of Eugene, too":* Bob Payne. "Oregon's Prefontaine: 'Great'—not yet the 'greatest,'" *Spokesman-Review*, April 27, 1971, page 18.

129 *"a crack at Ryun"*: Tom McGuire. "Prefontaine: The training and the competition," *The World,* September 18, 1970, page 10.

130 *"we'll see what happens"*: "Dream mile due—Pre vs. Ryun," *Oregon Journal,* May 3, 1971, page 22.

130 *"learned how to lose"*: Neil Amdur. "Jim Ryun may resume career," *New York Times* (Salina Journal), January 3, 1971, page 17.

130 *racing weight of 155:* Neil Amdur. "Jim Ryun may resume career," *New York Times* (Salina Journal), January 3, 1971, page 17.

130 *one hundred miles per week:* Neil Amdur. "Jim Ryun may resume career," *New York Times* (Salina Journal), January 3, 1971, page 17.

131 *the rain at all:* Howard Applegate. "Big races approaching for Ryun," *The World,* May 10, 1971, page 19.

131 *"what keeps you going"*: Karol Stonger. "What makes Ryun run—his wife does," *Sunday News,* May 9, 1971, page 42.

131 *"That's fine"*: Howard Applegate. "Big races approaching for Ryun," *The World,* May 10, 1971, page 19.

131 *"Mile of the Century"*: "Big races approaching for Ryun," *Columbian,* May 10, 1971, page 19.

131 *"Mile for a change"*: Pat Putnam. "A dream comes true," *Sports Illustrated,* May 24, 1971, page 21.

131 *"He's real tough now"*: Ken Doney. "Ryun-Prefontaine duel Twilight highlight," *Capital Journal,* June 2, 1971, page 27.

132 *"faster, a lot stronger"*: Ken Doney. "Ryun-Prefontaine duel Twilight highlight," *Capital Journal,* June 2, 1971, page 27.

132 *"running on pure guts"*: "UCLA surges past Webfoots for Pacific-8 track championship," *The World,* May 24, 1971, page 15.

132 *"smell, melting-tar smell"*: George Pasero. "Pasero says," *Oregon Journal,* May 24, 1971, page 21.

132 Is it worth it?: George Pasero. "Pasero says," *Oregon Journal,* May 24, 1971, page 22.

132 He'd be meeting eleven: "Fast Oregon mile promised Sunday," *The World,* June 5, 1970, page 14.

132 *upwards of 15,000 people:* Carl Cluff. "Pre gets 'workout,' eyes AAU before 'home folks,'" *Oregon Journal,* June 21, 1971, page 24.

133 *"that last 110 yards"*: Carl Cluff. "Pre says World won't end if I lose," *Oregon Journal,* June 5, 1971, page 13.

133 *"end of the world"*: Jerry Uhrhammer. "Ryun, Prefontaine talking little as mile confrontation nears," *Register-Guard,* June 3, page 1B.

133 *in for the race:* Carl Cluff. "Oregon 'family' promises fast 'fun race,'" *Oregon Journal,* June 4, 1971, page 22.

134 *medicine to take effect:* Jerry Uhrhammer. "Arne's kick nips Pre; Moore wins marathon," *Register-Guard,* June 7, 1971, page 3B.

134 *miffed by the pace:* Carl Cluff. "Kvalheim beats Pre; Ryun 10th," *Oregon Journal,* June 7, 1971, page 26.

134 the first two laps: Jerry Uhrhammer. "Arne's kick nips Pre; Moore wins marathon," *Register-Guard,* June 7, 1971, page 3B.

134 *cruised around the turn:* Photo, *Democrat-Herald,* June 7, 1971, page 18.

135 *media and quickly left:* Carl Cluff. "Ryun: Victory, not revenge, most important," *Oregon Journal,* January 27, 1972, page 22.

135 *"Jim Ryun the Runner"*: Jerry Uhrhammer. "Arne's kick nips Pre; Moore wins marathon," *Register-Guard,* June 7, 1971, page 3B.

136 *he crossed the finish:* Jerry Uhrhammer. "Pre ran three-mile according to plan," *Register-Guard,* June 20, 1971, page 3C.

136 next week, next week: Jerry Uhrhammer. "Bruins claim NCAA title; Oregon takes third," *Register-Guard,* June 20, 1971, page 1C.

136 *it was* next week: "Pre calls win a 'good workout,'" *Capital Journal,* June 21, 1971, page 30.

137 *"a good, hard workout"*: Neil Amdur. "Liquori retains title with 3:57.6," *New York Times,* June 20, 1971, page 4.

137 *"Bay, going for me"*: "Pre calls win a 'good workout,'" *Capital Journal,* June 21, 1971, page 30.

137 *"I don't disappoint them"*: Carl Cluff. "Pre gets 'workout,' eyes AAU before 'home folks,'" *Oregon Journal,* June 21, 1971, page 24.

138 *"American record should go"*: "Super three mile looms in Eugene," *Capital Journal,* June 24, 1971, page 19.

138 *"trouble all the time"*: Jerry Uhrhammer. "Sixteen to defend AAU track titles," *Register-Guard,* June 24, 1971, page 1D.

138 *"not counting him out"*: Pat Putnam and Skip Myslenski. "Firstest, fastest and mostest," *Sports Illustrated,* July 5, 1971, page 20.

138 *"the smug young man"*: Carl Cluff. "Pre makes good on vow—He's No. 1," *Oregon Journal,* June 26, 1971, page 13.

138 *he was totally calm:* Pat Putnam and Skip Myslenski. "Firstest, fastest and mostest," *Sports Illustrated,* July 5, 1971, page 20.

139 *"God's plan for me"*: Pat Putnam and Skip Myslenski. "Firstest, fastest and mostest," *Sports Illustrated,* July 5, 1971, page 21.

139 *"can run," he said:* Pat Putnam and Skip Myslenski. "Firstest, fastest and mostest," *Sports Illustrated,* July 5, 1971, page 20.

139 *"he's making a sales pitch"*: Pat Putnam and Skip Myslenski. "Firstest, fastest and mostest," *Sports Illustrated,* July 5, 1971, page 21.

140 *his words, all over:* Pat Putnam and Skip Myslenski. "Firstest, fastest and mostest," *Sports Illustrated,* July 5, 1971, page 21.

142 *"stronger I felt"*: Pat Putnam and Skip Myslenski. "Firstest, fastest and mostest," *Sports Illustrated,* July 5, 1971, page 21.

142 *it sounded like 12,000:* Jerry Uhrhammer. "World record, Pre, Meriwether top AAU," *Register-Guard,* June 26, 1971, page 1B.

142 *"Who's next?"*: Jerry Uhrhammer. "World record, Pre, Meriwether top AAU," *Register-Guard,* June 26, 1971, page 1B.

CHAPTER 9: ASSERTION

143 *"to be well represented"*: James H. Whitty. "Funds needed to send athletes to Olympic Games," *The World,* August 11, 1971, page 4.

144 *"of Coos Bay to see"*: "Former resident really shocked; 'Pre' says 'Thank you,'" *The World,* September 1, 1971, page 4.

144 *had raised only $1,000:* "Hatfield wins 2 races in Olympic fund meet," *Democrat-Herald,* August 30, 1971, page 16.

144 *other than Bill Bowerman:* Blaine Newnham. "Track capital Eugene to host Olympic Trials," *Register-Guard,* October 13, 1971, page 1A.

144 *"gets bigger," wrote the* Daily Emerald: "Bowerman tabbed," *Daily Emerald,* October 14, 1971, page 10.

144 *"country as a coach"*: Bill Mulflur. "Olympics now No. 1 priority for Bowerman," *Oregon Journal,* December 8, 1971, page 31.

144 *"can do in between"*: Tom McGuire. "Perspectives," *The World,* March 31, 1972, page 15.

144 *his pace quickened:* Kenny Moore. "The Pre Chronicles Part 5: What I'd like to do," *Track & Field News,* March 1972, page 2.

145 *"something up my sleeve"*: Harley Tinkham. "Downgrading U.S. Olympic team 'disgusting' to Steve Prefontaine," *Los Angeles Times,* January 23, 1972, page 47.

146 *"great and now rebounding"*: Al Lightner. "Sportslightner," *Statesman-Journal,* January 27, 1972, page 33.

146 *Manley, and Kerry Pearce:* Kenn Hess. "Injury might scratch Wilborn in mile race," *Democrat-Herald,* January 27, 1972, page 21.

146 *"going to be embarrassed":* Carl Cluff. "Ryun had better be ready," *Oregon Journal,* January 28, 1972, page 19.

146 *felt more meaningful:* George Pasero. "Pasero says," *Oregon Journal,* January 28, 1972, page 19.

146 *Olympic hopes started now:* George Pasero. "Pasero says," *Oregon Journal,* January 28, 1972, page 19.

146 *year's Twilight Mile outdoors:* Blaine Newnham. "Pre turns in brilliant two-mile," *Register-Guard,* January 30, 1972, page 1B.

147 *by the old guard:* photo, *Ventura County Star-Free Press,* January 31, 1972, page 12.

147 *admittedly, disappointed in Ryun:* Blaine Newnham. "Pre turns in brilliant two-mile," *Register-Guard,* January 30, 1972, page 1B.

147 *"places come to learn":* George Pasero. "Pasero says," *Oregon Journal,* January 31, 1972, page 22.

147 *of the previous generation:* Al Crombie. "Prefontaine meet's star as he routs Ryun in race," *The Columbian,* January 31, 1972, page 21.

148 *gave him more confidence:* "Steve Prefontaine 'outstanding' in Los Angeles two-mile event," *The World,* February 12, 1972, page 13.

148 *in Munich in September:* "Pre tops L.A. field," *Gazette-Times,* February 12, 1972, page 13.

148 *any runner in history:* Eddie Lopez. "Speed specialist," *Fresno Bee,* March 16, 1972, page 29.

148 *later called him "arrogant":* Eddie Lopez. "Wind irks Prefontaine," *Fresno Bee,* March 19, 1972, page 31.

149 *he spoke about openly:* Dan Berger. "Pre fires first shot," *Capital Journal,* March 27, 1972, page 30.

149 *didn't expect anything sensational:* Bob Baum. "Twilight Meet is low key," *Daily Emerald,* April 21, 1972, page 16.

149 *"psychological rocket":* Blaine Newnham. "Pre hits 3:56.7, Shmock 64-11 /12," *Register-Guard,* April 24, 1972, page 3B.

149 *Steve's turf, he flexed:* Bill Mulflur. "Pre's 3:56.7 miles plays second fiddle to Lindgren," *Oregon Journal,* April 24, 1972, page 24.

149 *hoped to meet Ebba:* Blaine Newnham. "Pre hits 3:56.7, Shmock 64-11 /12," *Register-Guard,* April 24, 1972, page 3B.

150 *off to the showers:* "Pre clicks off 3:56.7 mile," *Daily Emerald,* April 24, 1972, page 11.

150 *"or Abercombie and Fitch":* Joe Much. "Confrontation at one mile?" *Democrat-Herald,* April 26, 1972, page 21.

150 *"I love to compete":* Fire on the Track documentary.

150 *"with little competitive experience":* Bob Baum. "Wagner says 'much chance' for Beavers," *Daily Emerald,* May 4, 1972, page 10.

151 *pressure he was feeling:* Blaine Newnham. "Pre turns back Hailu as Ducks blitz Beavers," *Register-Guard,* May 7, 1972, page 1B.

151 *"had the most speed":* Blaine Newnham. "Pre turns back Hailu as Ducks blitz Beavers," *Register-Guard,* May 7, 1972, page 1B.

151 *"with the half-miler":* Carl Cluff. "Pre nips Hailu in one of all-time great duels," *Oregon Journal,* May 8, 1972, page 24.

151 *making him run mine:* Carl Cluff. "Pre nips Hailu in one of all-time great duels," *Oregon Journal,* May 8, 1972, page 24.

152 *"around if he had":* Blaine Newnham. "Pre turns back Hailu as Ducks blitz Beavers," *Register-Guard,* May 7, 1972, page 1B.

152 *"He never disappointed":* Dan Fouts interview with author, September 6, 2023.

152 *got a guts race:* Joe Much. "Wagner feels like Custer as Ducks swamp Beavers," *Democrat-Herald,* May 8, 1972, page 16.

152 *was no catching him:* Joe Much. "Wagner feels like Custer as Ducks swamp Beavers," *Democrat-Herald,* May 8, 1972, page 16.

153 *"inspired challenge of Hailu":* Blaine Newnham. "Pre turns back Hailu as Ducks blitz Beavers," *Register-Guard,* May 7, 1972, page 1B.

153 *a . . . swoosh?:* Joe Much. "Wagner feels like Custer as Ducks swamp Beavers," *Democrat-Herald,* May 8, 1972, page 16.

153 *"melted like butter"*: Phil Knight. *Shoe Dog.* New York: Simon & Schuster, 2018, page 110.

153 *"for the American market"*: Kenny Moore. *Bowerman and the Men of Oregon.* Rodale Press, 2006, page 265.

153 *"call it the Cortez"*: Phil Knight. *Shoe Dog.* New York: Simon & Schuster, 2018, page 111.

154 *"his or her wake"*: Phil Knight. *Shoe Dog.* New York: Simon & Schuster, 2018, page 181.

154 *"waffle-like surface"*: Phil Knight. *Shoe Dog.* New York: Simon & Schuster, 2018, pages 196–197.

155 *"someone going past you"*: Phil Knight. *Shoe Dog.* New York: Simon & Schuster, 2018, page 202.

155 *"a totally satisfactory answer"*: Phil Knight. *Shoe Dog.* New York: Simon & Schuster, 2018, page 210.

155 *"the paradigmatic Nike athlete"*: Phil Knight. *Shoe Dog.* New York: Simon & Schuster, 2018, page 211.

CHAPTER 10: ASCENSION

156 *"It's here, too"*: George Pasero. "Pasero says," *Oregon Journal,* June 6, 1972, page 24.

156 *"well with the kids"*: Tom McGuire. "Life team follows Pre," *The World,* June 16, 1972, page 17.

156 *"second father"*: Tom McGuire. "Life team follows Pre," *The World,* June 16, 1972, page 17.

157 *"more awesome than mine"*: Pat Tyson interview with author, July 12, 2023.

157 Everything's right here: Pat Tyson interview with author, July 12, 2023.

157 keep from getting sick: George Pasero. "Pasero says," *Oregon Journal,* June 26, 1972, page 20.

157 cut his mileage down: "Prefontaine confident for Olympic Trials," *Gazette-Times,* June 27, 1972, page 20.

158 which suited his temperament: Carl Cluff. "Prefontaine opens trial bid tonight in 5,000 meter heat," *Oregon Journal,* July 6, 1972, page 33.

158 *"It's a psyche"*: John Jeansonne. "Old Pre provides Olympic preview," *Newsday,* July 7, 1972, page 97.

158 *"is a satisfying thing"*: Dick Kunkle. "Keeping track," *Tacoma News Tribune,* July 9, 1972, page 70.

158 *"the great moment came"*: George Pasero. "Mum Pre will talk Sunday 'If I win,'" *Oregon Journal,* July 7, 1972, page 23.

159 pleasure in the race: Blaine Newnham. "Prefontaine-Young duel looms in 5,000 final," *Register-Guard,* July 7, 1972, page 1B.

159 *"that to happen now"*: John Jeansonne. "Old Pre provides Olympic preview," *Newsday,* July 7, 1972, page 97.

159 *"too many," Steve said:* Charles Maher. "Cold beer helps Prefontaine keep his cool," *Los Angeles Times,* January 18, 1974, page 43.

159 best in the country: George Pasero. "Mum Pre will talk Sunday 'If I win,'" *Oregon Journal,* July 7, 1972, page 25.

159 *"to run, I hope"*: Blaine Newnham. "Prefontaine-Young duel looms in 5,000 final," *Register-Guard,* July 7, 1972, page 1B.

159 face like the Grinch: Carl Cluff. "Pre just 5,000 meters from Munich," *Oregon Journal,* July 7, 1972, page 23.

160 *"else do the work"*: Blaine Newnham. "Prefontaine-Young duel looms in 5,000 final," *Register-Guard,* July 7, 1972, page 1B.

160 he was in good shape: Carl Cluff. "Pre just 5,000 meters from Munich," *Oregon Journal,* July 7, 1972, page 23.

160 joints did as well: Gerry Lindgren text exchange with author, November 17, 2023.

160 *"thing I've ever seen"*: John Jeansonne. "Old Pre provides Olympic preview," *Newsday,* July 7, 1972, page 97.

160 *"want to beat him"*: Blaine Newnham. "Prefontaine-Young duel looms in 5,000 final," *Register-Guard,* July 7, 1972, page 1B.

160 *"freak Pre out"*: Gerry Lindgren text exchange with author, November 17, 2023.

160 *"Coliseum," wrote Track & Field News:* "The Pre Chronicles—Part 7, Summer 72, The Olympic Campaign," *Track & Field News,* 1972, page 6.

161 *"dual meets and everything"*: Blaine Newnham. "Warmly wooed," *Register-Guard*, July 10, 1972, page 3B.

161 *he doubted himself*: Paul Buker. "Pre tops Young," *Daily Emerald*, July 10, 1972, page 6.

161 *the first three laps*: Carl Cluff. "Duck star shatters U.S. mark," *Oregon Journal*, July 10, 1972, page 26.

161 *me, he burns me*: Blaine Newnham. "Pre wears down Young in 5,000 final," *Register-Guard*, July 10, 1972, page 1B.

162 *"cheers are for you"*: Dick Kunkle. "Keeping track," *Tacoma News Tribune*, July 9, 1972, page 70.

162 *record for forty years*: https://www.wbur.org/hereandnow/2012/06/29/steve-prefontaines-olympic.

162 *some eighty yards*: Pat Putnam. "The high and the mighty," *Sports Illustrated*, July 17, 1972, page 15.

162 *"Munich here comes 'PRE'"*: George Pasero. "Steve thinks world record," *Oregon Journal*, July 10, 1972, page 25.

162 *"think I'll wear it"*: Pat Putnam. "The high and the mighty," *Sports Illustrated*, July 17, 1972, page 15.

162 *"For sure"*: Blaine Newnham. "Warmly wooed," *Register-Guard*, July 10, 1972, page 3B.

163 *"is off my shoulders"*: John Dixon. "Olympic Trials conclude," *The Independent*, July 10, 1972, page 34.

163 *"was in another world"*: Tom Jordan. *Pre: The Story of America's Greatest Running Legend*. Rodale Press, 1997, page 75.

163 *"I'm on the team"*: George Pasero. "Steve thinks world record," *Oregon Journal*, July 10, 1972, page 26.

163 *if it was all worth it*: George Pasero. "Steve thinks world record," *Oregon Journal*, July 10, 1972, page 26.

163 *Why run this hard?*: Paul Buker. "Fans helped," *Daily Emerald*, July 10, 1972, page 6.

163 *light jogging, nothing strenuous*: Bob Payne. "Olympic veterans sidelined by young, powerful team," *Spokesman-Review*, July 11, 1972, page 16.

163 *of his boyhood neighborhood*: Keith Topping. "Familiar sight," *The World*, July 19, 1972, page 1.

164 *to the Paddock Tavern*: Pat Tyson interview with author, July 12, 2023.

164 *"days so thanks a lot"*: Steve Prefontaine. "Pre says thank you," *The World*, July 29, 1972, page 4.

164 *"going to miss Eugene"*: Pat Tyson interview with author, July 12, 2023.

165 *of a pre-Olympic meet*: Neil Amdur. "Prefontaine is heading for last lap—Munich," *New York Times*, July 30, 1972, page 5.

165 *"this work for nothing"*: Neil Amdur. "Prefontaine is heading for last lap—Munich," *New York Times*, July 30, 1972, page 5.

165 *his career in 3:39.4*: Neil Amdur. "Prefontaine loses impressively in Oslo with his fastest 1,500," *New York Times*, August 3, 1972, page 39.

165 *for the Norwegian team*: "Pre helps Kvalheim qualify," *Oregon Journal*, August 3, 1972, page 32.

165 *"out of my system"*: Pat Putnam. "Experience may not be necessary," *Sports Illustrated*, August 28, 1972, page 36.

166 *"not even tired now"*: https://www.youtube.com/watch?v=mg5IlJdfXRc.

166 *in 8:28.2 or faster*: "Munich Pre-view," *Oregon Journal*, August 15, 1972, page 26.

CHAPTER 11: SHIELD

167 *"Germany's biggest frying pan"*: "Olympic stadium has heat problem," *Register-Guard*, July 27, 1972, page 2B.

167 *($52 million in 1972)*: "Olympic stadium has heat problem," *Register-Guard*, July 27, 1972, page 2B.

167 *for the XX Olympiad*: "Olympic stadium has heat problem," *Register-Guard*, July 27, 1972, page 2B.

167 *"of continually watered brick"*: Blaine Newnham. "Olympic spirit," *Register-Guard*, August 27, 1972, page 1B.

168 *"women of the street"*: Blaine Newnham. "Bowerman slaps Games security," *Register-Guard*, September 7, 1972, page 1A.

168 *"for that gold medal"*: "McSwain to Pre: Listen to me, you'll win," *The World,* September 6, 1972, page 1.

168 *"tucked beneath black Africa"*: "Black American athletes threaten pullout," *Register-Guard,* August 19, 1972, page 1B.

168 *"with our African brothers"*: "Black American athletes threaten pullout," *Register-Guard,* August 19, 1972, page 1B.

168 *"we are staying here"*: "Black American athletes threaten pullout," *Register-Guard,* August 19, 1972, page 1B.

168 *"not because he's older"*: Pat Putnam. "Experience may not be necessary," *Sports Illustrated,* August 28, 1972, page 36.

169 not at the beginning of his first: "Dellinger knows of waiting game," *Gazette-Times,* August 22, 1972, page 15.

169 *"is the only problem"*: Blaine Newnham. "Going crazy," *Register-Guard,* August 28, 1972, page 3B.

169 *"hit a stone wall"*: Blaine Newnham. "Going crazy," *Register-Guard,* August 28, 1972, page 3B.

169 *"his race 200,000 times"*: "Dellinger knows of waiting game," *Gazette-Times,* August 22, 1972, page 15.

170 *"they're puttin' on me"*: Robert Musel. "People back home pressure Coos Bay's Prefontaine," *The World,* August 23, 1972, page 1.

170 *"much inside of me"*: "Prefontaine's workouts are so good they scare him," *New York Times,* August 24, 1972, page 55.

171 *"was ready to go"*: Dave Wottle interview with author, September 20, 2023.

171 *"saying—no bad races"*: "Emotional 'Pre' sees only gold," *Democrat-Herald,* August 24, 1972, page 25.

171 *"bronze, only gold"*: "Emotional 'Pre' sees only gold," *Democrat-Herald,* August 24, 1972, page 25.

171 *"confident without being cocky"*: "Prefontaine's workouts are so good they scare him," *New York Times,* August 24, 1972, page 55.

171 *"cards on the table"*: "Prefontaine's workouts are so good they scare him," *New York Times,* August 24, 1972, page 55.

171 *"in workouts for nothing"*: "Prefontaine's workouts are so good they scare him," *New York Times,* August 24, 1972, page 55.

171 *"run a world record"*: Pat Putnam. "Experience may not be necessary," *Sports Illustrated,* August 28, 1972, page 36.

172 penicillin for a week: "Pre labels cocky reputation as undeserved," *Oregon Journal,* August 23, 1972, page 26.

172 nervous, upset: Blaine Newnham. "Prefontaine hedges on chances in 5,000," *Register-Guard,* September 4, 1972, page 1B.

172 *"good on that day"*: Robert Musel. "People back home pressure Coos Bay's Prefontaine," *The World,* August 23, 1972, page 1.

172 even make the finals: Blaine Newnham. "Prefontaine hedges on chances in 5,000," *Register-Guard,* September 4, 1972, page 1B.

172 *"to happen out there?"*: Blaine Newnham. "Prefontaine hedges on chances in 5,000," *Register-Guard,* September 4, 1972, page 1B.

172 *"dang thing over with"*: Blaine Newnham. "Prefontaine hedges on chances in 5,000," *Register-Guard,* September 4, 1972, page 1B.

172 *"I don't think so"*: Blaine Newnham. "Prefontaine hedges on chances in 5,000," *Register-Guard,* September 4, 1972, page 1B.

173 *"in the 5,000 meters"*: Bill Dellinger. "Munich report: Virén looms as Pre's top threat," *Oregon Journal,* September 5, 1972, page 30.

173 *"that's all that counts"*: Blaine Newnham. "Prefontaine hedges on chances in 5,000," *Register-Guard,* September 4, 1972, page 1B.

173 *"win that gold medal"*: Kenny Moore. *Bowerman and the Men of Oregon.* Rodale Press, 2006, page 284.

173 *"home bearing my shield"*: "Pre labels cocky reputation as undeserved," *Oregon Journal,* August 23, 1972, page 33.

173 *"something was wrong"*: Frank Shorter. *My Marathon.* Rodale Press, 2016, page 104.

173 *"too shocking to believe"*: Frank Shorter. *My Marathon.* Rodale Press, 2016, page 104.

173 *"took nine persons hostage"*: "Olympics suspended after bloody raid," *Register-Guard,* September 5, 1972, page 1A.

174 *could train without burden:* Bill Dellinger. "Pre bails out of village," *Oregon Journal,* September 8, 1972, page 36.

174 *"us home, I'd go":* Kenny Moore. *Bowerman and the Men of Oregon.* Rodale Press, 2006, page 296.

174 *"thing. A full year":* Ed Levitt. "He can't forget," *Oakland Tribune,* January 31, 1974, page 33.

174 *"just couldn't take it":* Ed Levitt. "He can't forget," *Oakland Tribune,* January 31, 1974, page 33.

174 *"it just won't go":* "The Pre Chronicles, Part 15, the 74 Outdoor Season," *Track & Field News,* August 1974, page 9.

175 *Saturday, May 24, 1969:* "Eight injured in accidents," *The Cottage Grove Sentinel,* May 29, 1969, page 1.

175 *passing vehicle "cut sharply":* "Eight injured in accidents," *The Cottage Grove Sentinel,* May 29, 1969, page 1.

175 *could likely never unsee:* Ron Apling interview with author, April 14, 2023.

176 *looking over both shoulders:* "Pre survives first test," *Oregon Journal,* September 7, 1972, page 28.

176 *"easy for him":* Bill Dellinger. "Pre bails out of village," *Oregon Journal,* September 8, 1972, page 36.

176 *His people found him:* Blaine Newnham. "Prefontaine places 2nd but makes finals," *Register-Guard,* September 7, 1972, page 1A.

176 *He was relieved:* Blaine Newnham. "Prefontaine places 2nd but makes finals," *Register-Guard,* September 7, 1972, page 1A.

176 *60 seconds a lap:* John Dixon. "Olympic 5,000 meters: Pre's race, or is it?" *Independent,* September 6, 1972, page 46.

176 *"the bloody gold medal":* John Dixon. "Olympic 5,000 meters: Pre's race, or is it?" *Independent,* September 6, 1972, page 46.

177 *is almost over:* Ed Levitt. "He can't forget," *Oakland Tribune,* January 31, 1974, page 33.

177 *to run this race:* Ed Levitt. "He can't forget," *Oakland Tribune,* January 31, 1974, page 33.

178 *and tore his shoe: Los Angeles Times,* September 11, 1972, page 43.

178 *"to make a move":* https://www.youtube.com/watch?v=RlpbZ6FMzNc.

178 *it up for Virén:* Blaine Newnham. "Pre's warning for 1976: 'He'd better watch out,'" *Register-Guard,* September 11, 1972, page 3B.

179 *of an inch deep:* Blaine Newnham. "Pre's warning for 1976: 'He'd better watch out,'" *Register-Guard,* September 11, 1972, page 3D.

180 *"set the pace":* Jerry Uhrhammer. "Prefontaine ties college two-mile mark," *Register-Guard,* March 21, 1971, page 1B.

181 *runners wouldn't take charge:* Blaine Newnham. "Pre's warning for 1976: 'He'd better watch out,'" *Register-Guard,* September 11, 1972, page 3D.

185 *even after he lost:* Blaine Newnham. "Pre's warning for 1976: 'He'd better watch out,'" *Register-Guard,* September 11, 1972, page 3D.

CHAPTER 12: BROKEN

189 *crushed, crestfallen: Fire on the Track,* 1995.

189 *"I run for myself":* Blaine Newnham. "Pre wears down Young," *Register-Guard,* July 10, 1972, page 3D.

190 *"I'll kick your butt": Fire on the Track,* 1995.

190 *"Games are all about?":* Blaine Newnham. "Pre's warning for 1976: 'He'd better watch out,'" *Register-Guard,* September 11, 1972, page 3D.

190 *"his unflagging confidence"*: Blaine Newnham. "Pre's warning for 1976: 'He'd better watch out,'" *Register-Guard,* September 11, 1972, page 3D.

191 *"his greatest achievement"*: Blaine Newnham. "Pre's warning for 1976: 'He'd better watch out,'" *Register-Guard,* September 11, 1972, page 3D.

191 *"was running to win"*: Blaine Newnham. "Pre's warning for 1976: 'He'd better watch out,'" *Register-Guard,* September 11, 1972, page 3D.

191 *ran roughly a 4:01:* Harry Missildine. "Olympic report from Caviness," *Spokesman-Review,* October 10, 1972, page 16.

191 *4:04 to 4:02 in another:* Kenny Moore. *Bowerman and the Men of Oregon.* Rodale Press, 2006, page 301.

191 Would he kill himself?: Kenny Moore. *Bowerman and the Men of Oregon.* Rodale Press, 2006, page 301.

191 *"he'll be fine"*: Kenny Moore. *Bowerman and the Men of Oregon.* Rodale Press, 2006, page 301.

192 *didn't have the spirit:* Ron Reid. "Search your soul, then run like blazes," *Sports Illustrated,* January 29, 1973, page 50.

192 *"started me to thinking"*: "Prefontaine set for 2-mile race in Times Games," *Los Angeles Times,* February 4, 1973, page 50.

192 *"have it all over"*: Bill Dellinger. "Munich experience will make Pre tougher in 76," *Oregon Journal,* September 11, 1972, page 28.

192 *"quiet moment in Eugene"*: Pat Tyson interview with author, July 12, 2023.

193 *"He'd better be ready"*: Blaine Newnham. "Pre's warning for 1976: 'He'd better watch out,'" *Register-Guard,* September 11, 1972, page 3D.

193 *every day since 1968:* Blaine Newnham. "Pre wears down Young," *Register-Guard,* July 10, 1972, page 3D.

193 *"to be ashamed of"*: Blaine Newnham. "Pre's warning for 1976: 'He'd better watch out,'" *Register-Guard,* September 11, 1972, page 3D.

193 *borrowed for a caravan:* Frank Taylor. "He goes for gold on tooth-brush," *Daily Mirror,* August 23, 1972, page 26.

193 *Steve's favorite watering hole:* Charles Maher. "Cold beer helps Prefontaine keep his cool," *Los Angeles Times,* January 18, 1974, page 43.

193 *"many, many years"*: Charles Maher. "Cold beer helps Prefontaine keep his cool," *Los Angeles Times,* January 18, 1974, page 43.

193 *"as soon stop breathing"*: *Los Angeles Times,* January 20, 1975, page 30.

194 *"drink really cheap beer"*: Pete Shmock interview with author, May 17, 2023.

194 *"and search for money"*: Georgia Pope interview with author, November 29, 2023.

194 *"through in the end"*: Pete Shmock interview with author, May 17, 2023.

194 *"just open his throat"*: Craig Blackman interview with author, March 11, 2024.

194 *"running on the streets"*: Harvey Winn interview with author, August 14, 2023.

195 *"take care of us"*: Craig Blackman interview with author, March 11, 2024.

195 *"to cook the burgers"*: Vince Buford interview with author, July 31, 2023.

195 *"Pre was her favorite"*: Doug Chapman interview with author, August 25, 2023.

195 *"'Step aside, step aside!'"*: Craig Blackman interview with author, March 11, 2024.

195 *"depended on the season"*: Georgia Pope interview with author, November 29, 2023.

195 *"So there you go"*: Dan Fouts interview with author, September 6, 2023.

195 *"couldn't get enough of him"*: Harvey Winn interview with author, August 14, 2023, 3:25.

195 *"to people. Very relaxing"*: Charles Maher. "Cold beer helps Prefontaine keep his cool," *Los Angeles Times,* January 18, 1974, page 43.

196 *"salts you burn up"*: Charles Maher. "Cold beer helps Prefontaine keep his cool," *Los Angeles Times,* January 18, 1974, page 51.

196 *"than he used to"*: Kenny Moore. *Bowerman and the Men of Oregon.* Rodale Press, 2006, page 306.

196 *Fifteen "Go Pre" sweatshirts: The World,* September 28, 1972, page 18.

196 *at the Timber Inn:* Tom McGuire. "Wednesday potpourri," *The World,* September 27, 1972, page 15.

196 *"a bit to Earth":* Steve Bence interview with author, May 24, 2023.

197 *"step of the way":* Gerry Lindgren text exchange with author, November 17, 2023.

197 *"that's so far away":* Mark Feig interview with author, June 26, 2023.

197 *"ignored him, disowned him":* Ray Arndt interview with author, May 18, 2023.

197 *dog Steve ever had:* Bill Mulflur. "'Track isn't main thing in my life,' says Pre," *Oregon Journal,* January 12, 1973, page 21.

197 *"what place you got":* Pat Tyson interview with author, July 12, 2023.

198 *"strapped by their dad?":* Ray Arndt interview with author, May 18, 2023.

198 *"don't have any goals":* Bill Mulflur. "'Track isn't main thing in my life,' says Pre," *Oregon Journal,* January 12, 1973, page 21.

199 *Olympics in four years:* "Pre's thinking Olympics again," *Capital Journal,* January 25, 1973, page 35.

199 *"A full year":* Ed Levitt. "He can't forget," *Oakland Tribune,* January 31, 1974, page 33.

CHAPTER 13: REBUILT

200 *"exhausted and discouraged":* Kenny Moore. *Bowerman and the Men of Oregon.* Rodale Press, 2006, page 307.

200 *saw sitting before him:* Phil Knight. *Shoe Dog.* New York: Simon & Schuster, 2016, page 214.

200 *"I took the job":* Blaine Newnham. "Bowerman: 'I'm disappointed I took the job," *Register-Guard,* August 27, 1972, page 1B.

200 *"the University of Oregon":* Blaine Newnham. "Bowerman: 'I'm disappointed I took the job," *Register-Guard,* August 27, 1972, page 1B.

200 *dealing without "toilet articles":* Blaine Newnham. "Bowerman: 'I'm disappointed I took the job,'" *Register-Guard,* August 27, 1972, page 1B.

200 *"Where have I succeeded?":* Blaine Newnham. "Bowerman slaps Games security," *Register-Guard,* September 7, 1972, page 1A.

201 *"suddenly, dramatically, unexpectedly, conclusively":* Blaine Newnham. "Bowerman retires; Dellinger takes helm," *Register-Guard,* page 1B.

201 *code, no longer "patchable":* Kenny Moore. *Bowerman and the Men of Oregon.* Rodale Press, 2006, page 307.

201 *"athletes, students, and community":* "Bill Bowerman quits; Dellinger gets UO job," *Capital Journal,* March 24, 1973, page 21.

201 *the $600,000 fundraising project:* "Bill Bowerman quits; Dellinger gets UO job," *Capital Journal,* March 24, 1973, page 21.

202 *off the American record:* Leonard Koppett. "Prefontaine wins two-mile run," *New York Times,* January 21, 1973, page 223.

202 *"track meet in my life":* Ron Reid. "Search your soul, then run like blazes," *Sports Illustrated,* January 29, 1973, page 51.

202 *again with his signature warmth:* Transcript of post-*LA Times* Mile 1973 interview with Pre.

203 *"cocky after [the Olympics]":* Steve Bence interview with author, May 24, 2023.

203 *"and he liked that":* Scott Daggatt interview with author, October 6, 2023.

203 *nerve in his back:* Bill Mulflur. "Pre, Ebba will compete in Pac-8," *Oregon Journal,* May 16, 1973, page 34.

204 *a dozen under 4:07:* Ken Wheeler. "Record mile figures at UO," *Oregon Journal,* April 27, 1973, page 42.

204 *"Up for grabs":* Ken Wheeler. "Record mile figures at UO," *Oregon Journal,* April 27, 1973, page 42.

204 *his legs were "dead":* "The Pre Chronicles, Part 11, His senior outdoor campaign," *Track & Field News,* May 1973, page 5.

204 *"to see you run":* "The Pre Chronicles, Part 11, His senior outdoor campaign," *Track & Field News,* May 1973, page 5.

204 *with the signature swoosh:* Blaine Newnham. "Pre's talking records after 3:55.0 mile," *Register-Guard*, April 28, 1973, page 1B.

204 *"[Pre] wearing our shoes":* Phil Knight. *Shoe Dog*. New York: Simon & Schuster, 2016, page 220.

205 *"recovery [from the Olympics]":* Phil Knight. *Shoe Dog*. New York: Simon & Schuster, 2016, page 220.

205 *"I hope you understand":* Letter from Bill Bowerman to Phil Knight, U of O Special Collections, May 17, 1973.

206 *"Pre is in pain":* Art Bushnell. "Pre ailing," *Daily Emerald*, May 11, 1973, page 21.

207 *according to Steve's doctor:* Art Bushnell. "Pre ailing," *Daily Emerald*, May 11, 1973, page 21.

207 *"helped me win it":* Ron Reid. "Pre's last duck-waddle," *Sports Illustrated*, May 28, 1973, page 84.

208 *"the good times, Pre":* Ron Reid. "Pre's last duck-waddle," *Sports Illustrated*, May 28, 1973, page 84.

208 *"a long love affair":* Ron Reid. "Pre's last duck-waddle," *Sports Illustrated*, May 28, 1973, page 84.

208 *and raised it high:* George Pasero. "Pasero says," *Oregon Journal*, May 21, 1973, page 23.

208 *"to go with it":* Ron Reid. "Pre's last duck-waddle," *Sports Illustrated*, May 28, 1973, page 84.

208 *of them one day:* Mark Feig interview with author, July 5, 2023.

208 *"go have a beer":* Mark Feig interview with author, July 5, 2023.

209 *"yards in 51 seconds":* Jerry Byrd. "Prefontaine's mind is set," *Shreveport Journal*, June 8, 1973, page 20.

209 *"put in the cake":* Carl Cluff. "Pre steps off record 13:19.0," *Oregon Journal*, June 8, 1973, page 25.

209 *"but I didn't":* Blaine Newnham. "Knut, Feig in fast mile company," *Register-Guard*, June 8, 1973, page 1D.

209 *"racing is all about":* Jerry Estill. "Best yet to come for Prefontaine," *Town Talk*, June 8, 1973, page 9.

209 *"the voluble Oregonian":* Bob Payne. "Thunder, rain, heat fail to stop Bruins, Prefontaine," *Spokesman-Review*, June 10, 1973, page 43.

209 *"Olympics-worth of maturity":* Bob Payne. "Thunder, rain, heat fail to stop Bruins, Prefontaine," *Spokesman-Review*, June 10, 1973, page 43.

210 *a "warm feeling":* "Ducks second to Bruins; Ebba 4th," *Statesman Journal*, June 10, 1973, page 33.

210 *(eventually cast off altogether):* "Scoreboard tells story," *Spokesman Review*, June 12, 1973, page 19.

210 *but PRE, 13:05.3:* "Pre ends his collegiate career in win," *The World*, June 11, 1973, page 11.

210 *"to run for me":* Blaine Newnham. "Jim, Kip vs. Pre?" *Register-Guard*, June 10, 1973, page 1C.

211 *"don't need it, really":* Blaine Newnham. "Jim, Kip vs. Pre?" *Register-Guard*, June 10, 1973, page 1C.

211 *"2:56 for three-quarters":* Dave Wottle interview with author, September 20, 2023.

211 a rabbit? Why not?: Dave Wottle interview with author, September 20, 2023.

212 *was his best event:* Paul Buker. "Pre-Wottle mile battle stirs speculation of world record," *Daily Emerald*, June 20, 1973, page 6.

212 *"and break me early":* Paul Buker. "Pre-Wottle mile battle stirs speculation of world record," *Daily Emerald*, June 20, 1973, page 6.

212 *summer, balmy and windless:* Carl Cluff. "Wottle 3:53.3, Pre 3:54.6," *Oregon Journal*, June 21, 1973, page 26.

212 *was set to go:* "Wottle wins the mile," *The World*, June 21, 1973, page 15.

212 *him sir or not:* Dave Wottle interview with author, September 20, 1973.

212 rabbit who usually wins: Carl Cluff. "Wottle 3:53.3, Pre 3:54.6," *Oregon Journal*, June 21, 1973, page 30.

212 *Wottle began to tingle:* Paul Buker. "Super mile, world high hurdle record serve final rites for packed stands," *Daily Emerald*, June 21, 1973, page 14.

213 *he wanted to explode:* John Conrad. "Wottle (3:53.3) still king of milers," *Register-Guard*, June 21, 1973, page 1B.

213 *He had no snap:* Blaine Newnham. "Pre planned to explode, but there was no snap," *Register-Guard*, June 21, 1973, page 1B.

213 *off a fast pace:* John Conrad. "Wottle (3:53.3) still king of milers," *Register-Guard*, June 21, 1973, page 1B.

213 *"Don't worry about it!":* Steve Wynne. "Pre still heads their list," *Capital Journal,* June 21, 1973, page 19.

213 *"a weakness I had":* Dave Wottle interview with author, September 20, 2023.

213 *"he was absolutely right":* Dave Wottle interview with author, September 20, 2023.

214 *"it up for them":* Blaine Newnham. "Pre planned to explode, but there was no snap," *Register-Guard,* June 21, 1973, page 1B.

214 *"always grateful for that":* Dave Wottle interview with author, September 20, 2023.

214 *appreciatively, took a swig:* Blaine Newnham. "Pre planned to explode, but there was no snap," *Register-Guard,* June 21, 1973, page 1B.

CHAPTER 14: GALVANIZED

215 *1976 Olympics in Montreal:* Dave Wottle interview with author, September 20, 2023.

215 *to work for Nike:* Kenny Moore. *Bowerman and the Men of Oregon.* Rodale Press, 2006, page 218.

216 *"he can run fast":* Phil Knight. *Shoe Dog.* Scribner, 2016, page 221.

216 *of Nike shoes:* Phil Knight. *Shoe Dog.* Scribner, 2016, page 221.

216 *"them to see Pre":* Phil Knight. *Shoe Dog.* Scribner, 2016, page 221.

217 *the winner, Filbert Bayi:* "Prefontaine 11th," *The World,* June 29, 1973, page 15.

217 *"people ahead of me":* Blaine Newnham. "Pre's year ends early," *Register-Guard,* July 22, 1973, page 1C.

217 *in a walk, 13:40.6:* "Prefontaine wins 5,000m," *The World,* July 5, 1973, page 19.

218 *"them off my head":* Dave Wottle interview with author, September 20, 2023.

218 *a quality Minolta camera:* Dave Wottle interview with author, September 20, 2023.

218 *they were too political:* "Extra dimension added U.S.-German dual meet," *Statesman Journal,* July 11, 1973, page 21.

219 *back still bothered him:* "Prefontaine, Geis run 2-3," *Oregon Journal,* July 13, 1973, page 45.

219 *had nothing to give:* Blaine Newnham. "Pre's year ends early," *Register-Guard,* July 22, 1973, page 1C.

219 *"leading the way":* Dave Wottle interview with author, September 21, 2023.

219 *"after the Olympic Games":* Blaine Newnham. "Pre's year ends early," *Register-Guard,* July 22, 1973, page 1C.

220 *10,000 meters in 27:43.6:* John Conrad. "Pre steals show with U.S. marks," *Register-Guard,* April 28, 1974, page 1B.

220 *3,000 meters to 10,000 meters:* "The Pre Chronicles, Part 15, The 1974 Outdoor Season," *Track & Field News,* August 1974.

221 *running shoe for $14.30:* Fred Westerlund. "He's more than just a runner," *Democrat-Herald,* August 30, 1973, page 20.

221 *"have to understand individuals":* Fred Westerlund. "He's more than just a runner," *Democrat-Herald,* August 30, 1973, page 20.

222 *"him coach me sooner":* Maryl Barker interview with author, June 16, 2023.

222 *"rather than overtrain him":* "Practical Running Psychology," Mountain View, CA: *World Publications,* page 47.

223 *"be her best years":* Dave Distel. "Fame hasn't been a bane to Orange HS sophomore," *Capital Journal,* March 6, 1974.

223 *"I did with those":* Debra Roth and Maryl Barker interviews with author, June 29, 2023.

223 *"you have to run!":* Janet Heinonen. "Tough act to follow," *Register-Guard,* November 14, 1974, page 3B.

223 *"It felt so free":* Maryl Barker interview with author, June 16, 2023.

224 *"and the bad weather":* Jim Williams. "Prefontaine ends career in a blaze," *The World,* May 21, 1973, page 9.

224 *"sprinters in the world":* Jim Williams. "Fran Sichting: 'Great to have someone around you know cares,'" *The World,* May 23, 1973, page 9.

224 *"was a passing fad"*: Fran Worthen interview with author, May 5, 2023.

224 *"of the pretty brunette"*: Jim Williams. "Sit up and take notice," *The World,* May 29, 1973, page 4.

224 *"19-year-old freckled lovely"*: Ron Reid. "It's no go for the new go-go girl," *Sports Illustrated,* July 2, 1973, page 53.

225 staying in *"plush hotels"*: Neil Amdur. "Olympic storm stirring," *New York Times,* August 3, 1971, page 19.

225 *"men than I am?"*: Jim Williams. "Athletes getting 'raw deal' says Prefontaine," *The World,* March 8, 1973, page 17.

225 *"wouldn't have any jobs"*: Jim Williams. "Athletes getting 'raw deal' says Prefontaine," *The World,* March 8, 1973, page 17.

225 *"an idea for themselves"*: Blaine Newnham. "Bowerman slaps Games security," *Register-Guard,* September 7, 1972, page 1A.

226 *"corner hot dog stand"*: Jim Williams. "Athletes getting 'raw deal' says Prefontaine," *The World,* March 8, 1973, page 17.

226 *"monetary rewards for performing"*: "Pro track is formed," *Fresno Bee* (Munich AP), September 11, 1972, page 18.

227 *"itself in my mind"*: "O'Hara's dream coming true," *Progress Bulletin,* December 25, 1972, page 50.

227 *field to the forefront:* "O'Hara's dream coming true," *Progress Bulletin,* December 25, 1972, page 50.

227 *laughed and Ryun smiled:* Dave Anderson. "Jim Ryun takes the money runs," *New York Times,* November 15, 1972, page 55.

227 *$18,000 to $25,000:* Dave Anderson. "Jim Ryun takes the money runs," *New York Times,* November 15, 1972, page 55.

227 *"to the Olympic code"*: Dave Anderson. "Jim Ryun takes the money runs," *New York Times,* November 15, 1972, page 55.

228 *and pocket the cash:* Dave Anderson. "Jim Ryun takes the money runs," *New York Times,* November 15, 1972, page 55.

228 *"don't think they haven't"*: Dave Anderson. "Jim Ryun takes the money runs," *New York Times,* November 15, 1972, page 55.

228 *"to 3:45 or something"*: Ron Reid. "It wasn't small potatoes in Pocatello," *Sports Illustrated,* March 12, 1973, page 64.

228 *"with the different organizations"*: Rod Hunt. "Minidome boosts Idaho," *Idaho Statesman,* March 9, 1973, page 7.

229 *"money out of it"*: "Bowerman not a pro track fan," *Register-Guard,* November 24, 1972, page 2D.

229 *over the hill, anyway:* "Bowerman not a pro track fan," *Register-Guard,* November 24, 1972, page 2D.

229 *"years if things go"*: Tom McGuire. "Prefontaine favors professional track," November 25, 1972, page 13.

229 *"way they are now"*: Tom McGuire. "Prefontaine favors professional track," November 25, 1972, page 13.

229 *"mighty strong bargaining point"*: Tom McGuire. "Prefontaine favors professional track," November 25, 1972, page 13.

229 *limit on his future:* Tom McGuire. "Prefontaine favors professional track," November 25, 1972, page 13.

230 *"takes care of them"*: Bill Mulflur. "Track isn't main thing in my life," says Pre," *Oregon Journal,* January 12, 1973, page 21.

230 *"in our own world"*: Bill Mulflur. "'Track isn't main thing in my life,' says Pre," *Oregon Journal,* January 12, 1973, page 21.

230 *"coach from a book"*: Bill Mulflur. "'Track isn't main thing in my life,' says Pre," *Oregon Journal,* January 12, 1973, page 21.

230 *running at world-record pace:* Ron Reid. "It wasn't small potatoes in Pocatello," *Sports Illustrated,* March 12, 1973, page 64.

231 *"in all of us"*: Ron Reid. "It wasn't small potatoes in Pocatello," *Sports Illustrated,* March 12, 1973, page 64.

231 *"we can make ITA"*: Ron Reid. "It wasn't small potatoes in Pocatello," *Sports Illustrated,* March 12, 1973, page 64.

231 *"I run for Kip"*: "ITA opens tonight," *Progress Bulletin,* March 24, 1973, page 18.

232 *"they're giving Kip Keino"*: "Pre does it again with six-mile mark," *Register-Guard,* March 25, 1973, page 2B.

232 *lot to be desired:* "Prefontaine attacks both AAU, NCAA as well as the Munich Olympics," *The World,* March 27, 1973, page 13.

232 *earned the title "talkative"*: "Prefontaine attacks both AAU, NCAA as well as the Munich Olympics," *The World,* March 27, 1973, page 13.

232 *"had enough of that"*: "Prefontaine attacks both AAU, NCAA as well as the Munich Olympics," *The World,* March 27, 1973, page 13.

232 *"Just fine, Jim"*: Neil Cawood. "This is money," *Register-Guard,* April 1, 1973, page 1B.

232 *"get the larger crowds"*: Neil Cawood. "This is money," *Register-Guard,* April 1, 1973, page 1B.

232 *for Ryun and Keino:* Neil Cawood. "This is money," *Register-Guard,* April 1, 1973, page 1B.

232 *hadn't "reached Mecca yet"*: Carl Cluff. "Pre's pro price: Zeroes lots of em," *Oregon Journal,* March 31, 1973, page 14.

233 *"wait for more bodies"*: Carl Cluff. "Pre's pro price: Zeroes lots of em," *Oregon Journal,* March 31, 1973, page 14.

233 *"Zeroes . . . lots of 'em"*: Neil Cawood. "This is money," *Register-Guard,* April 1, 1973, page 1B.

233 *to increase the competition:* "Pro track expanding," *New York Times,* December 20, 1973, page 52.

233 *"in our first year"*: "Pro sprinter reports $5,000 bribe offer," *Idaho Statesman,* April 4, 1973, page 23.

234 *"he is a senior"*: Robert Fachet. "Pro track survives—so far," *Washington Post,* June 20, 1973, page 22.

234 *"he opens his mouth"*: Robert Fachet. "Pro track survives—so far," *Washington Post,* June 20, 1973, page 22.

234 *"jury is still out"*: "ITA still hopeful of signing Pre," *Oregon Journal,* December 24, 1974, page 14.

234 *"but then what's money"*: Letter from Steve Prefontaine to Pat Tyson, October 11, 1974.

235 *"a lamb in Europe"*: Carl Cluff. "Pre may go pro Sunday," *Oregon Journal,* December 18, 1974, page 27.

235 *"intentionally imprecise"*: Phil Knight. *Shoe Dog.* Simon & Schuster, 2016, page 223.

235 *sign with the ITA:* Kenny Moore. *Bowerman and the Men of Oregon.* Rodale Press, 2006, page 322.

CHAPTER 15: ROGUE

237 *"grant the AAU sanction"*: Kenny Moore. *Bowerman and the Men of Oregon.* Rodale Press, 2006, page 324.

238 *"entire meet, if necessary"*: Dennis Anstine. "Pre to race Finns at home," *The World,* February 7, 1975, page 6.

238 *barely 2,000 people:* https://en.wikipedia.org/wiki/Madras,_Oregon.

239 *"would make the difference"*: Danny Gauthier interview with author, September 13, 2023.

240 *"would make us keep going"*: Greg Kemper interview with author, September 14, 2023.

240 *"That damn MGB"*: Ralph Mann interview with author, March 13, 2024.

240 *of a car accident:* Dan Gauthier interview with author, September 13, 2023.

240 *"to work extra jobs"*: Desiree Kelly interview with author, September 12, 2023.

240 *"walls made of paper"*: Tom McGuire. "Perspectives," *The World,* August 10, 1971, page 11.

240 *with Bud and Maxine:* Desiree Kelly interview with author, September 12, 2023.

241 *in Colorado that winter:* Frank Shorter interview with author, June 26, 2024.

242 *"and I are right now"*: Frank Shorter. *My Marathon.* Rodale Books, 2016, page 132.

242 *"tomorrow if he could"*: Mike Monroe. "Prefontaine would rather switch than starve," *Denver Post,* March 21, 1975, page 69.

243   *"taken out of context"*: *Los Angeles Times,* April 1, 1975, page 26.

243   *"the way he does"*: Bill R. Justus. "Doesn't appreciate athlete's attitude," *Democrat-Herald,* April 3, 1975, page 4.

243   *"if given the chance"*: "Steve Prefontaine is tired of being a poor man," *Capital Journal,* March 27, 1975, page 25.

243   *"dislike for the military"*: "Prefontaine misses the point," *Oregon Journal,* March 29, 1974, page 4.

244   *his words in print:* Blaine Newnham. "Apologies, apple pies," *Register-Guard,* April 20, 1975, page 1B.

244   *"taken out of context"*: Blaine Newnham. "Apologies, apple pies," *Register-Guard,* April 20, 1975, page 1B.

244   *"I'd say darn right"*: Blaine Newnham. "Apologies, apple pies," *Register-Guard,* April 20, 1975, page 1B.

245   *in their respective events:* "Finnish track team in meet here Sunday," *Madras Pioneer,* May 1, 1975.

245   *"meet in the country"*: "Finnish athletes arrive for Northwest track tour," *Democrat Herald,* May 2, 1975, page 19.

245   *"in quite good shape"*: "Finnish athletes arrive for Northwest track tour," *Democrat Herald,* May 2, 1975, page 19.

246   *hoped for 2,000 people:* Carl Cluff. "Weather frowns on Pre, Finns," *Oregon Journal,* May 5, 1975, page 16.

246   *times, some good performances:* "Pre eyes more big meets for cities in Central Oregon," *Bend Bulletin,* May 2, 1975, page 11.

246   *Wilkins by three feet:* Carl Cluff. "Weather frowns on Pre, Finns," *Oregon Journal,* May 5, 1975, page 16.

246   *"put this on"*: Robert Gauthier interview with author, September 11, 2023.

247   *"For an old man"*: John Craig. "Prefontaine wins 3,000 meters; crowd poor for all-star track meet," *Bend Bulletin,* May 5, 1975, page 13.

247   *Laird recalled, some "toughies"*: Bruce Laird interview with author, April 28, 2023.

248   *wouldn't in his backyard:* Dennis Anstine. "Pre to race Finns at home," *The World,* February 7, 1975, page 6.

248   *"come, you come here"*: Neta Prefontaine interview with author, December 8, 2023.

249   *"do anything like that"*: John Conrad. "Pre's homecoming a big success," *Register-Guard,* May 10, 1975, page 1D.

249   *"to complain about it"*: Dennis Anstine. "Pre delivers . . . an American record for hometown fans," *The World,* page 8.

249   *"talk to your uncle"*: Cathal Dennehy, "On anniversary of Prefontaine's death, his family shares touching memories," *Runner's World,* May 29, 2015.

249   *"little guy came through"*: Dennis Anstine. "Pre delivers . . . an American record for hometown fans," *The World,* page 8.

249   *"a pretty outstanding record"*: John Conrad. "Pre's homecoming a big success," *Register-Guard,* May 10, 1975, page 1D.

250   *kids could think of:* Dennis Anstine. "Pre delivers . . . an American record for hometown fans," *The World,* page 8.

250   *"nice to be home"*: Dennis Anstine. "Pre delivers . . . an American record for hometown fans," *The World,* page 8.

250   *"on other continents, too"*: Dan Stinson. "Prefontaine gets no challenge," *Vancouver Sun,* May 16, 1975, page 21.

250   *"is not working out"*: John Conrad. "Virén won't run against Pre," *Register-Guard,* May 20, 1975, page 1C.

251   *"didn't look beyond laps"*: Kenny Moore. *Bowerman and the Men of Oregon.* Rodale Press, 2006, page 324.

251   *"to run against him"*: Kenny Moore. *Bowerman and the Men of Oregon.* Rodale Press, 2006, page 324.

251 *"prepared no matter what"*: John Conrad. "Virén won't run against Pre," *Register-Guard*, May 20, 1975, page 1C.

CHAPTER 16: FIRE

252 *"and the international meets"*: Kenny Moore. "A final drive to the finish," *Sports Illustrated*, June 9, 1975.

253 *"to reinforce his statement"*: Frank Shorter interview with author, June 26, 2024.

253 *"you! You drive crazy"*: Roscoe Divine interview with author, June 21, 2023.

254 *"it's a constitutional violation"*: Blaine Newnham. "Bizarre boycott?" *Register-Guard*, May 27, 1975, page 1C.

254 *"cards to settle him"*: Steve Bence. "1972: Pre, UO track, Nike shoes, and my life with them all," AO Creative, 2021.

254 *several hours to rest*: Jerry Uhrhammer. "Pre's last hours," *Register-Guard*, "May 30, 1975, page 3D.

254 *"all this is over"*: Jeff Kiehl. "Omens of death in final hours," *Tacoma News Tribune*, May 31, 1975, page 15.

255 *"pressure isn't on me"*: John Conrad. "It's Pre and Shorter left in 5,000," *Register-Guard*, May 27, 1975, page 3C.

255 *best 5,000 in 13:32.2*: John Conrad. "Pre's last one a good one," *Register-Guard*, May 30, 1975, page 3D.

256 *"and then we'll see"*: Paul Daquilante. "Writer recalls visit with Pre," *Democrat-Herald*, June 3, 1975, page 19.

256 *"you can't listen in"*: Dennis Antsine. "Pre, warm, genuine," *The World*, May 30, 1975, page 6.

256 *future as a promoter?*: Paul Daquilante. "Writer recalls visit with Pre," *Democrat-Herald*, June 3, 1975, page 19.

256 *"there's a next time"*: Dennis Anstine. "Prefontaine runs well in last duel against Shorter," *The World*, May 30, 1975, page 6.

256 *"I think that's great"*: Scott Daggatt interview with author, October 6, 2023.

256 *Oregon's outstanding senior trackman*: "UO awards go to Barger and Daggatt," *Register-Guard*, May 30, 1975, page 4D.

256 *class the following morning*: Scott Daggatt interview with author, October 6, 2023.

257 *"a couple of beers"*: Jerry Uhrhammer. "Pre's last hours," *Register-Guard*, "May 30, 1975, page 3D.

257 *"be willing to party"*: Harvey Winn interview with author, August 15, 2023.

257 *own words, "super drunk"*: Robert Gauthier interview with author, September 11, 2023.

257 *"Enticing, isn't it?"*: Rick Bailey interview with author, September 14, 2023.

258 *A-frame house in Madras*: John Conrad. "Most popular track athlete," *Register-Guard*, May 30, 1975, page 1D.

258 *Steve, tired*: "Friends recall Pre's last hours," *Bend Bulletin*, May 30, 1975, page 10.

258 *"with the American system"*: Kenny Moore. "A final drive to the finish," *Sports Illustrated*, June 9, 1975.

258 *the three-hour drive*: John Conrad. "Most popular track athlete," *Register-Guard*, May 30, 1975, page 1D.

258 *and super tired himself*: Robert Gauthier interview with author, September 11, 2023.

258 *two beers that evening*: Rick Bailey interview with author, September 14, 2023.

258 *three or four beers*: Kenny Moore. *Bowerman and the Men of Oregon*. Rodale Press, 2006, page 332.

259 *"the signs of drunkenness"*: Frank Shorter. *My Marathon*. Rodale, 2016.

259 *"enough to affect his driving"*: Jerry Uhrhammer. "Pre's last hours," *Register-Guard*, "May 30, 1975, page 3D.

259 *two or three minutes*: Jerry Uhrhammer. "Pre's last hours," *Register-Guard*, "May 30, 1975, page 3D.

259 *"our heads are clear"*: Kenny Moore. "A final drive to the finish," *Sports Illustrated*, June 9, 1975.

260 *streetlight 100 feet away*: Police report.

260 *At 12:30 a.m.*: Police report.

260 *"thump, and then silence":* Police report.

260 *"rapidly dressed":* Police report.

260 *"high rate of speed":* Police report.

260 *"gasping," "choking":* Mary Pilon. "Steve Prefontaine's last run," Grantland, May 30, 2015.

261 *back would ache well:* Blaine Newnham and Don Mack. "Pre's death the end of an era," *Register-Guard,* May 30, 1975, page 1A.

261 *hoping it wasn't him:* Blaine Newnham and Don Mack. "Pre's death the end of an era," *Register-Guard,* May 30, 1975, page 1A.

261 *Loveall found no pulse:* Blaine Newnham and Don Mack. "Pre's death the end of an era," *Register-Guard,* May 30, 1975, page 1A.

261 *Leonard Jacobson, confirmed it:* Blaine Newnham and Don Mack. "Pre's death the end of an era," *Register-Guard,* May 30, 1975, page 1A.

261 *contributed to his death:* Dave Frei. "He was Bill Bowerman's kind of guy," *Register-Guard,* May 31, 1975, page 1B.

261 *a half-block away:* Mary Pilon. "Steve Prefontaine's last run," Grantland, May 30, 2015.

261 *acrid scent of "vomitus":* Kenny Moore. *Bowerman and the Men of Oregon.* Rodale Press, 2006, page 333.

261 *feet of skid marks:* Blaine Newnham and Don Mack. "Pre's death the end of an era," *Register-Guard,* May 30, 1975, page 1A.

261 *into the tape deck:* Blaine Newnham and Don Mack. "Pre's death the end of an era," *Register-Guard,* May 30, 1975, page 1A.

262 *He was "shook up":* Blaine Newnham and Don Mack. "Pre's death the end of an era," *Register-Guard,* May 30, 1975, page 1A.

262 *"over the whole nation":* "Most popular track athlete," *Register-Guard,* May 30, 1975, page 1D.

262 *"in an ordinary sense":* "Most popular track athlete," *Register-Guard,* May 30, 1975, page 1D.

263 *"a lot of people":* "Most popular track athlete," *Register-Guard,* May 30, 1975, page 1D.

263 *"he was our boy":* Bill Dixon. "His absence is felt with sharpness," *The World,* May 29, 1976, page 11.

263 *"week as that meet":* Ralph Mann interview with author, March 13, 2024.

263 *"or five seconds less":* Mary Pilon. "Steve Prefontaine's last run," Grantland, May 30, 2015.

263 *"my dad like that":* Desiree Kelly interview with author, September 12, 2023.

263 *"soon. Take care, Steve":* Letter from Steve Prefontaine to the Gauthiers, March 21, 1974.

263 *"to my house Monday":* "Most popular track athlete," *Register-Guard,* May 30, 1975, page 1D.

264 *"shock of hearing that":* Pete Shmock interview with author, May 17, 2023.

264 *"urge to return home":* Mike Jordan. "Pre was just too alive to die," *Tacoma News Herald,* May 31, 1975, page 16.

264 *of life to die:* Mike Jordan. "Pre was just too alive to die," *Tacoma News Herald,* May 31, 1975, page 16.

264 *"wallet all those years":* Neta Prefontaine interview with author, December 8, 2023.

265 *bumper along Seventh Street:* "They came to pay Pre final tribute," *The World,* page 12.

265 *and forest green ferns:* Blaine Newnham. "Pre's last lap back where it began," *Register-Guard,* June 3, 1975, page 1C.

265 *"through our national organization":* Carl Cluff. "Pre's People pay tearful tribute to favorite son," *Oregon Journal,* June 3, 1975, pages 17 and 18.

265 *"the deed, the act":* Blaine Newnham. "Pre's last lap back where it began," *Register-Guard,* June 3, 1975, page 1C.

265 *the flag of Finland:* Dave Bushnell. "Coos Bay pays final tribute to Steve Prefontaine," *Daily Emerald,* June 3, 1975, page 6.

266 *"can't leave my people":* Carl Cluff. "Pre's People pay tearful tribute to favorite son," *Oregon Journal,* June 3, 1975, pages 17 and 18.

266 *She never quit:* Dave Bushnell. "Coos Bay pays final tribute to Steve Prefontaine," *Daily Emerald,* June 3, 1975, page 6.

266 *"meters . . . nobody but me'":* Paul Daquilante. "That 12:36.2 . . . it was all Prefontaine," *Democrat-Herald,* June 5, 1975, page 22.

266 *stands clapped and cheered:* Paul Daquilante. "That 12:36.2 . . . it was all Prefontaine," *Democrat-Herald,* June 5, 1975, page 22.

EPILOGUE: A HIGHER STANDARD THAN VICTORY

268 *"unbelievable will to win":* Phil Knight email to author, February 5, 2024.

268 *"step of the way":* Bill Bowerman, Prefontaine eulogy, Hayward Field, June 3, 1975.

269 *"can keep it going":* Pat Tyson interview with author, July 12, 2023.

269 *"ones we keep repeating":* Howard Bryant interview with author, Creative Nonfiction Podcast, Episode 320.

269 *"not get seventy years":* Marty Liquori interview with author, December 6, 2023.

271 *"to be around him":* Ralph Mann interview with author, March 13, 2024.

272 *"just strive for that":* Pete Shmock, interview with author, October 7, 2024.

272 *"United States Olympic Committee":* Joseph M. Turrini, *The End of Amateurism in American Track and Field,* University of Illinois Press, 2010, page 147.

272 *"for track and field":* Joseph M. Turrini, *The End of Amateurism in American Track and Field,* University of Illinois Press, 2010, page 147.

272 *"twenty percent active athletes":* Joseph M. Turrini, *The End of Amateurism in American Track and Field,* University of Illinois Press, 2010, page 148.

272 *"form our own federation":* "Pre felt sluggish after win," *Capital Journal,* May 30, 1975, page 29.

272 *"because people saw that":* Ken Popejoy interview with author, May 20, 2023.

INDEX

ABOUT

MARINER BOOKS

MARINER BOOKS traces its beginnings to 1832 when William Ticknor cofounded the Old Corner Bookstore in Boston, from which he would run the legendary firm Ticknor and Fields, publisher of Ralph Waldo Emerson, Harriet Beecher Stowe, Nathaniel Hawthorne, and Henry David Thoreau. Following Ticknor's death, Henry Oscar Houghton acquired Ticknor and Fields and, in 1880, formed Houghton Mifflin, which later merged with venerable Harcourt Publishing to form Houghton Mifflin Harcourt. HarperCollins purchased HMH's trade publishing business in 2021 and reestablished their storied lists and editorial team under the name Mariner Books.

Uniting the legacies of Houghton Mifflin, Harcourt Brace, and Ticknor and Fields, Mariner Books continues one of the great traditions in American bookselling. Our imprints have introduced an incomparable roster of enduring classics, including Hawthorne's *The Scarlet Letter,* Thoreau's *Walden,* Willa Cather's *O Pioneers!,* Virginia Woolf's *To the Lighthouse,* W.E.B. Du Bois's *Black Reconstruction,* J.R.R. Tolkien's *The Lord of the Rings,* Carson McCullers's *The Heart Is a Lonely Hunter,* Ann Petry's *The Narrows,* George Orwell's *Animal Farm* and *Nineteen Eighty-Four,* Rachel Carson's *Silent Spring,* Margaret Walker's *Jubilee,* Italo Calvino's *Invisible Cities,* Alice Walker's *The Color Purple,* Margaret Atwood's *The Handmaid's Tale,* Tim O'Brien's *The Things They Carried,* Philip Roth's *The Plot Against America,* Jhumpa Lahiri's *Interpreter of Maladies,* and many others. Today Mariner Books remains proudly committed to the craft of fine publishing established nearly two centuries ago at the Old Corner Bookstore.